Graphis Mission Statement: Graphis is commited to presenting exceptional work in international design, advertising, illustration and photography. Since 1944 we have presented individuals and companies in the visual communications industry who have consistently demonstrated excellence and determination in overcoming economic, cultural and creative hurdles to produce brilliance.

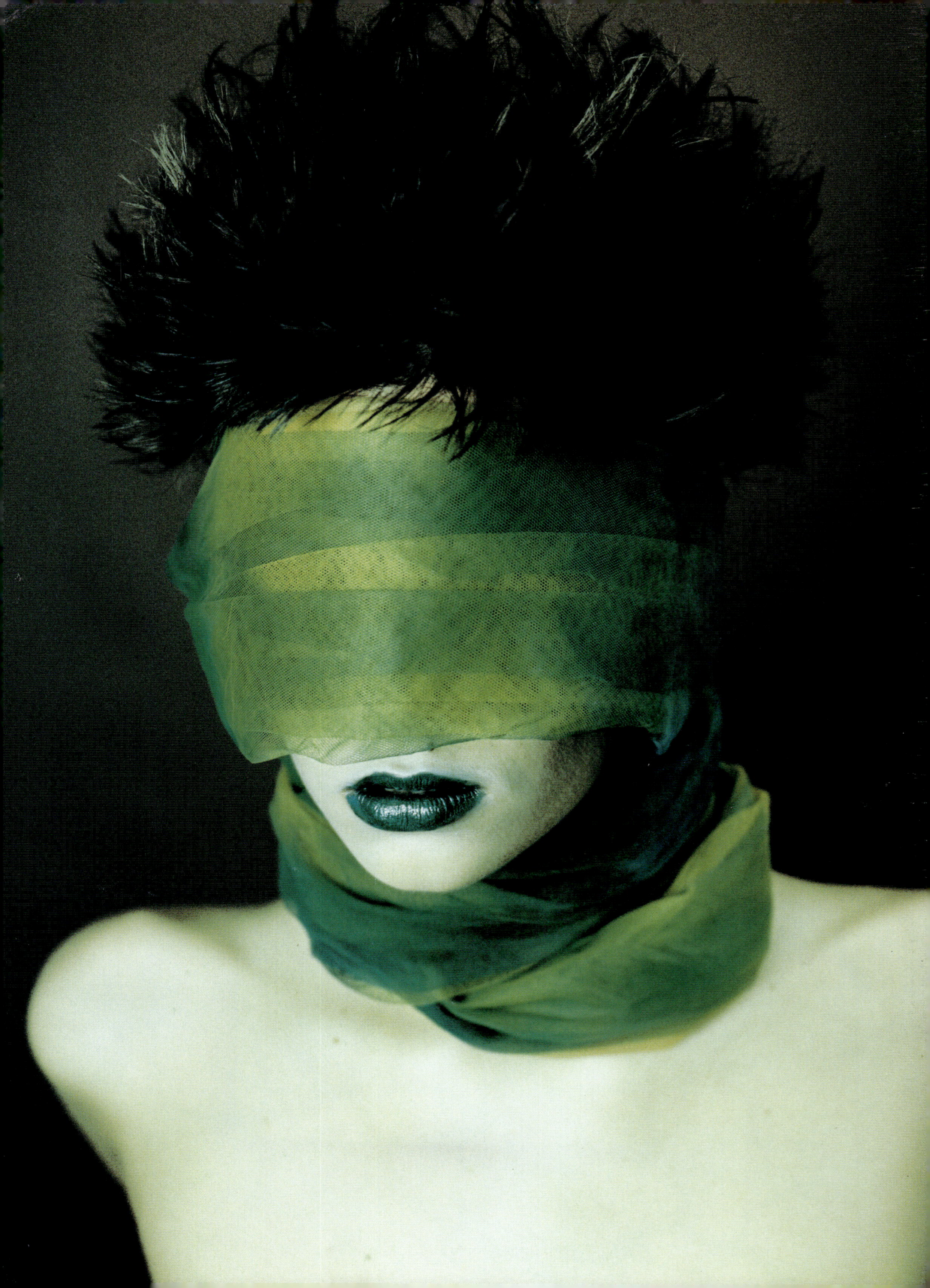

Graphis Photo Annual 2003

An International Annual of Photography
Das internationale Jahrbuch der Photographie
Le répertoire internationale de la photographie

CEO & Creative Director: B. Martin Pedersen

Editor: Michael Porciello
Photo Editor: Sarah Hasted

Art Director: Lauren Prigozen
Design & Production: Nicole Recchia, Luis Diaz,
Alexia Leitich, and Joanne Sullivan

Published by Graphis Inc.

This book is dedicated to
Robert Nettarp

(opposite) Rafter

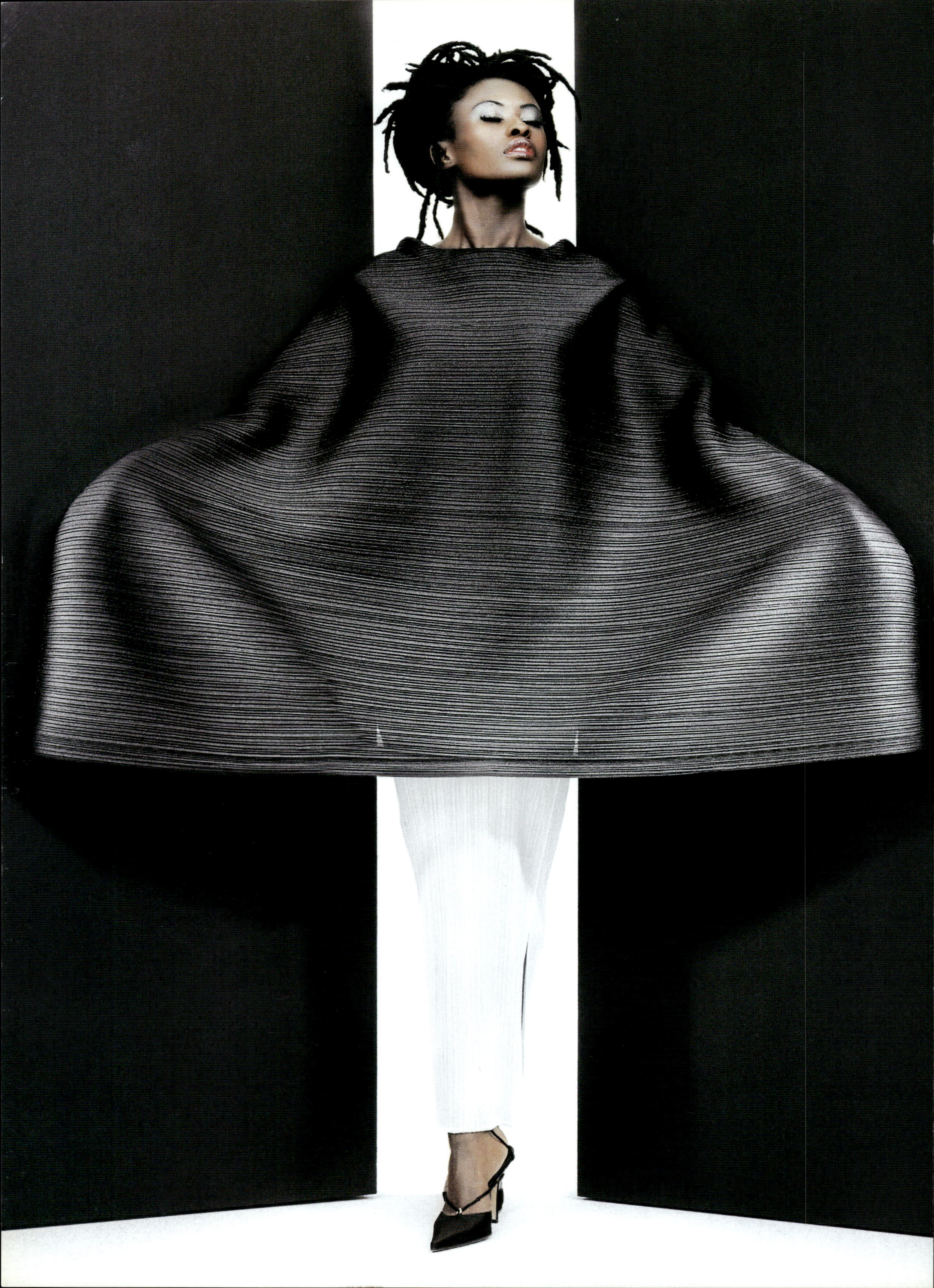

Contents Inhalt Sommaire

Remarks: We extend our heartfelt thanks to contributors throughout the world who have made it possible to publish a wide and international spectrum of the best work in this field. Entry instructions for all Graphis Books may be requested from: **Graphis Inc.**, 307 Fifth Avenue, Tenth Floor, New York, NY 10016, or visit our Web site at www.graphis.com. *Anmerkungen*: Unser Dank gilt den Einsendern aus aller Welt, die es uns ermöglicht haben, ein breites, internationales Spektrum der besten Arbeiten zu veröffentlichen. Teilnahmebedingungen für die Graphis-Bücher sind erhältlich bei: **Graphis Inc.**, 307 Fifth Avenue, Tenth Floor, New York, NY 10016. Die aktu- ellsten Einsendetermine finden Sie unter: www.graphis.com. *Remerciements*: Nous remercions les participants du monde entier qui ont rendu possible la publication de cet ouvrage offrant un panorama complet des meilleurs travaux. Les modalités d'inscription peuvent être obtenues auprès de: **Graphis Inc.**, 307 Fifth Avenue, Tenth Floor, New York, NY 10016. Pour les dates limites les plus actuelles consultez www.graphis.com. ISBN: 1-931241-16-3 Printed in Hong Kong. Distributed in North America by Publishers Group West. Distributed in all other countries by HBI/HarperCollins.

(opposite) Howard Schatz

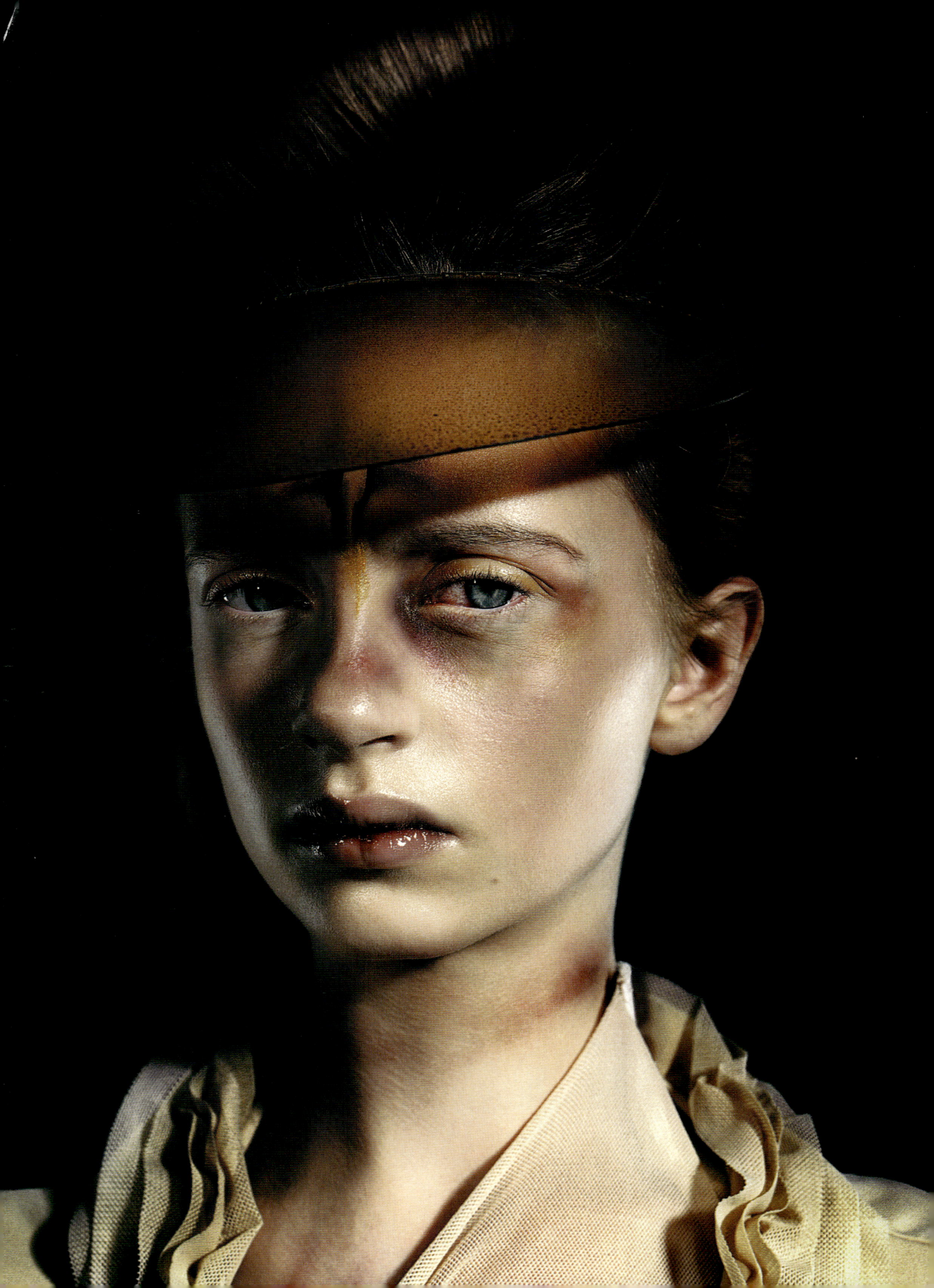

ROBERT NETTARP

(1970-2002)

This article was originally published in Graphis magazine #337 (Jan/Feb 2002)

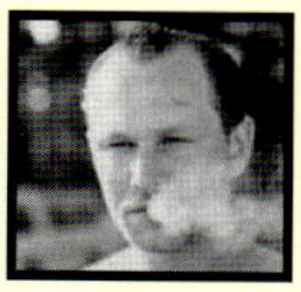

In the laboratory of fashion photography, Robert Nettarp's photography is an eccentric mix of roughness and epic mise en scène. An odd ball in the game of fashion—too often caught in its own self-conscious clichés—Swedish Nettarp disturbs. With an inspired energy and sexy spontaneity, he creates high-impact imagery imbued with a sentiment of ill-being. There is a discomforting directness in his images, a violent evidence that something had to happen. Frontal portraits, distorted faces staring at the camera, gaping and shouting mouths. Most of the scenes seem like interrupted film stills, written and composed with a touch of a classic film noir in Technicolor. Nettarp has just completed this Fall, his second series of in-store commercials for Hugo, the sub-brand of Hugo Boss. The latest film portrays a group of young people walking down the street to the beat of Depeche Mode, ignoring the danger of burning flames that surround them.

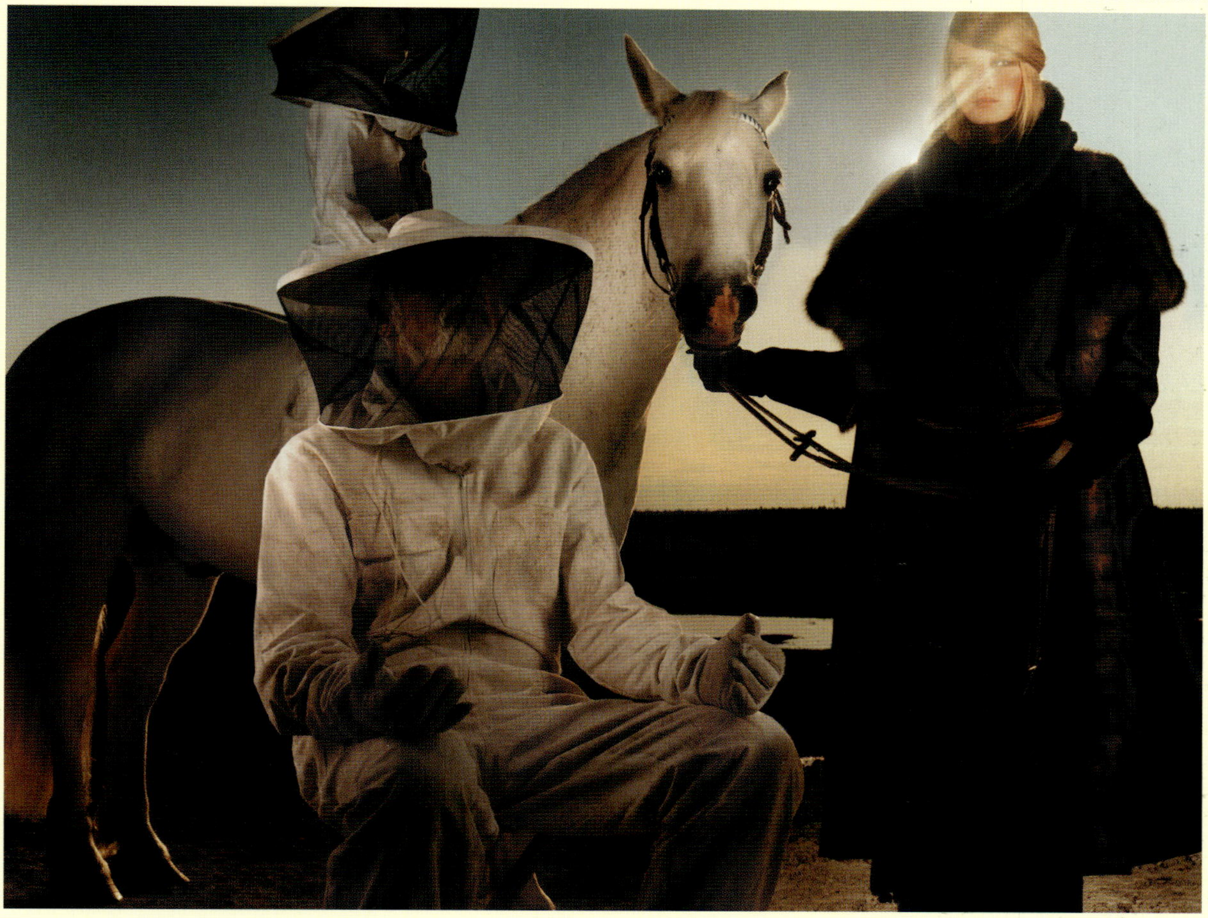

Very much like an advertising creative, Nettarp starts with an idea, a simple idea he has drafted swiftly in his sketchbook during his wanderings throughout Stockholm. Inspiration? He finds it on the street, or, in the daily newspaper's latest passion crime. Lots of them come on the shooting spot. With a natural intuition, he responds to the odds and ends of the location. "As soon as you step off the plane, you can smell, you can feel the light and the vibe of your location, and adjust your idea," says Nettarp. His French Vogue story on fur—which helped to launch his international career—depicts a place of surreal expectation, somewhere out of nowhere.

Generally, his ideas develop into a narrative often set in an incongruous decor, as if the camera had frozen as much information as possible into one frame. Not enough though to tell the whole story: it's up to you to imagine the action before and after. He captures the immediacy of a past or impending conflict. Not to take it literally, in the Bruised Lady—despite the controversial interpretation the photo has generated in the Swedish press—his intention was far from depicting a sexually abused woman. For years he had in mind a story about a group of strong, self-confident girls fighting till they bleed. For them, life is like a boxing ring. Odd but simple idea: Swedish Bible magazine published it.

Because he does not distinguish between personal and commercial work, at times the photographer gives his photography disconcerting directions in response to editorial assignments. Intense sexual practices, anti-military sentiments are some of the more violent topics he has addressed in his own New Romantic way—a feeling of dark self-confidence imprints his images. But when asked whether he feels his photos communicate violence, he prefers to speak about a "beauty always on the edge."

Nettarp was trained as a painter and his father's collection of modern art certainly influenced his sense of painterly composition: the Bruised Lady bears the gravity of a classic Dutch master. Although, he admits, he dropped painting because "he had all the ideas clear in [his] head, not in [his] hands. Just in the eyes." Photography was a logical shift, and he jumped into it accidentally at age 18. He had taken casual portraits of his top model friends, who had used them in their books, and in less than 2 months, with no agent, he was commissioned a billboard campaign for the now famous Swedish clothing brand H&M.

The photo industry in Sweden has changed enormously over the past 4 years—in Stockholm alone, 6 agents represent thousands of emerging photographers, highly sought after by award-winning art directors. But for editorial jobs, the fashion magazine stand was pretty much limited to the Swedish Elle. So, Nettarp crossed European borders. "A successful photographer has to be everywhere at once," states Julian Meijer, Nettarp's agent both in Paris and New York. Successful collaborations with French Vogue and Italy's Amica have kicked off his young career in a highly competitive market. Meijer admits he has taken a risk in representing Nettarp—"the Viking" as he likes to call him. His images are a hard sell to the shivery American editorial milieu (Nylon was an exception), but the agent is fully confident that advertising jobs will soon pick up. "Rich in multiple interpretations, his work does not belong to any trend. That's a long-term guarantee of success," concludes Julian Meijer. ■ *—Laetitia Wolff*

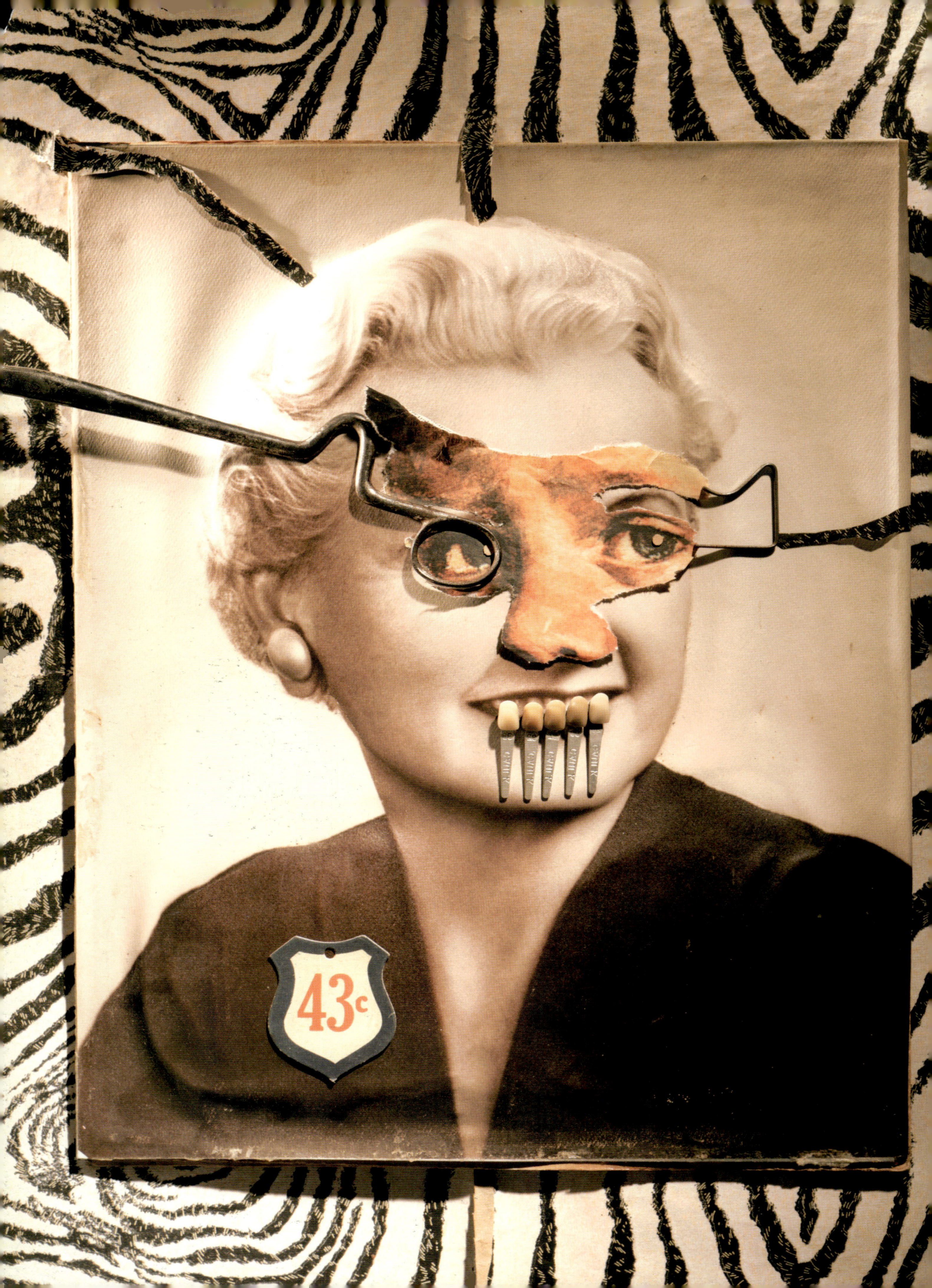
43c

20 Questions on Photography by Lyle Rexer

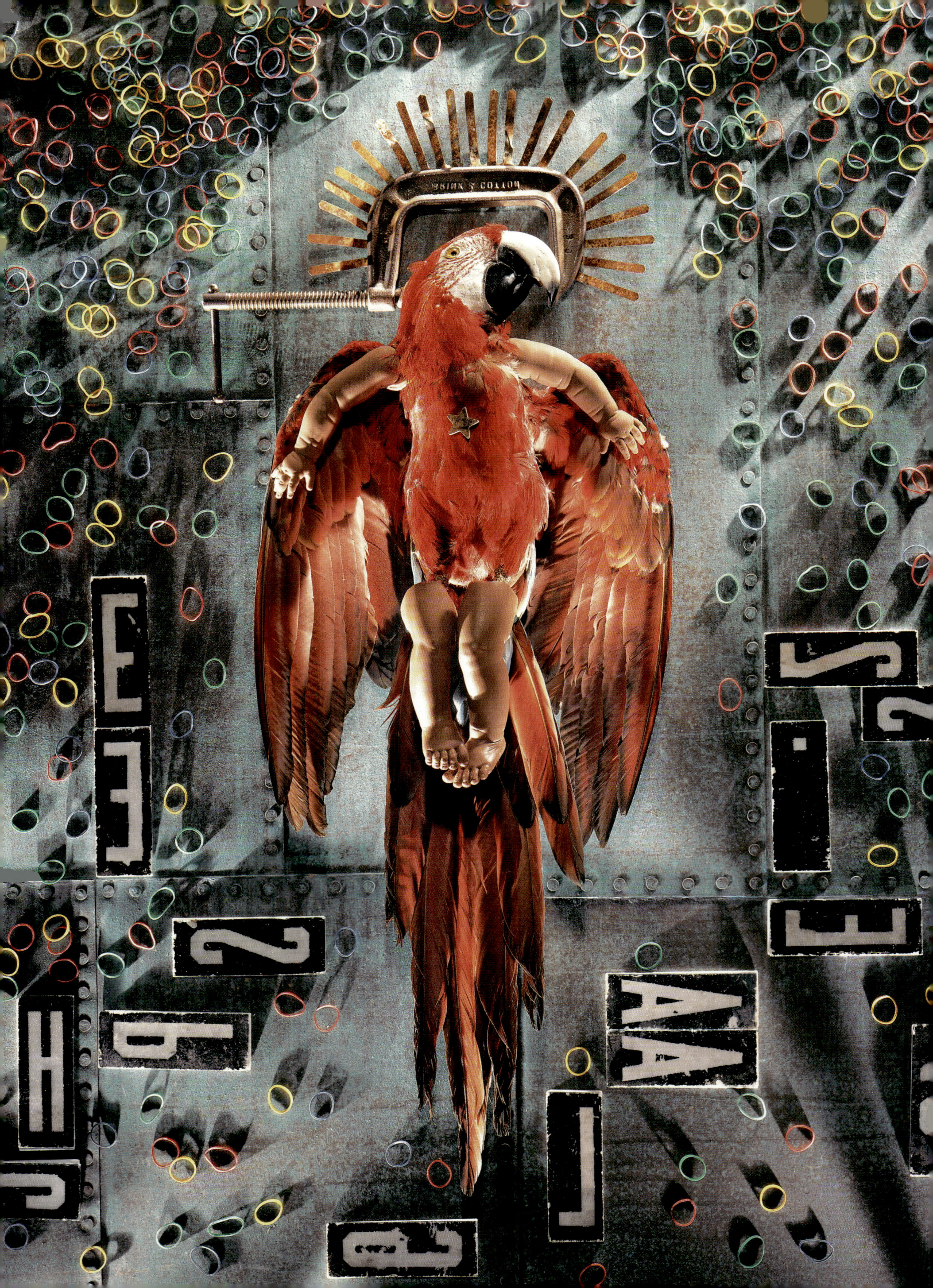

Have all the pictures been taken?
Whistle an imaginary tune and ask if all the music has been written. Imagination is infinite. I think the world will be forever increasingly hungry for more visual input. All the pictures that have been taken will hopefully inspire photographers like children do their parents.

Are there great future subjects for a photographer?
As long as there will be great future photographers.

Photography has always been a hands-on medium of expression. How do you see digital technology changing the relationship of the photographer to act of image-making?
There are many digits in a hand, a finger… I've always believed concept is a more important source.

The classic role of the photojournalist is to bear truthful witness to the moment. How can the photojournalist validify his or her credibility if the "truth value" of images is subverted by digital processing?
Integrity, the same as before digital enhancement.

What is the impact of the world's growing skepticism toward photographic images (and the people who make them)?
I'm not aware of it.

The rise of digital technology has gone hand-in-hand with the return of antique processes. Are the latter valid artistically and commercially?
The message must surpass the medium.

What are the implications of the Web for the photographers' ability to maintain commercial and artistic control of their images?
Reduced control of copyright.

Throughout photography's history, fine art photography has sought to separate itself from commercial and industrial applications (most recently, fashion and advertising). Is that separation valid or even possible today?
Doing it now is believing, seeing it now is rare.

People now see photographs occupying the same space in museums that paintings do. What is the current relationship between painting (and other arts) and photography and how does this influence photographic practice?
There is power in the unique—in every sense of the word; in this case relating directly to smaller editions—and their impact when it comes to large-scale photographic work. I applaud more photography in more museums. More, and bigger if necessary. If the technology is there, let's apply it. Digital or not. Photography has influenced painting and vice versa—that's not new, but it's an interesting area to revisit.

Many of the key artists using photography aren't photographers in the conventional sense and some even have others make the photos for them, which they then deploy. What are the implications for the traditional photographer—the person whose primary creative activity is to use a camera?
Want ads. Like: "Talented and technically able photographer needs artists with vision for creative collaboration. Copyright issues no problem."

Over the last two decades, more and more of the images we see depend on color. Is there a future for black and white imagery?
Did video ever really kill the radio star?

In many artistic works, photos gain their meaning in a series, project or concept. Is there a future for the single image as a significant communication?
The power of the single picture is and will be everlasting. See Marilyn Monroe under W for Warhol.

Does photography have a moral dimension?
Yes.

Where do you see yourself going in the future, and what are you presently striving for and perfecting?
I've just become an American citizen so I figure I'll hang around "stateside" for a while. Striving to leave a legacy of meaningful work while perfecting my patience to do so.

What photograph or series of photographs is your proudest achievement?
My first-ever exposed sheet of 8x10" film, with which I won the Kodak Young Photographer Award of the Year, in the UK.

Aside from photography, what is your favorite pastime?
Film.

Who is your past/present mentor (influence)?
At the moment: David Nebreda and Boris Mikhailov.

How do you predict the future of traditional photography given the new emergence of digital technology?
The two will go hand-in-hand.

What part of your work do you find most demanding?
Relying on others.

Over to you—any final words on photography?
Later, I have to run (it is morning now).

Hans Neleman is the author Moko Maori-Tattoo and Silence. His next book, Night Chicas, will be published by Graphis Press in January 2003. He works from his studio in SoHo, New York City and lives in Connecticut with his wife, daughter and son.

(opposite and opening page) Still lifes from Neleman's book Silence.

Have all the pictures been taken?
All but one: the next one.

Are there great future subjects for a photographer?
As long as the world turns around there'll be future subjects for a photographer—new ones or old subjects to be revisited in a different way.

Photography has always been a hands-on medium of expression. How do you see digital technology changing the relationship of the photographer to act of image-making?
Photography has also always been a medium based on technology, so the digital revolution is another step forward in this young medium just like color film, 35mm camera, or the invention of the fixer were new in the not so distant past.

The classic role of the photojournalist is to bear truthful witness to the moment. How can the photojournalist validify his or her credibility if the "truth value" of images is subverted by digital processing?
In the 21st century the printed image is almost always manipulated digitally and retouched. Honesty and dignity have to be part of this dilemma.

What is the impact of the world's growing skepticism toward photographic images (and the people who make them)?
I don't think there's growing skepticism toward the photographic image. There's a question and an interest about how images are created and put together. There is, however, an overwhelming feeling that too many images are out there, a feeling that can make one indifferent.

The rise of digital technology has gone hand-in-hand with the return of antique processes. Are the latter valid artistically and commercially?
Regardless of what the process is, a good image is a good image and a bad image is just that. I believe that digital technology keeps photography fresh and relevant and will take a central role in commercial and artistic projects. However, film will continue to be used by artists as well as commercial photographers as another tool on the palette.

What are the implications of the Web for the photographers' ability to maintain commercial and artistic control of their images?
The web enables photographers, young or established, to show their work anywhere, everywhere, all the time. The positive implications of the web for the photographer far outweigh the risks of being copied.

Throughout photography's history, fine art photography has sought to separate itself from commercial and industrial applications (most recently, fashion and advertising). Is that separation valid or even possible today?
On the highest level fine art and commercial photography are not separated.

People now see photographs occupying the same space in museums that paintings do. What is the current relationship between painting (and other arts) and photography and how does this influence photographic practice?
Photography and other forms of fine art feed and influence each other.

Many of the key artists using photography aren't photographers in the conventional sense and some even have others make the photos for them, which they then deploy. What are the implications for the traditional photographer—the person whose primary creative activity is to use a camera?
There are no implications.

Over the last two decades, more and more of the images we see depend on color. Is there a future for black and white imagery?
Yes.

In many artistic works, photos gain their meaning in a series, project or concept. Is there a future for the single image as a significant communication?
This is a good question. I think that it's harder and harder for one image to have huge significance in communication because we are exposed to an explosion of images around us every day. It takes tragic events like 9/11 to make the picture of the three firefighters standing with the American flag on top of the Twin Towers' rubbles an image that will not be erased from our minds.

Does photography have a moral dimension?
Yes, photography is the world's collective memory.

Where do you see yourself going in the future, and what are you presently striving for and perfecting?
I always strive for a better picture, for the next good idea for a great new project.

What photograph or series of photographs is your proudest achievement?
I really like the last series that I did. I shot a vase with tulips from the same spot for 40 days.

Aside from photography, what is your favorite pastime?
I like to spend my free time with my family.

Who is your past/present mentor (influence)?
Painting and art are Irving Penn and Tom Wesselman.

How do you predict the future of traditional photography given the new emergence of digital technology?
I believe that photography, like other art forms, will continue to go back to processes that are old. When my wife bought me a print of Irving Penn's print "Crossing the River Styx" I looked at the variations in the platinum and silver prints and found it impossible not to admire their beauty.

What part of your work do you find most demanding?
Coming up with new ideas and making them happen.

Over to you—any final words on photography?
I think it is a really exciting time in photography right now. A time of a lot of hope, change and also confusion. 1839-2002. photography is only beginning.

Ilan Rubin moved to New York from his native Israel 15 years ago. In addition to cover work for the Japanese, German, and Spanish editions of Vogue, his editorial clients have included Allure, GQ, Rolling Stone, Nylon and Arena. He has worked with the top advertising agencies for the likes of Nike, Sony, Isabella Rosselini and Coach.

(opposite page and overleaf) Editorial work for German Vogue and Amica magazine.

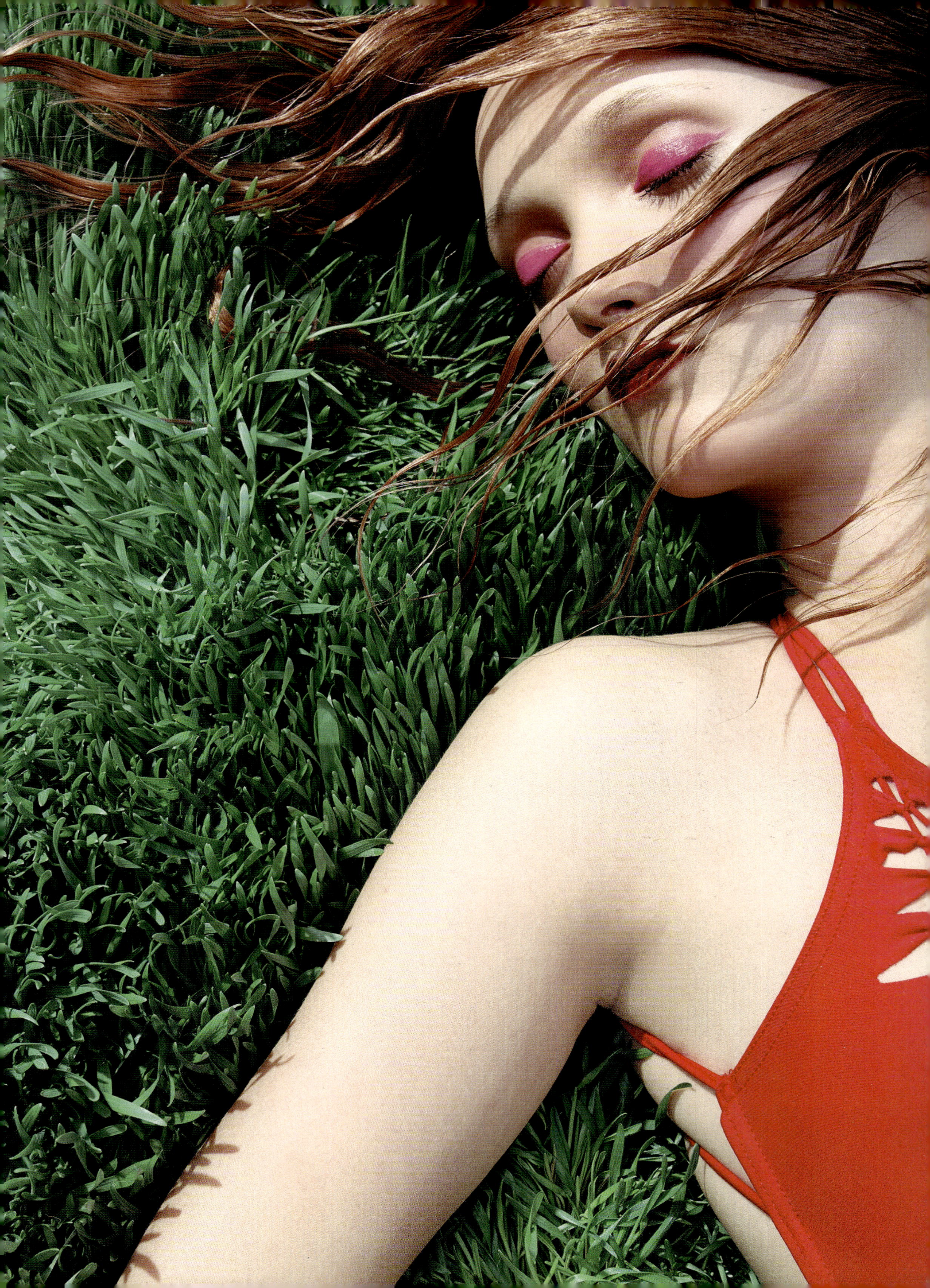

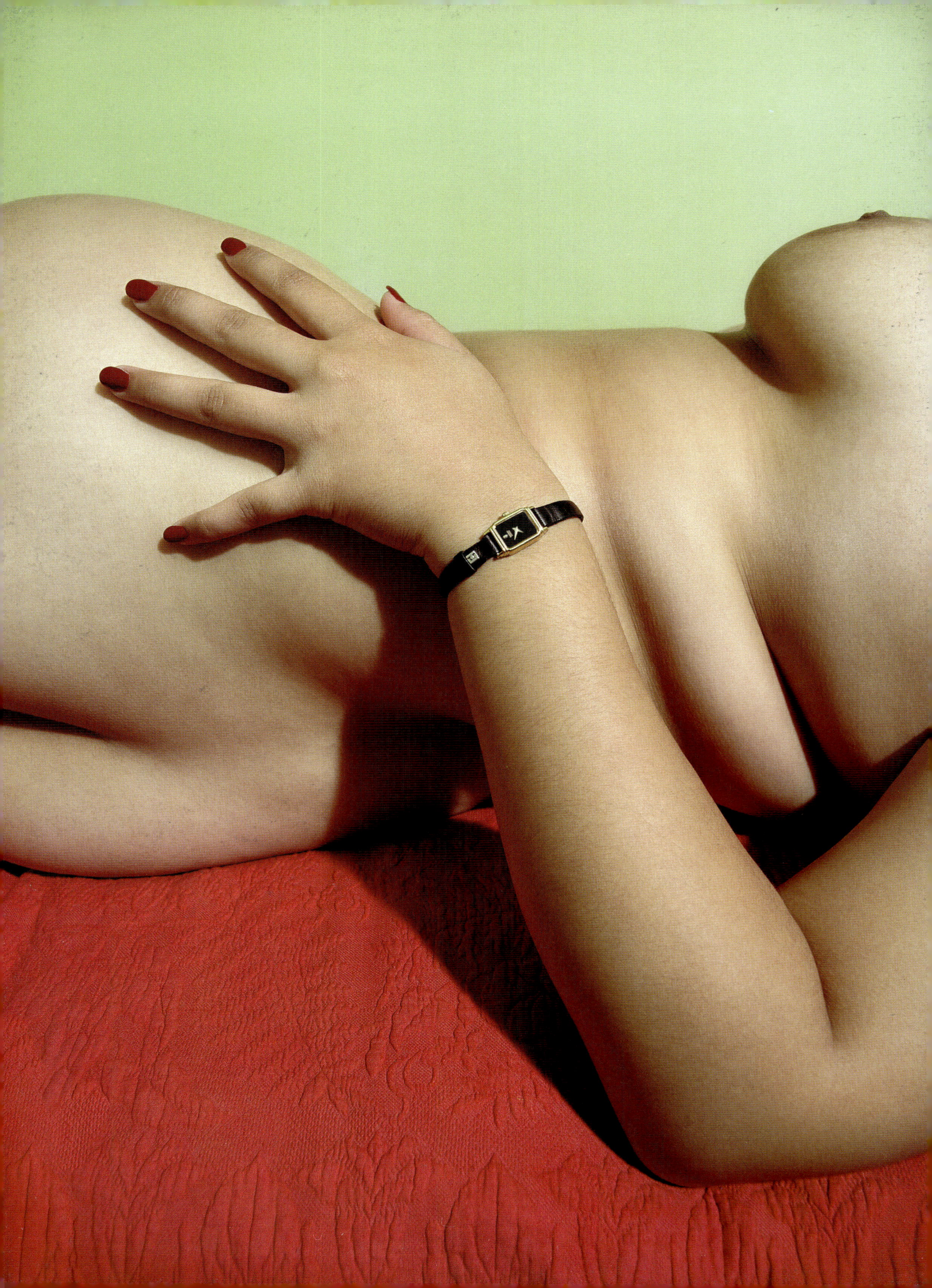

Photo Annual 2003

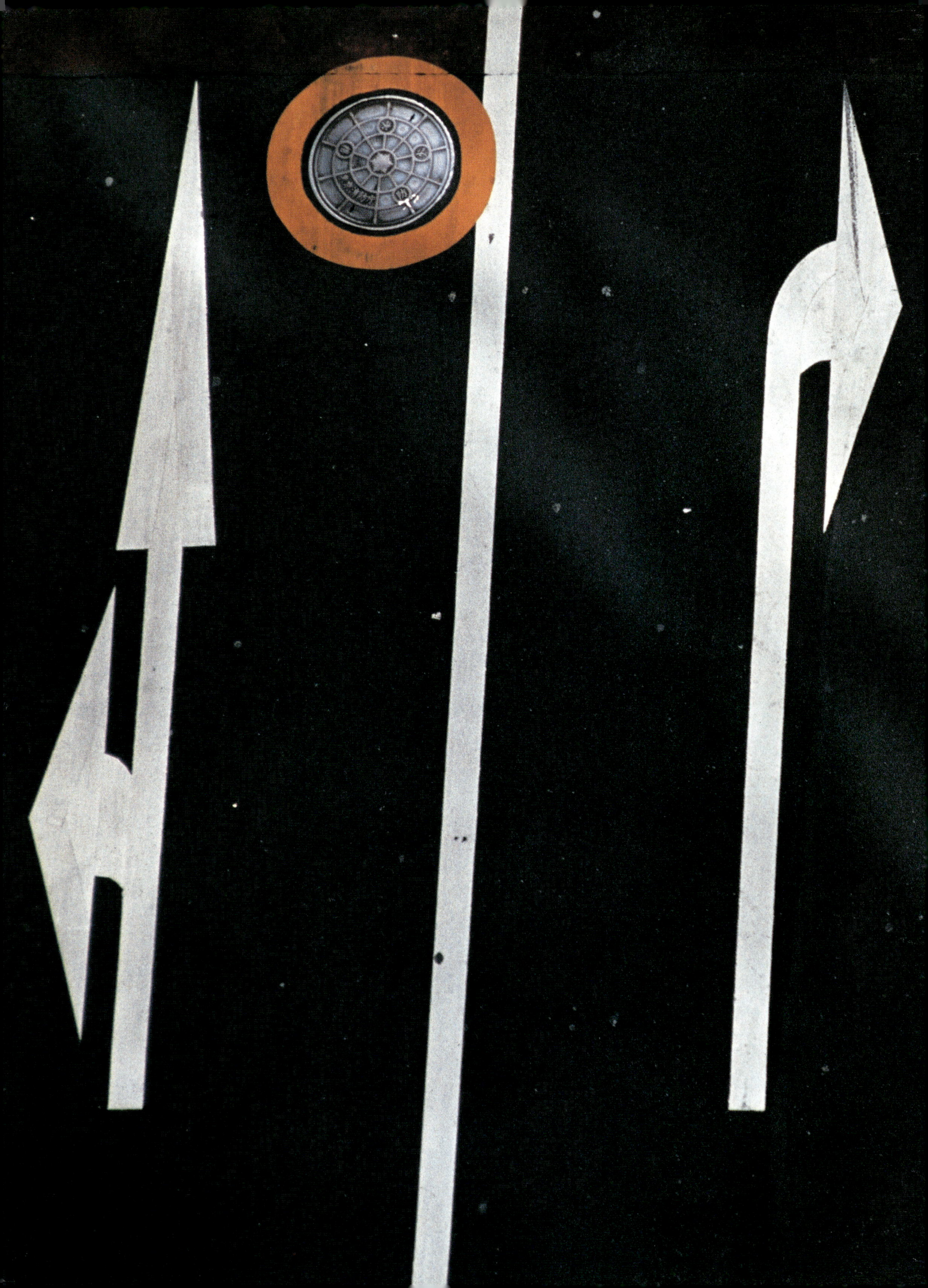

Architecture

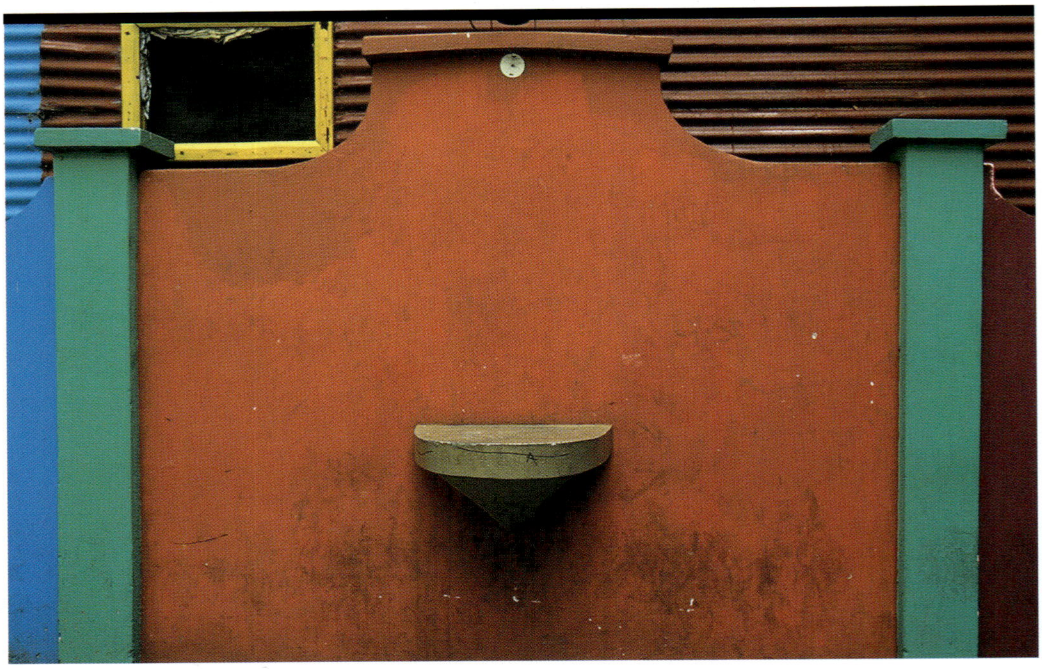

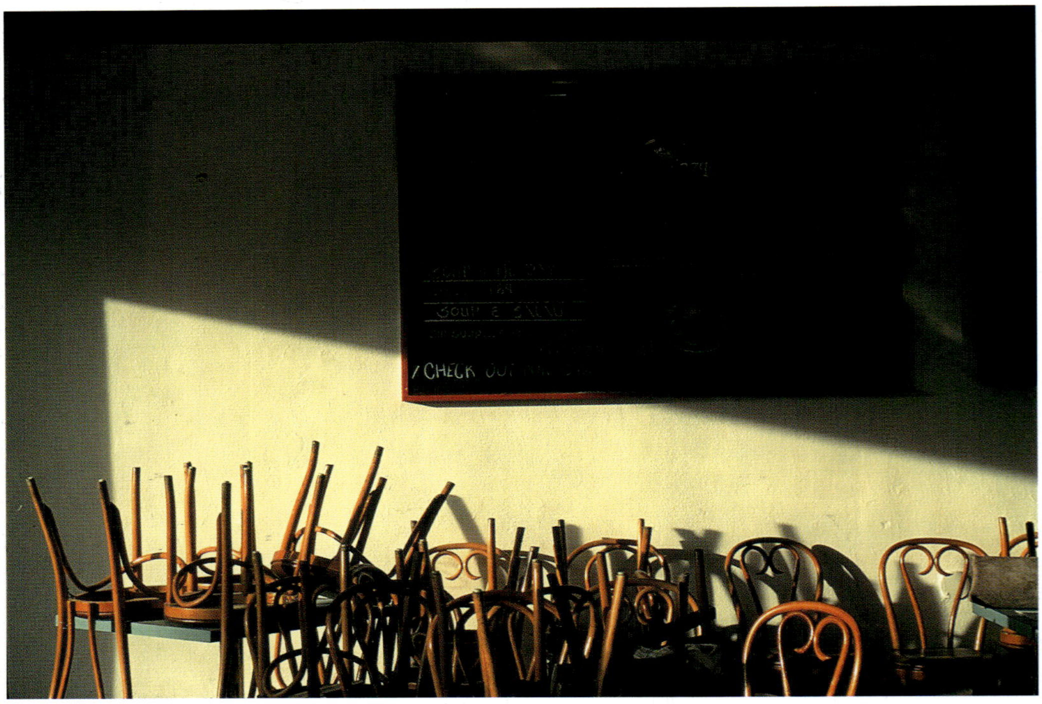

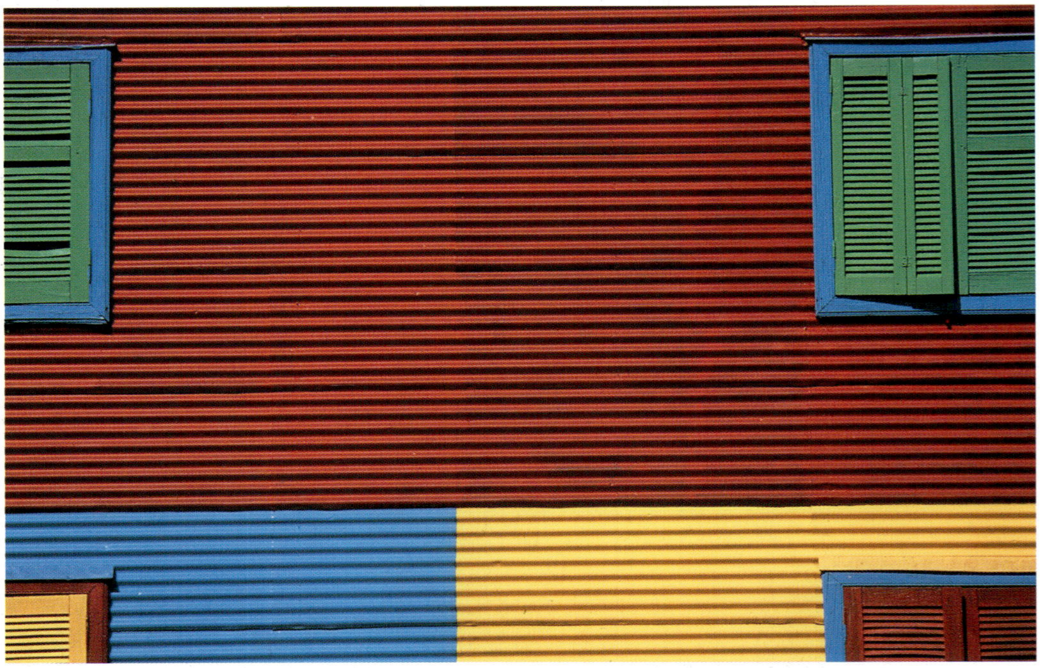

(this and opening page) Arthur Meyerson (opposite) Andrea Wells

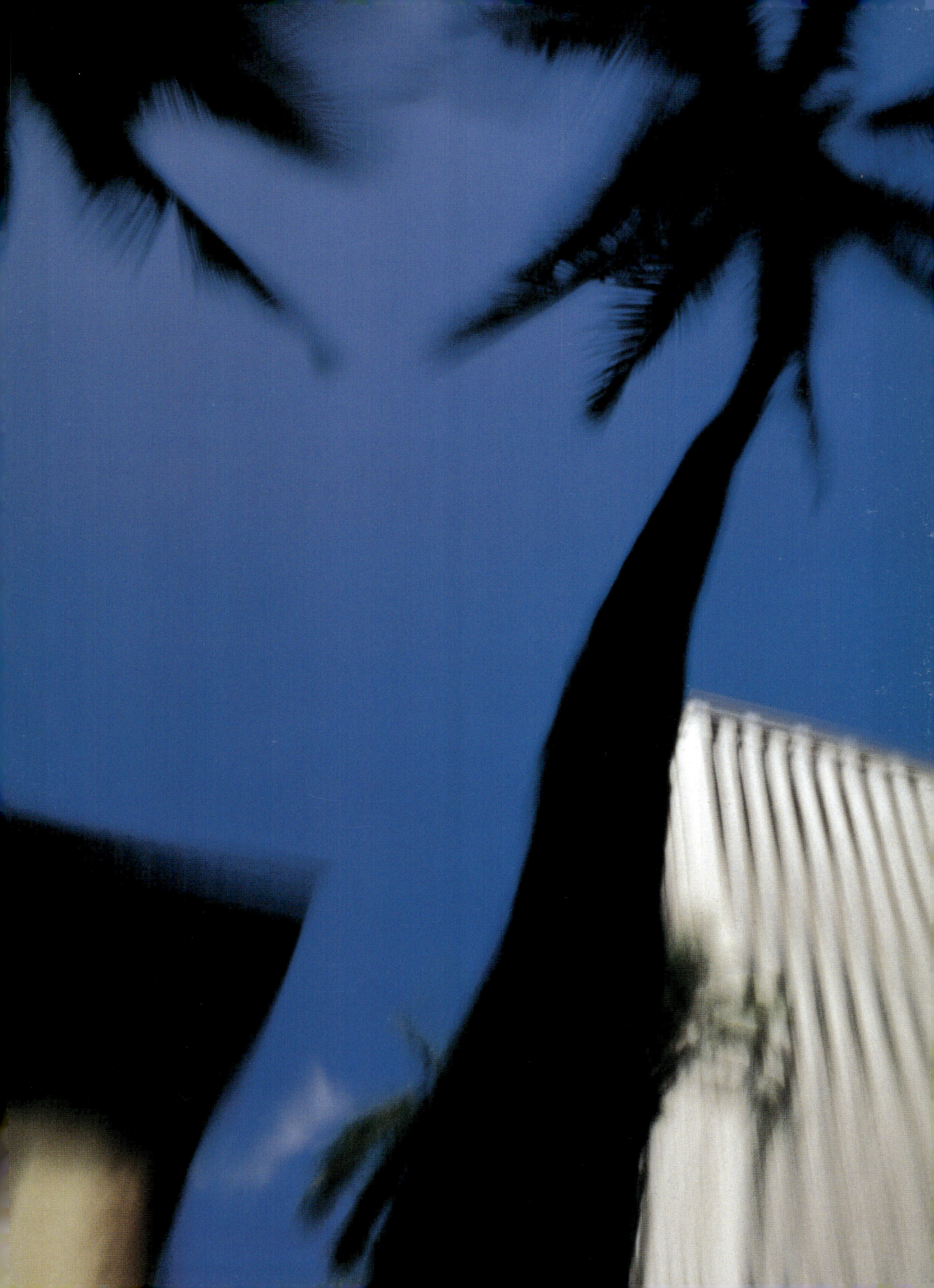

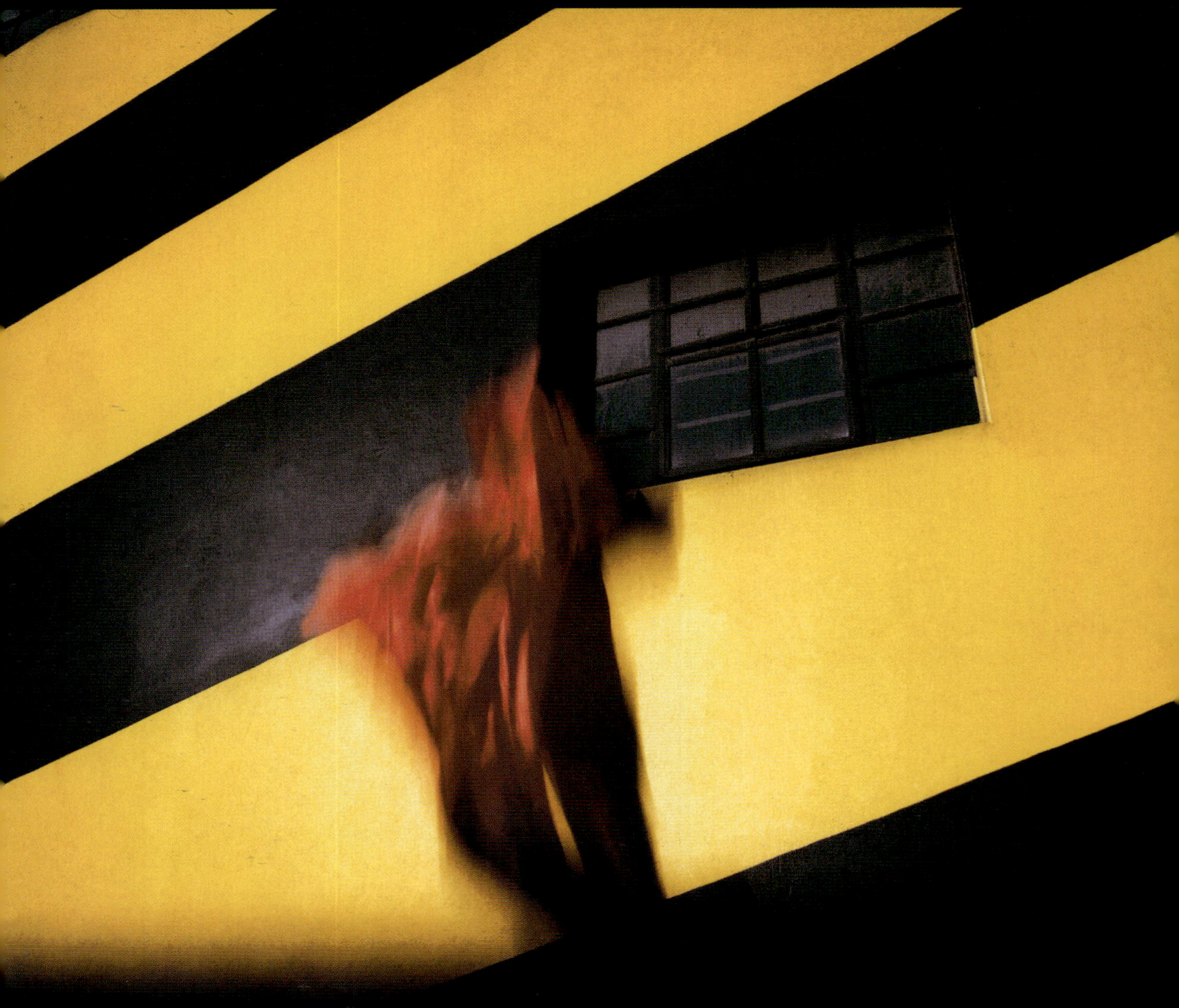

Phil Bekker

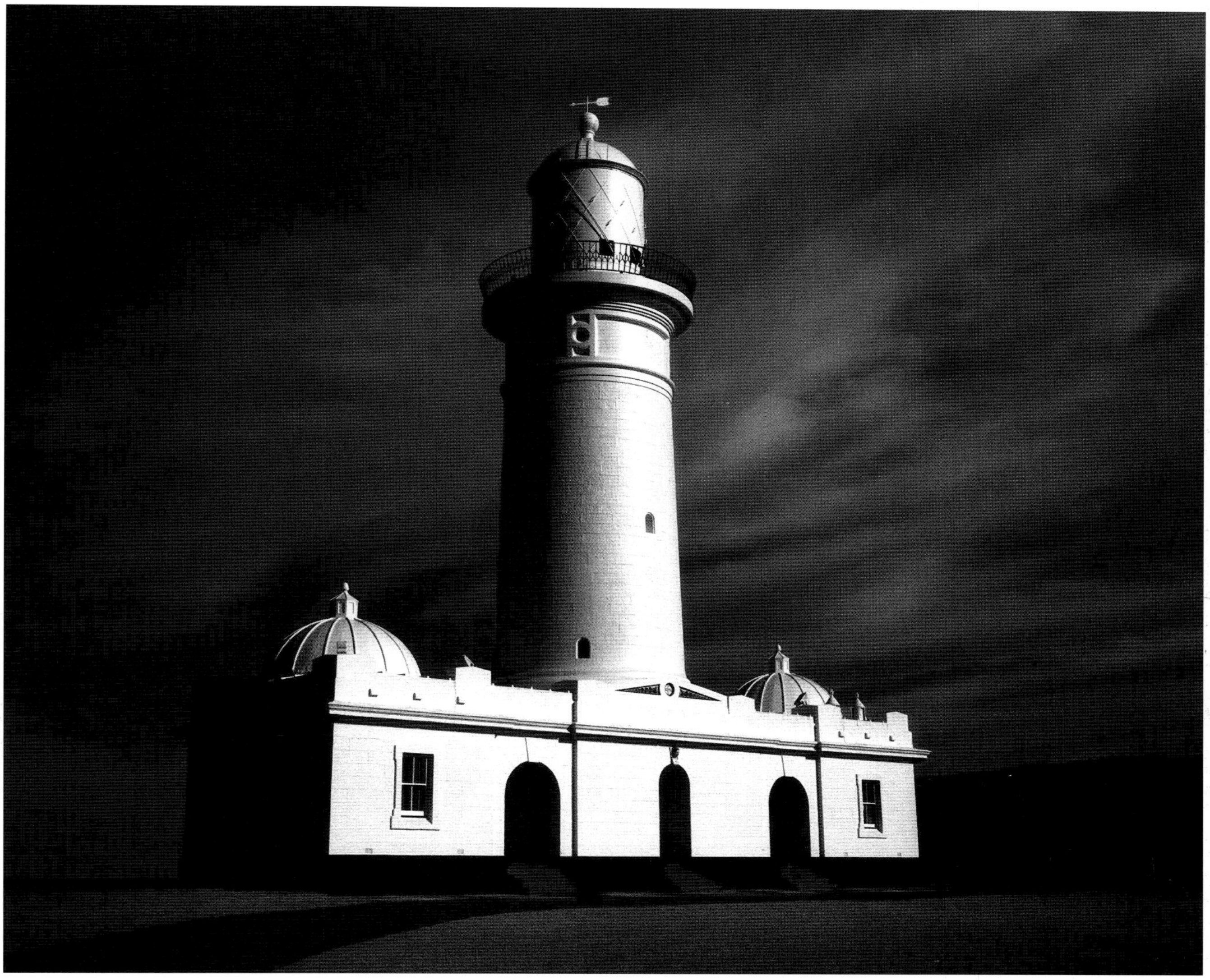

Walter Whitman

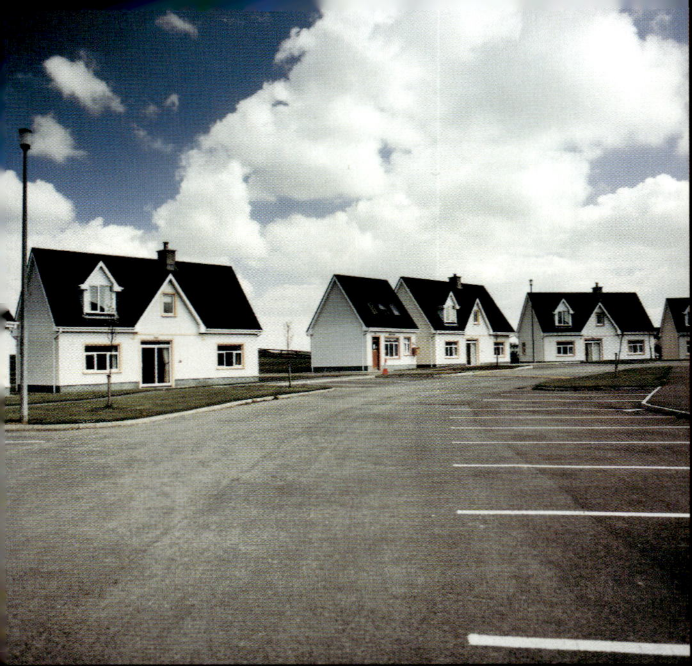

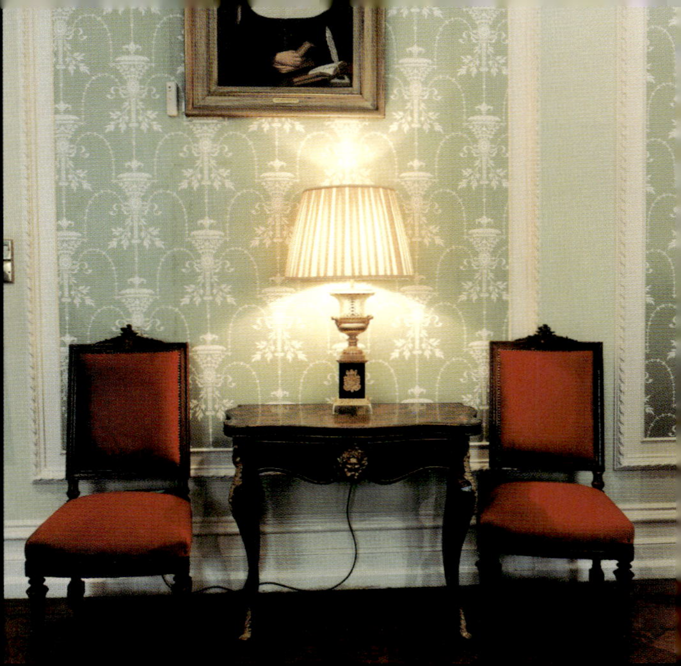

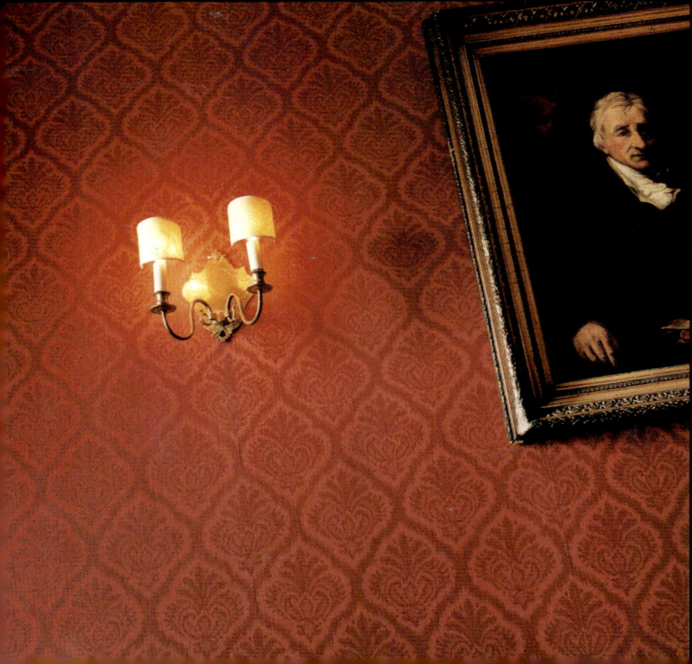

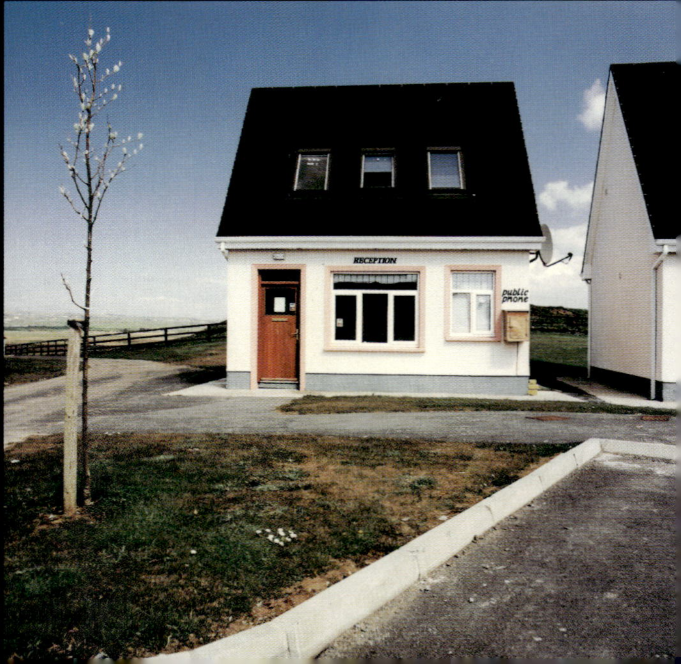
RECEPTION
public phone

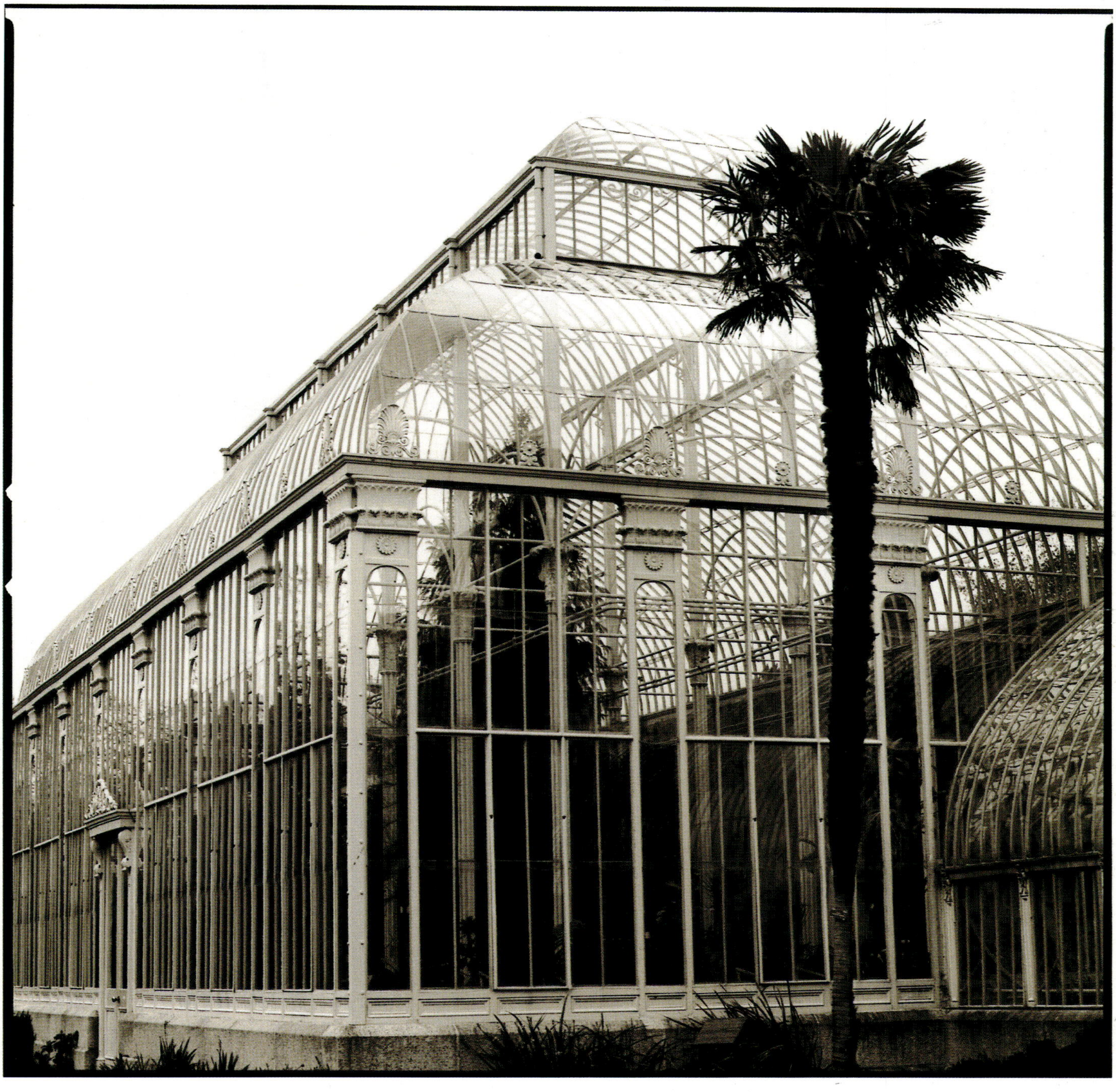

Craig Cutler

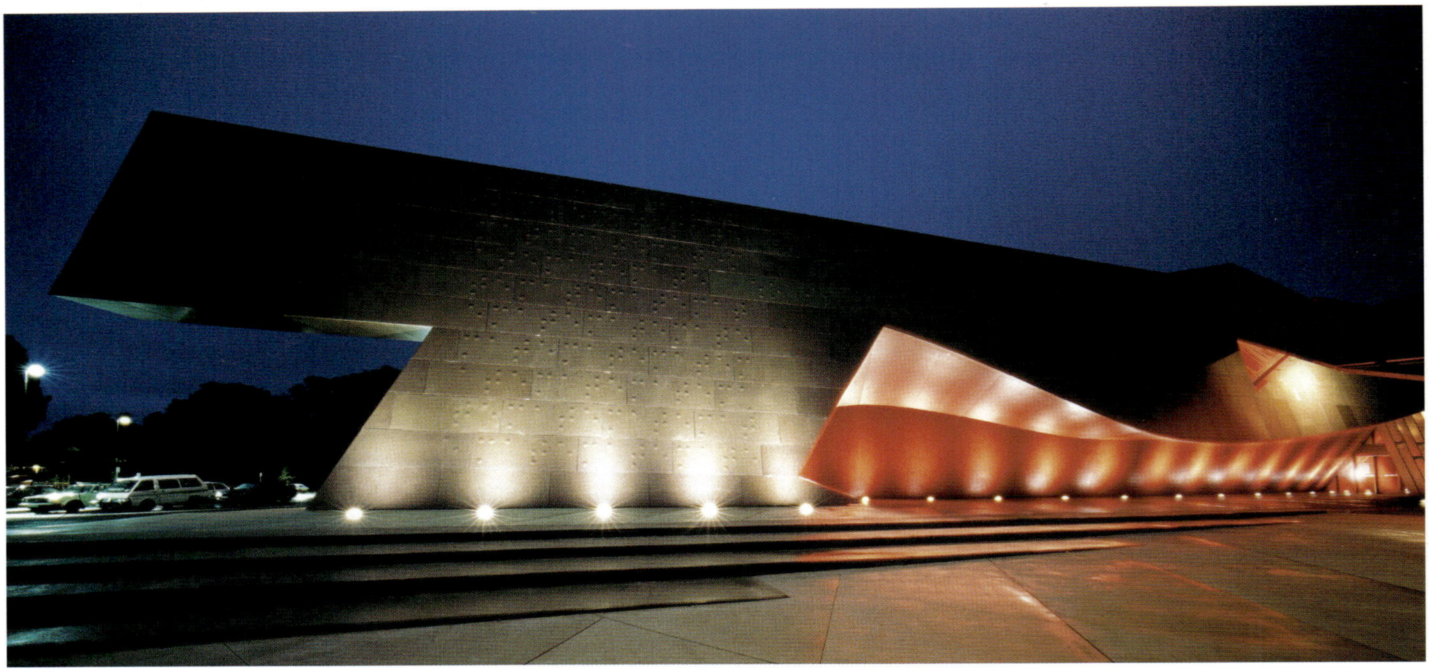

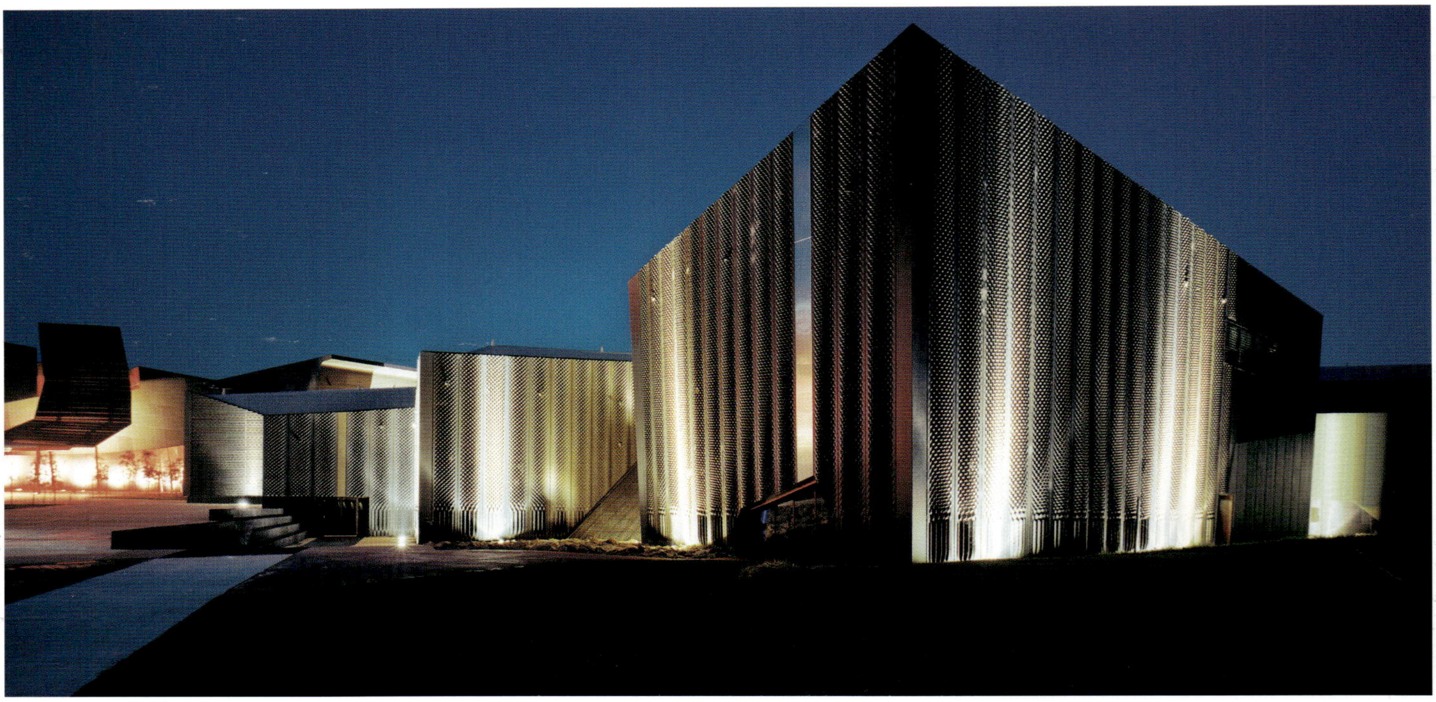

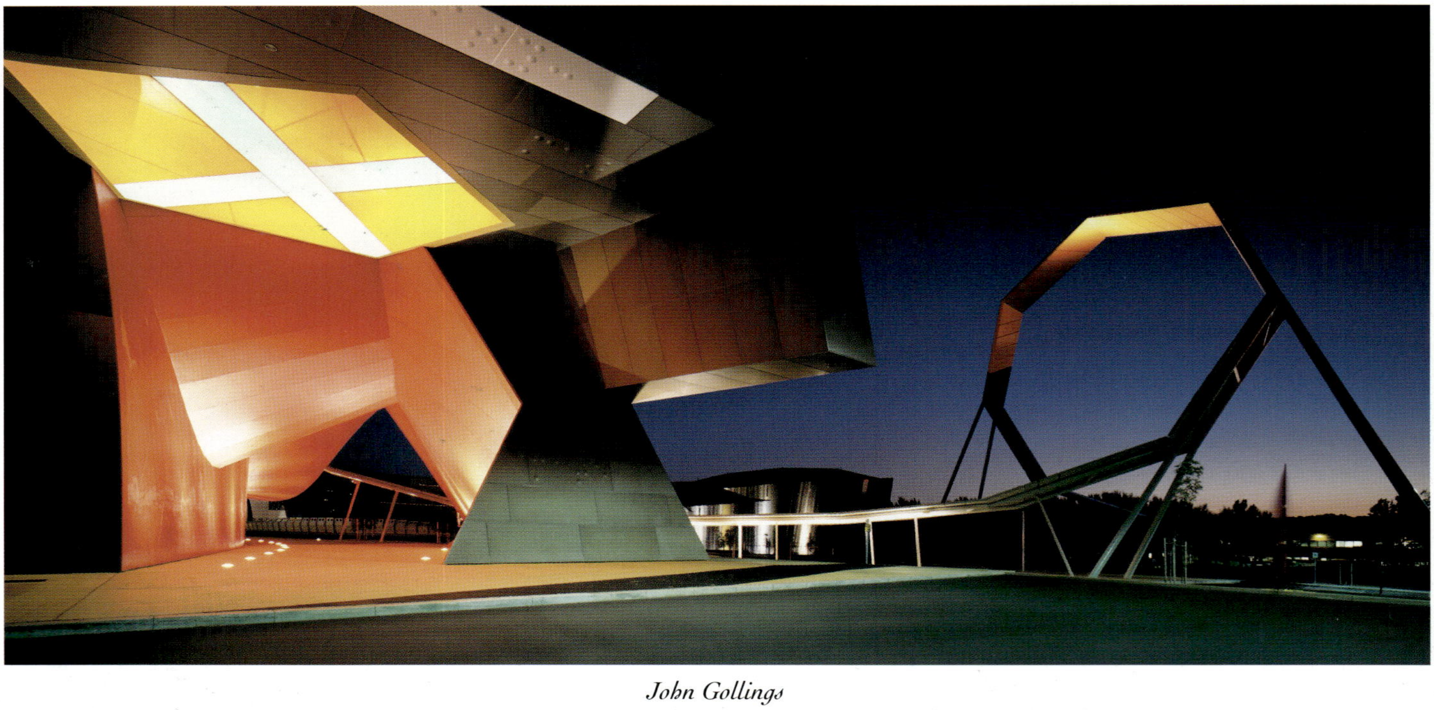

John Gollings

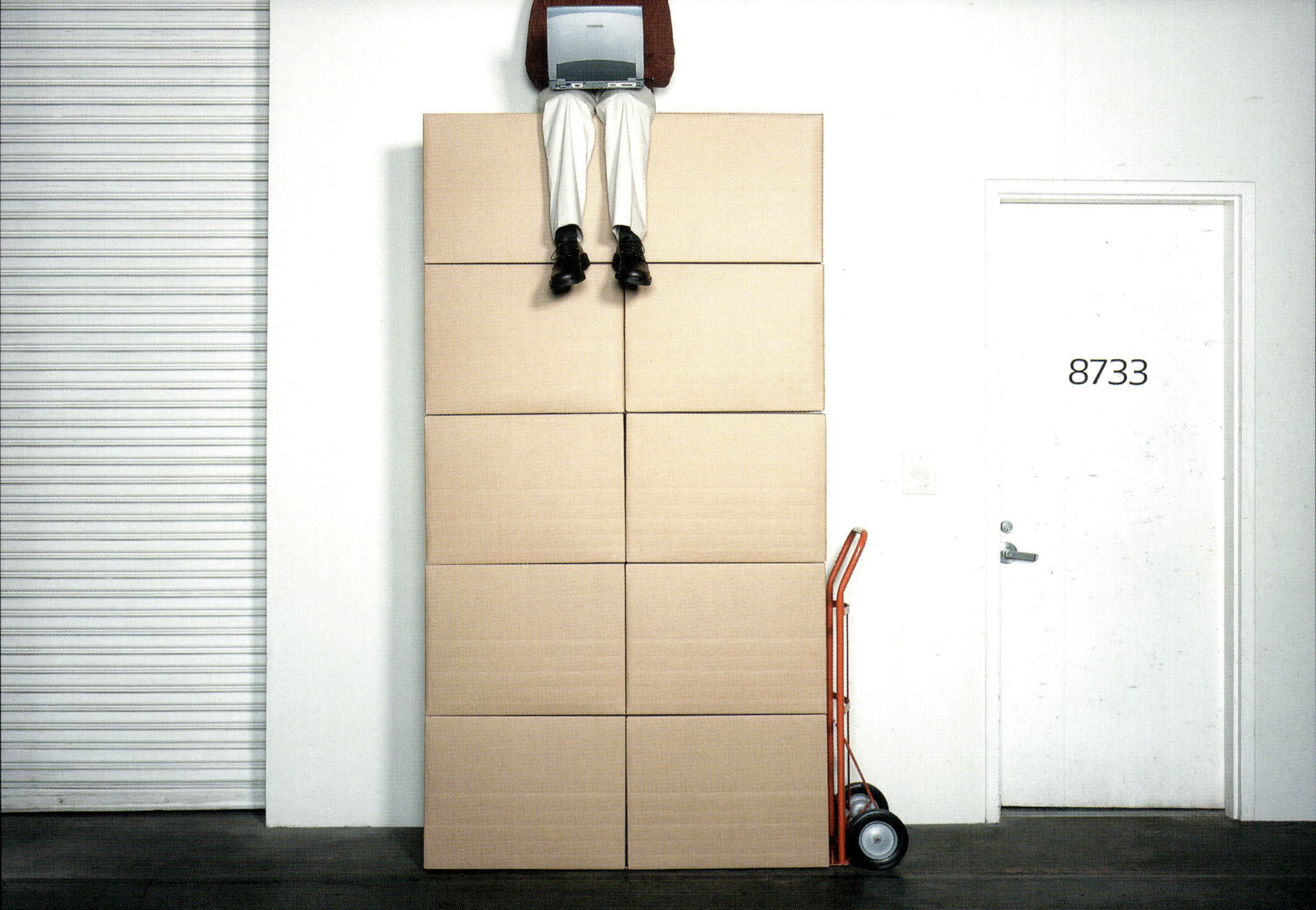
8733

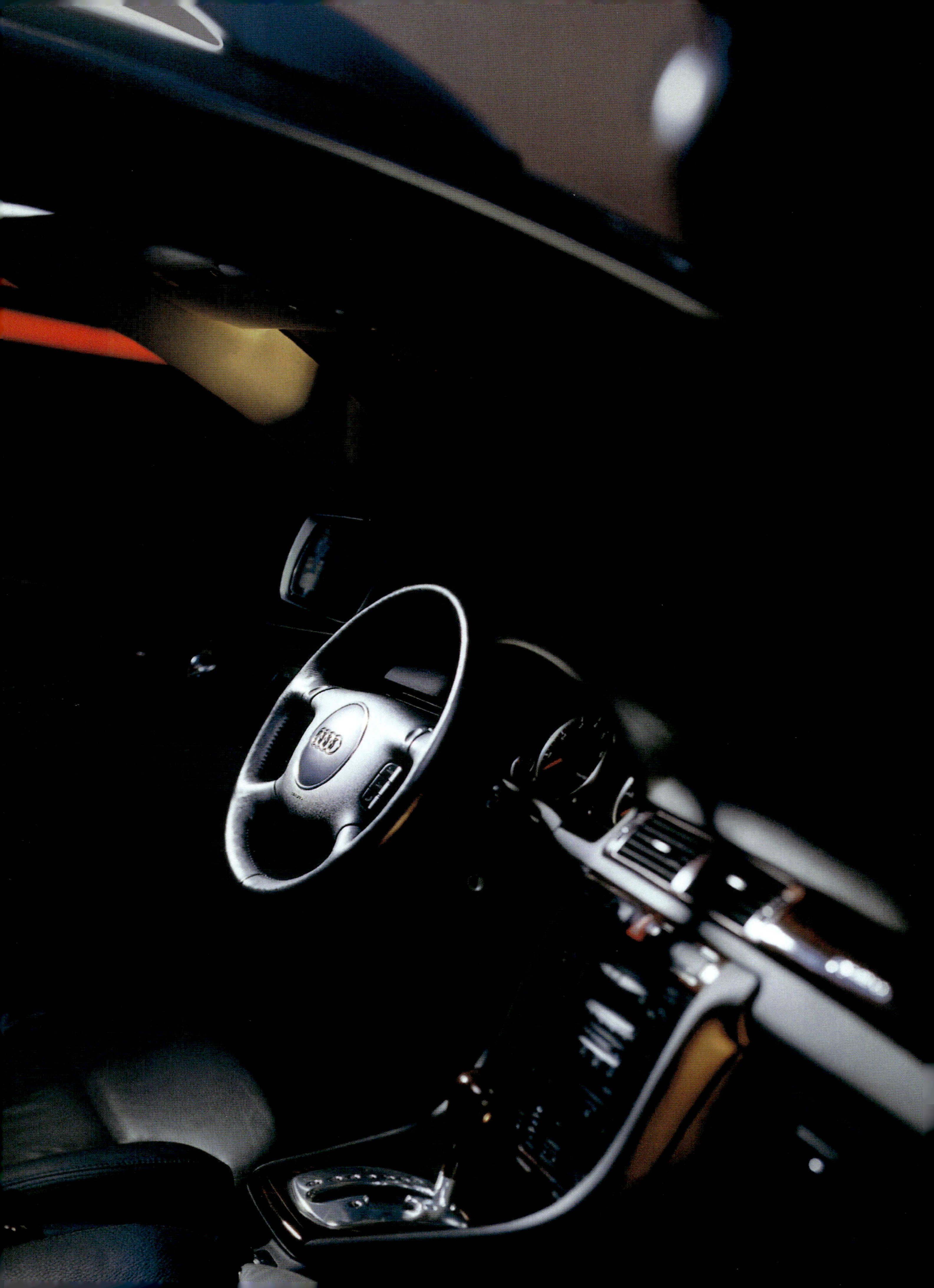

Automotive

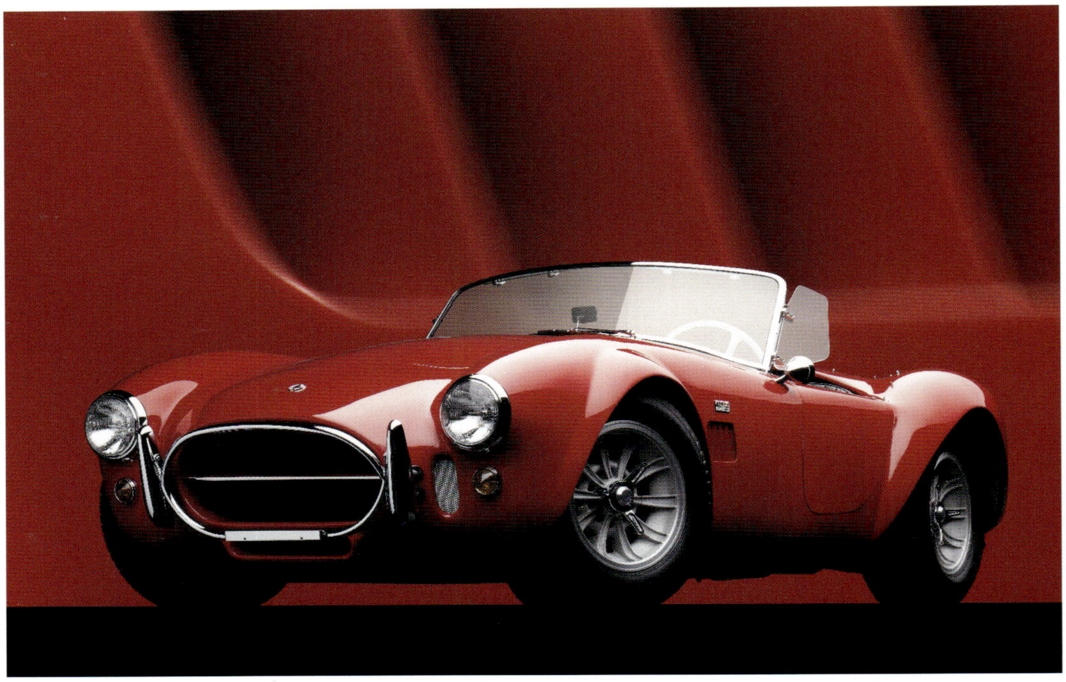

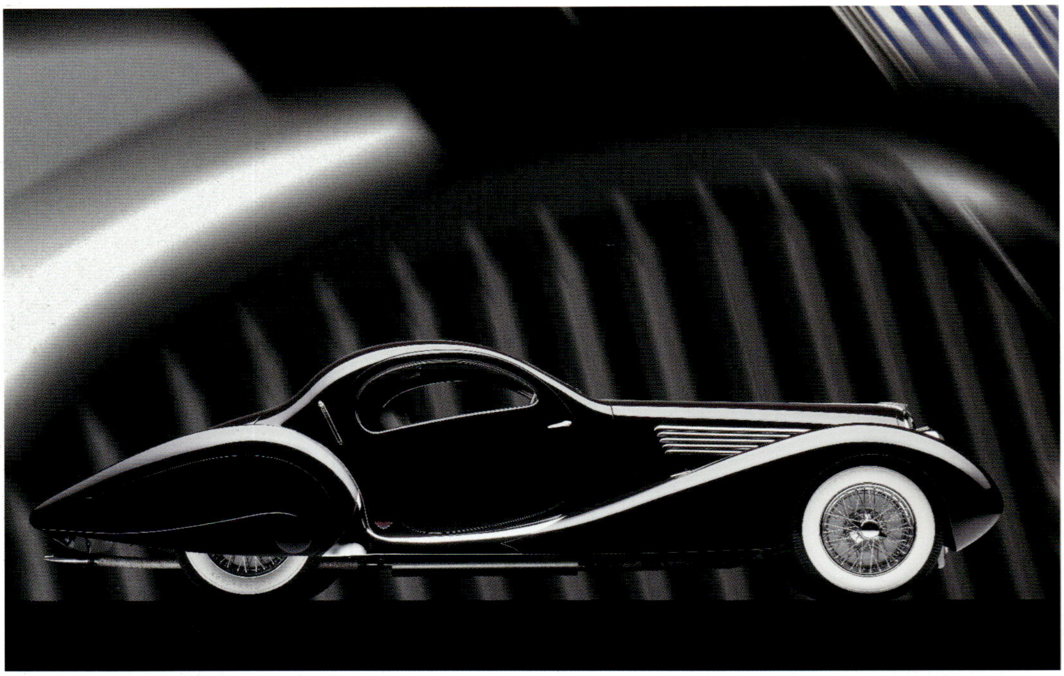

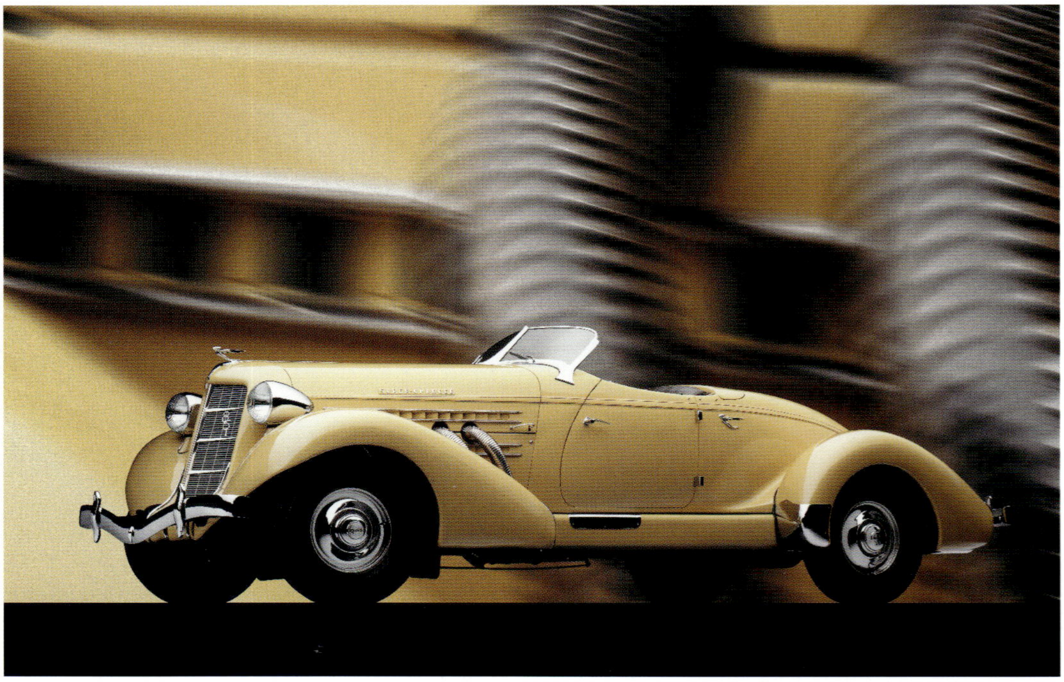

Michael Furman (opening page) Michael Moore

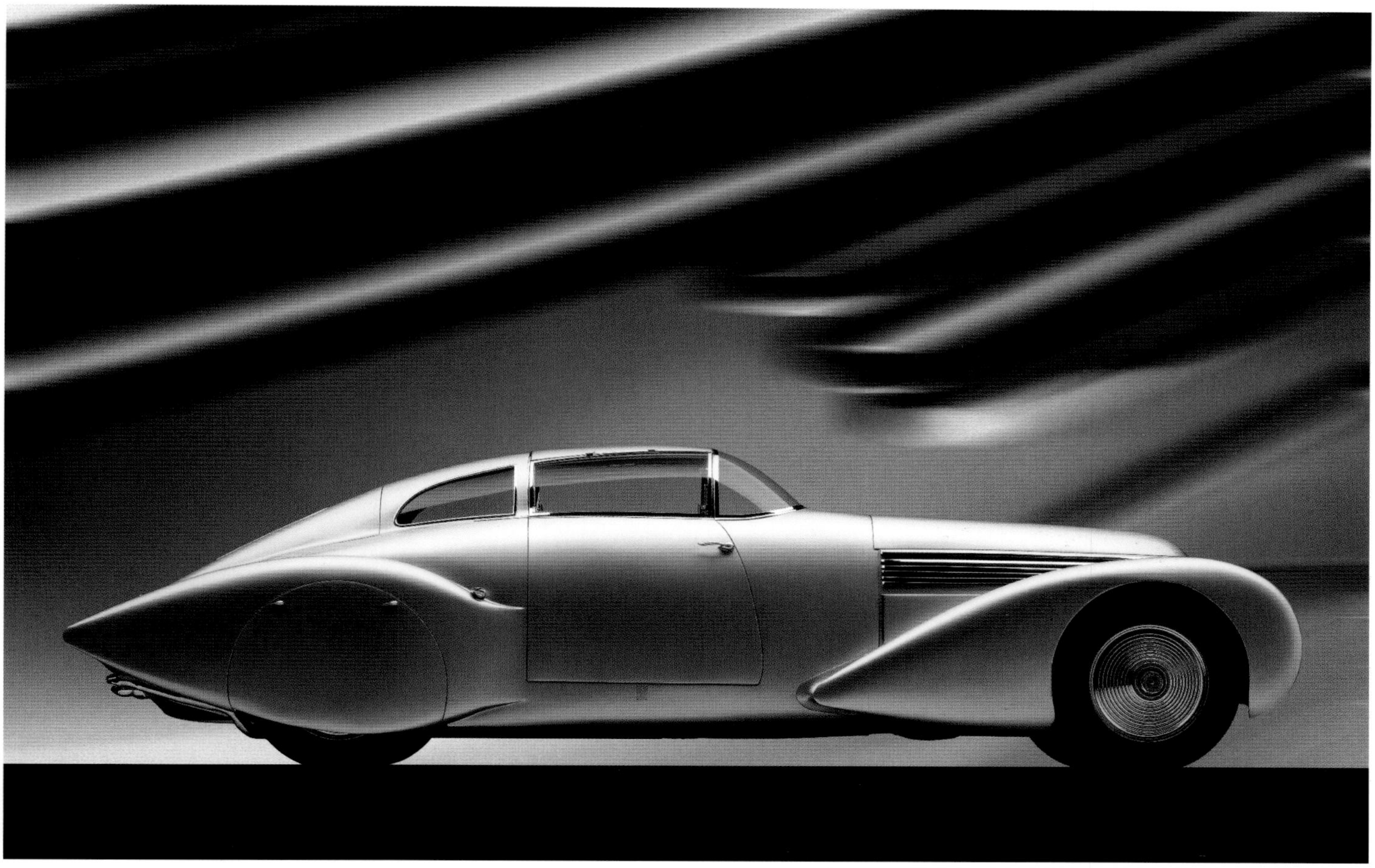

Michael Furman

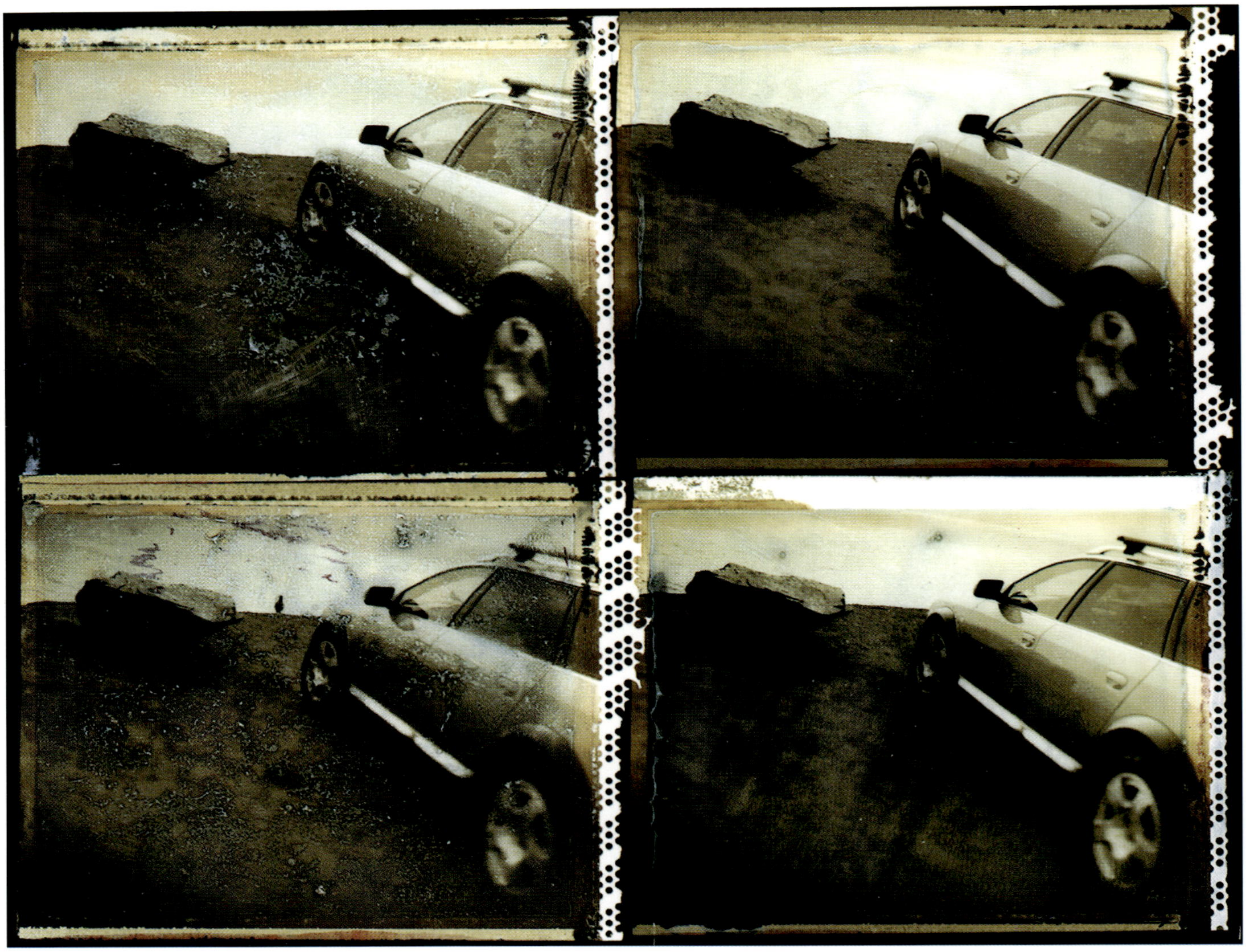

Michael Moore

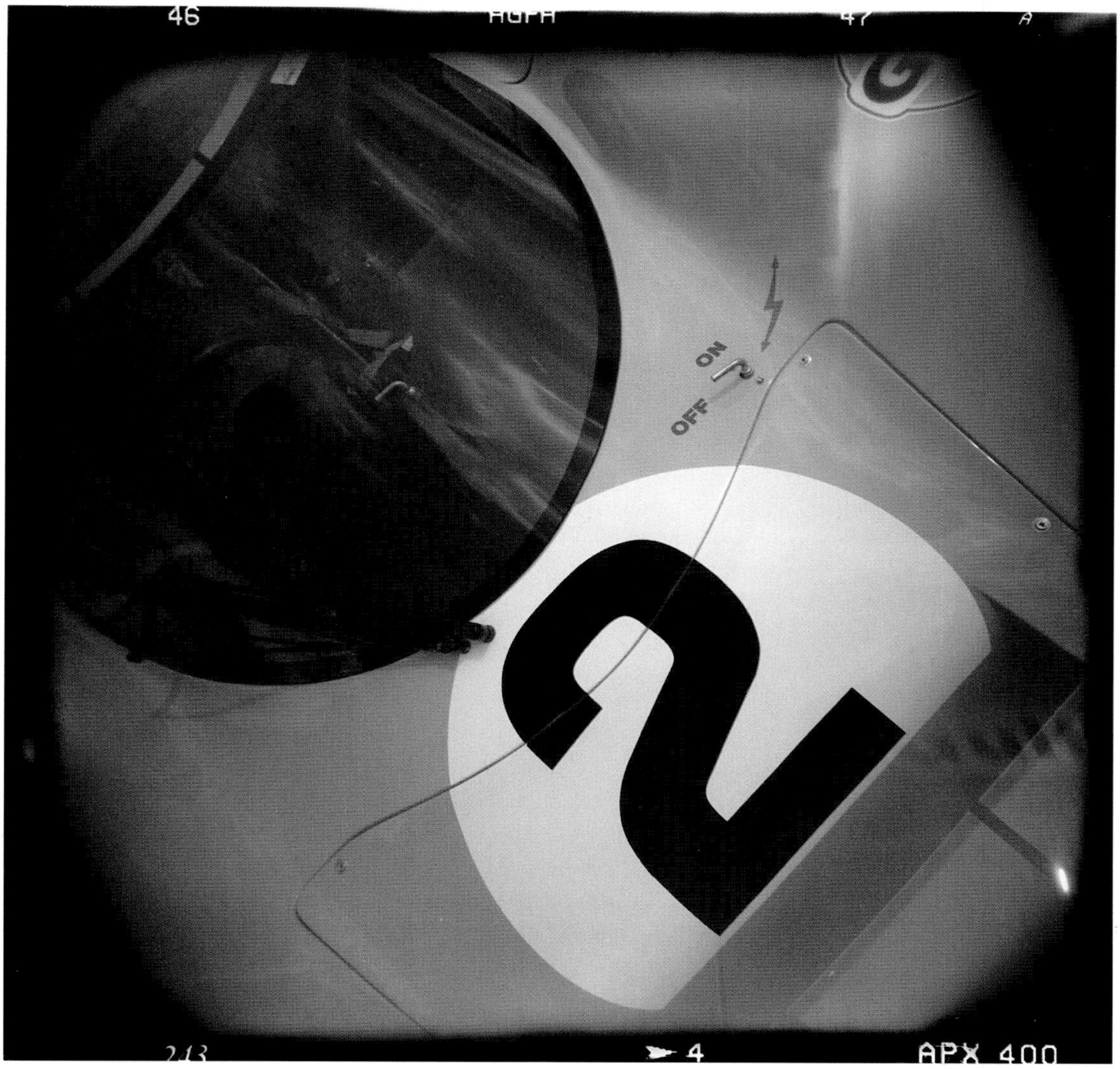

Greg Myhra

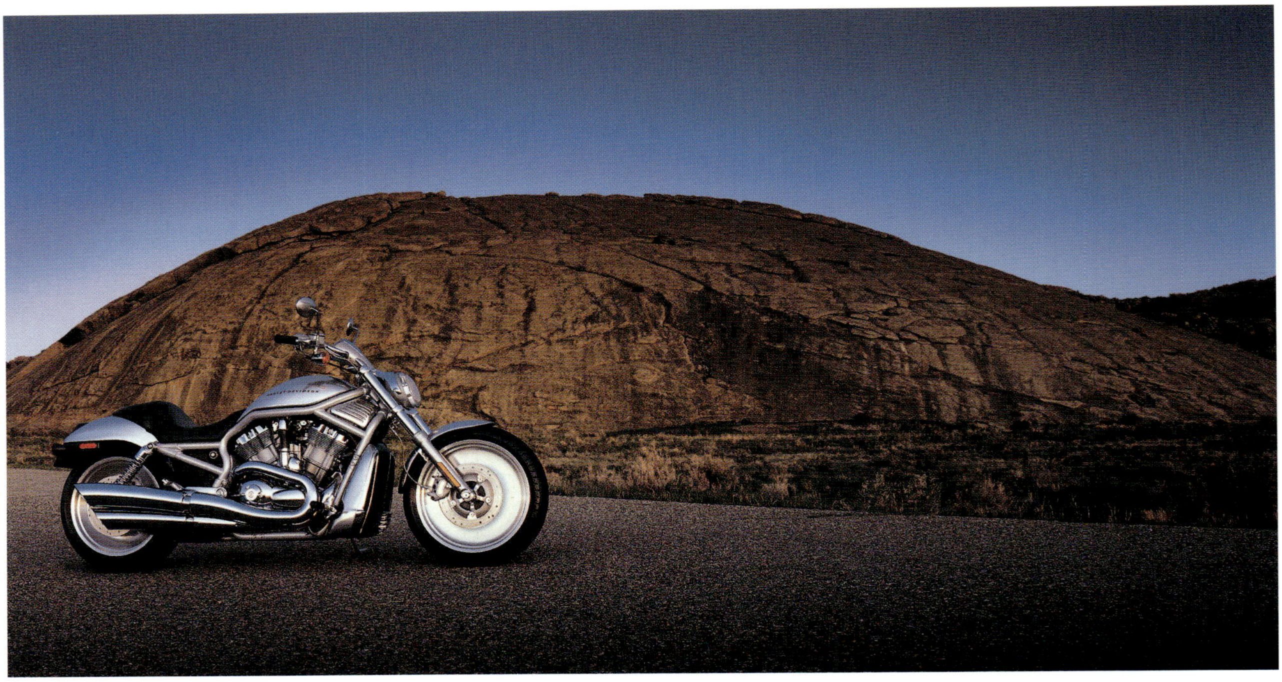

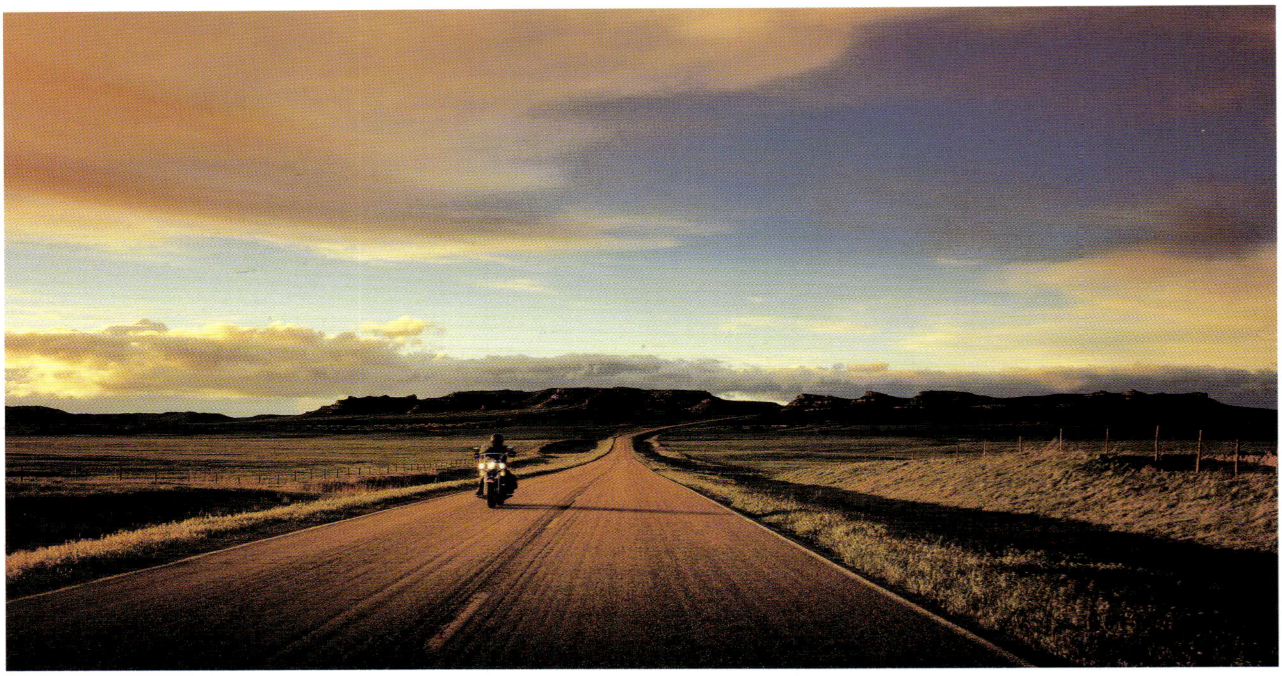

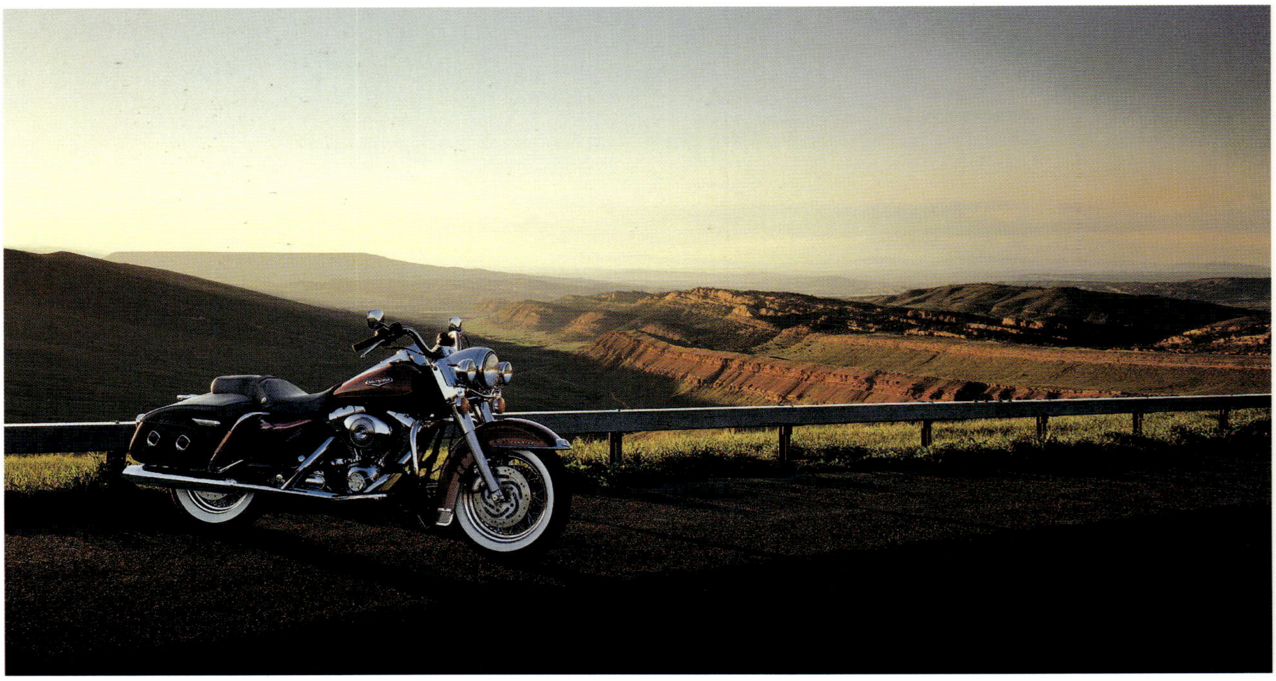

Chris Wimpey

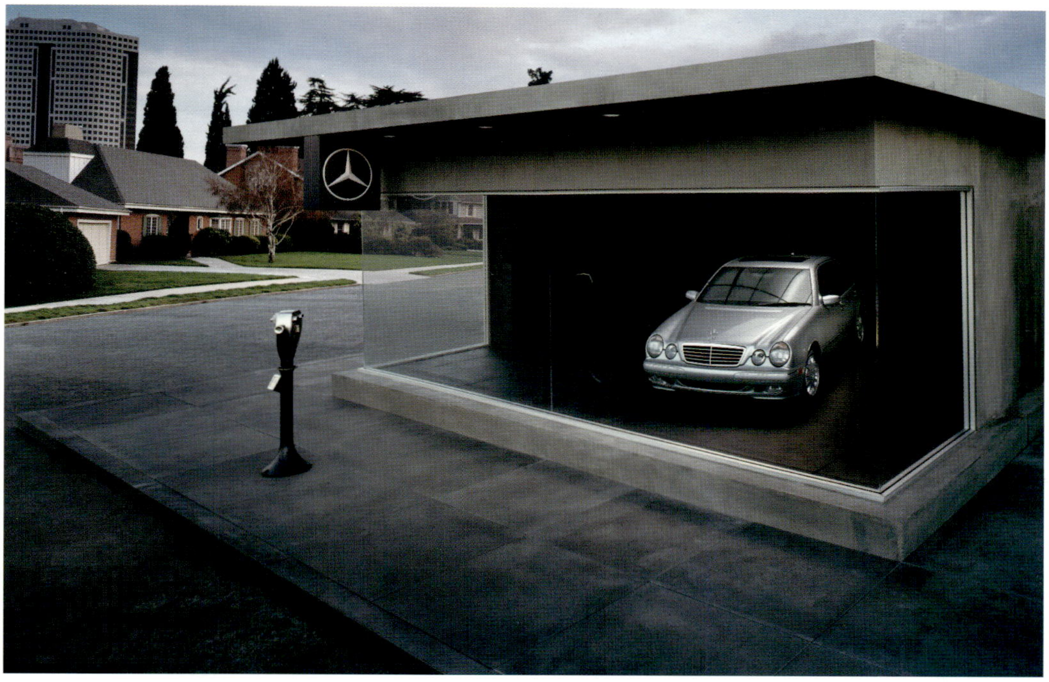

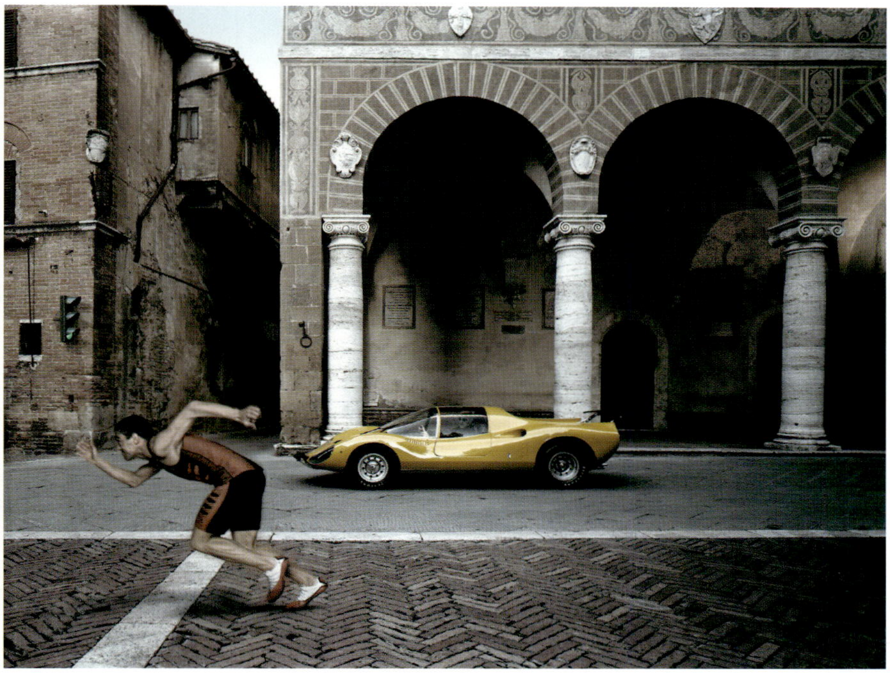

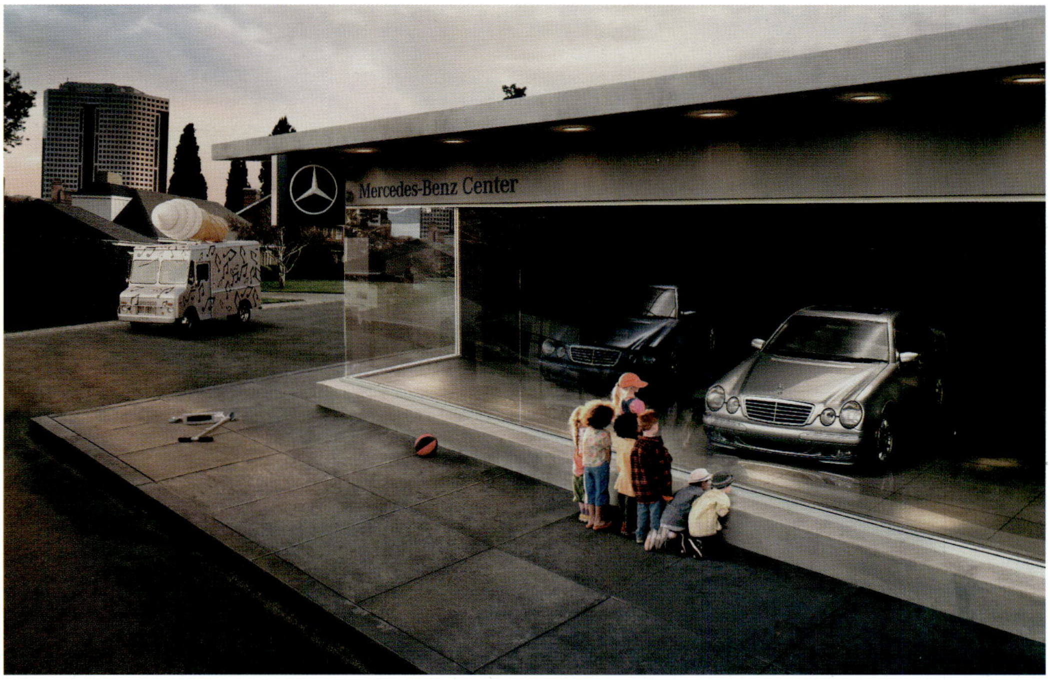

Stuart Hall

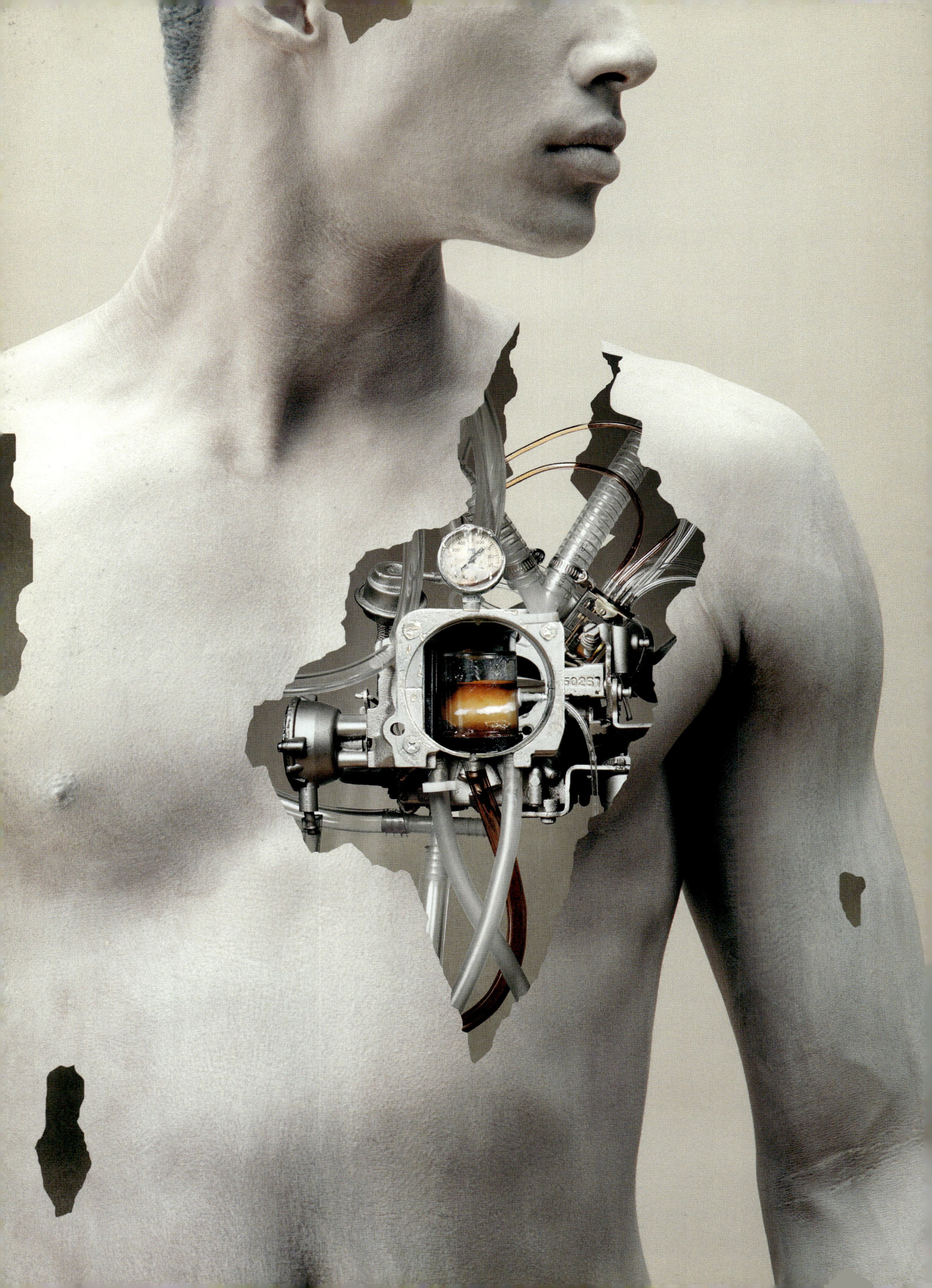

Digital

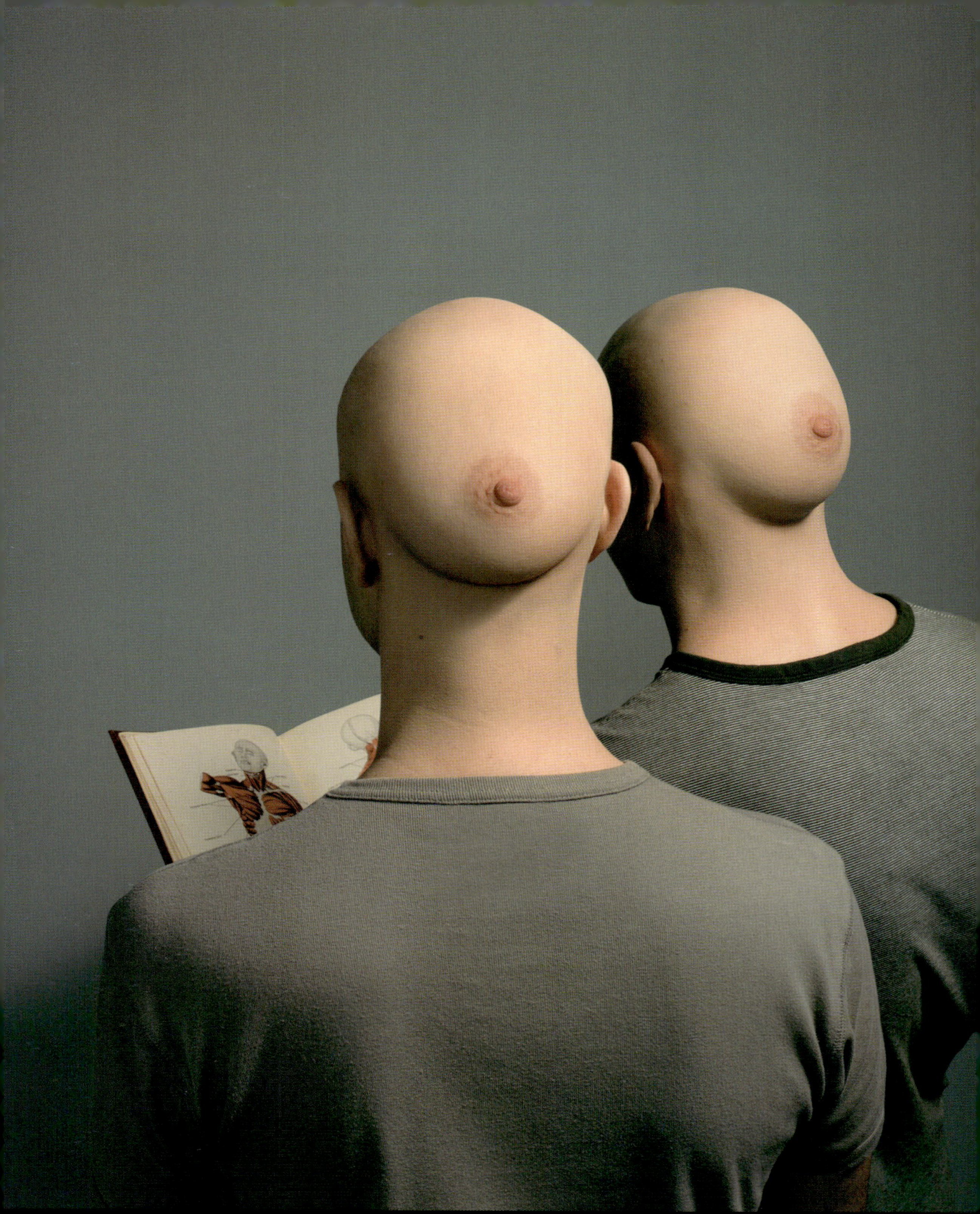

Hugh Kretschmer (opening page), Sanjay Kothari

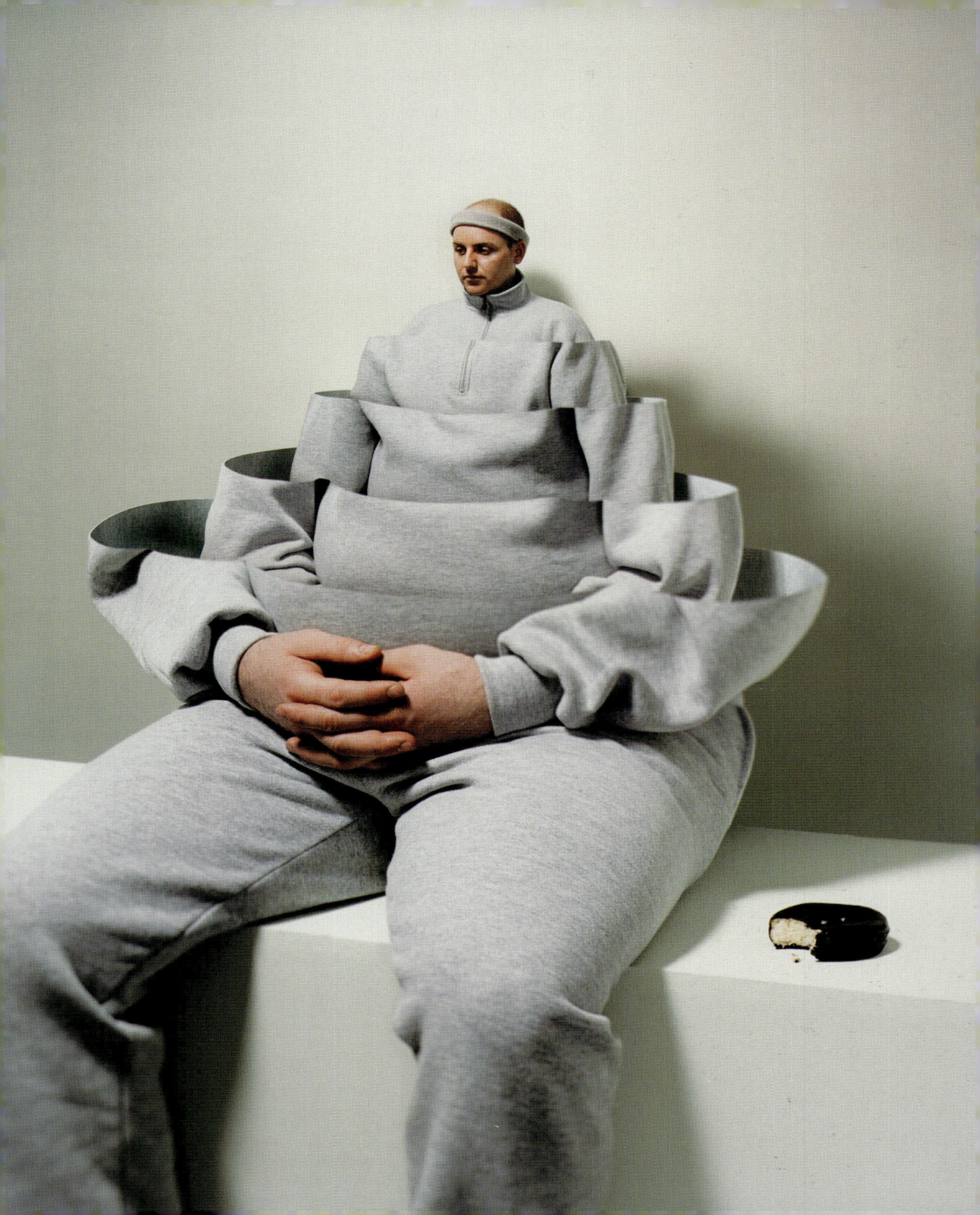

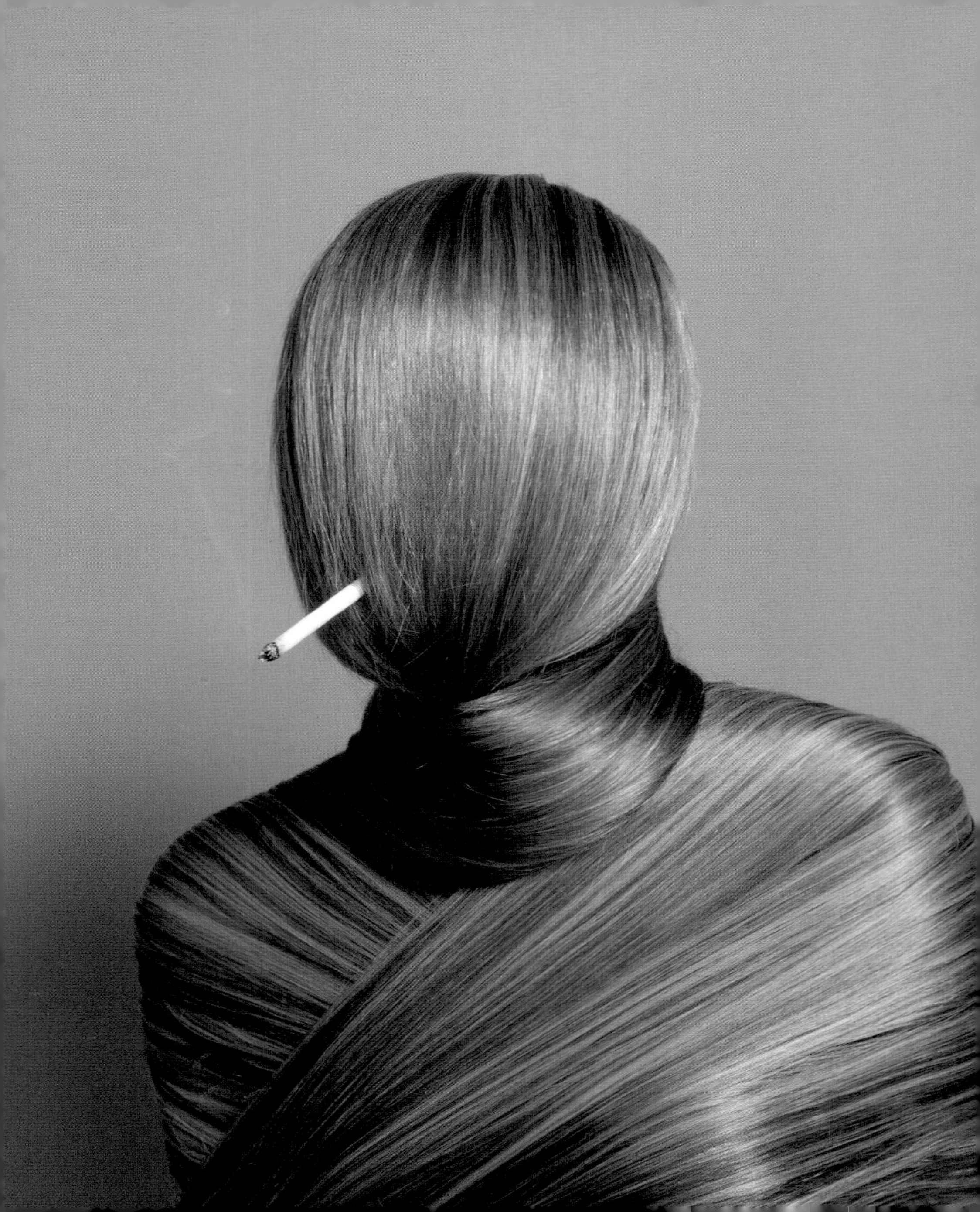

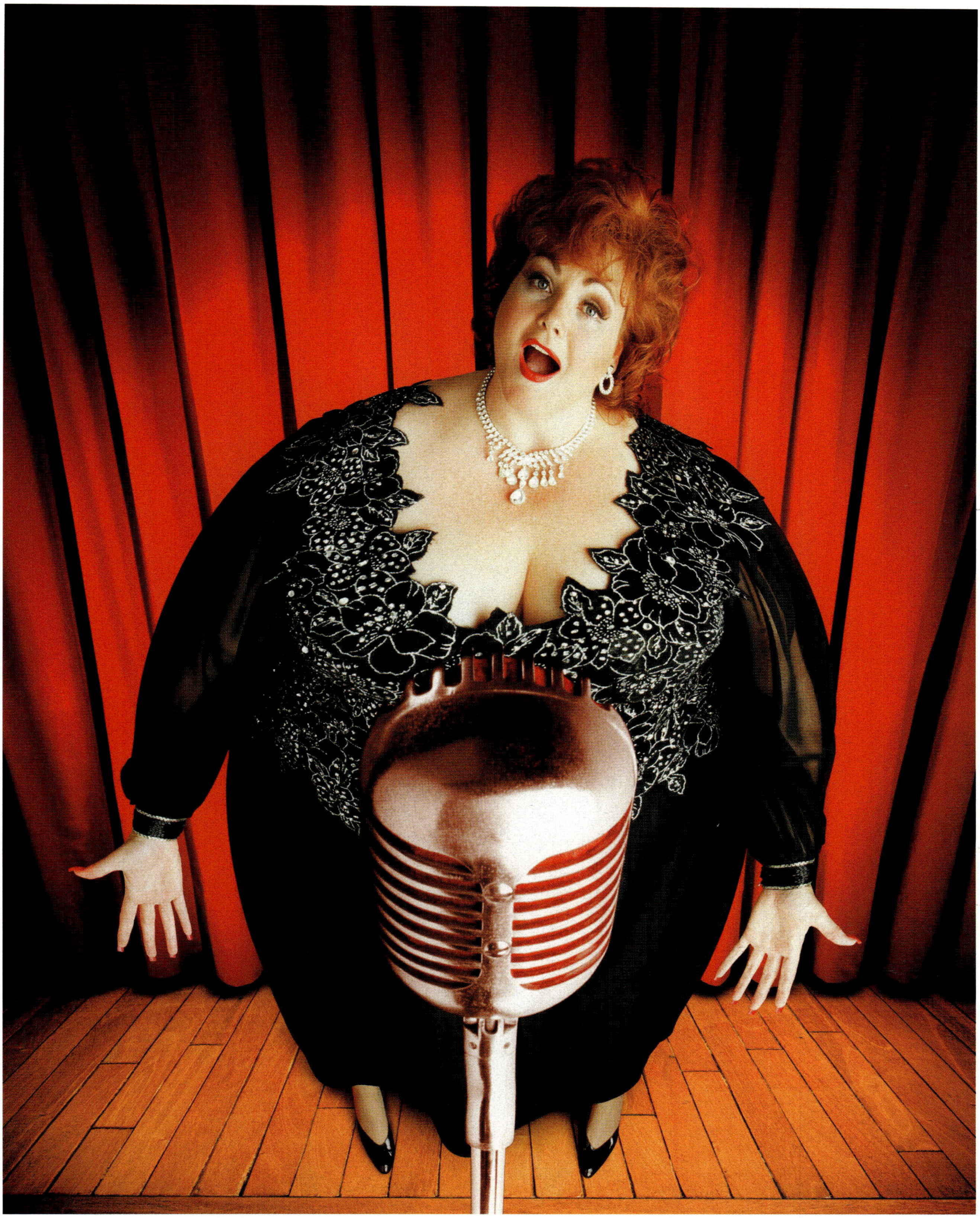

Graham French

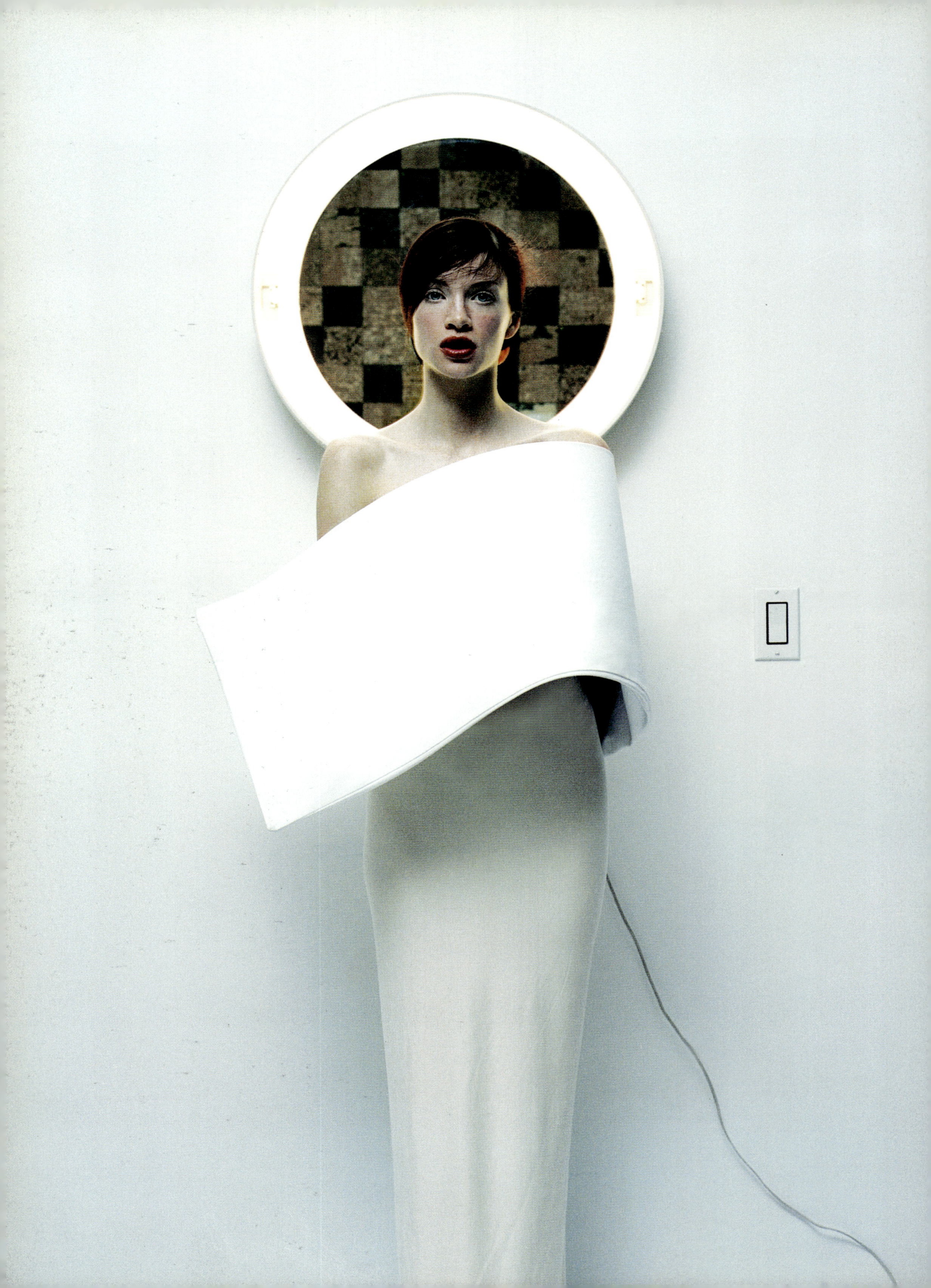

Fashion

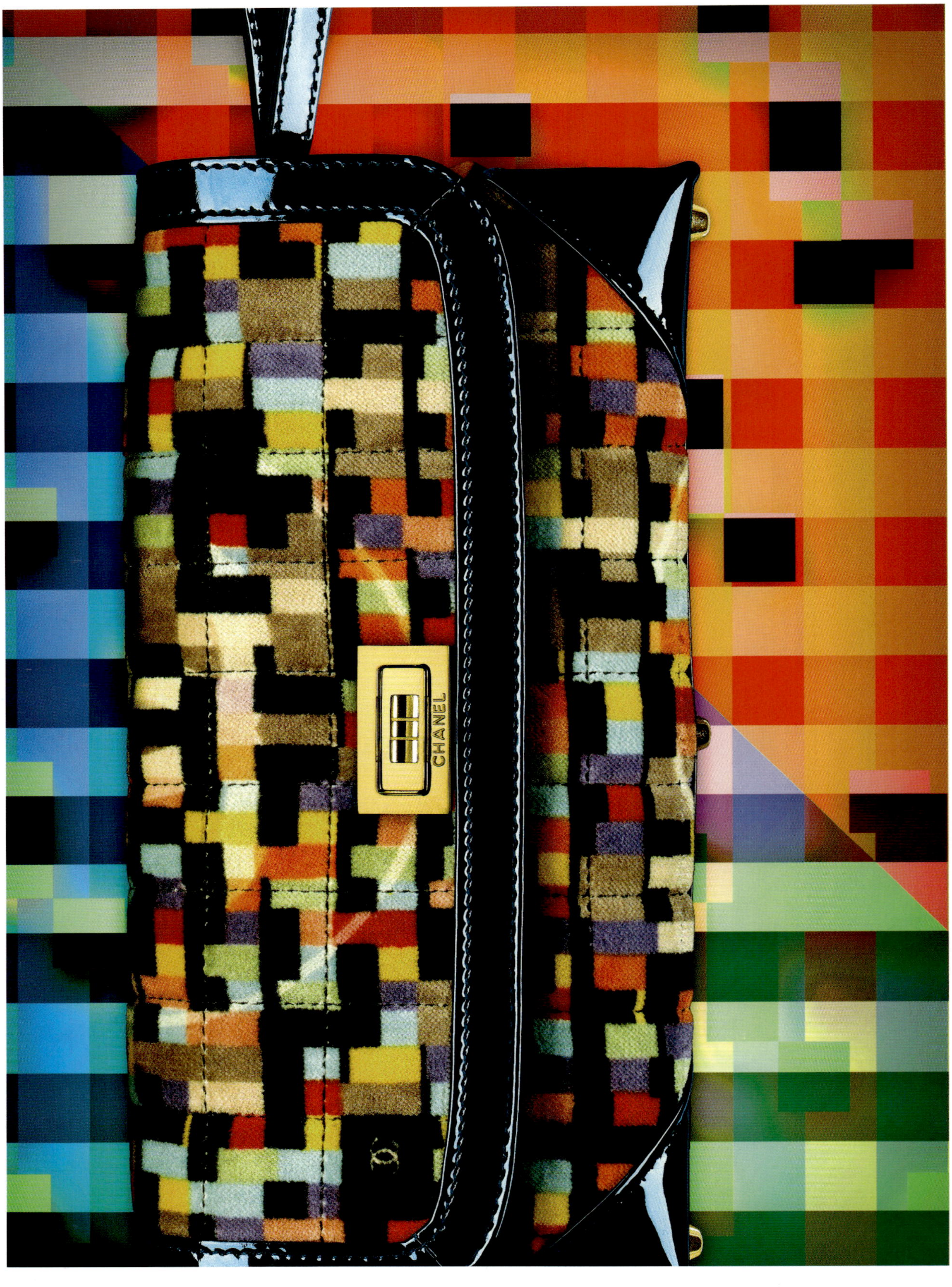

(this spread) Dan Forbes (opening page) Eva Mueller

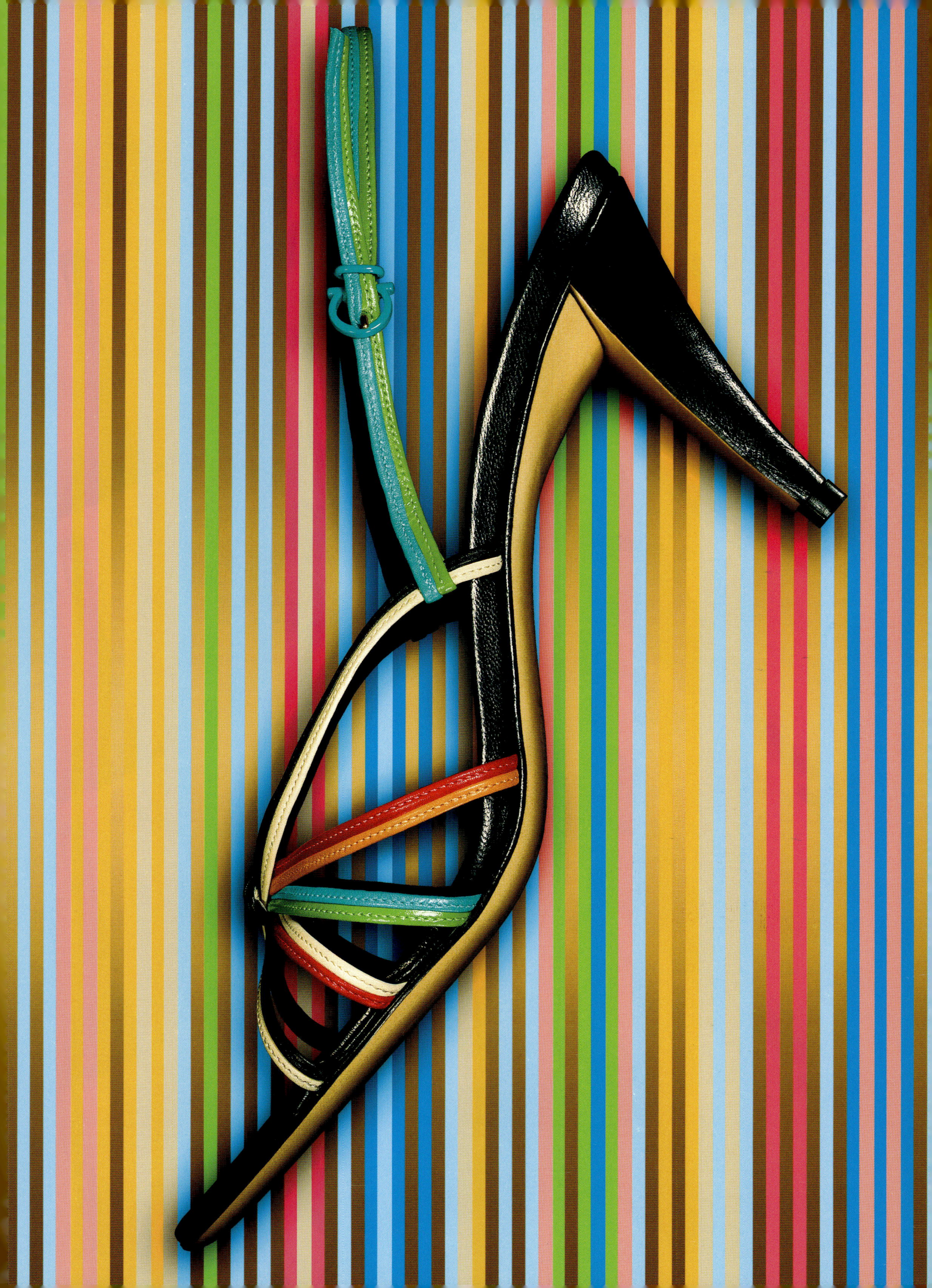

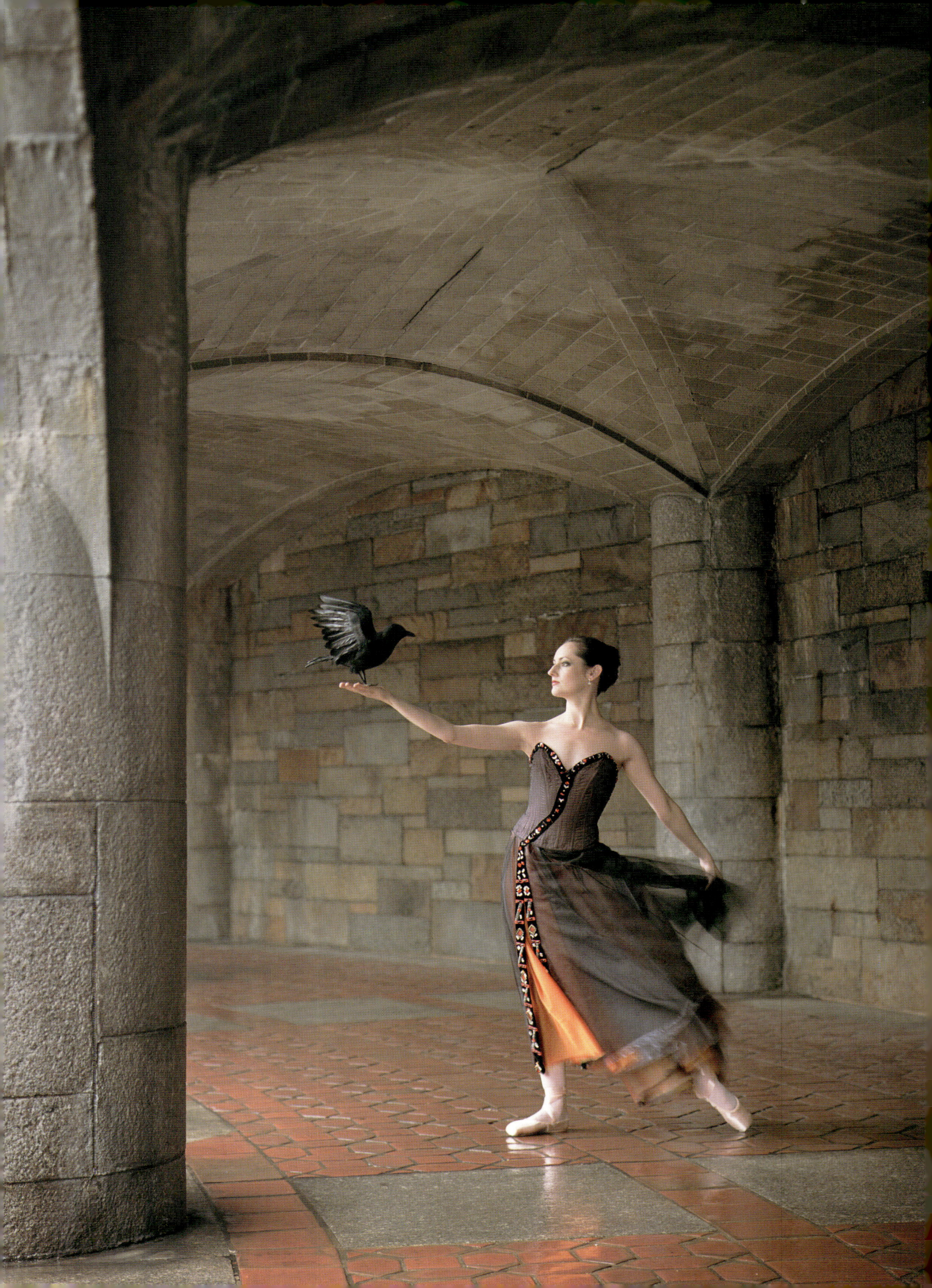

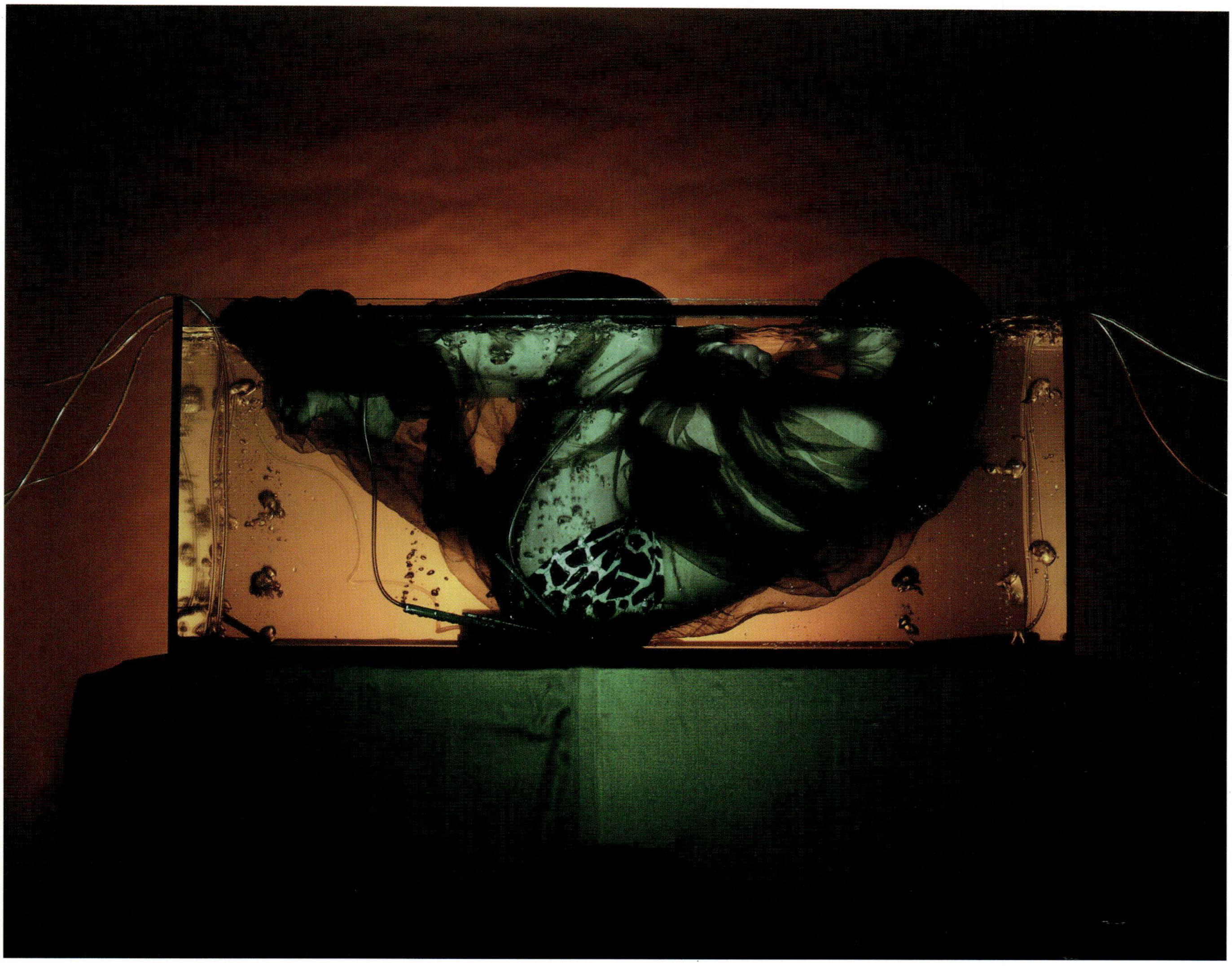

Rosanne Olson (opposite) Bryce Bennett

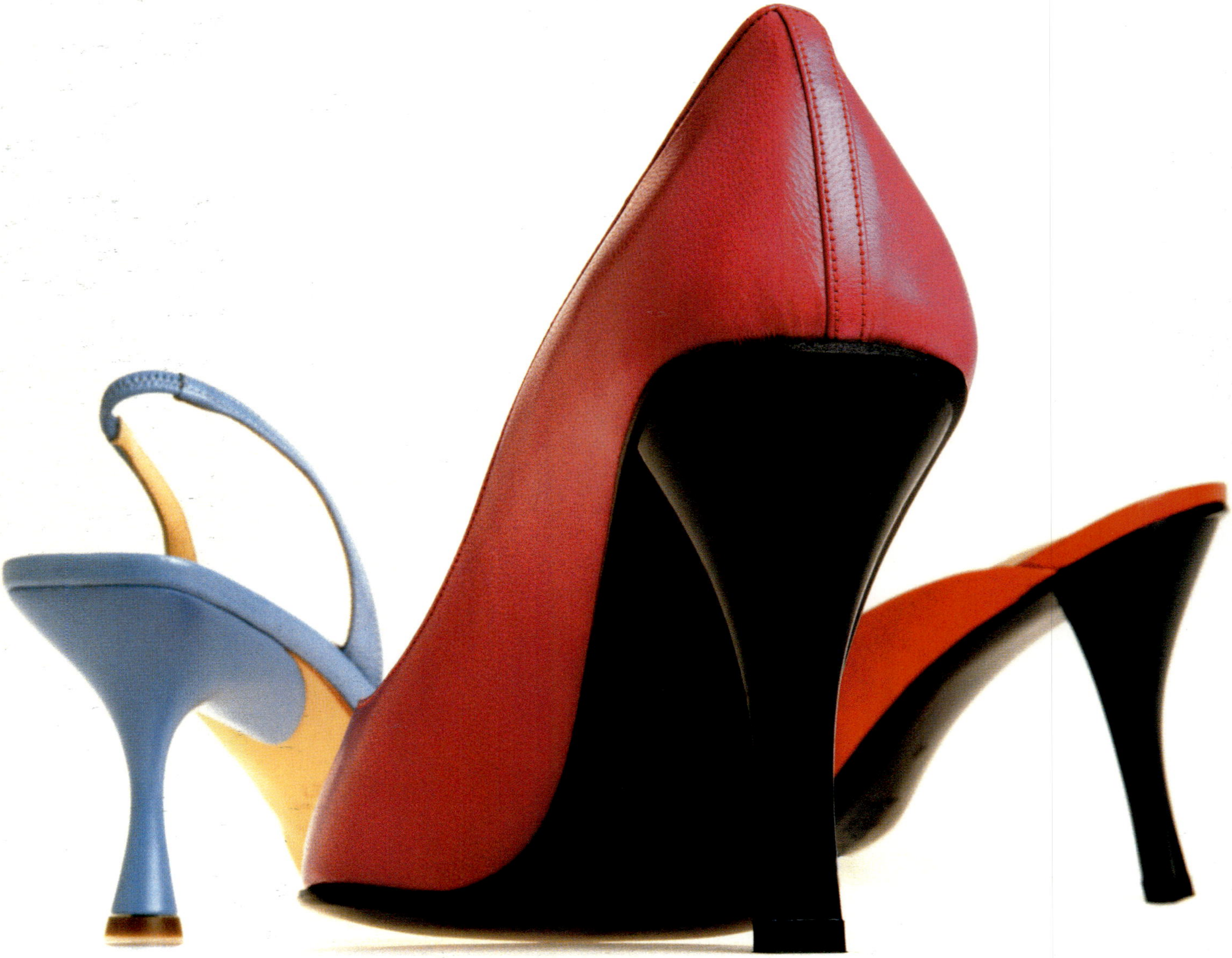

Jono Rotman

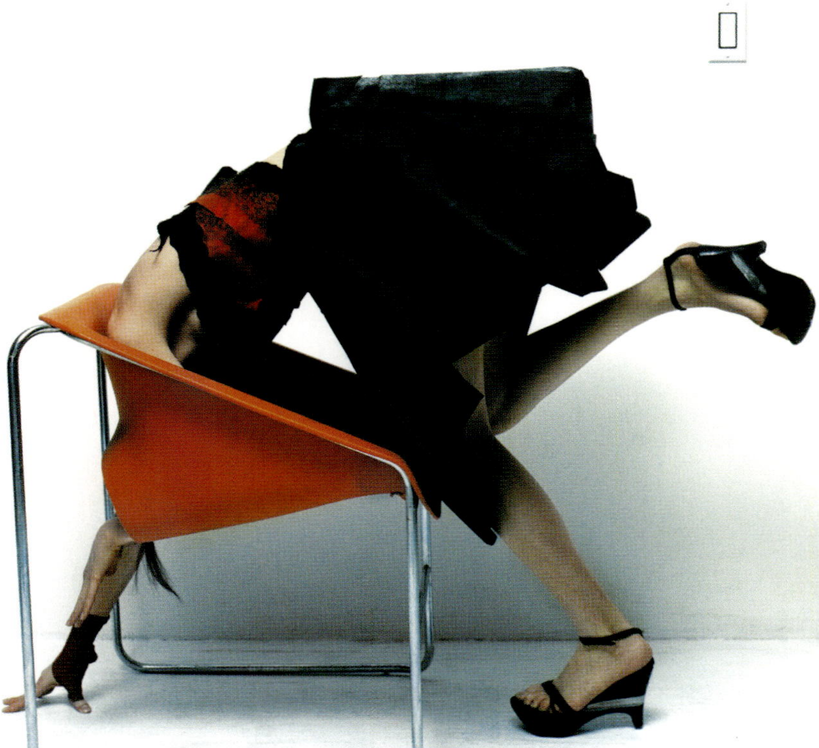

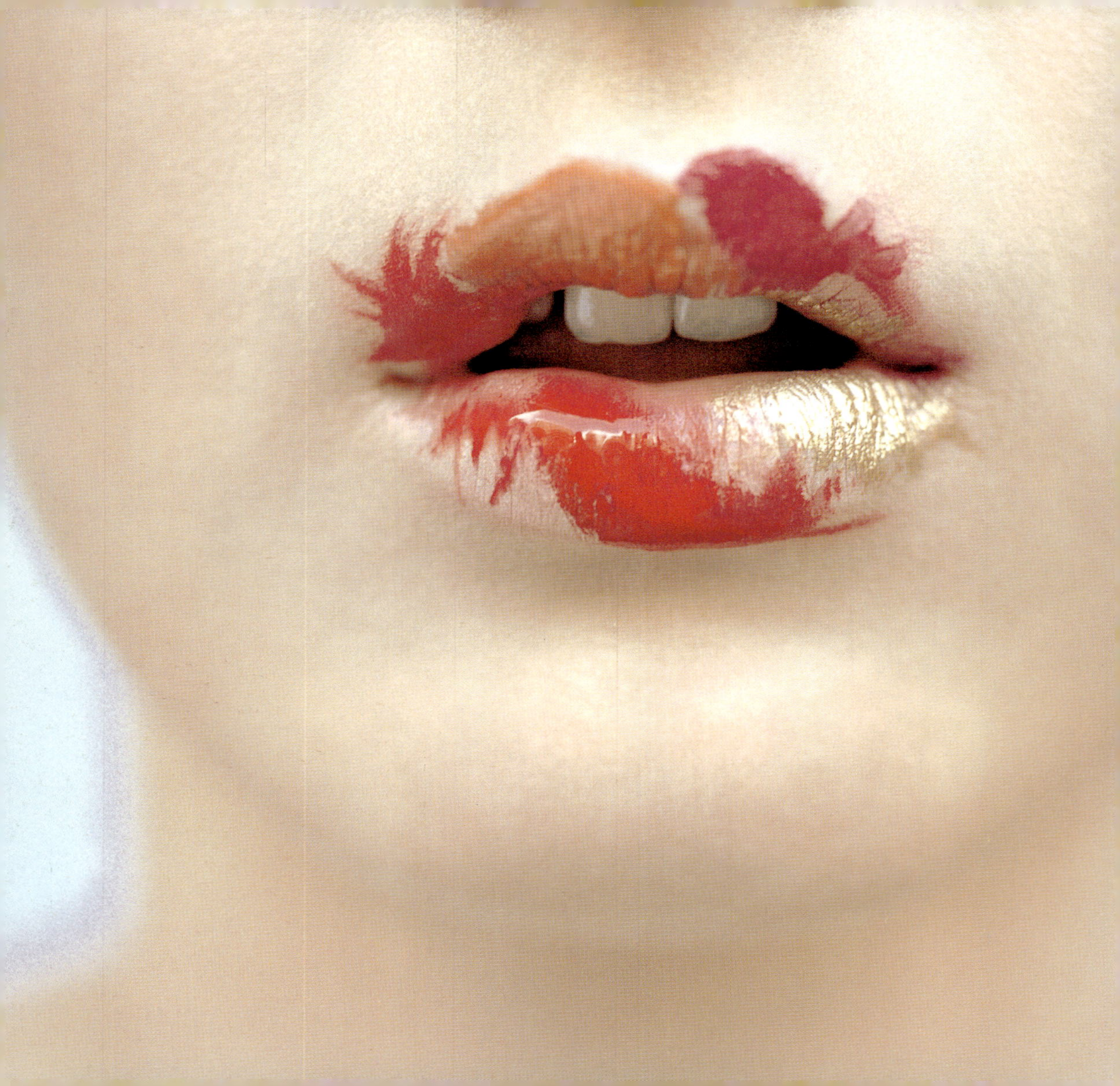

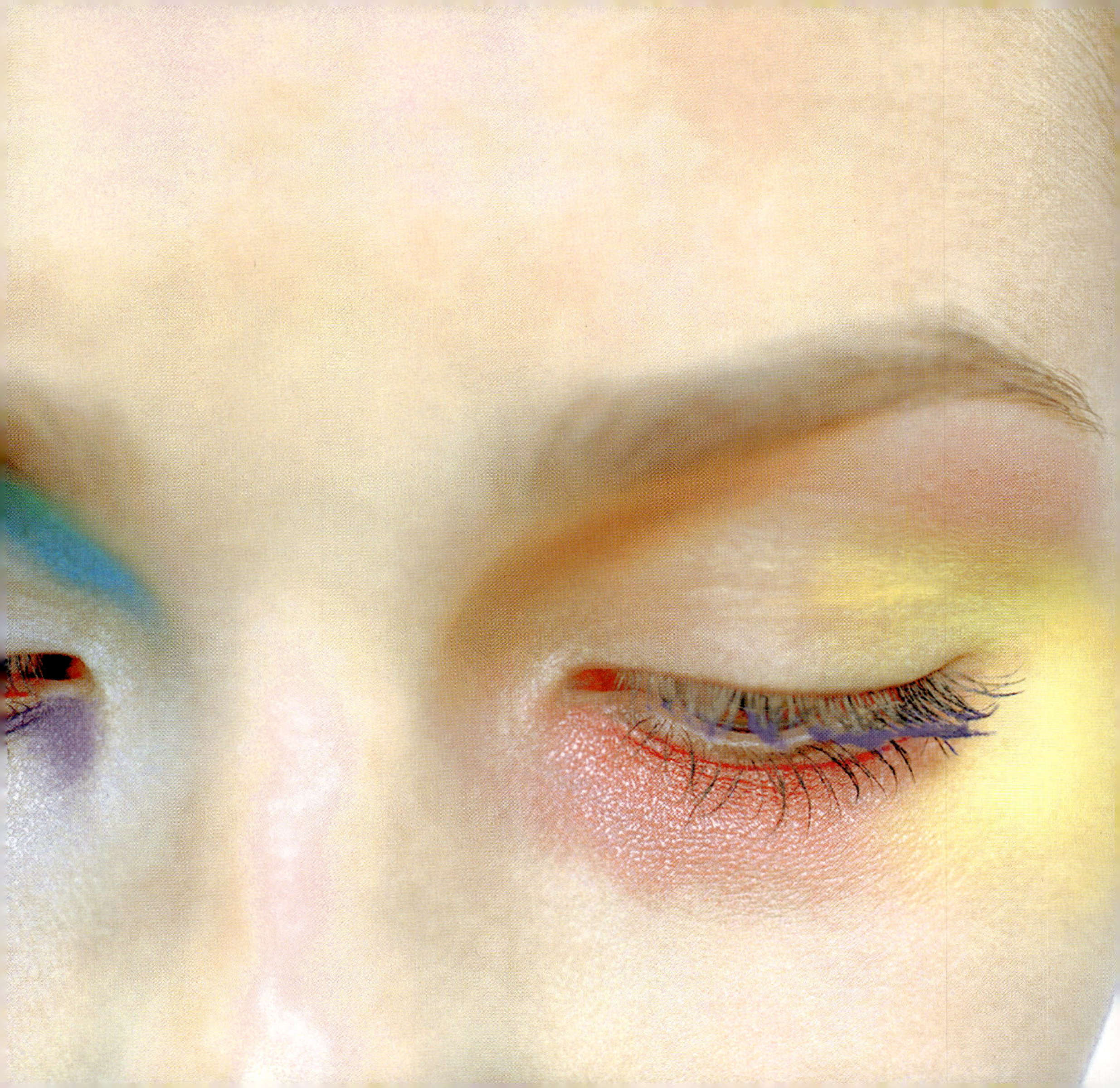

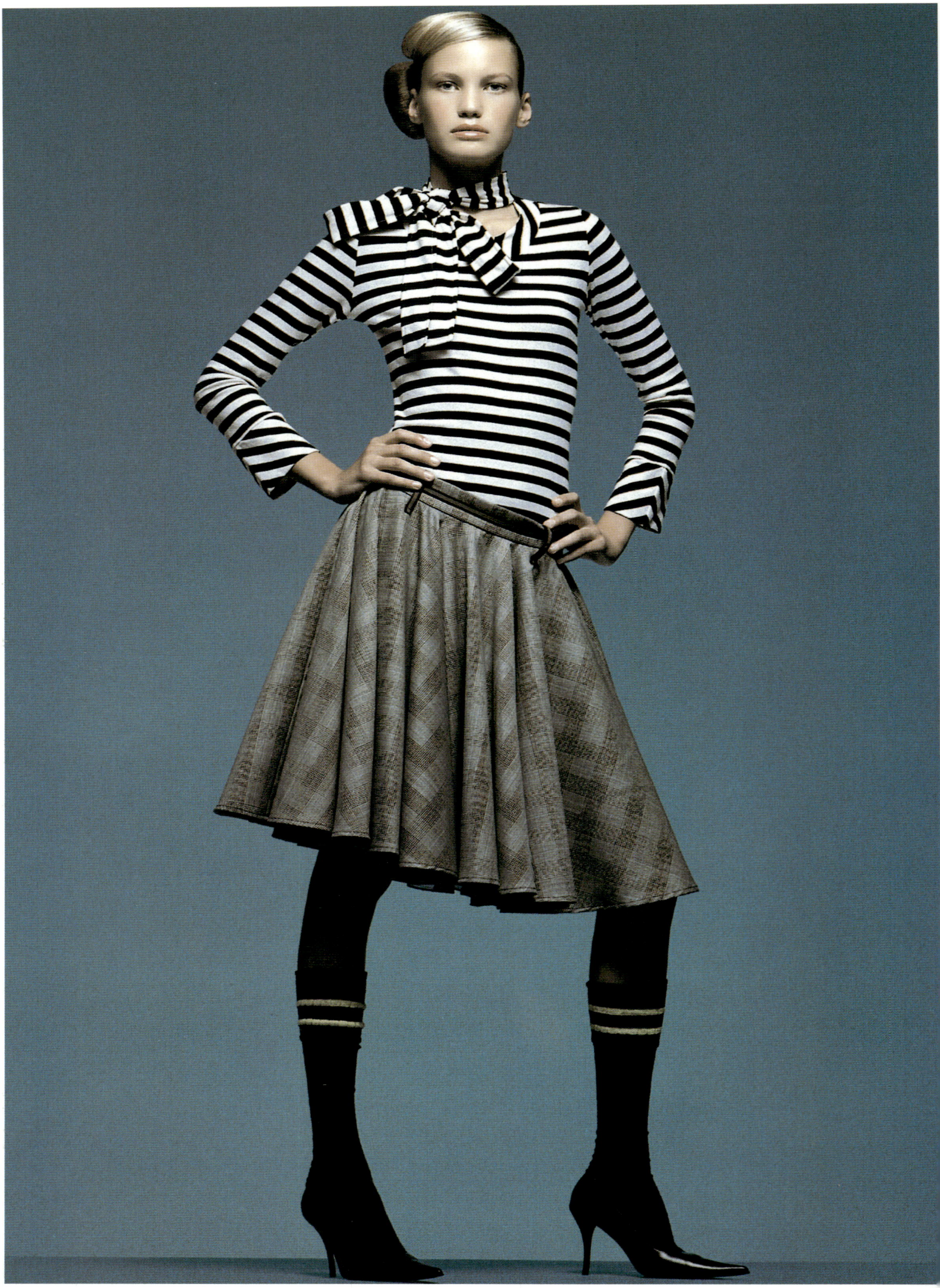

Kenneth Rimm

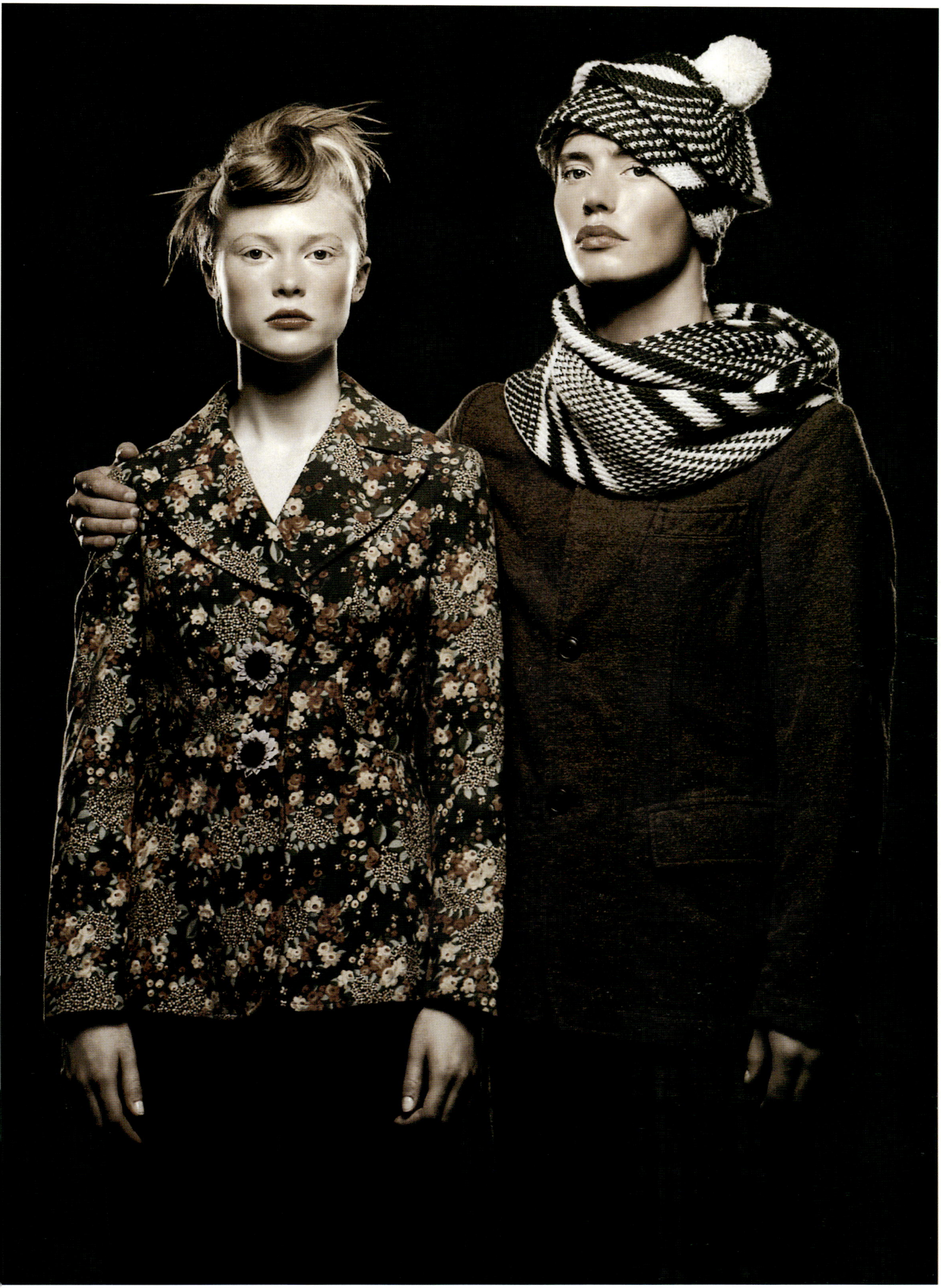

Kenneth Rimm

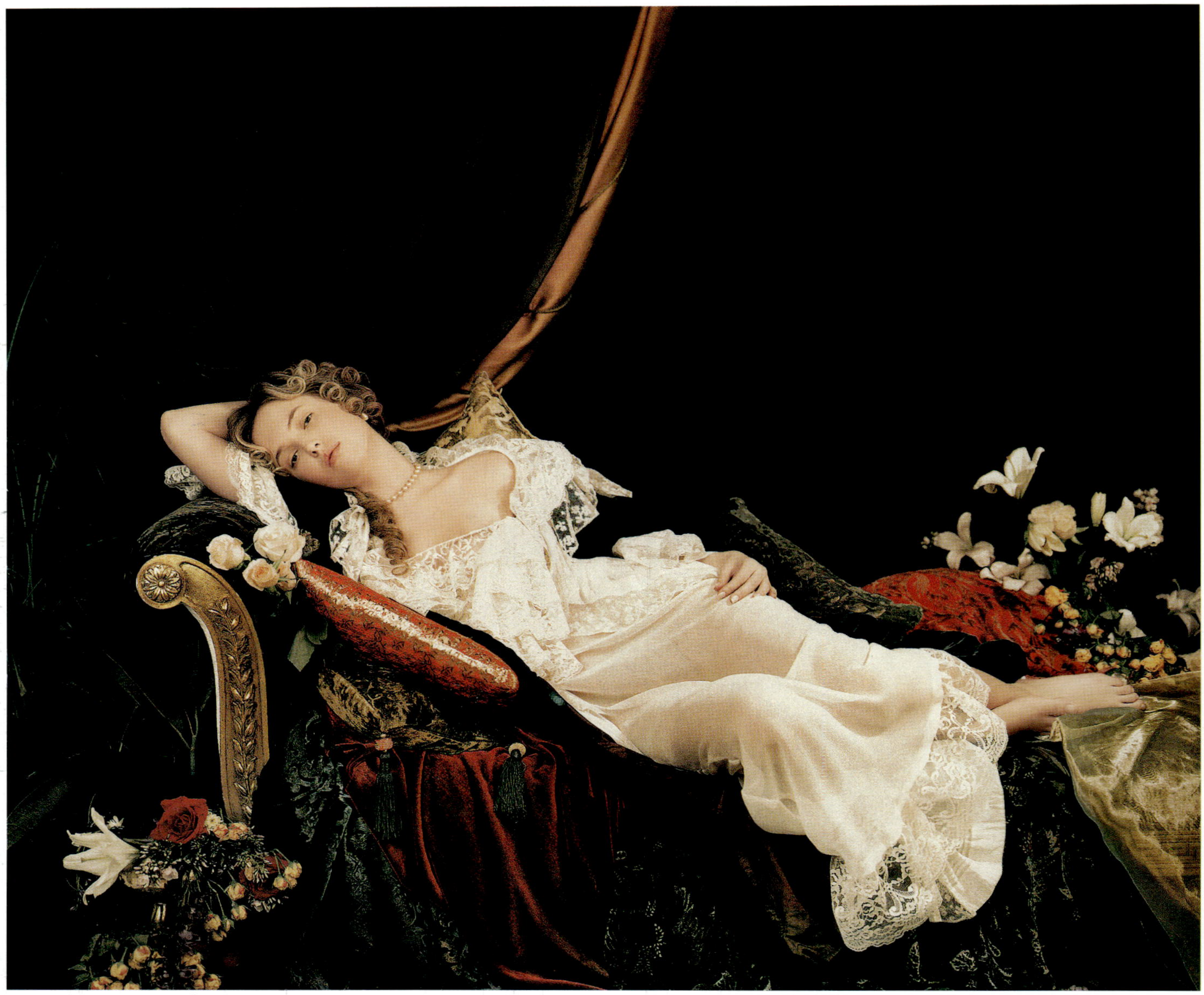

Sanjay Kothari (opposite) Eric Bottero

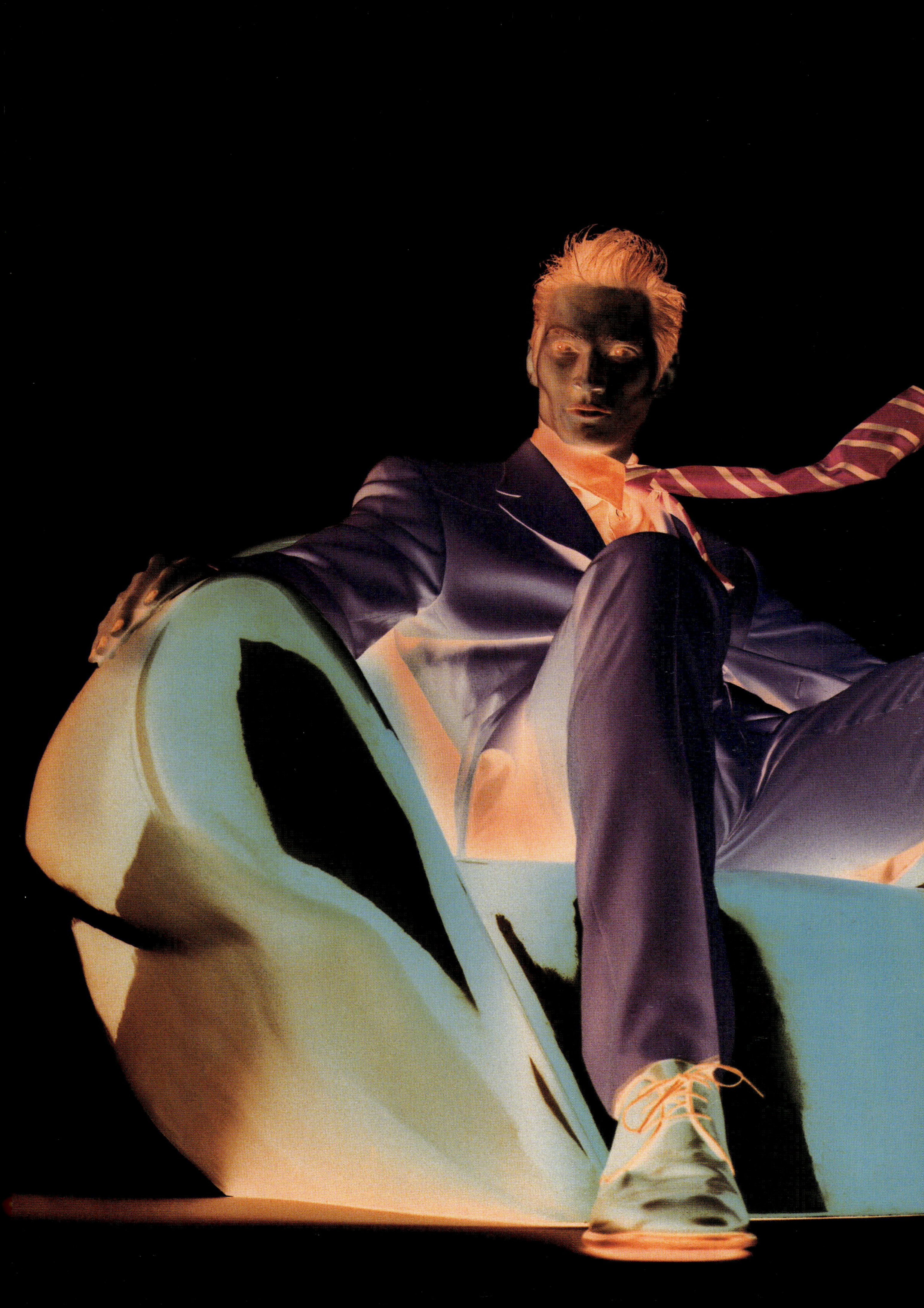

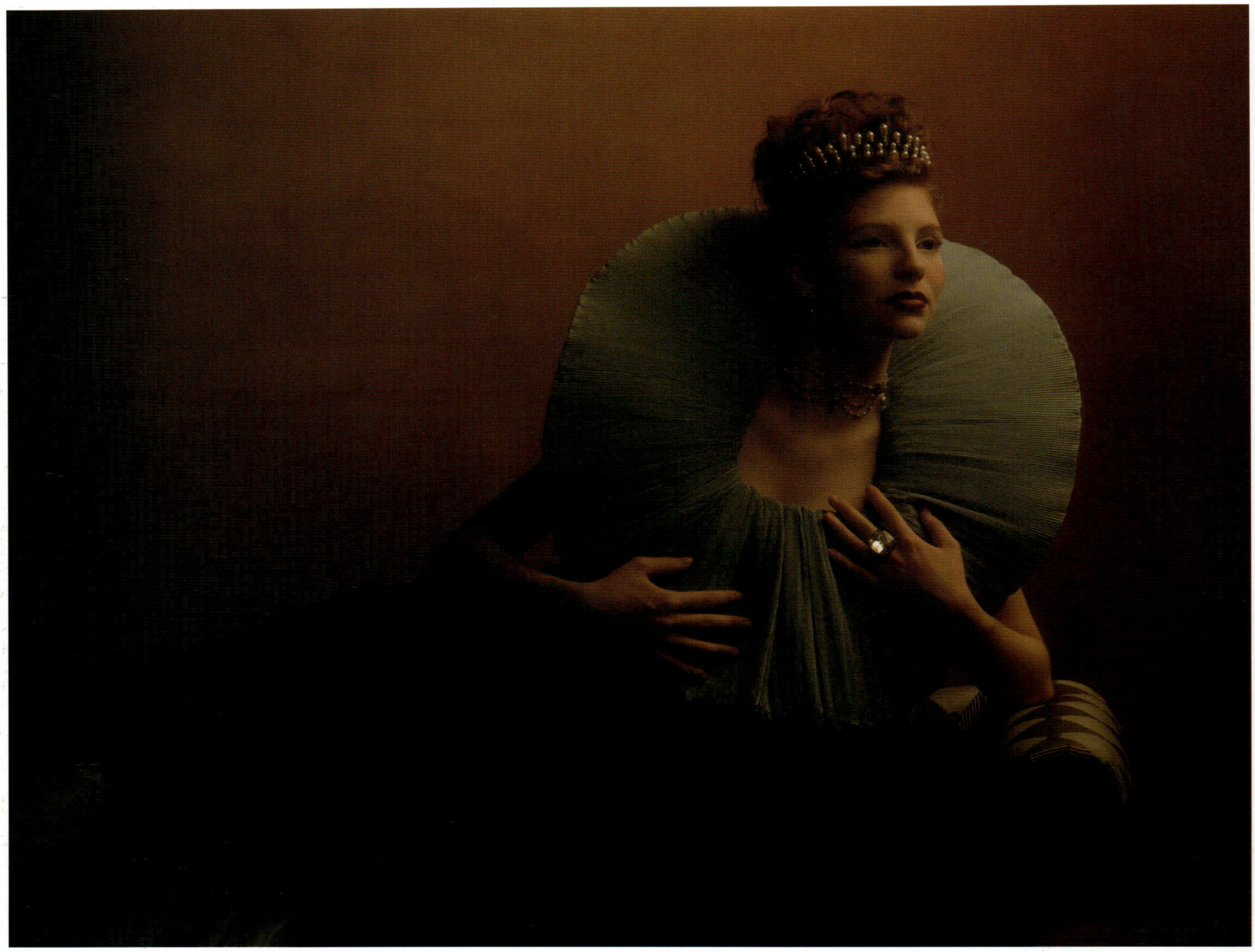

(this spread) Parish Kohanim

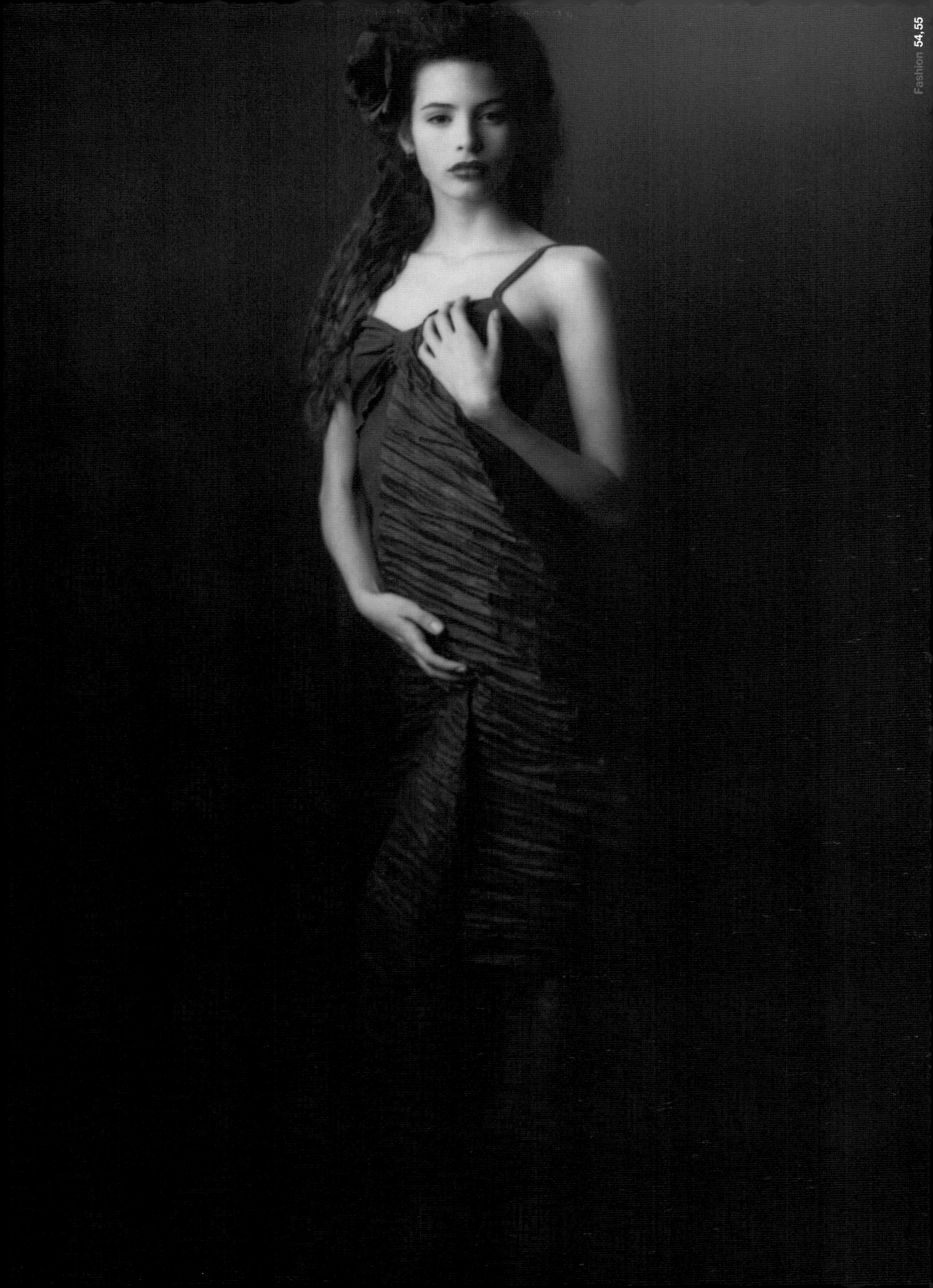

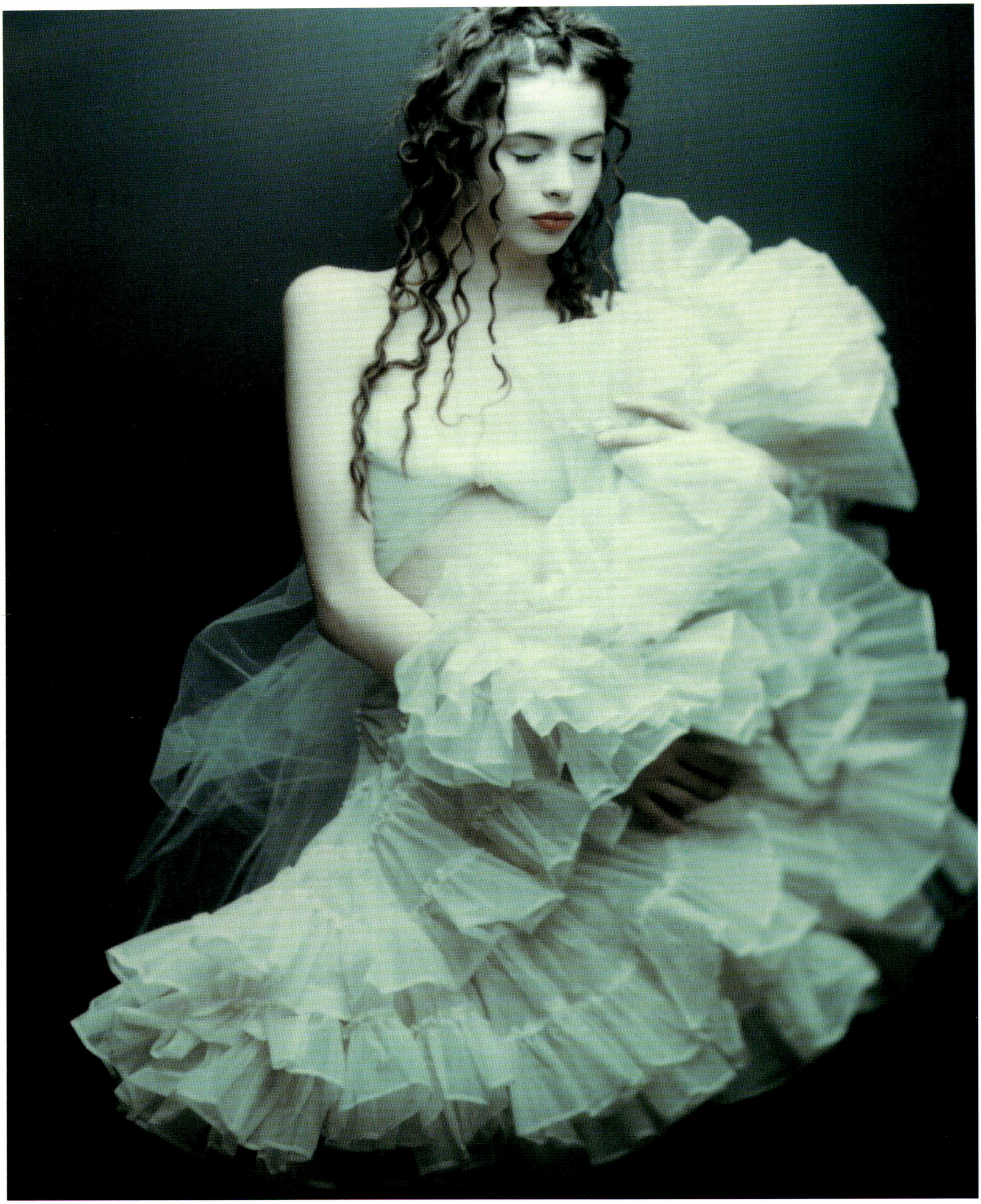

Parish Kohanim

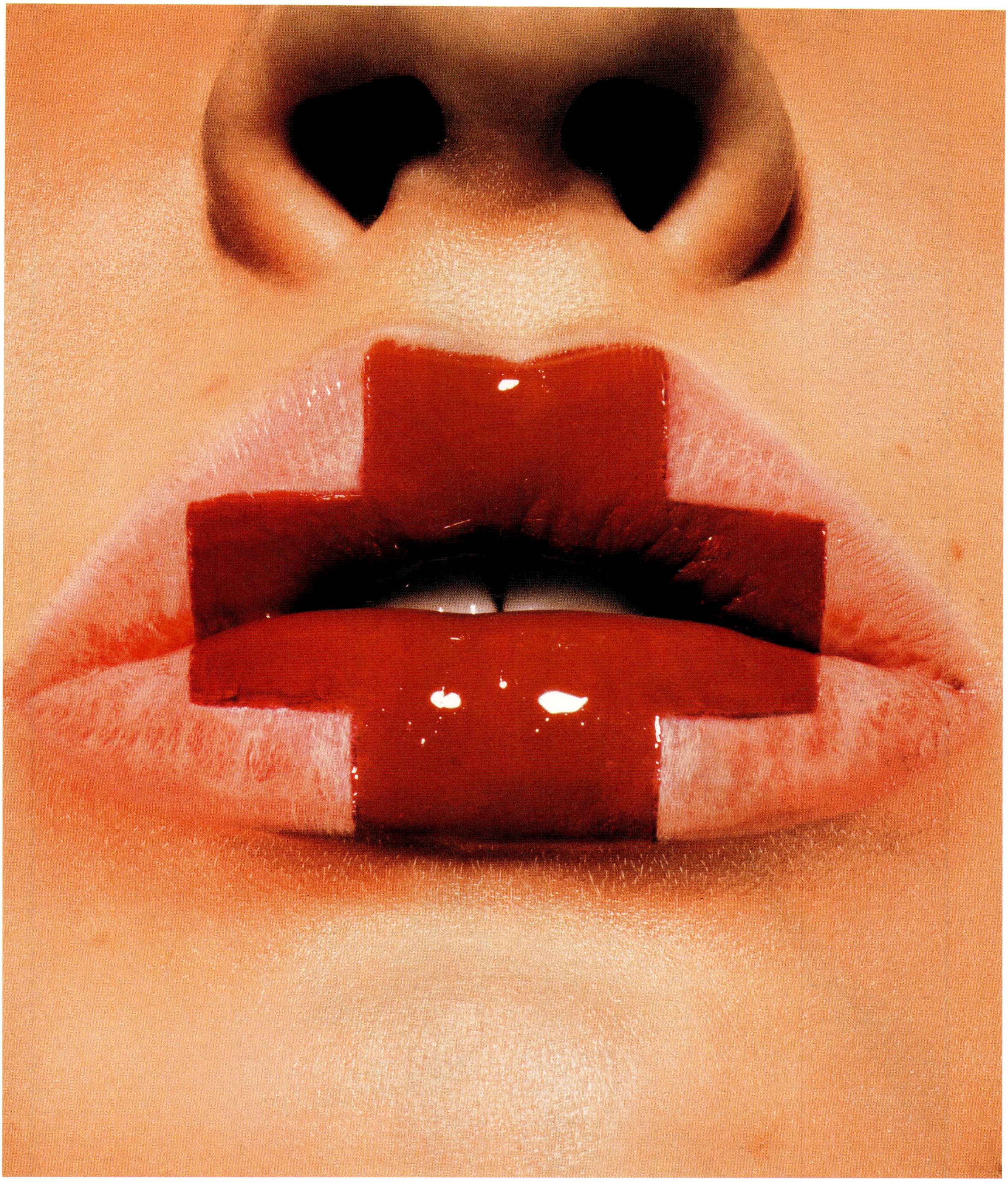

Donna Trope

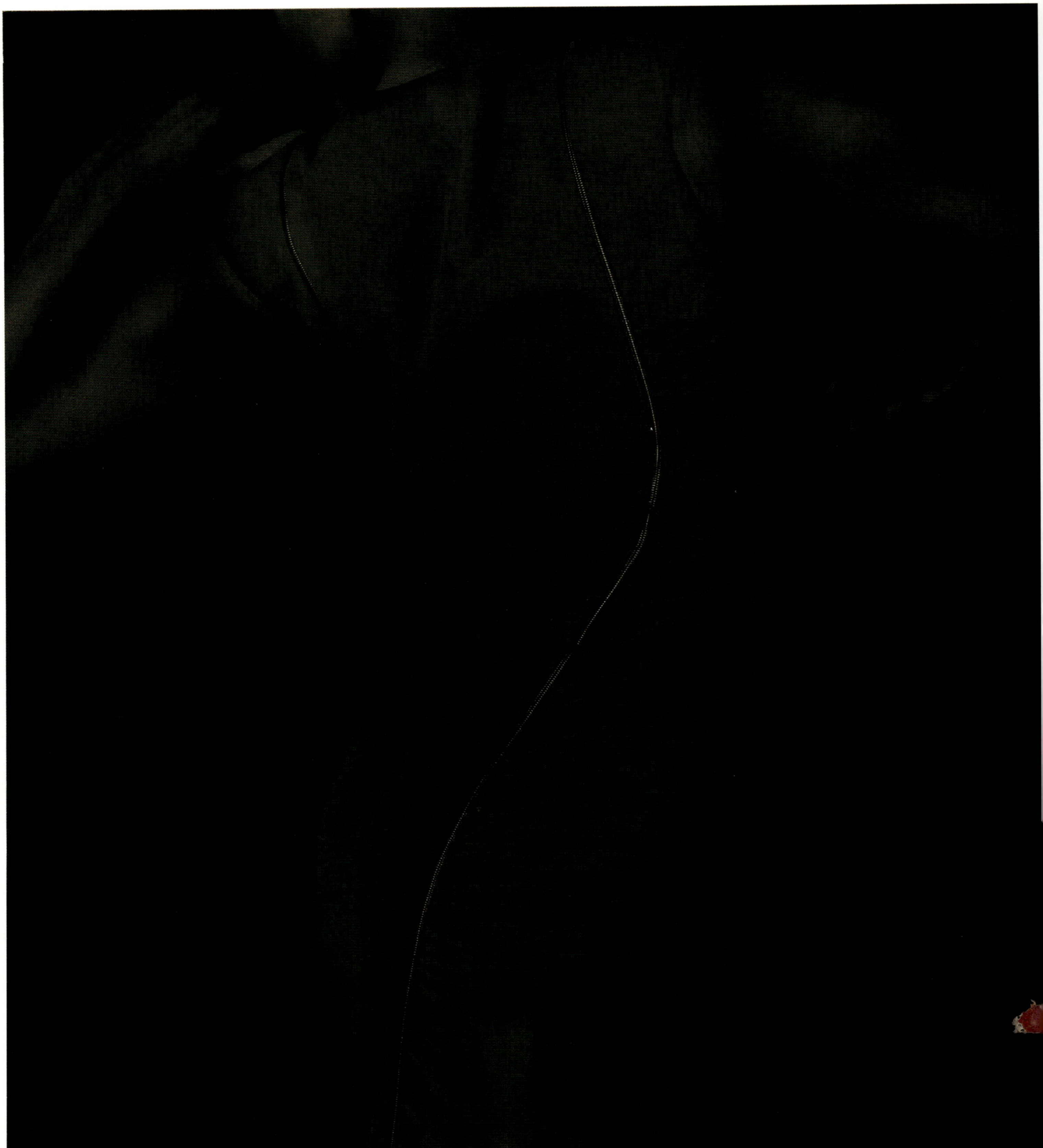

Gil Blank

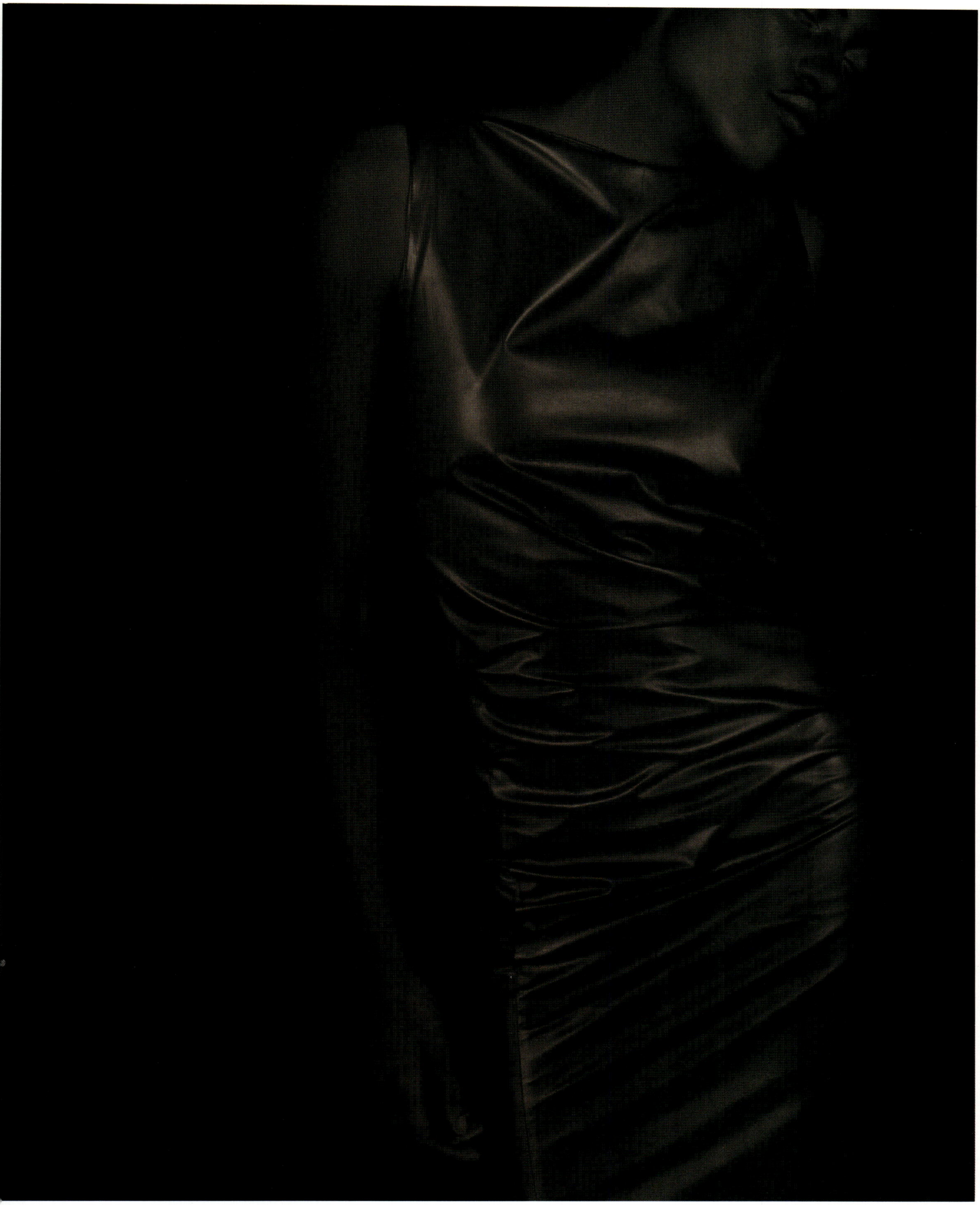

Gil Blank

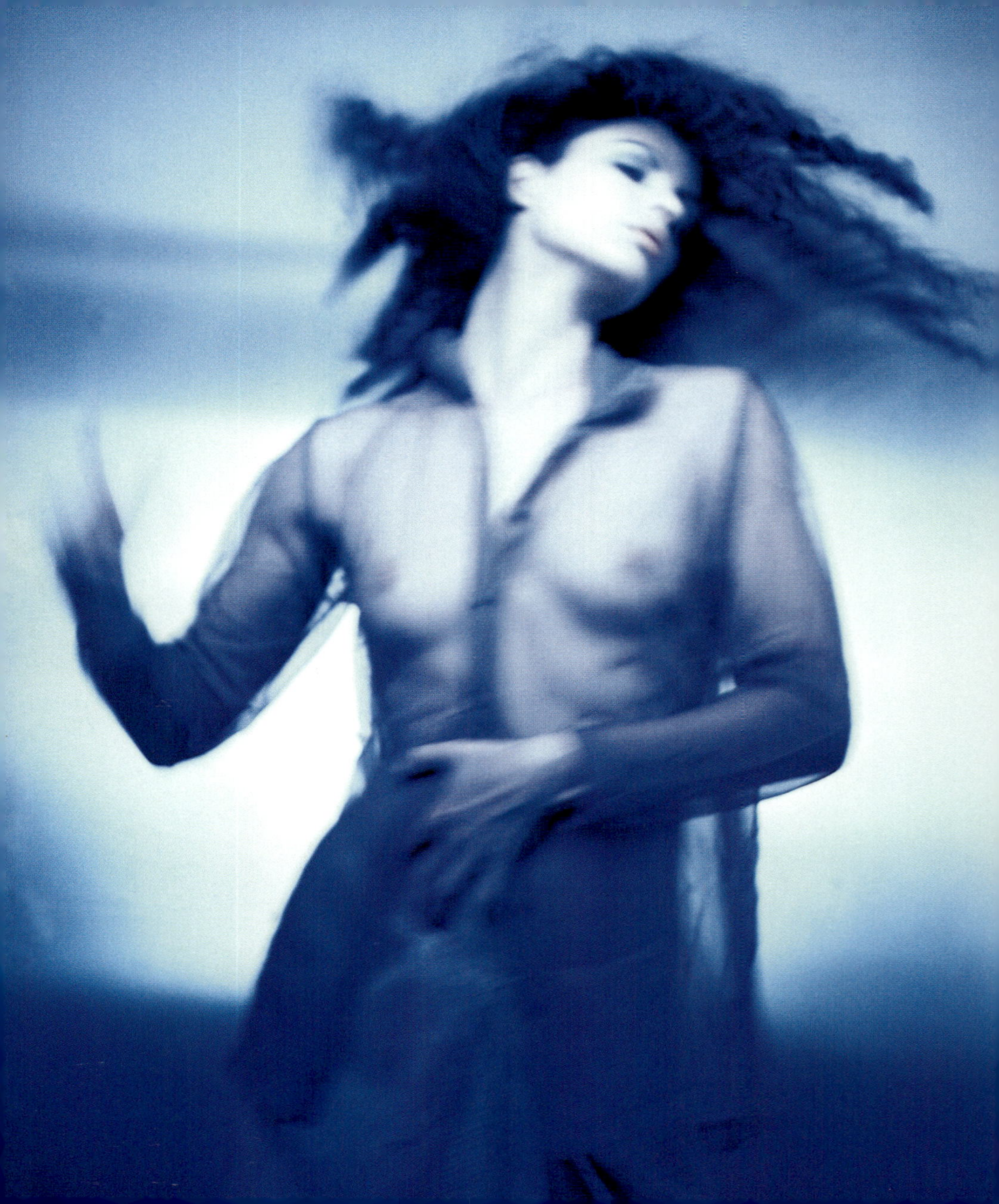

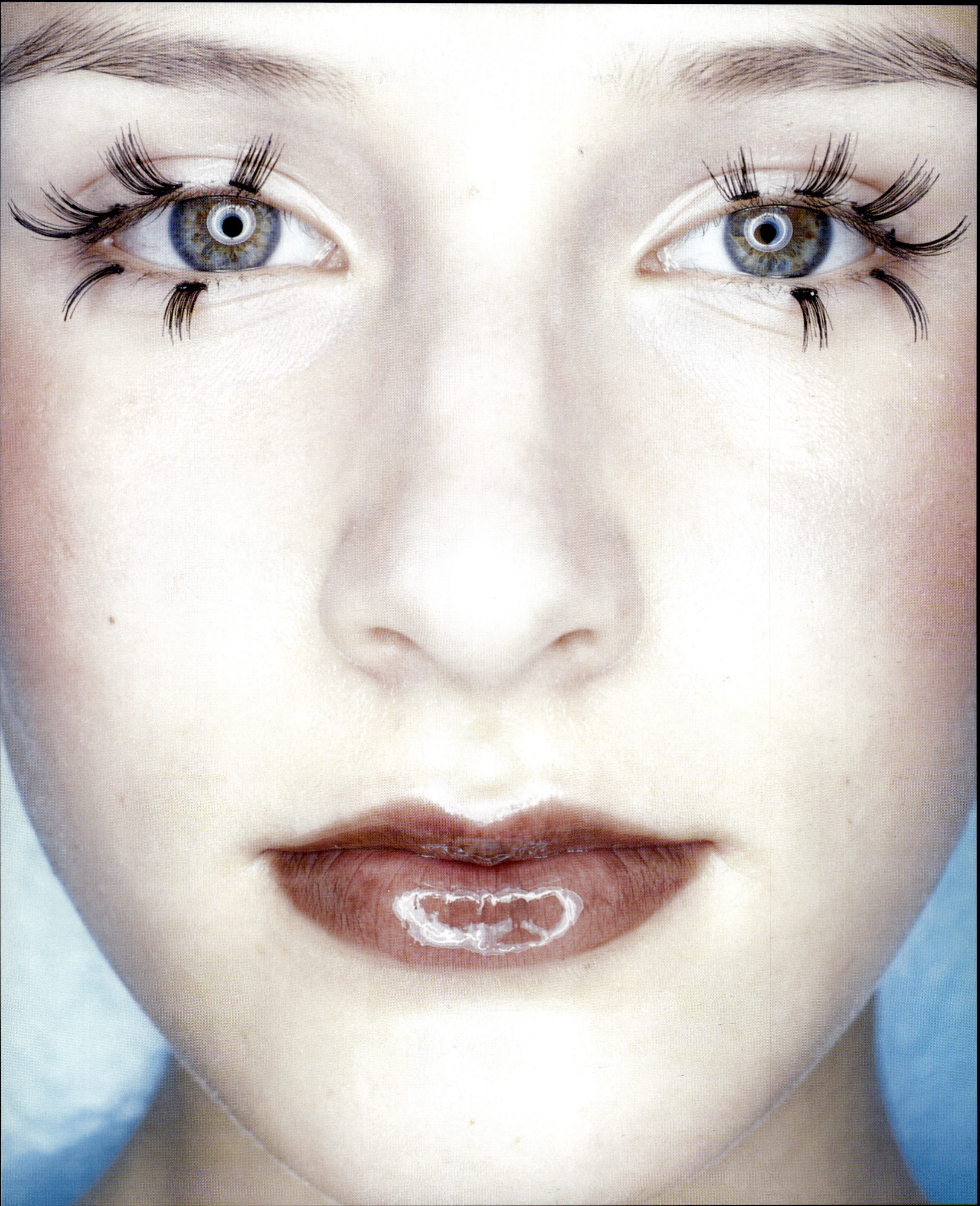

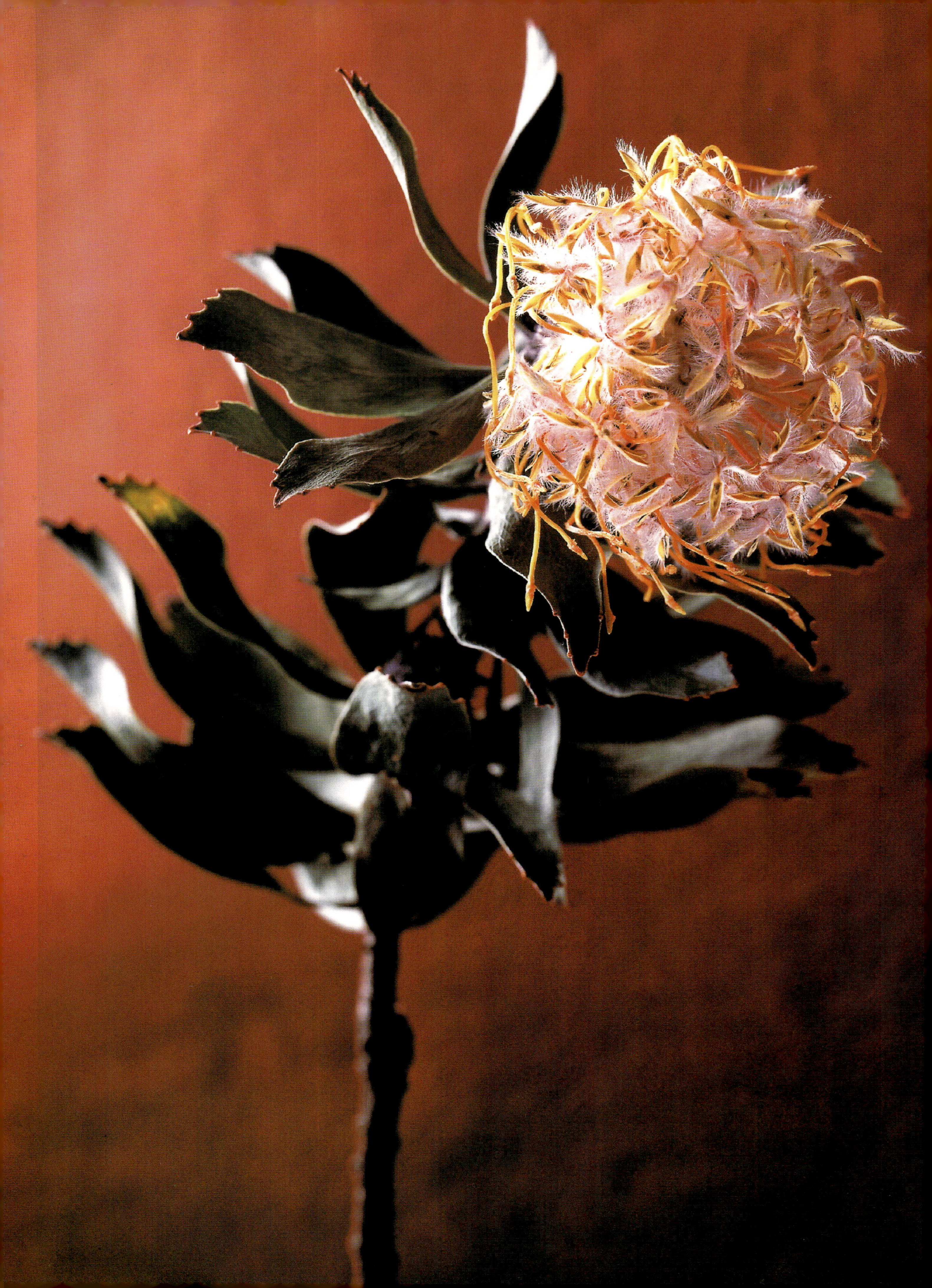

Flowers

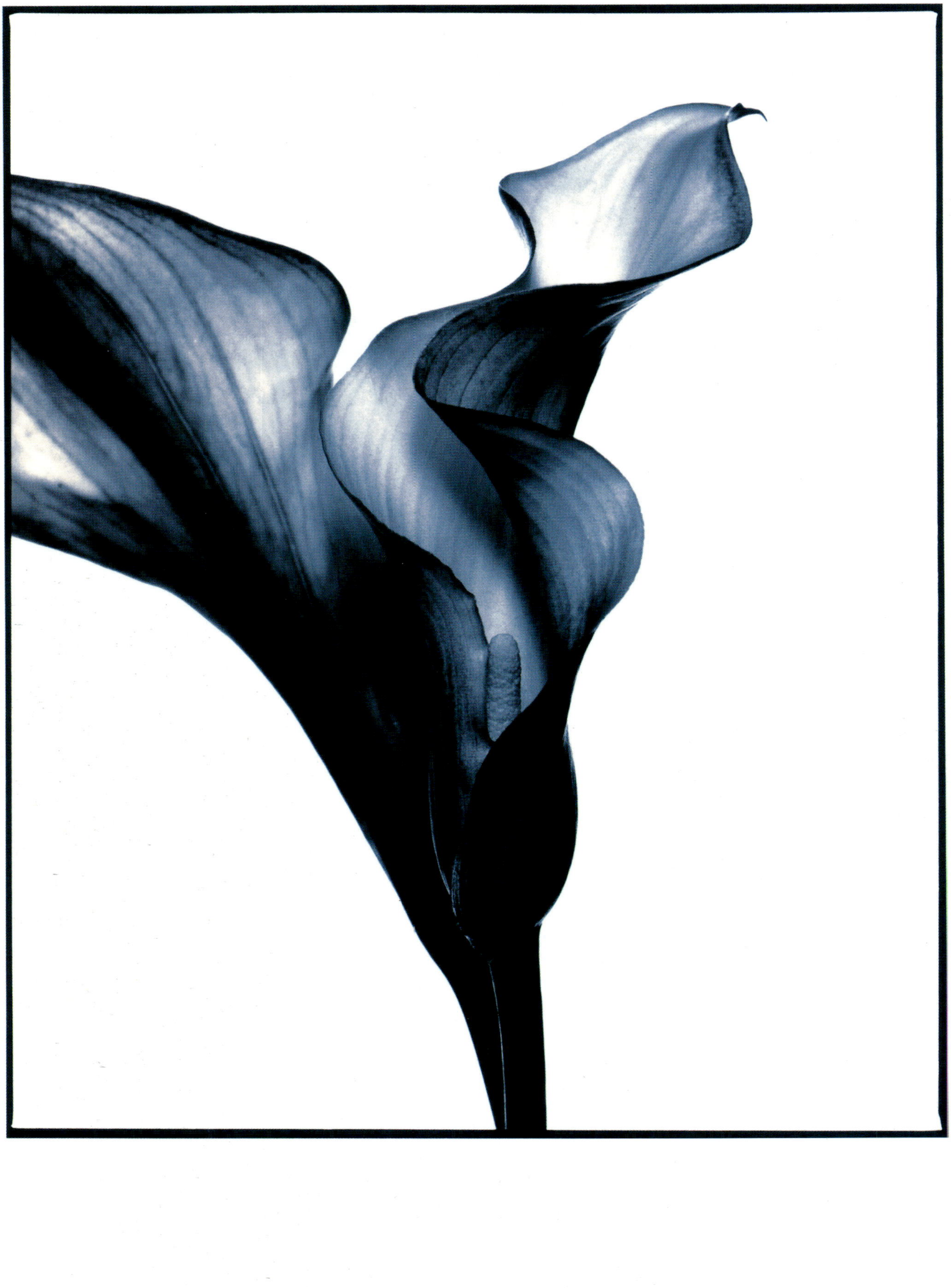

Jon Shireman (opening page) Bret Wills (opposite) André Baranowski

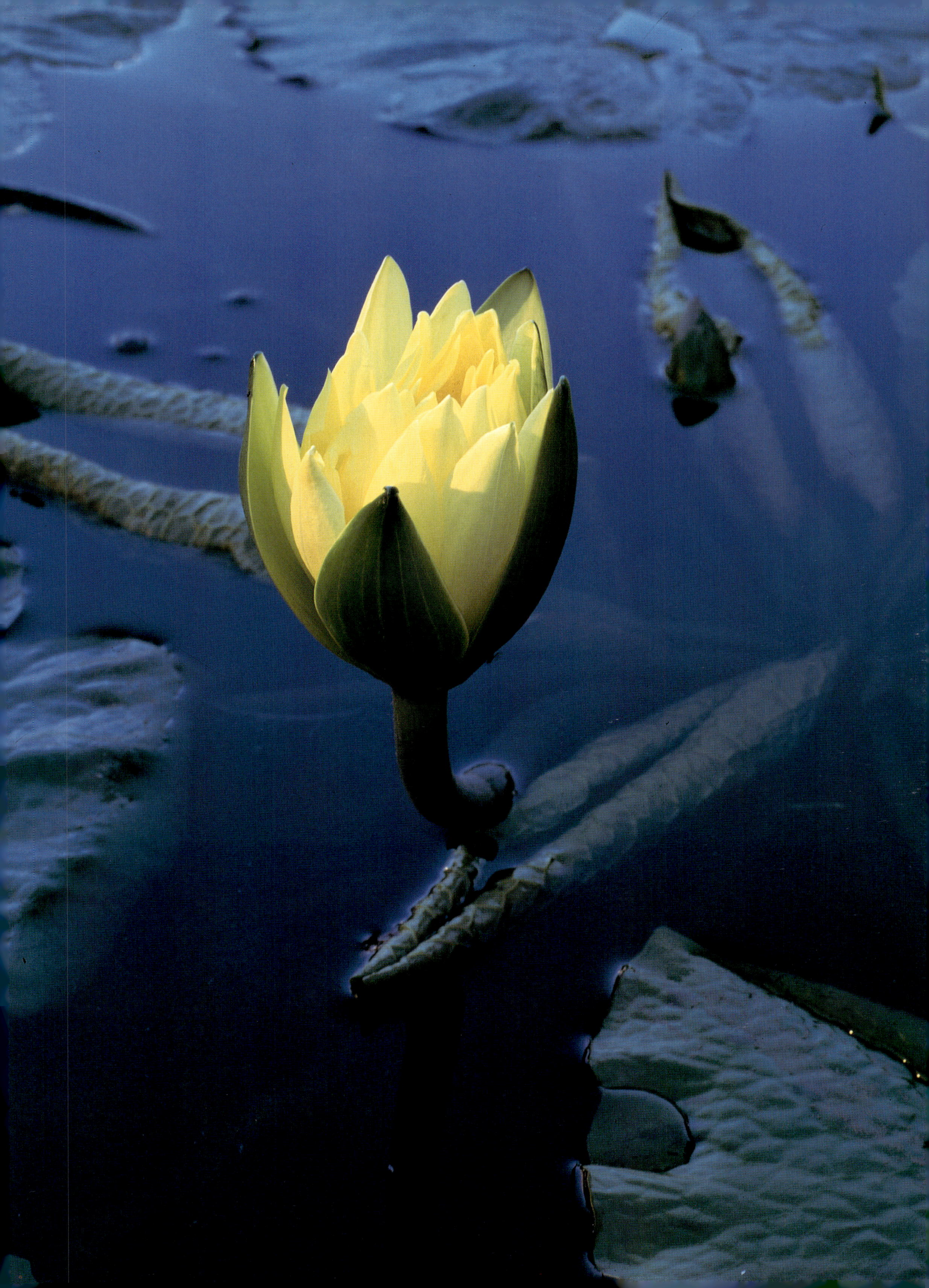

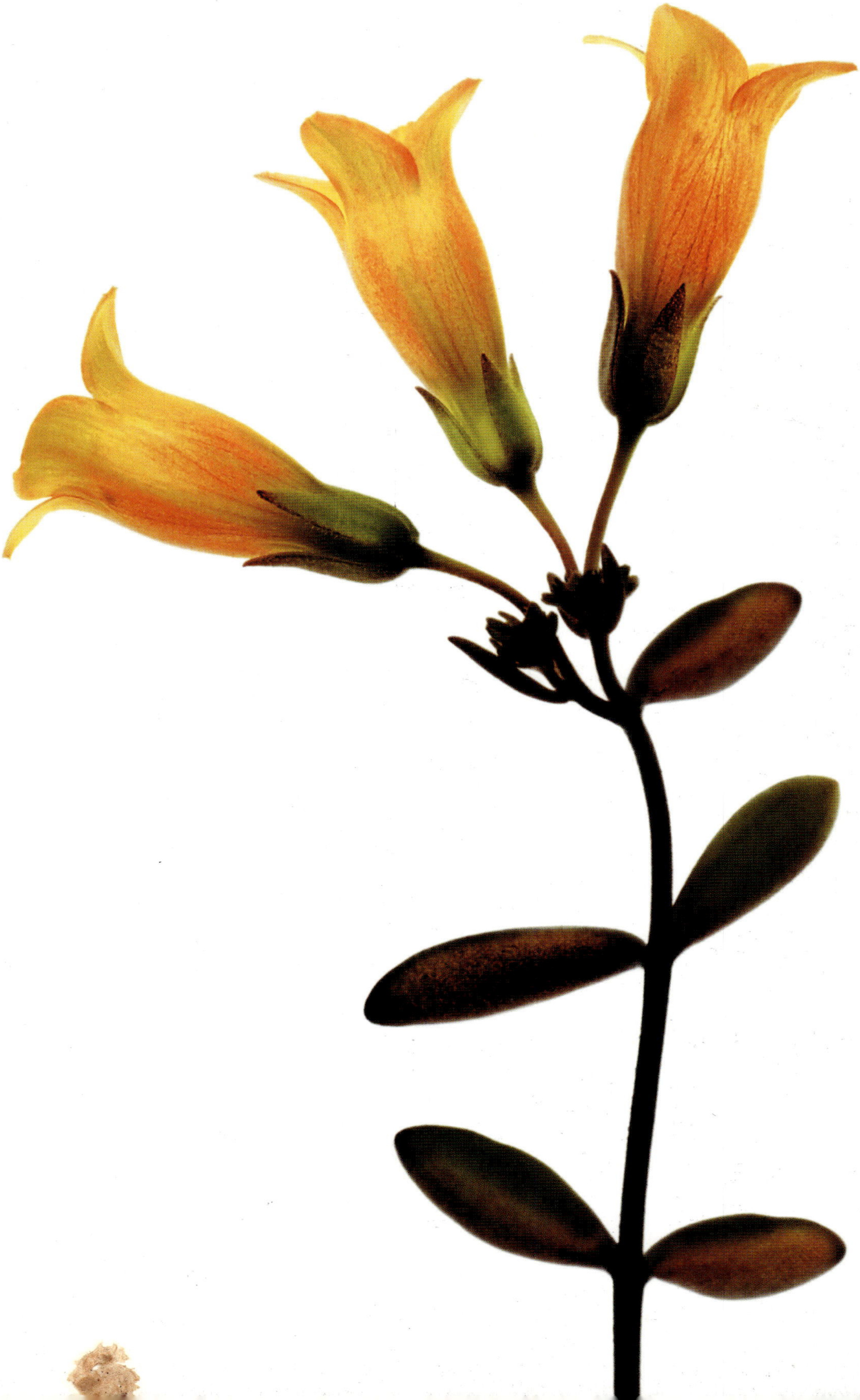

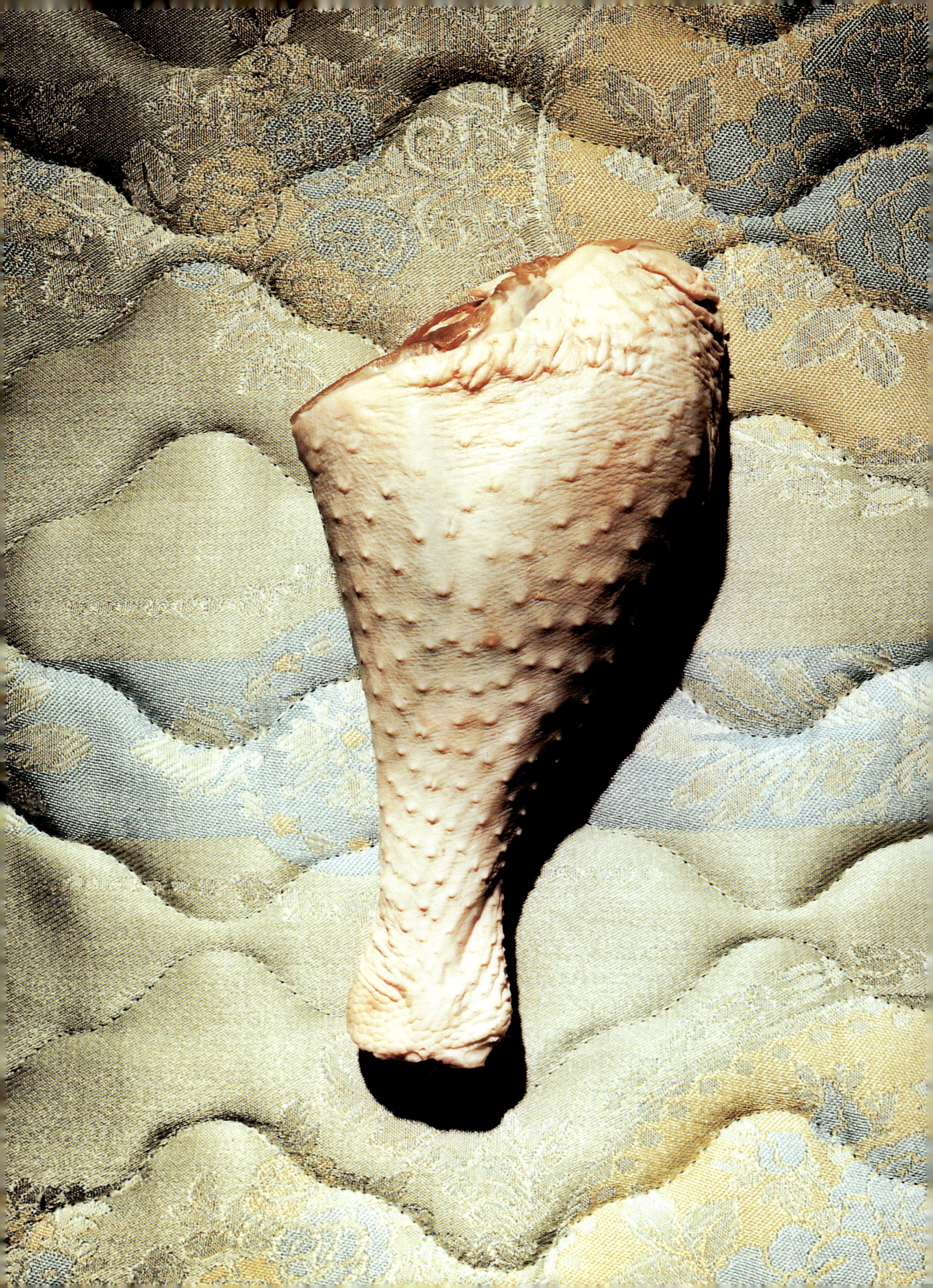

Food & Beverage

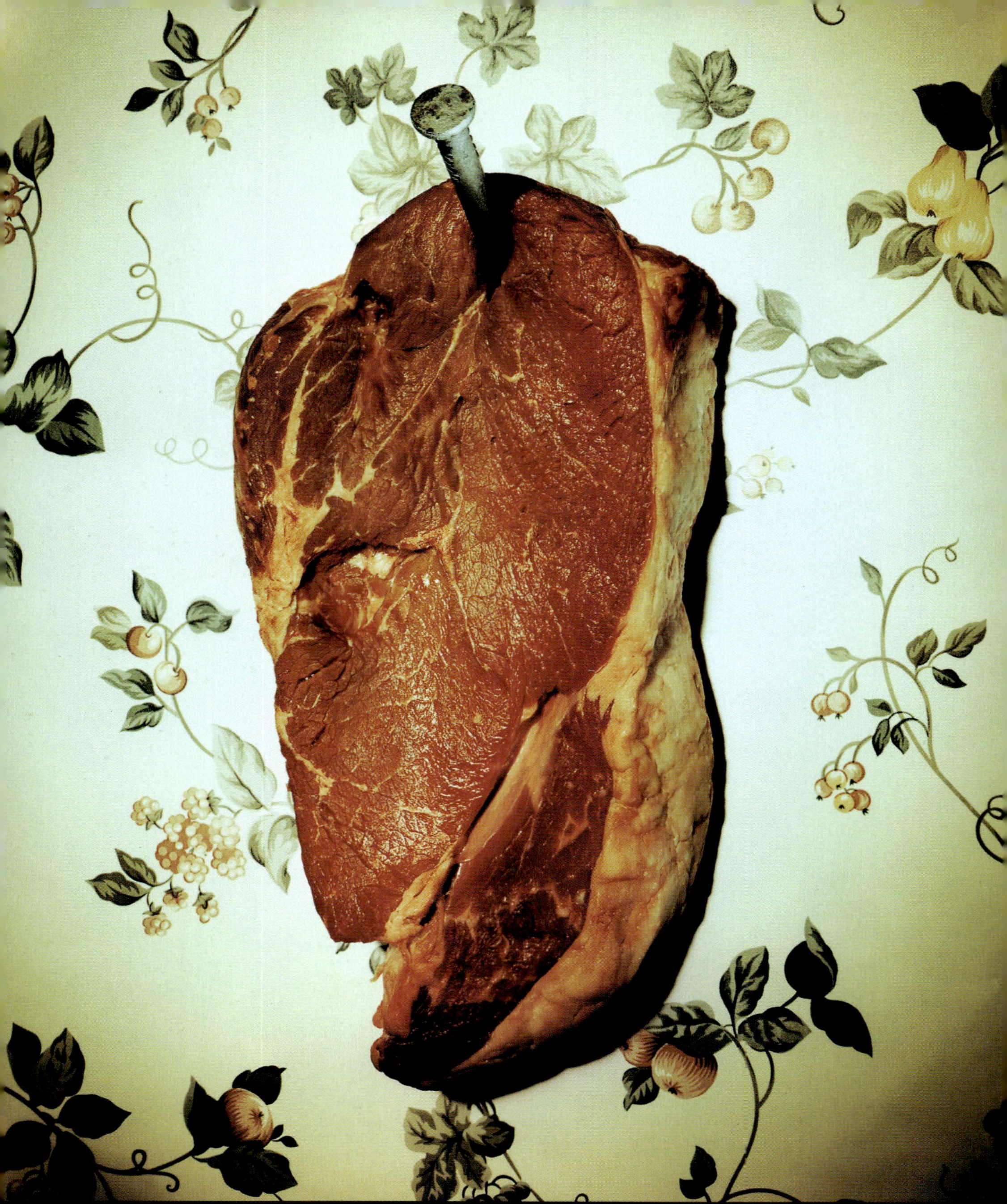

(this and opening page) David Emmite (opposite) Geoff Spear

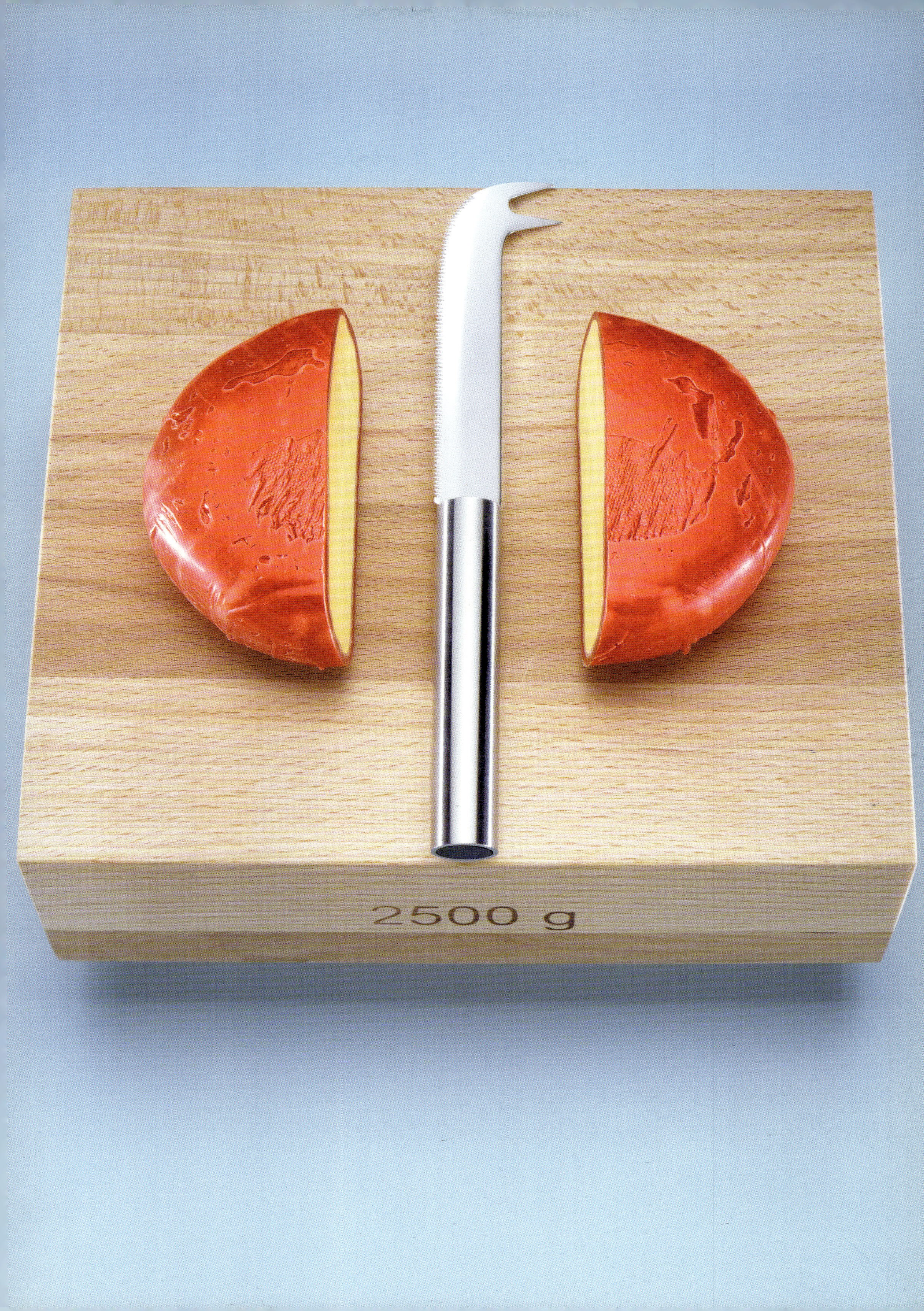
2500 g

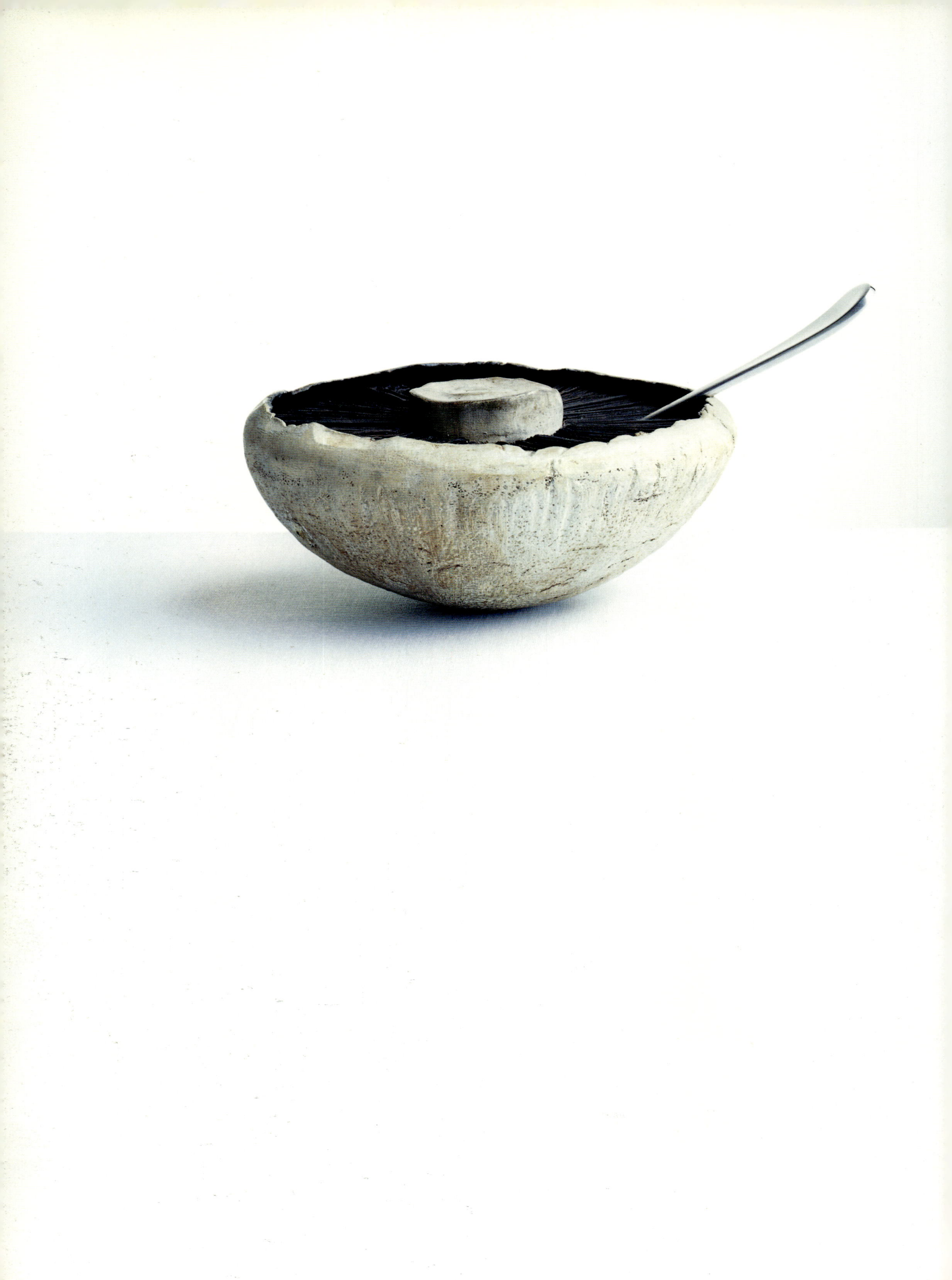

Jonathan Knowles (opposite) Phil Marco

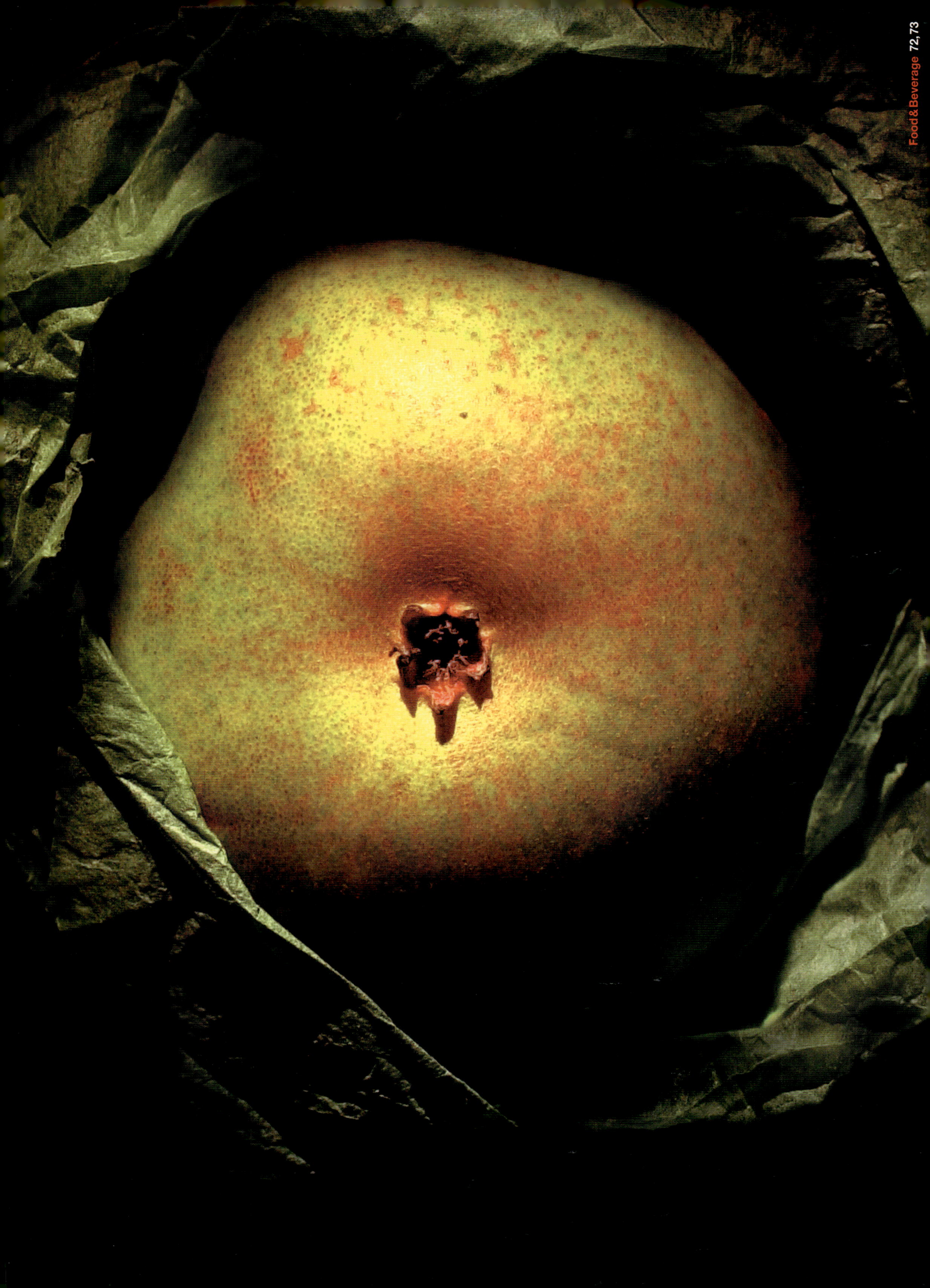

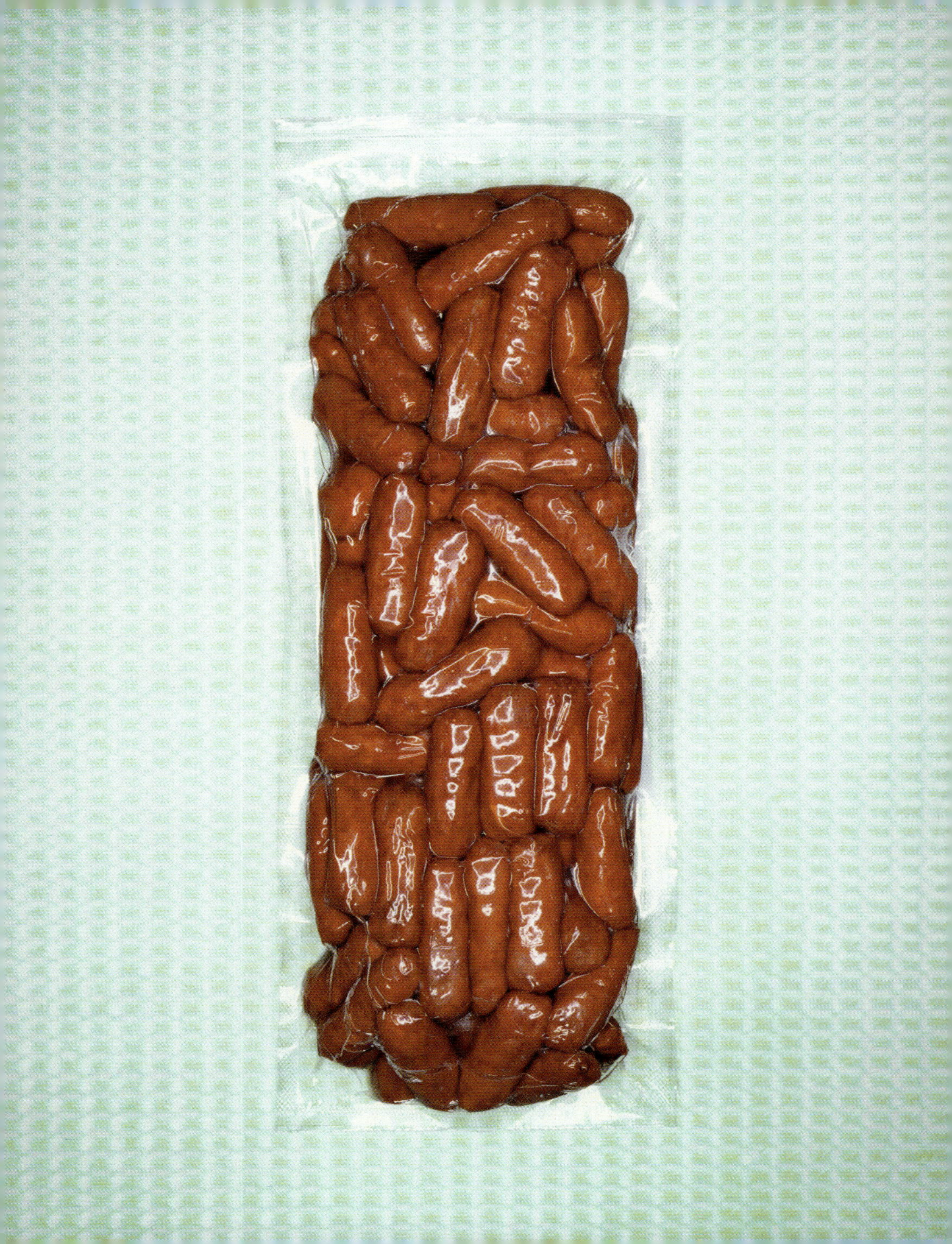

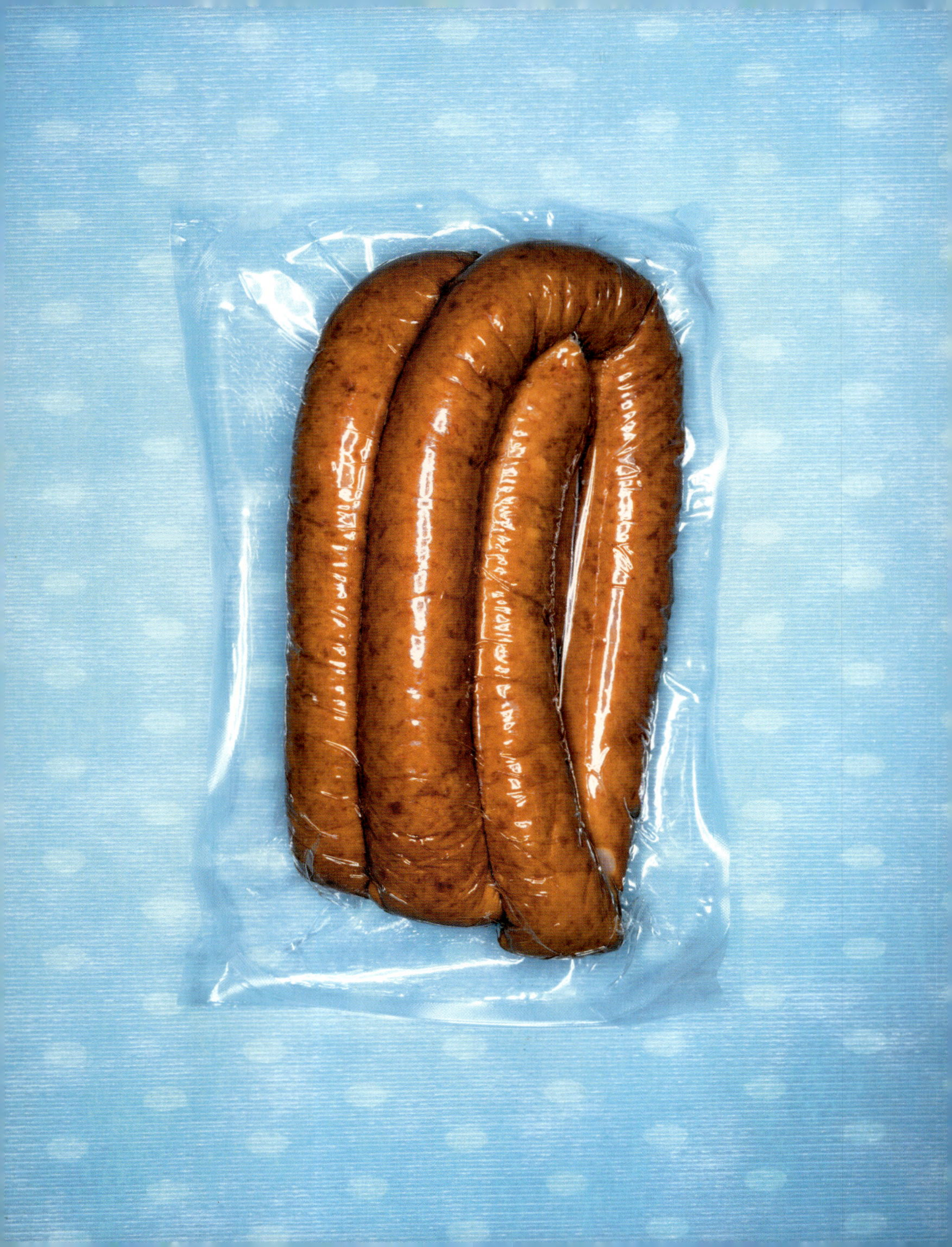

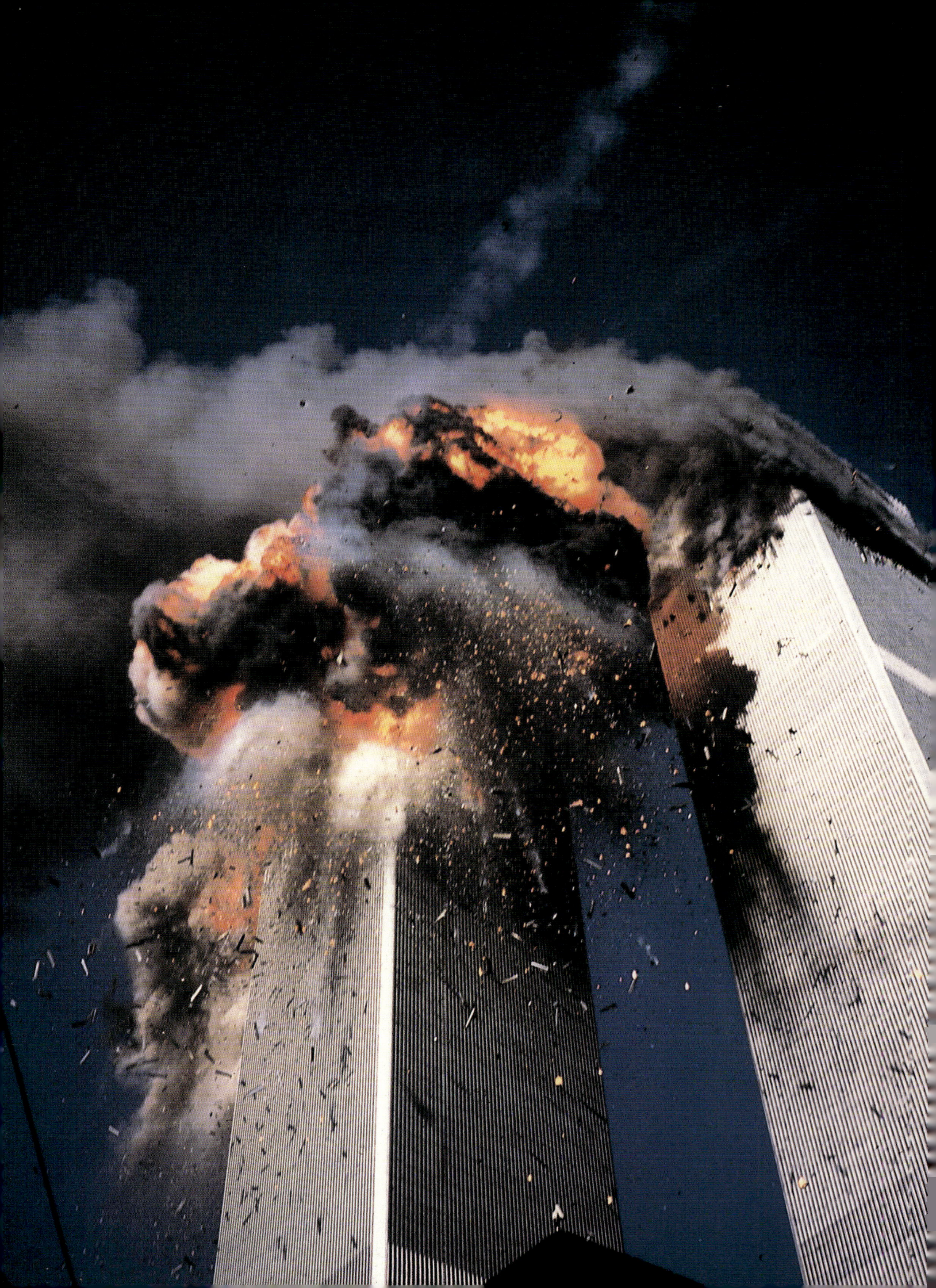

Journalism

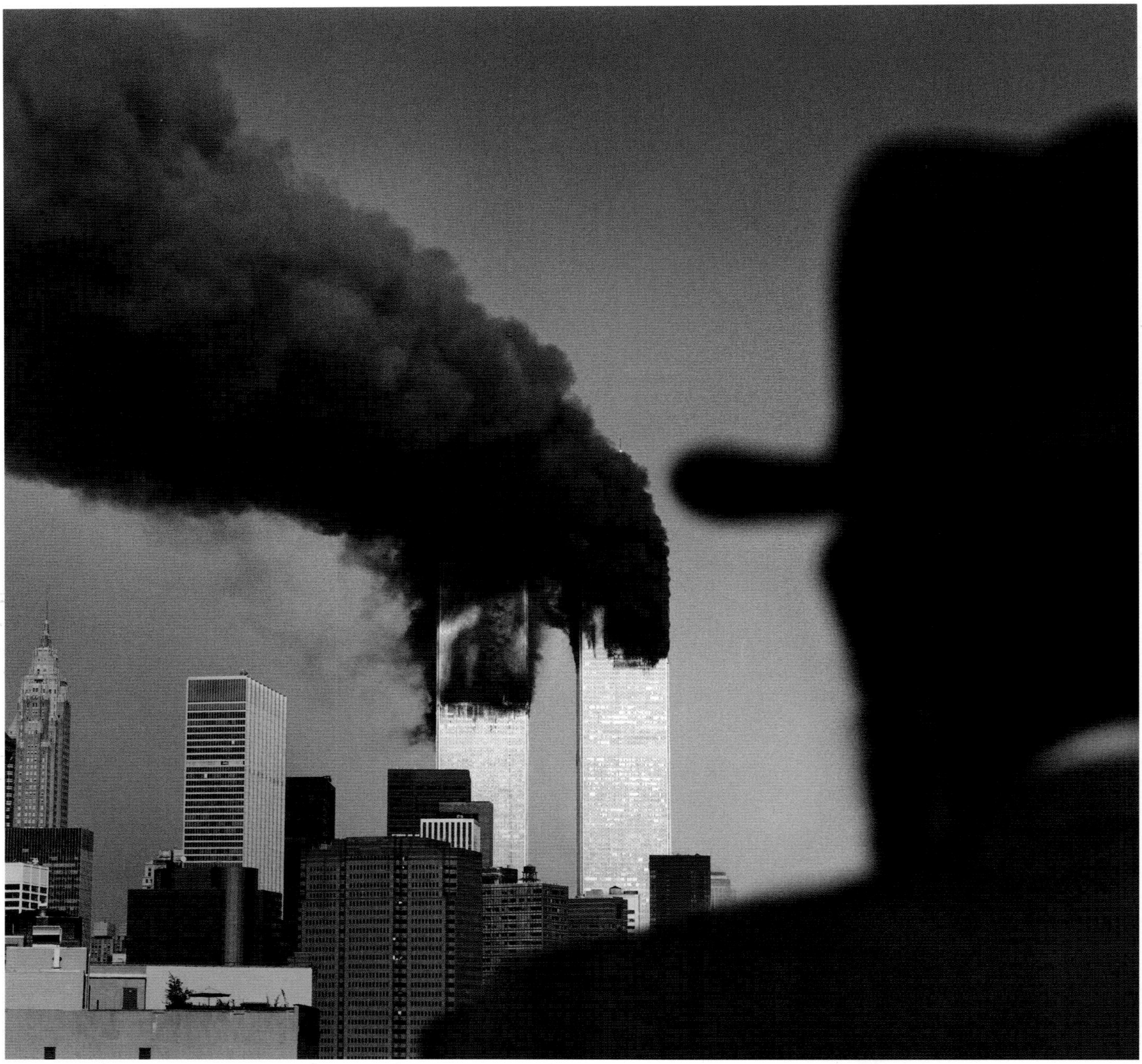

(opening page) Tower two of the World Trade Center at the moment of impact by hijacked United Airlines Flight 175 on the morning of September 11. (this page) Hugh Kretschmer: "Moments before the first tower collapsed, I photographed this Hasidic Jew watching the horror that was unfolding from across the East River. I couldn't help but wonder what he was thinking."

Hugh Kretschmer (opening page) Lyle Owerko

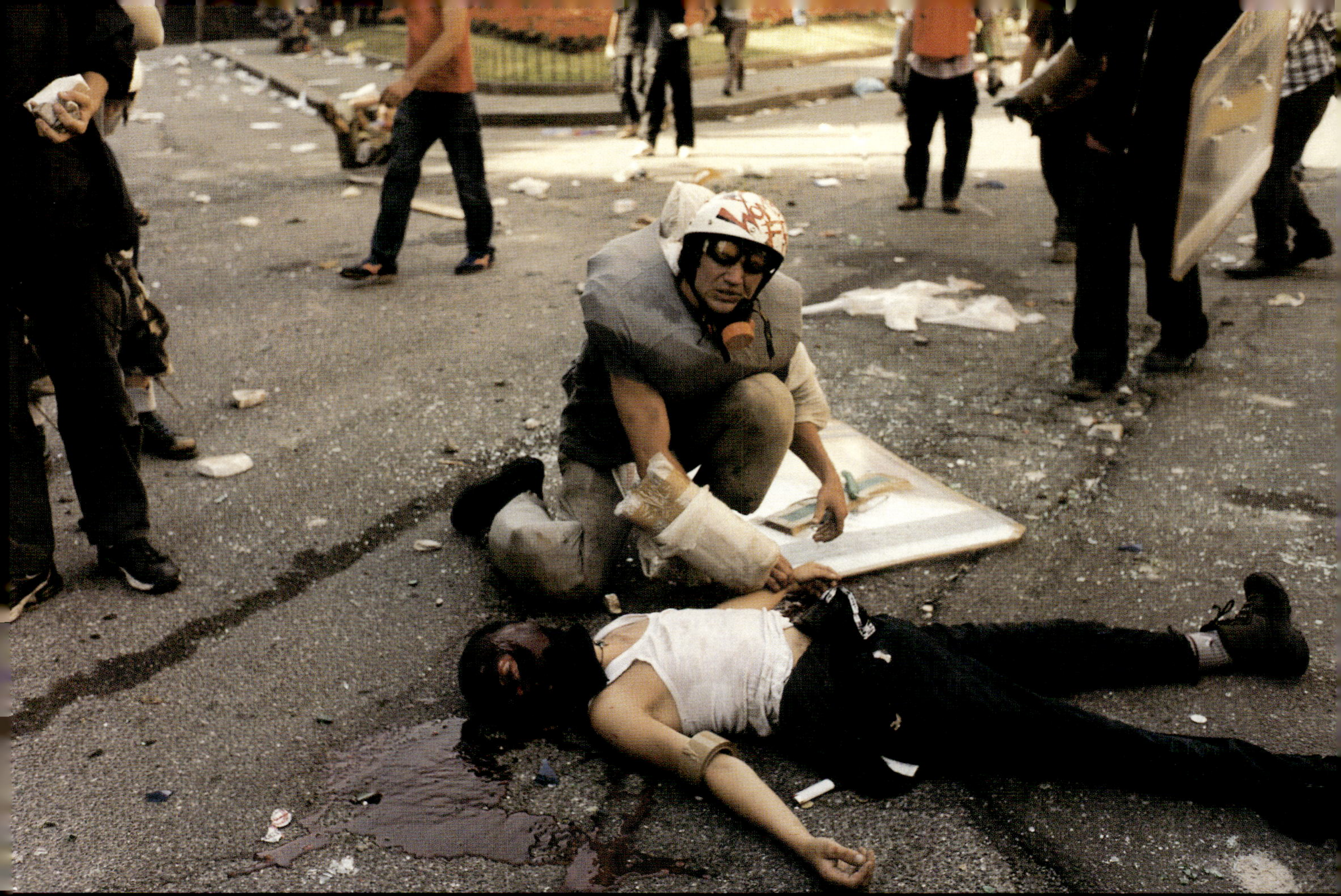

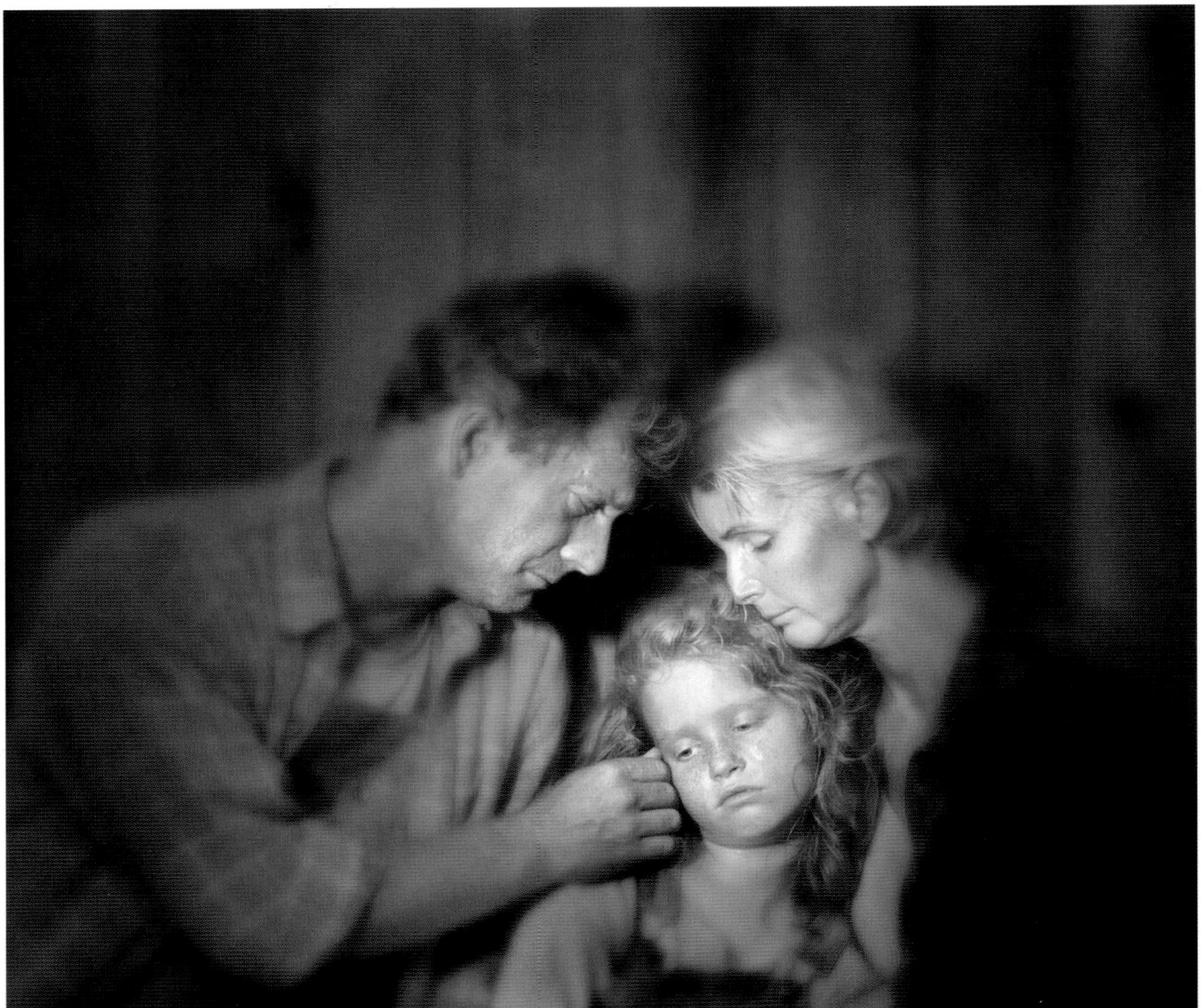

(this and following spread) As a society we have lost our connection to the sources of the food we eat. These farm images were meant to bridge that gap. All of the photographs were taken an hour outside of Detroit, Michigan.

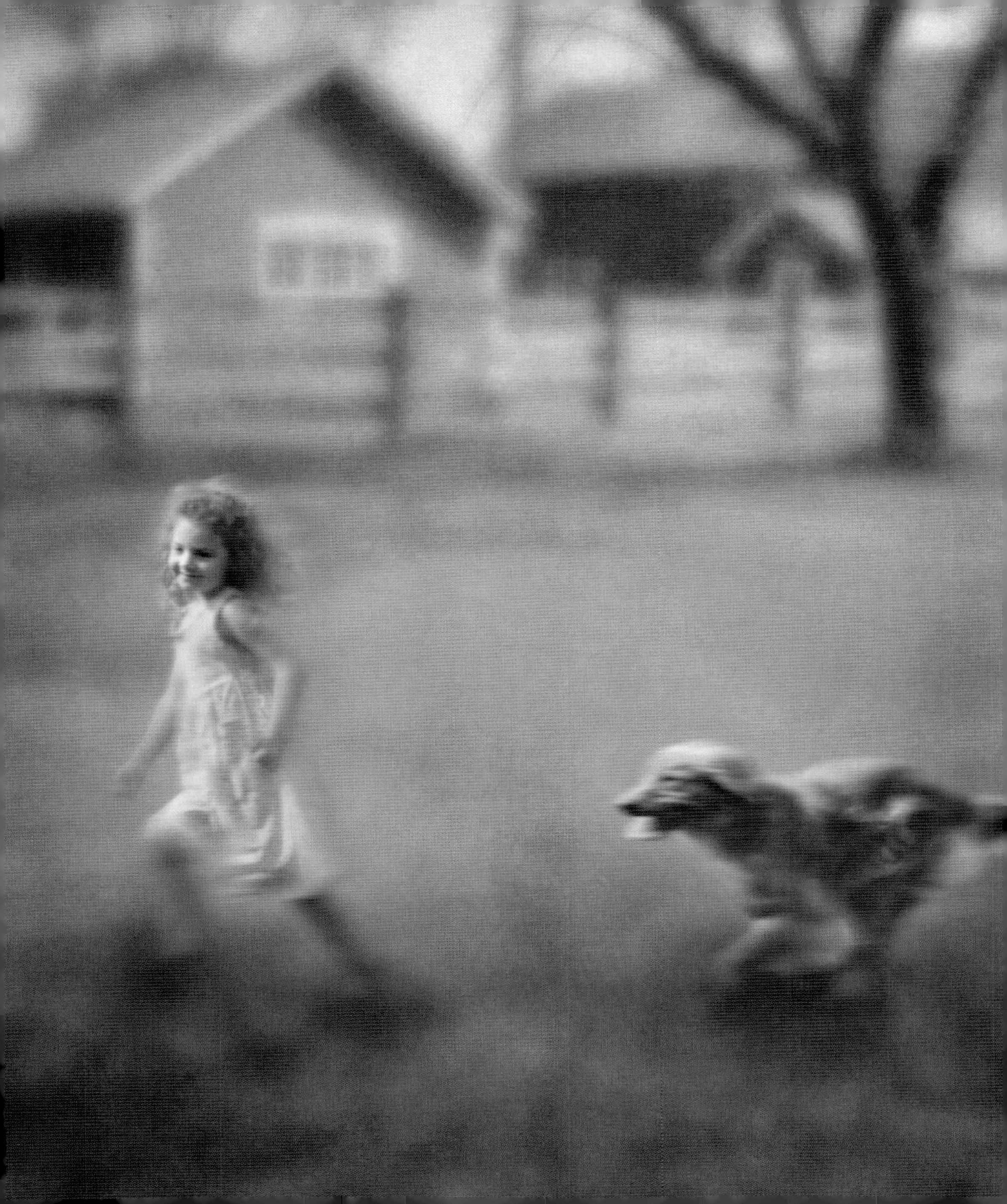

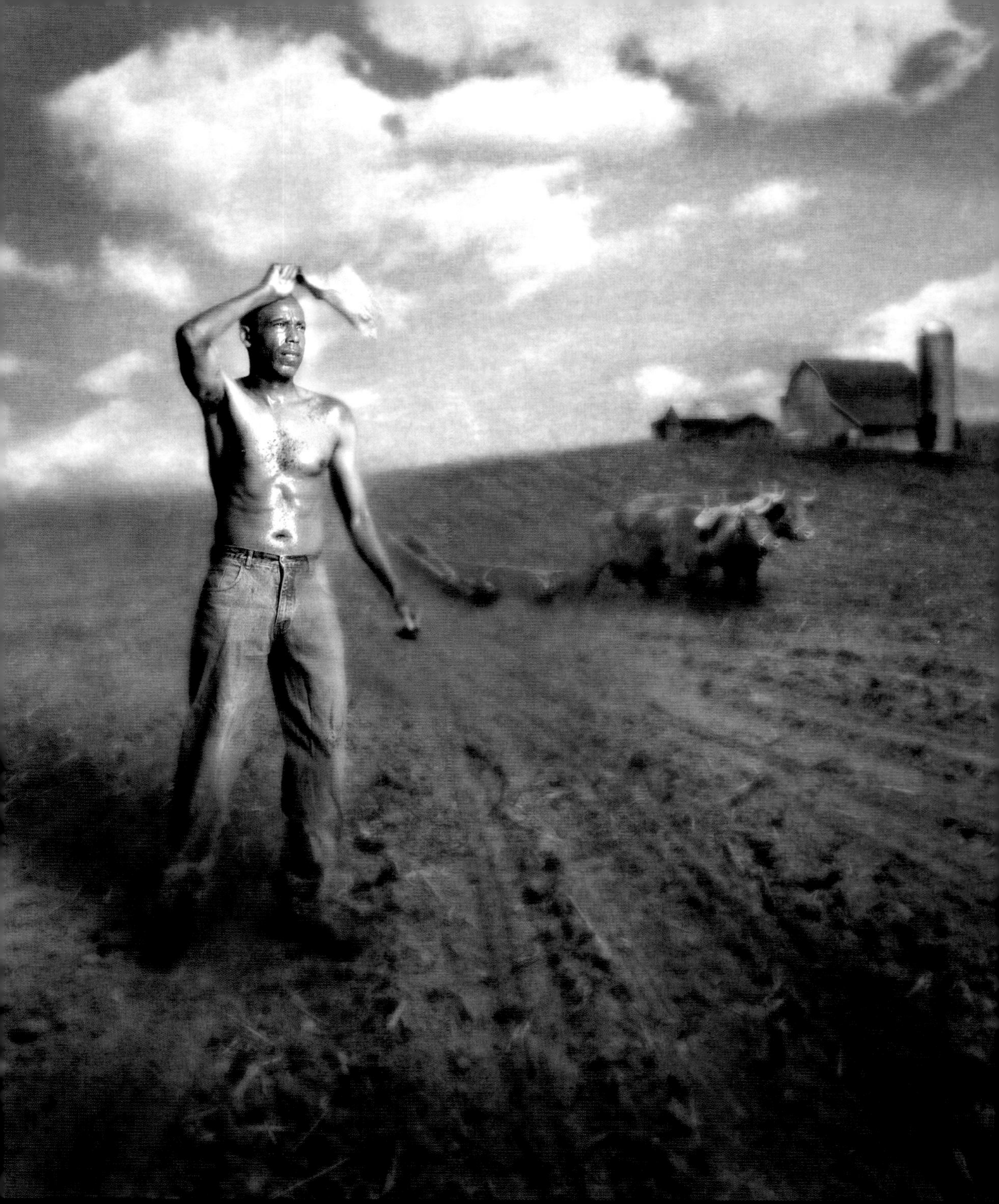

Reid Lincoln Ashton: "I spent a few days on a farm that eaches traditional farming techniques, such as how to arm using oxen and other primitive methods, to village elders from rural African tribes. These tribes are so poor and their locations so remote that if they were given a tractor, they wouldn't have the gas necessary to run it."

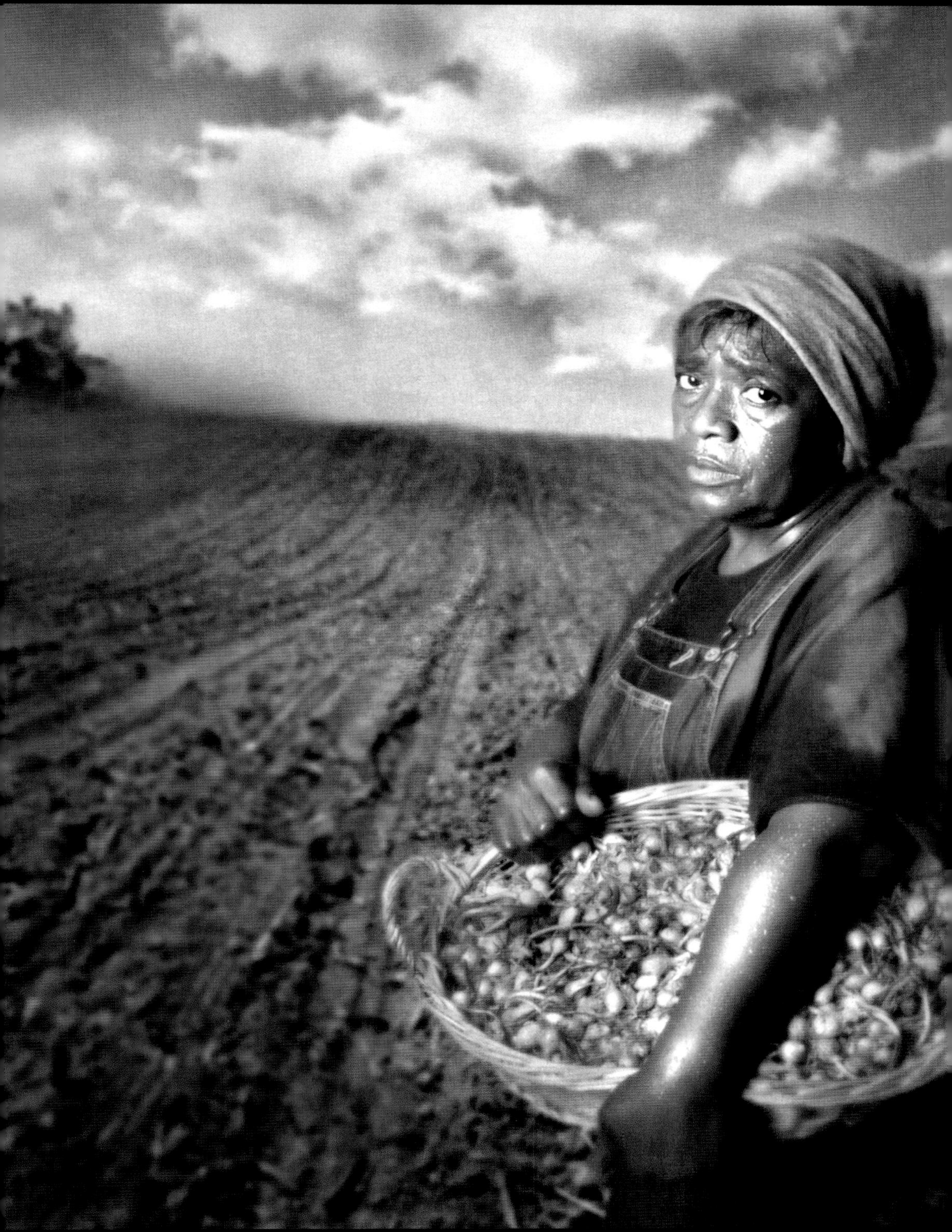

Reid Lincoln Ashton

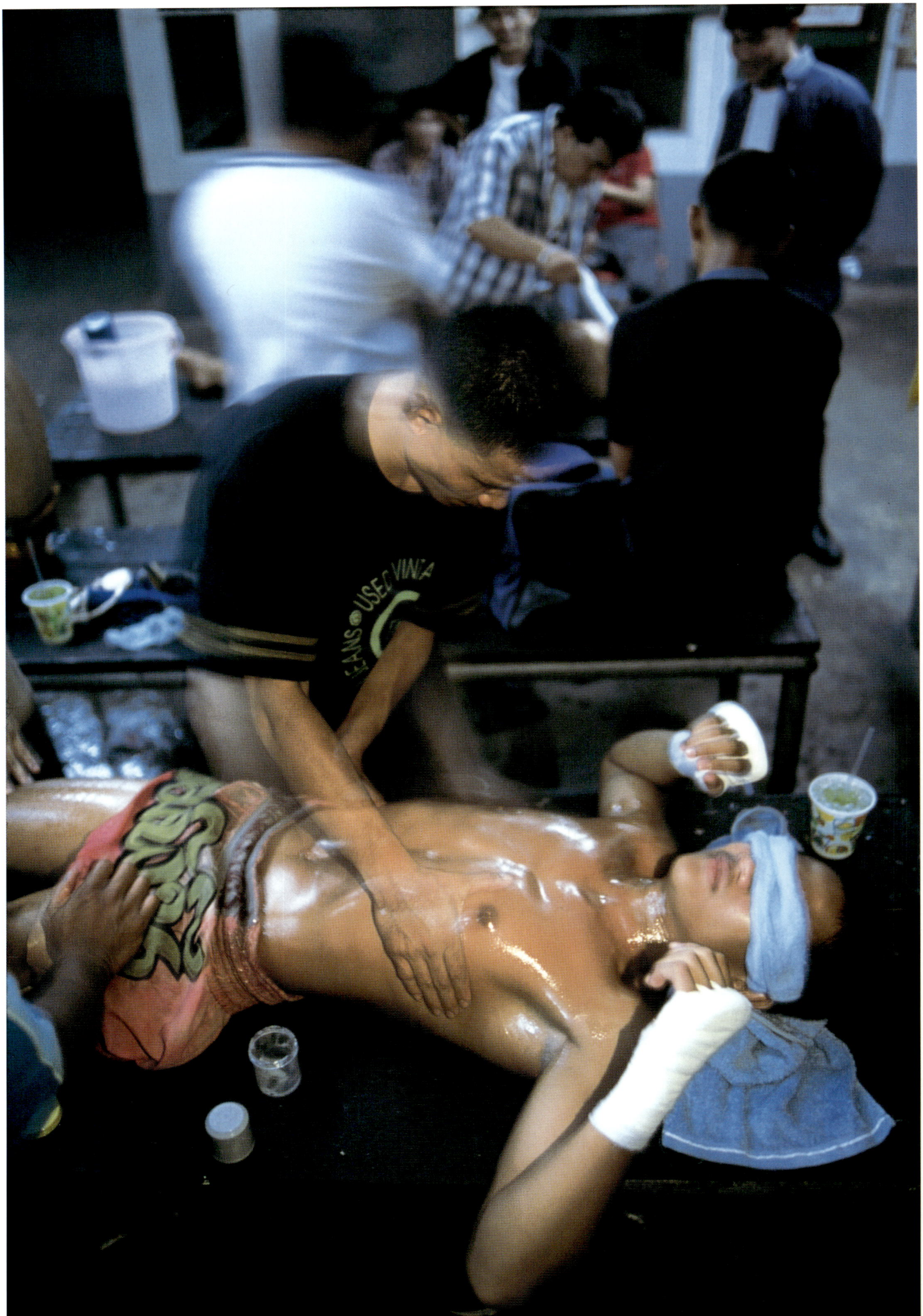

Jeffrey Aaronson

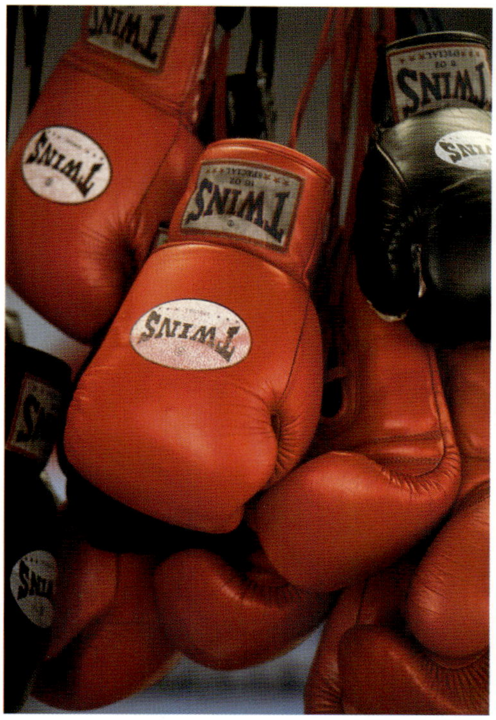

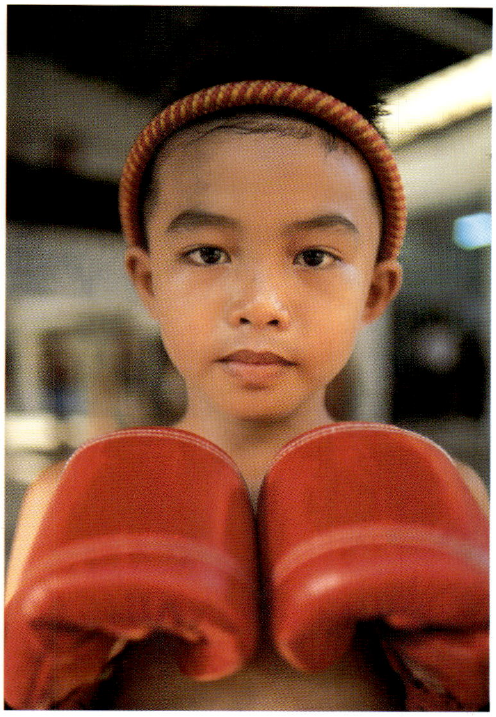

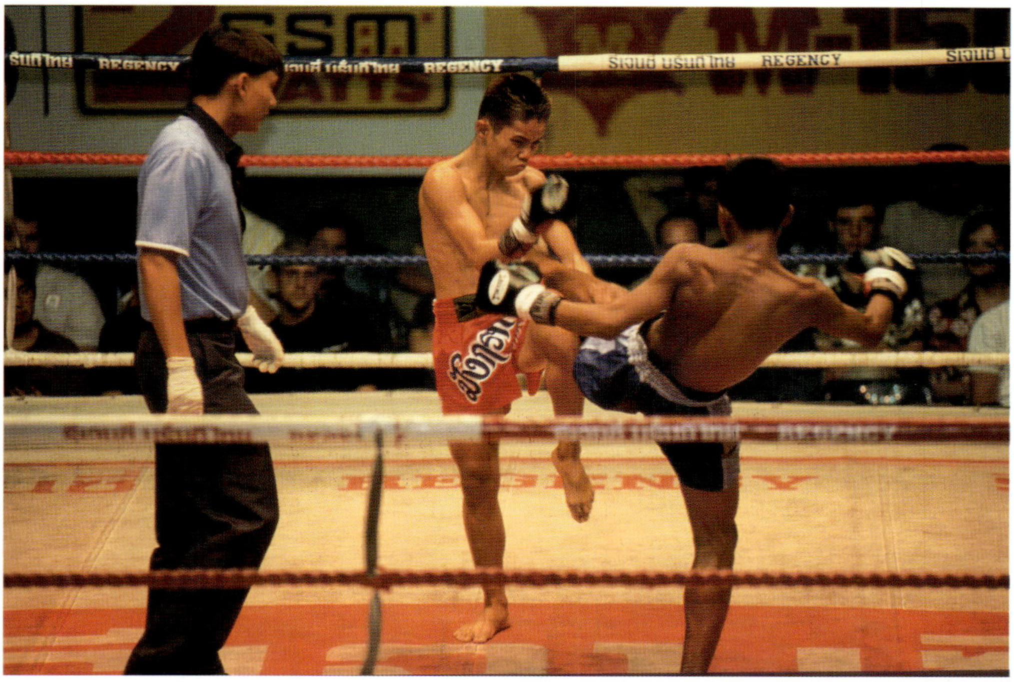

(this spread) "Crouching Tiger, Hidden Thailand" Feature story on Muay Thai (Thai Kickboxing) the sport that is King in Thailand.

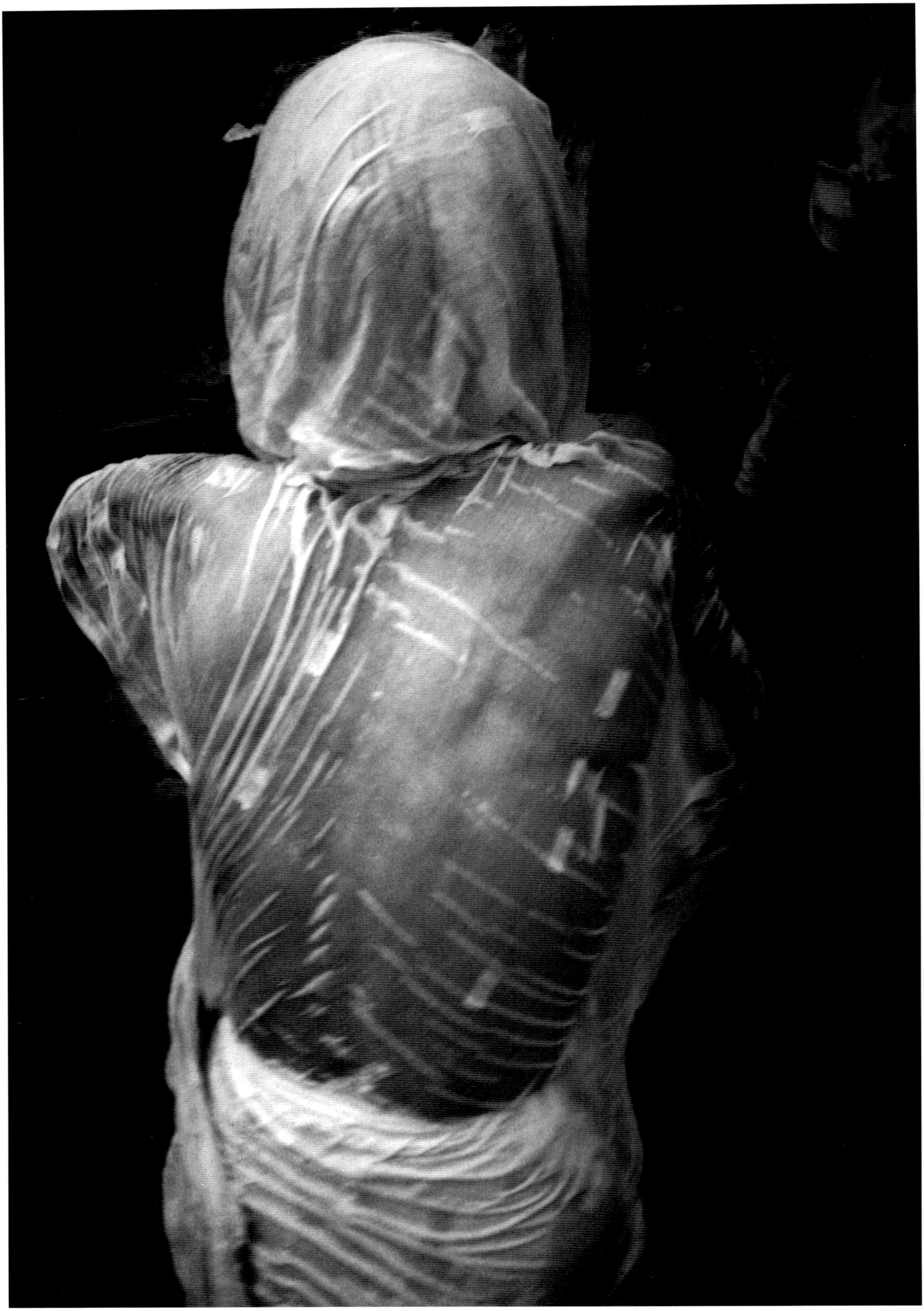

Stephanie Flack

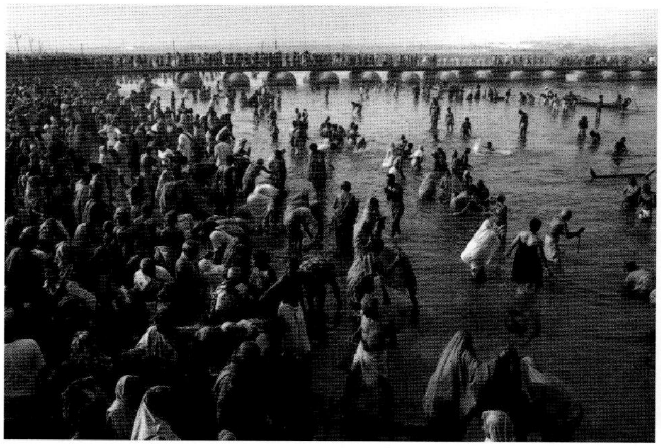
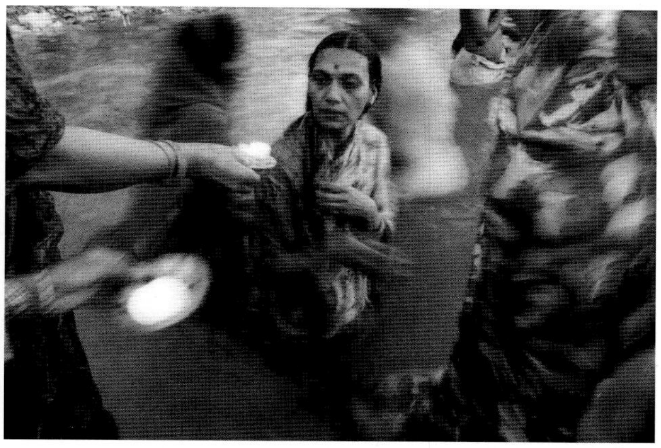
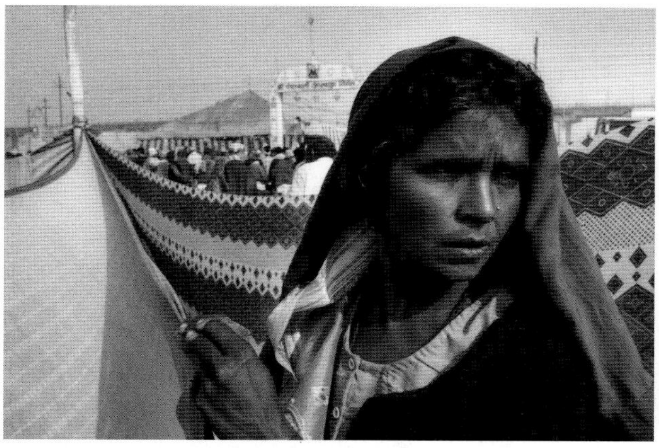
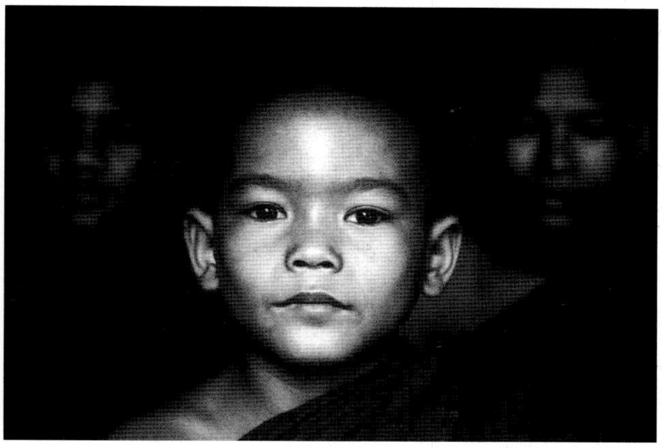
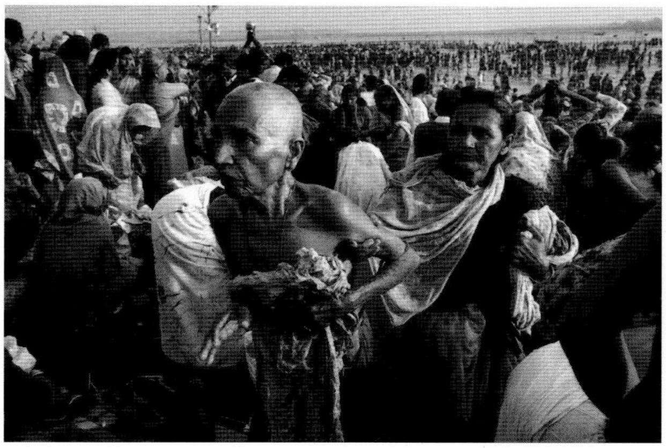
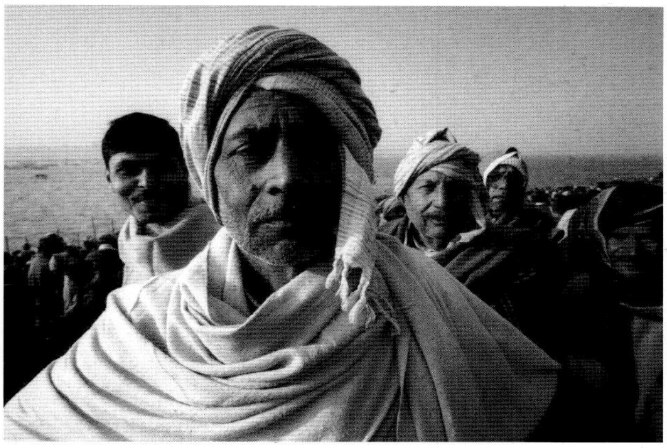
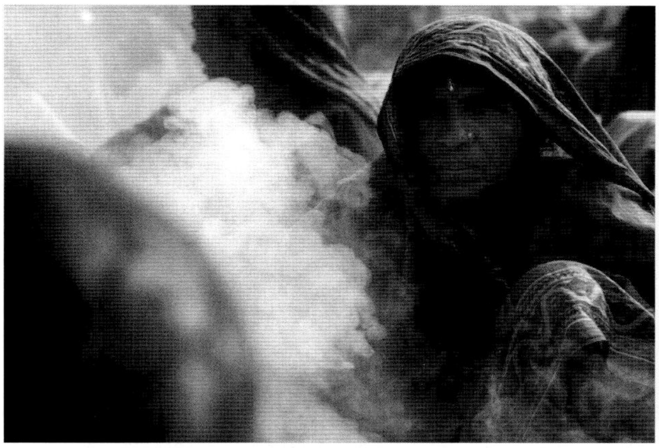
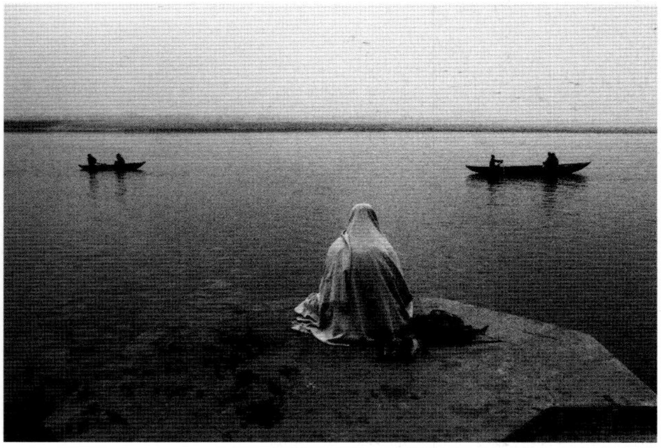

Clockwise from top left: (1) Hindu worshipers attending the Kumbh Mela Festival in India. (2) Pilgrims offer votives to the Ganges. (3) Young Buddhust monks in a Rangoon, Burma monastery. (4) Turbined Hindu pilgrims attending the festival. (5) Pilgrim meditating along the ghats of the river Ganges. (6) Women huddle around campfire at the festival. (7) Hindu couple make their way through the crowd at the Kumbh Mela Festival. (8) A women holds sari to dry in the breeze at the Kumbh Mela Festival. (opposite) Wet sari of worshipper who bathed in the Ganges River.

Stephanie Flack

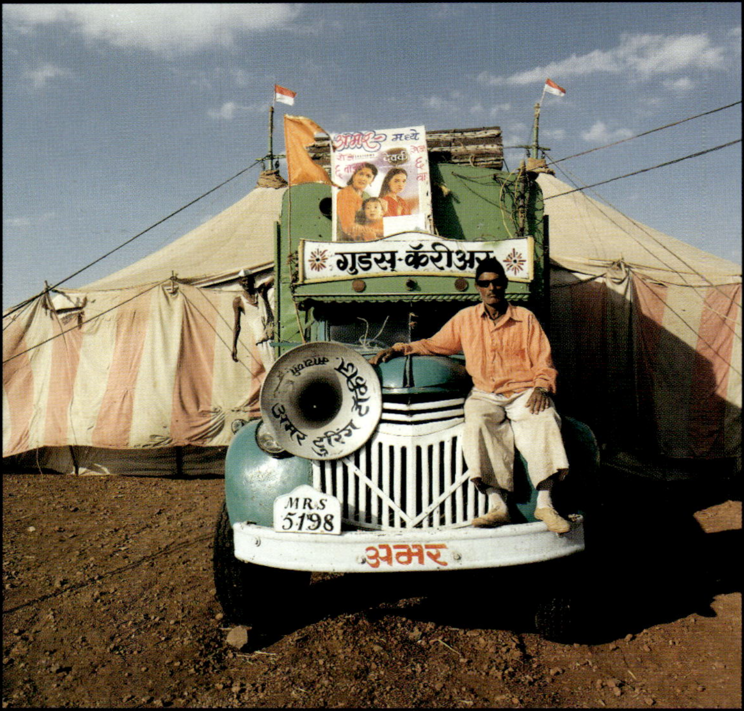

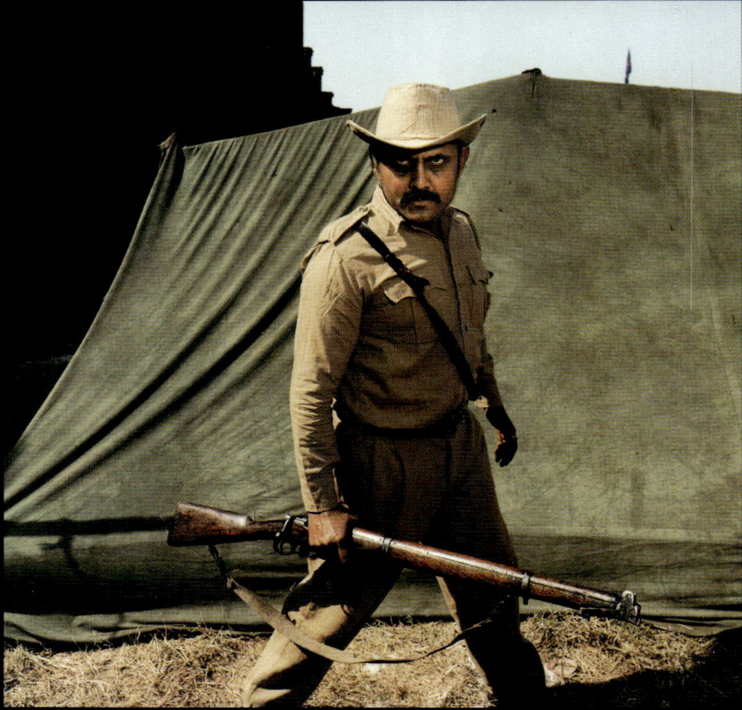

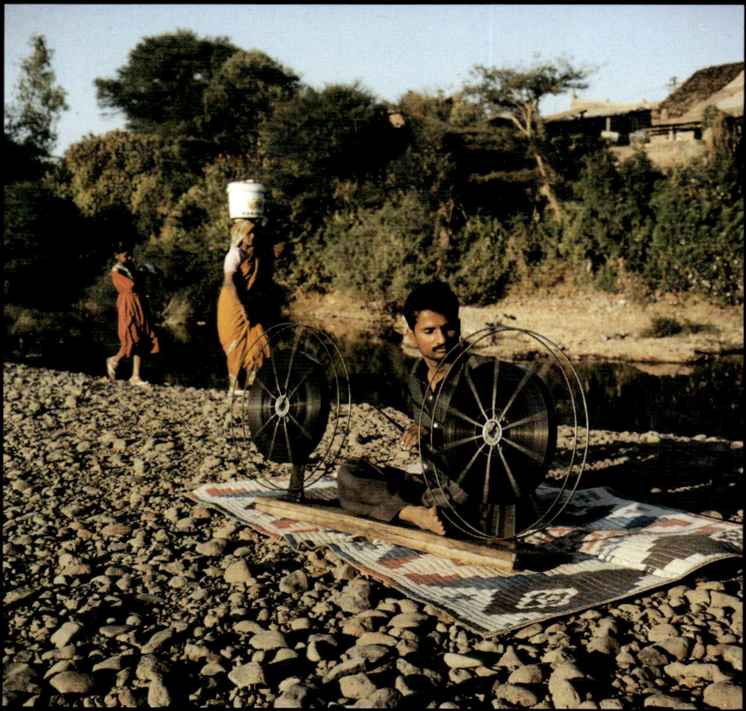

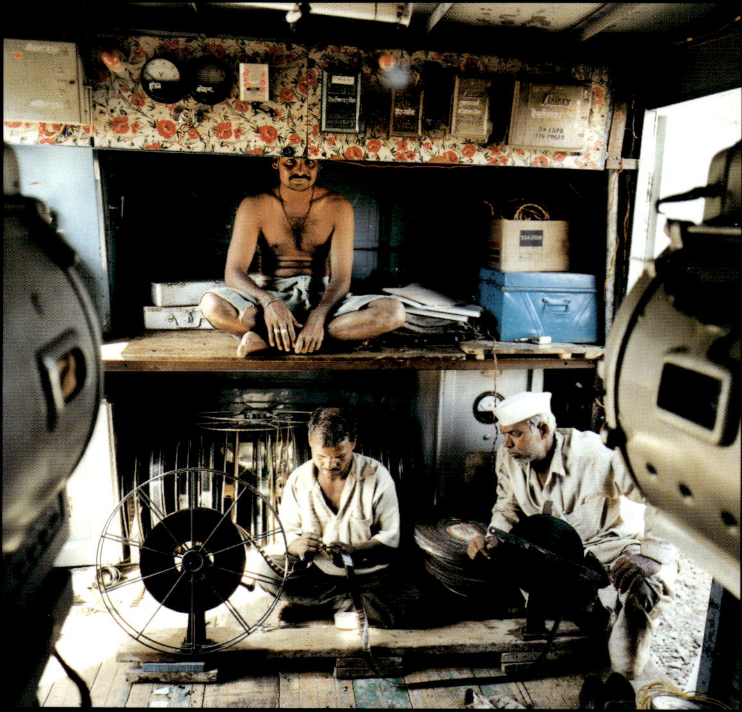

Clockwise from top left: (1) This old truck travels to remote areas in India to bring cinema to the people. A huge tent is set up for the screenings. (2) A character actor on the set of a Hindi film in Bombay, India. (3) In the belly of the truck with two projectors the cinema workers set up for the next show. (4) As they have very limited room in the projection truck a man rewinds the film reels on the ground near where the cinema set camp. (opposite) The interior of the touring cinema tent. Up to one thousand people from area villages can fit inside.

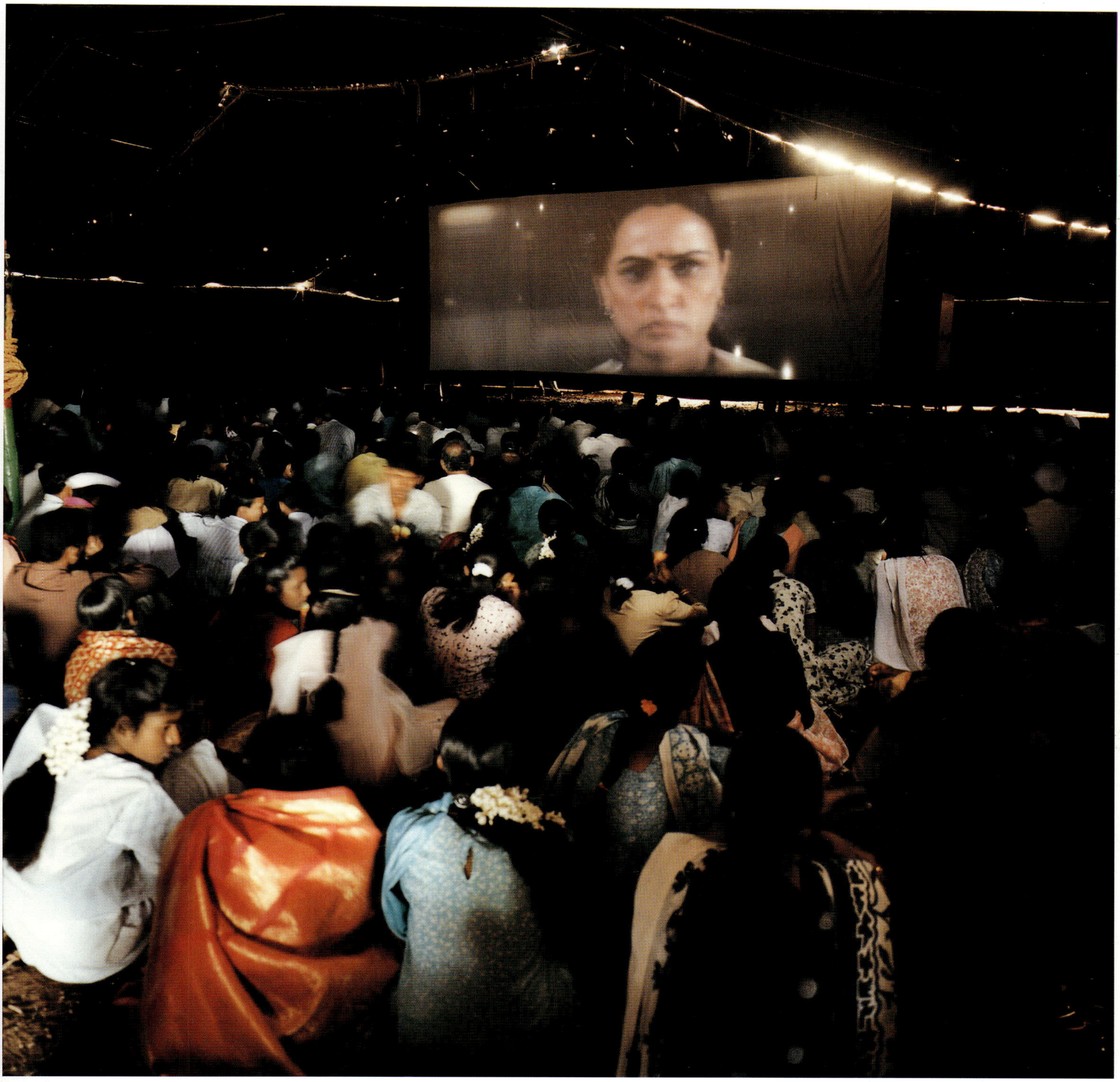

Jonathan Torgovnik

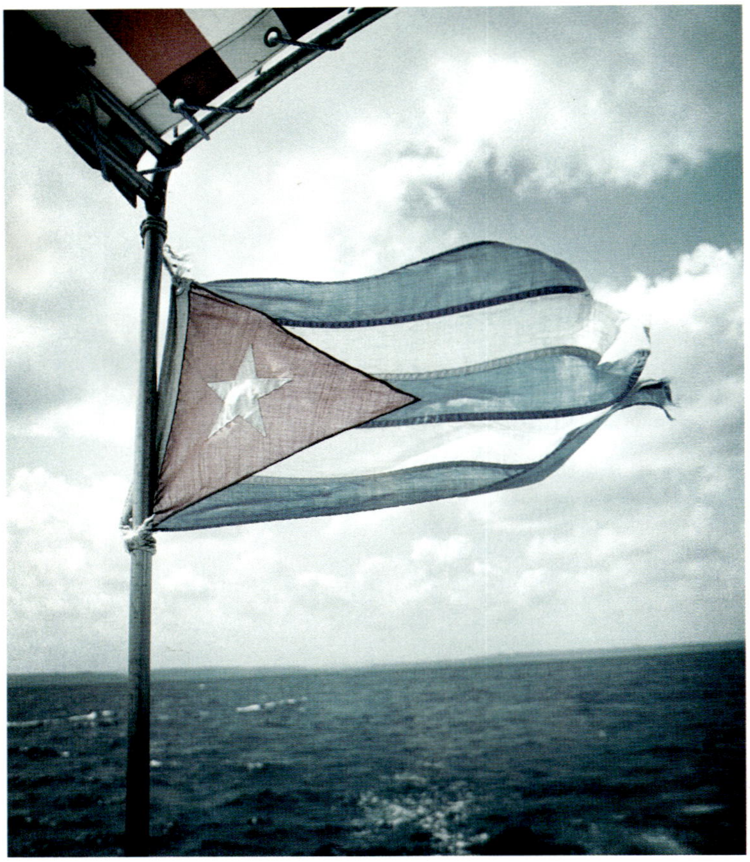

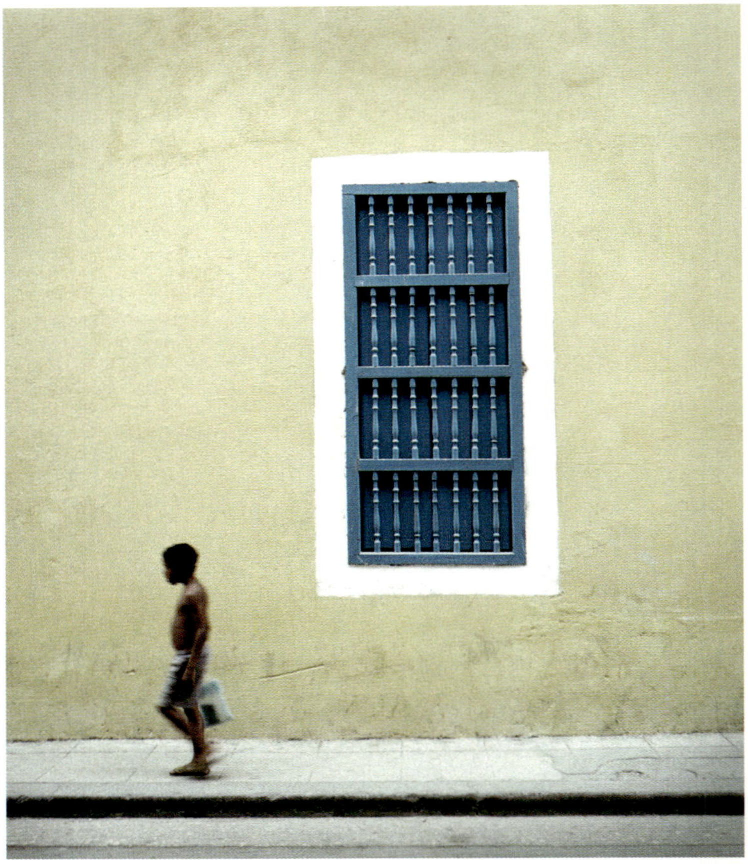

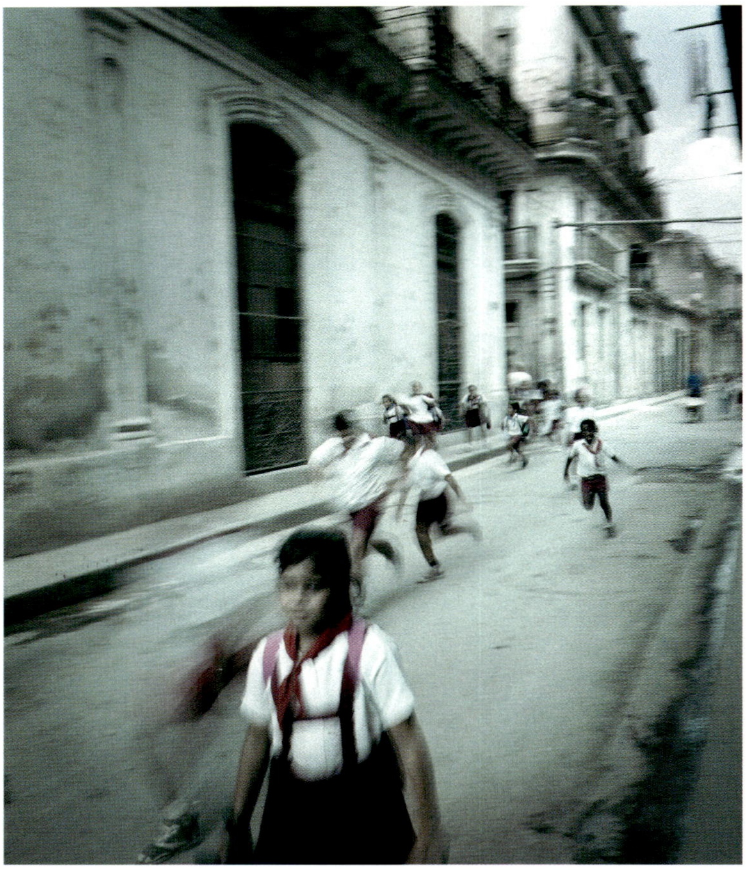

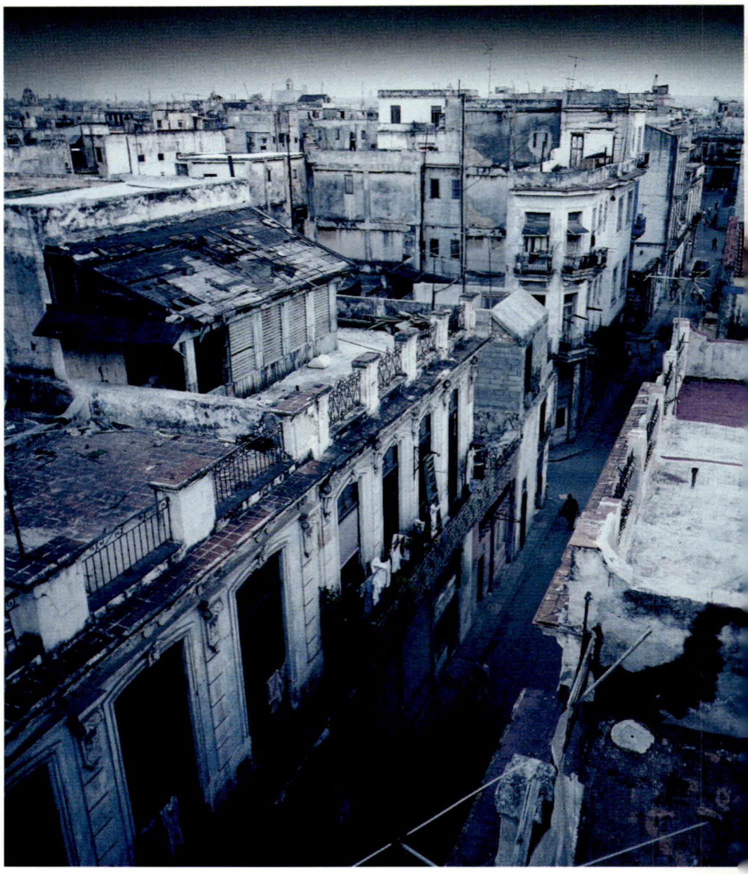

From left to right: (1) I went marlin fishing but didn't manage to catch anything. So I just sat staring at this flag all afternoon when it struck me what a nice image it would be. (2) Originally I had wanted to take a shot of just this window but then the boy walked by and I liked that image better so I asked him to walk by again and I took the shot. (3) I heard the kids yelling and running before I could see them. It sounded like they were heading towards me so I waited around the corner from where I thought they were and as they turned the corner, I took the shot. (4) I actually walked through an open door in someones house and then up onto their roof. This is what I saw when I got there

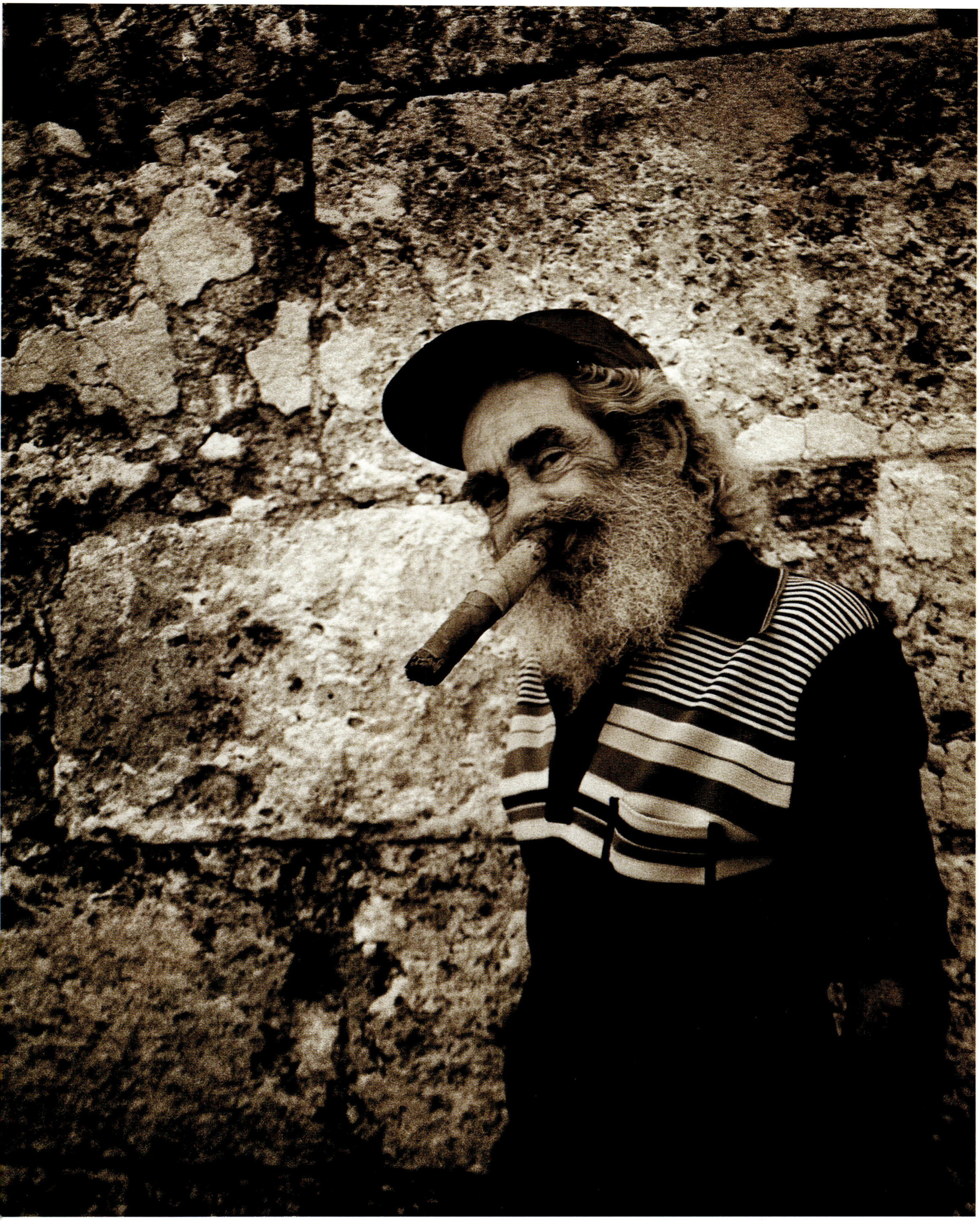

Chris Gordaneer

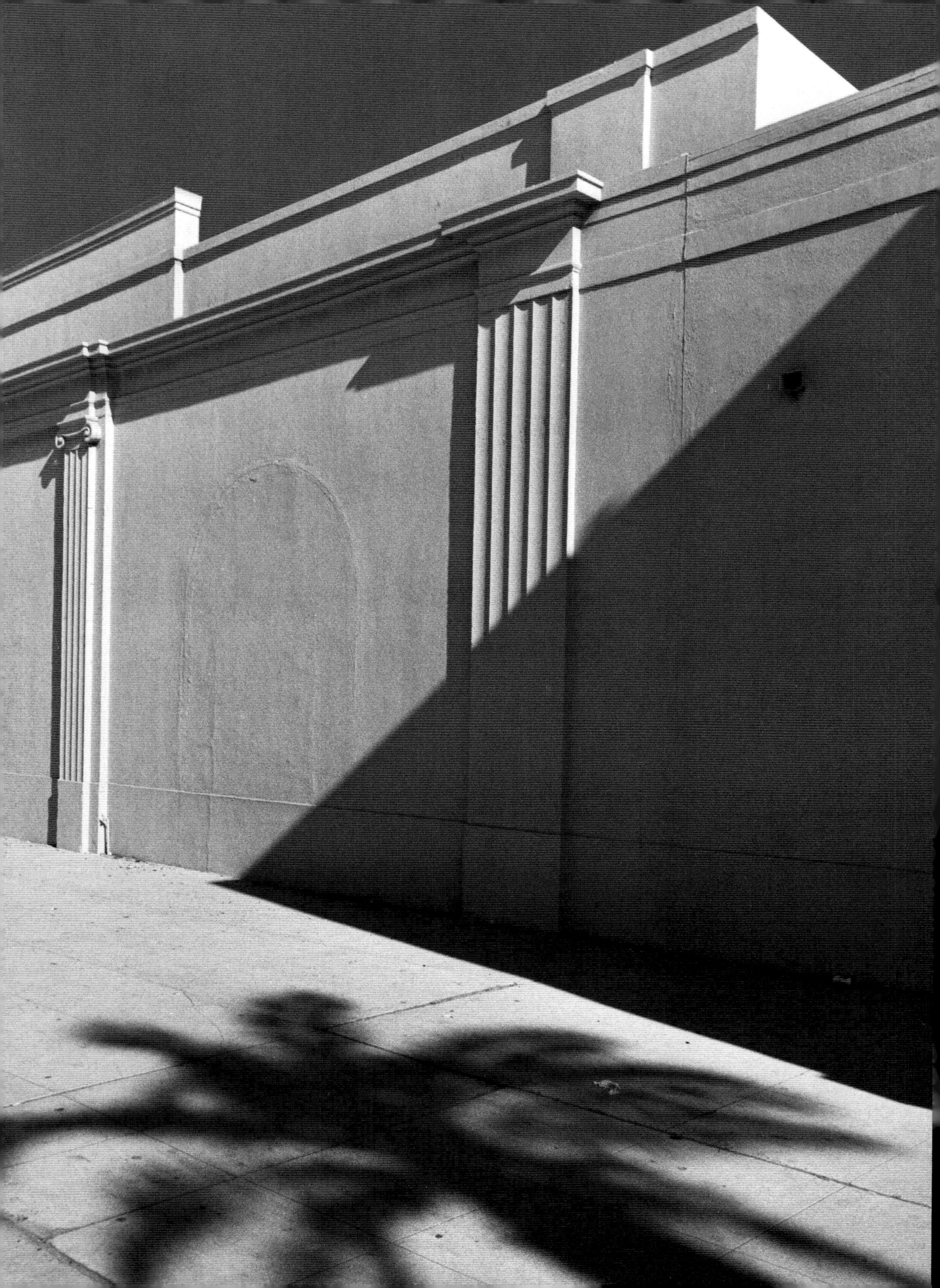

Landscape

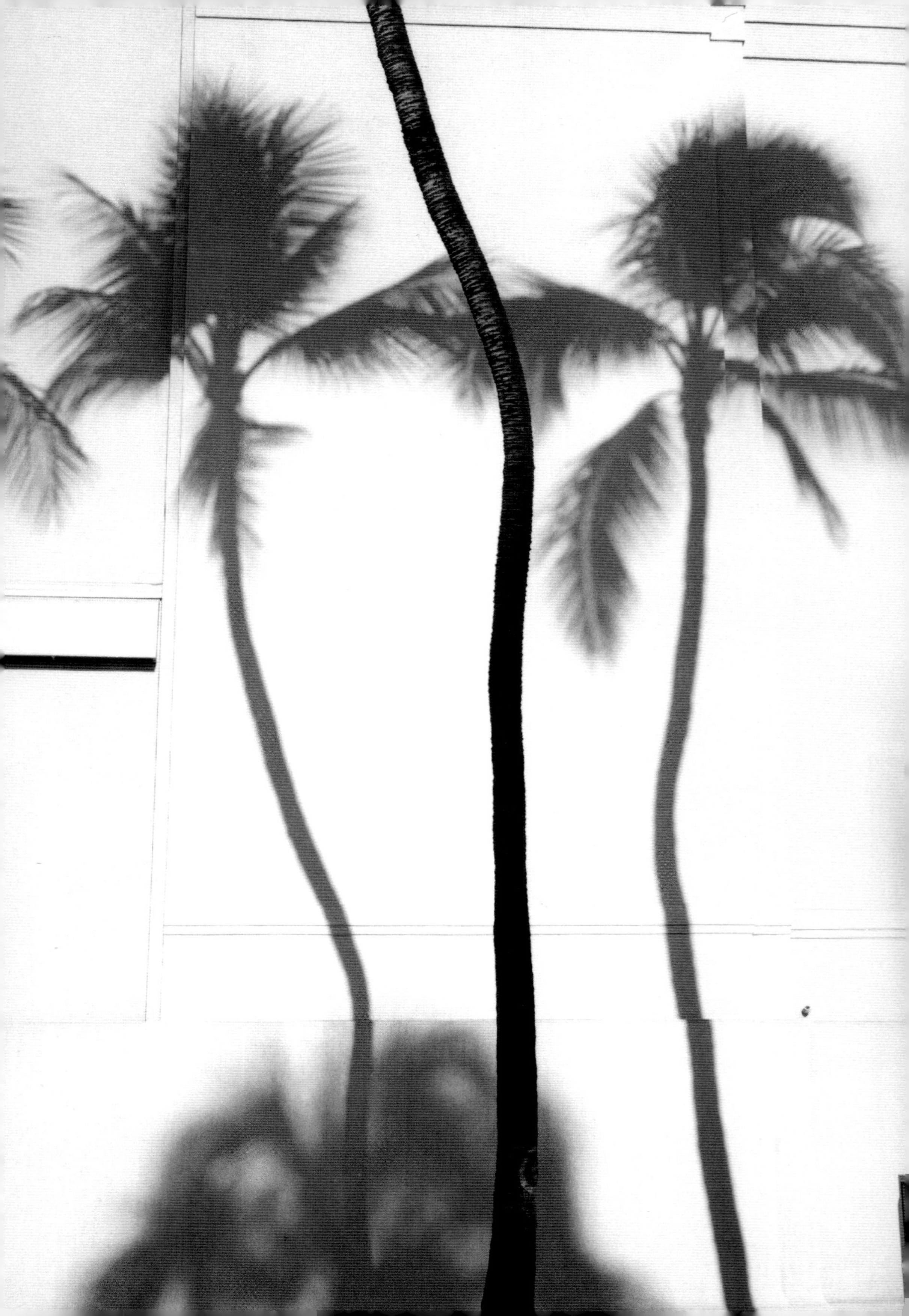

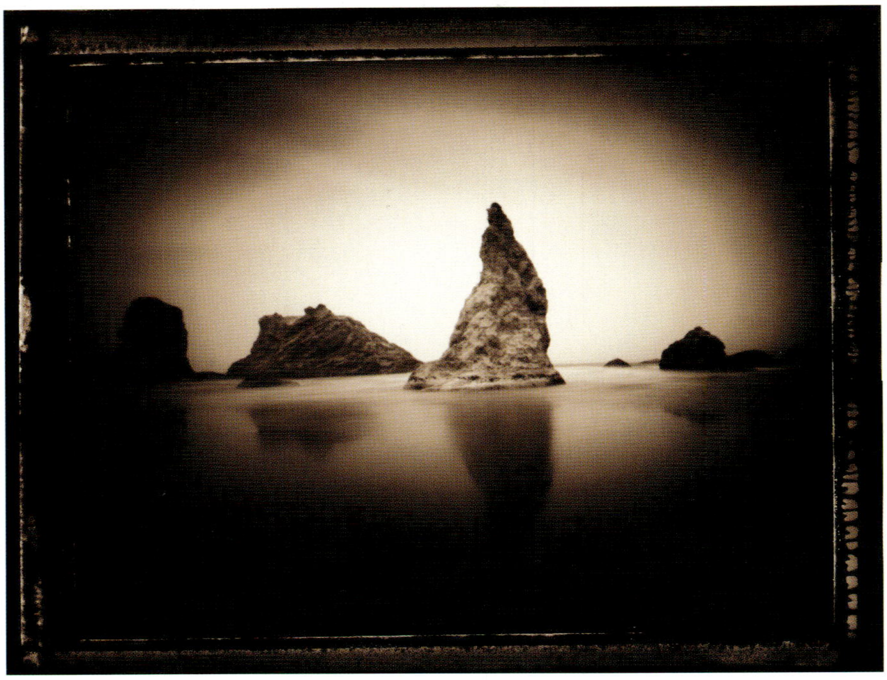

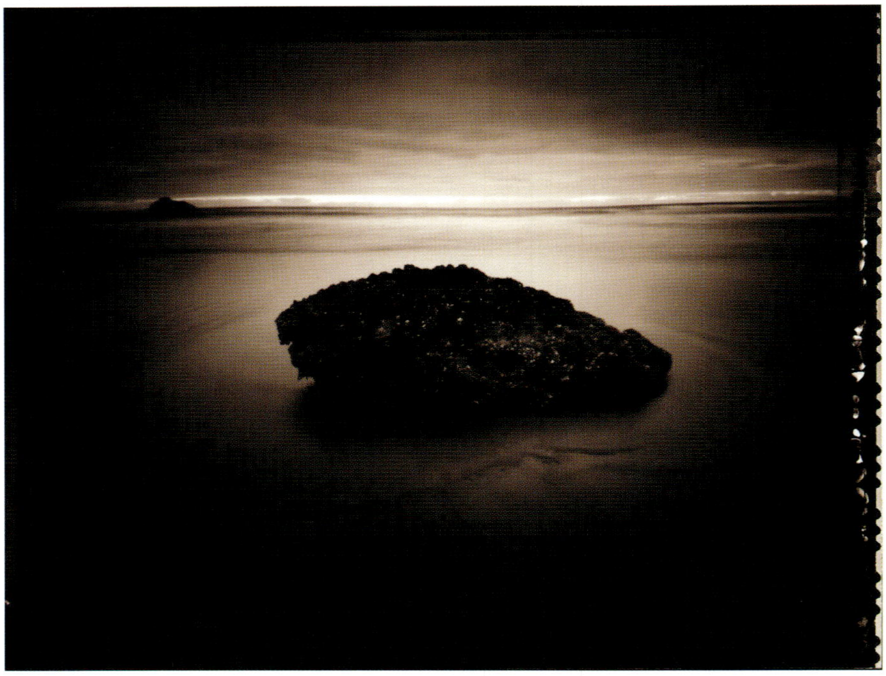

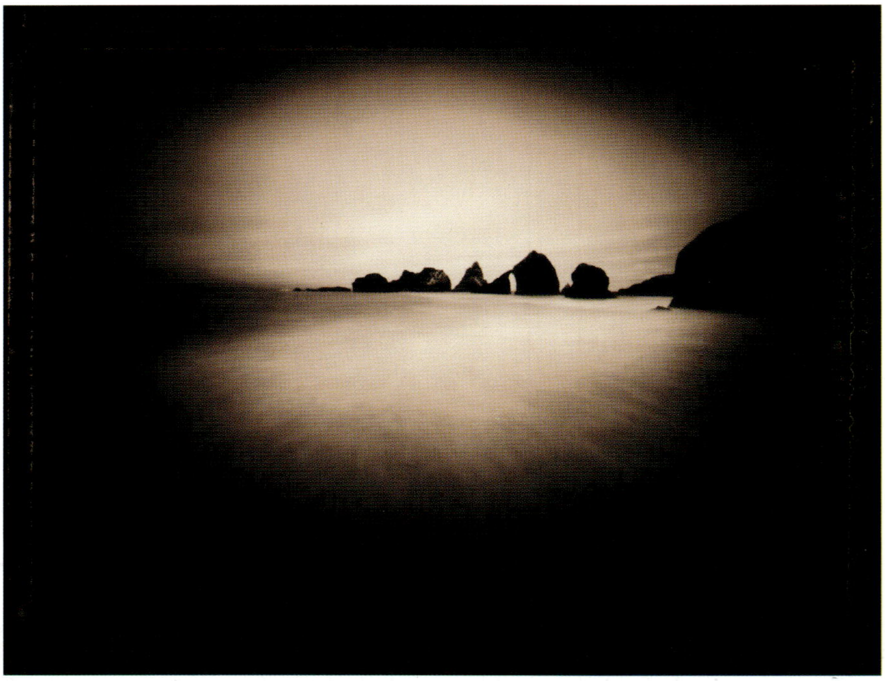

Lars Topelmann

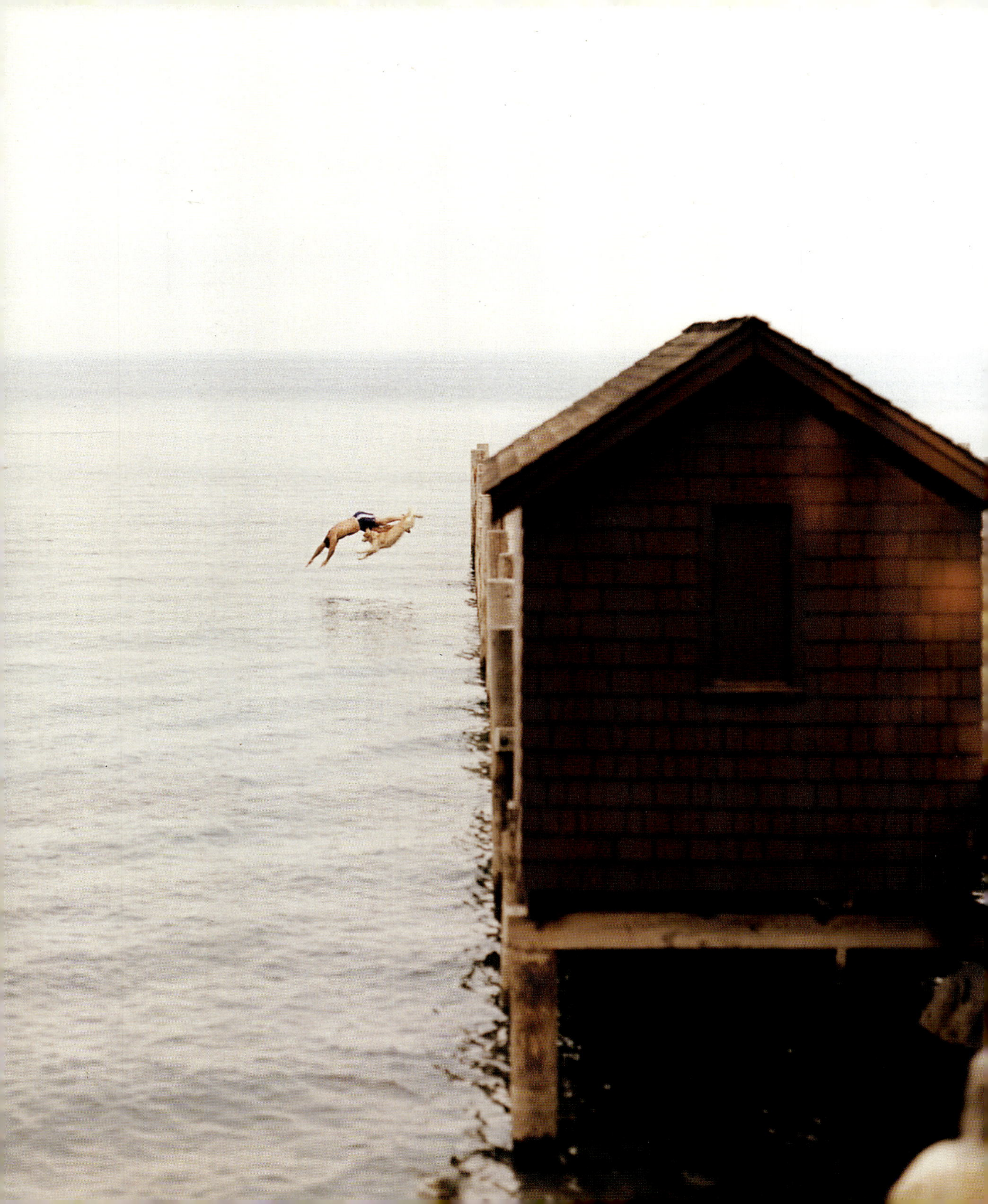

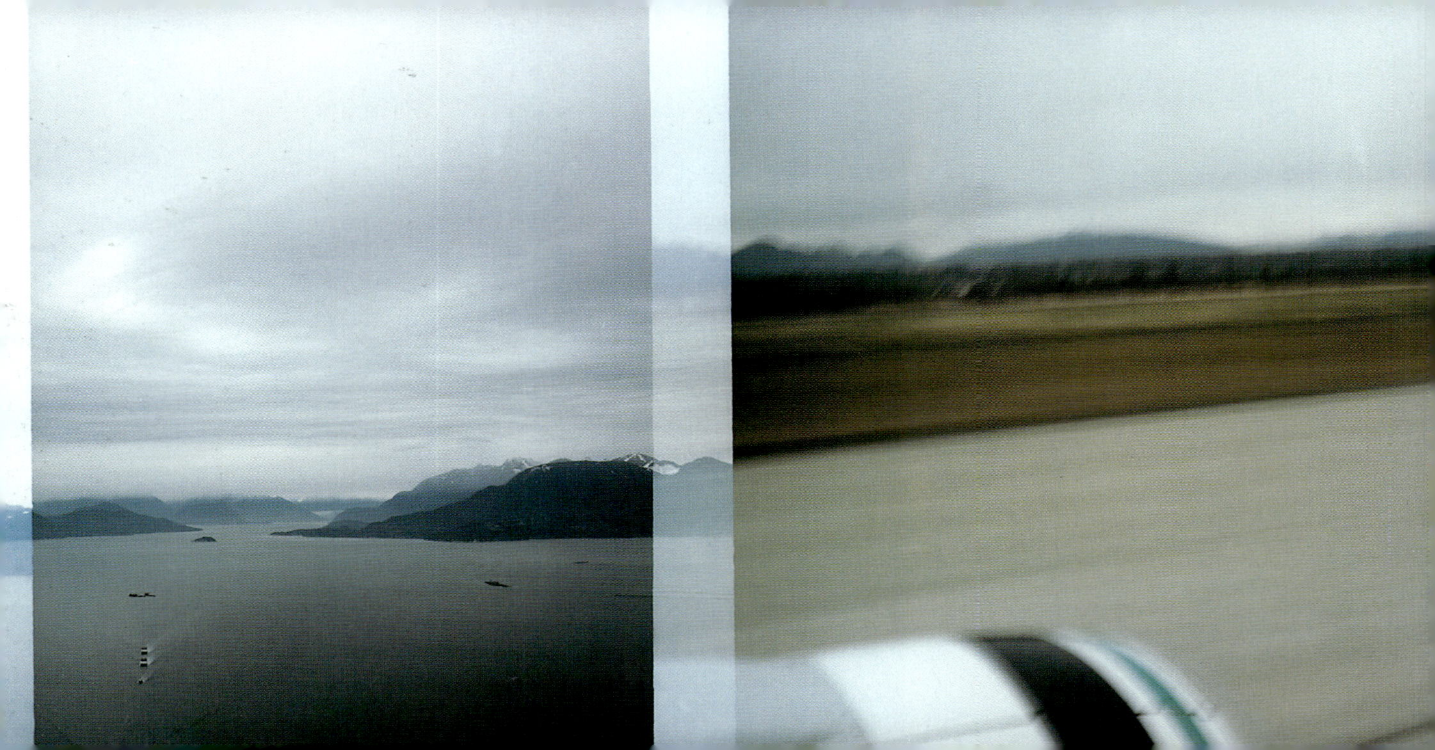

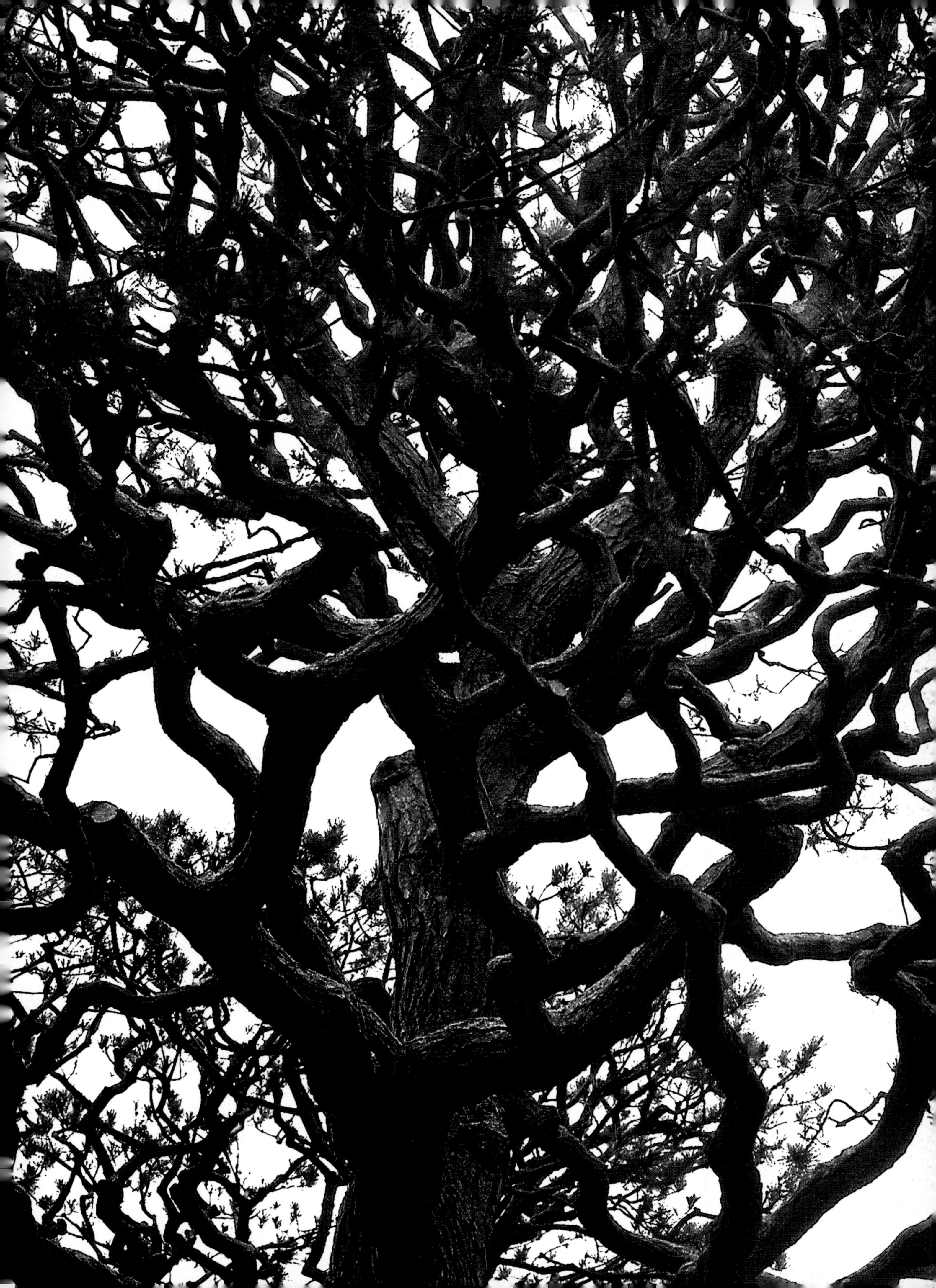

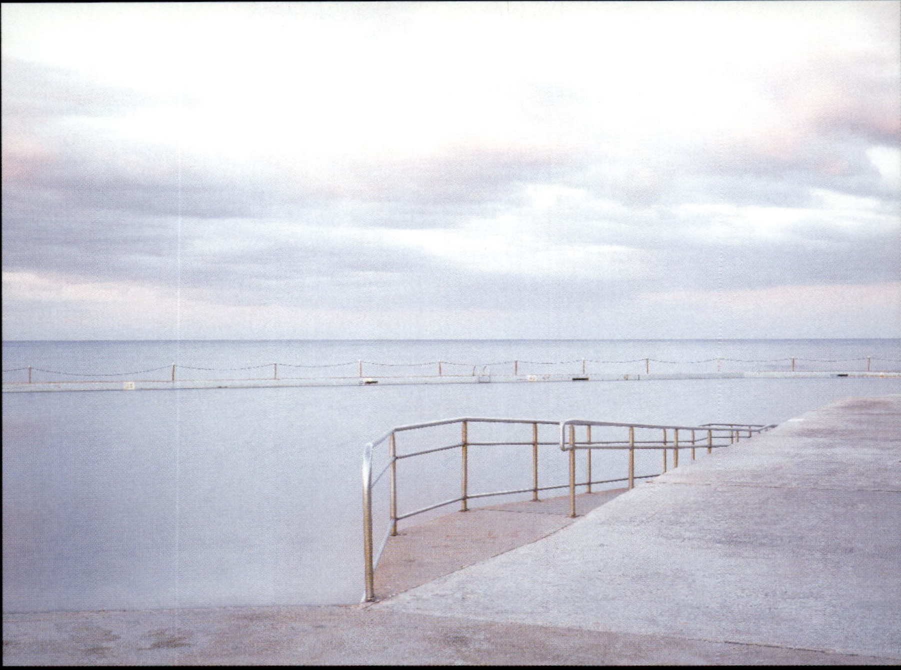

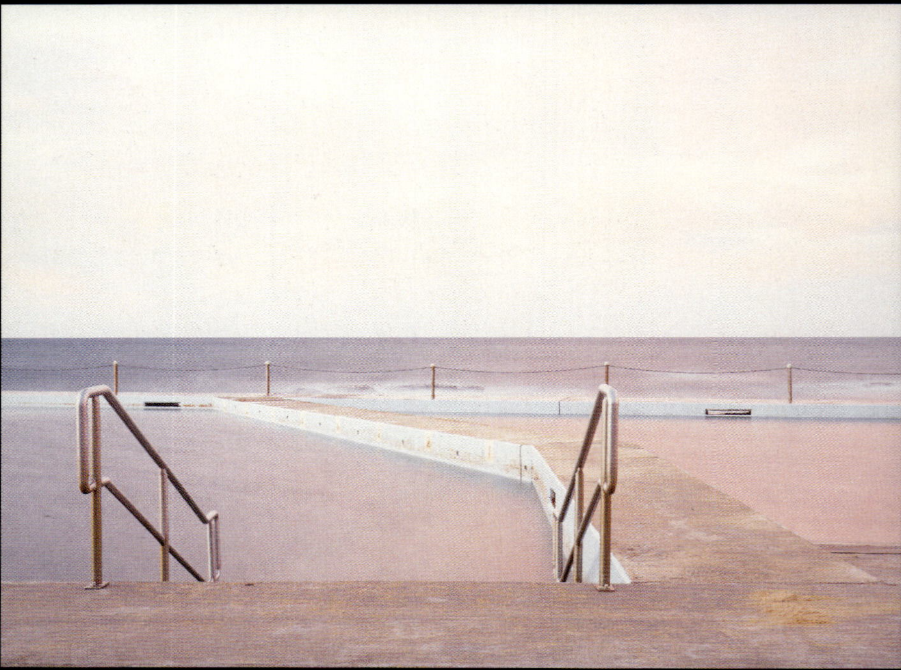

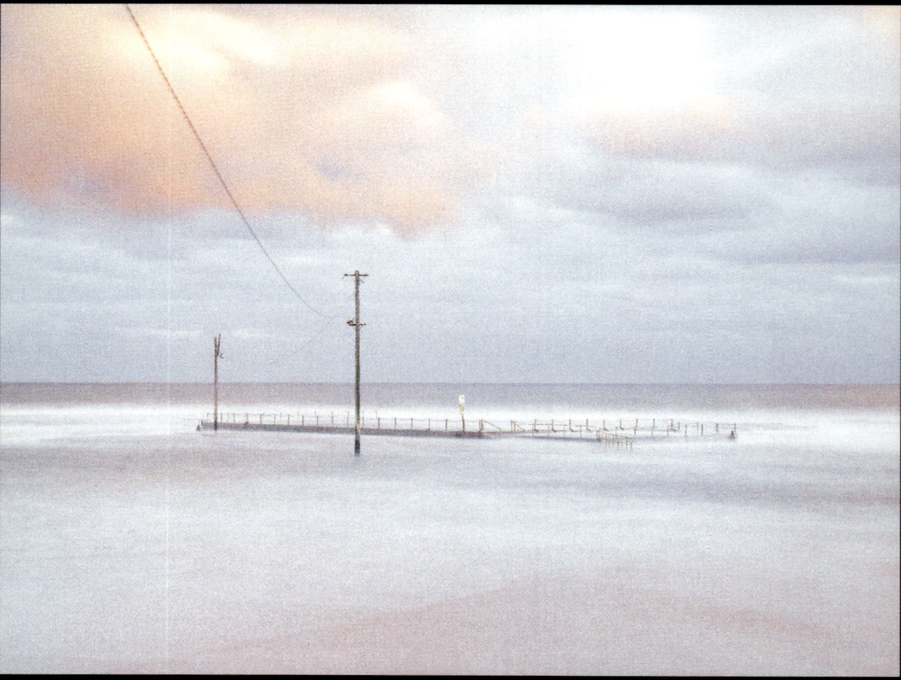

Michael Hall

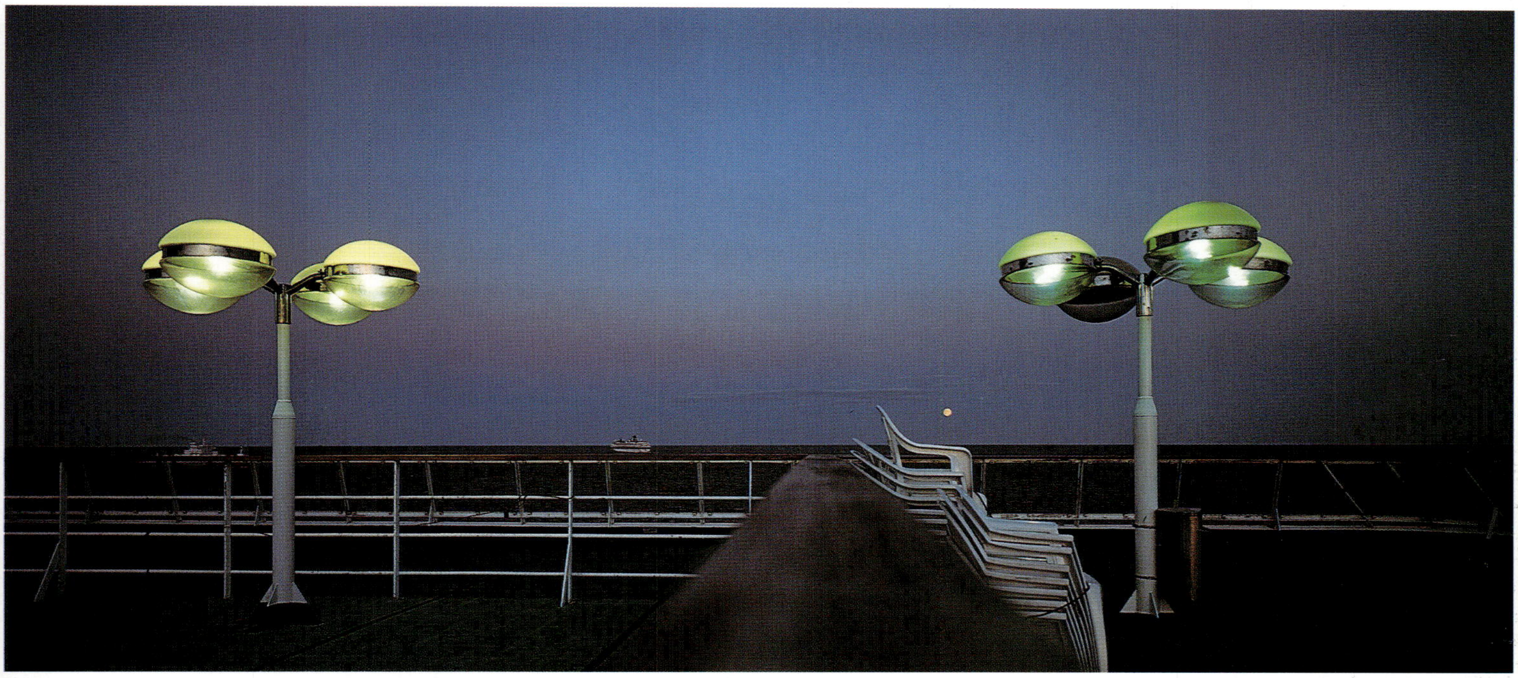

Markku Lahdesmaki

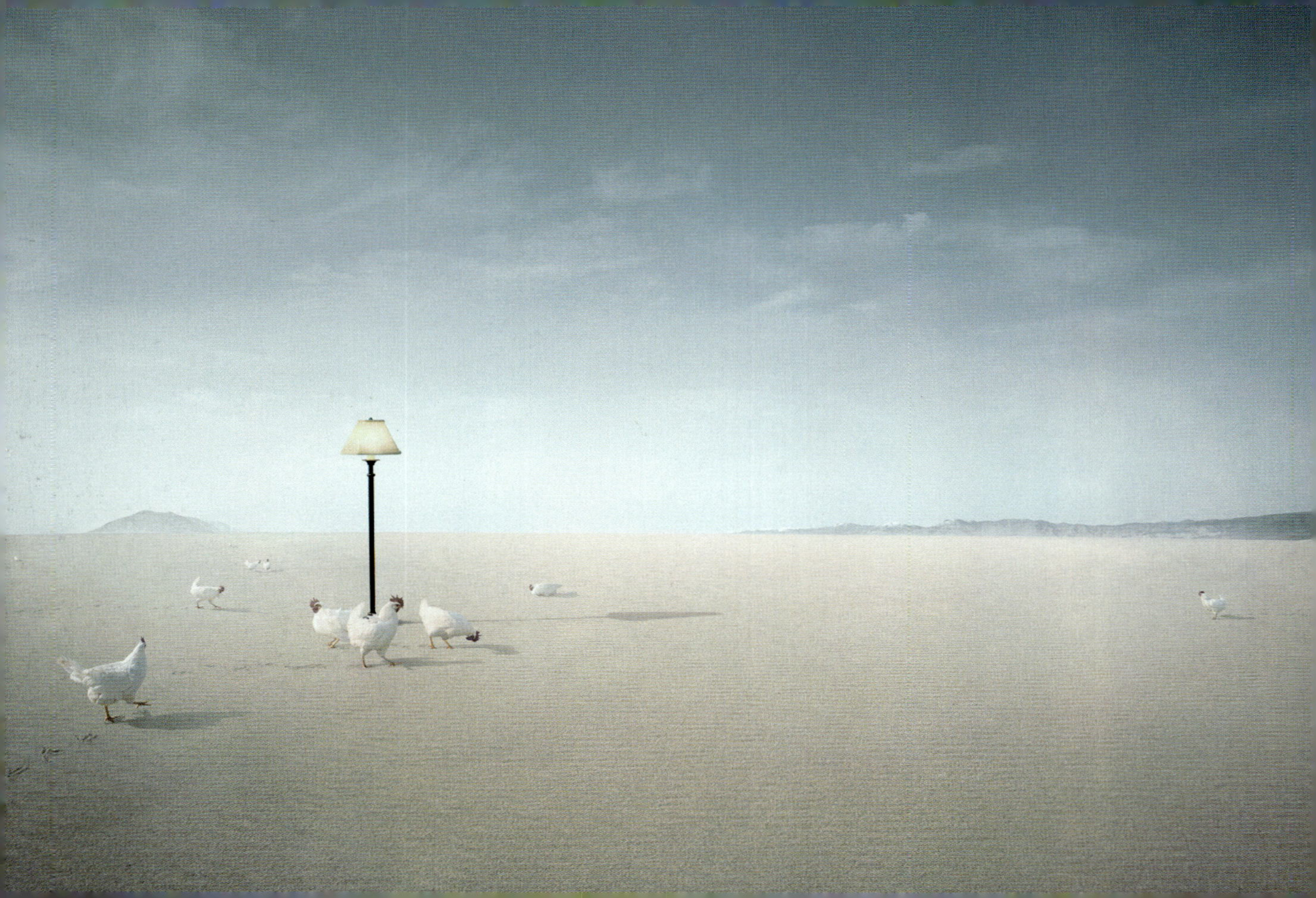

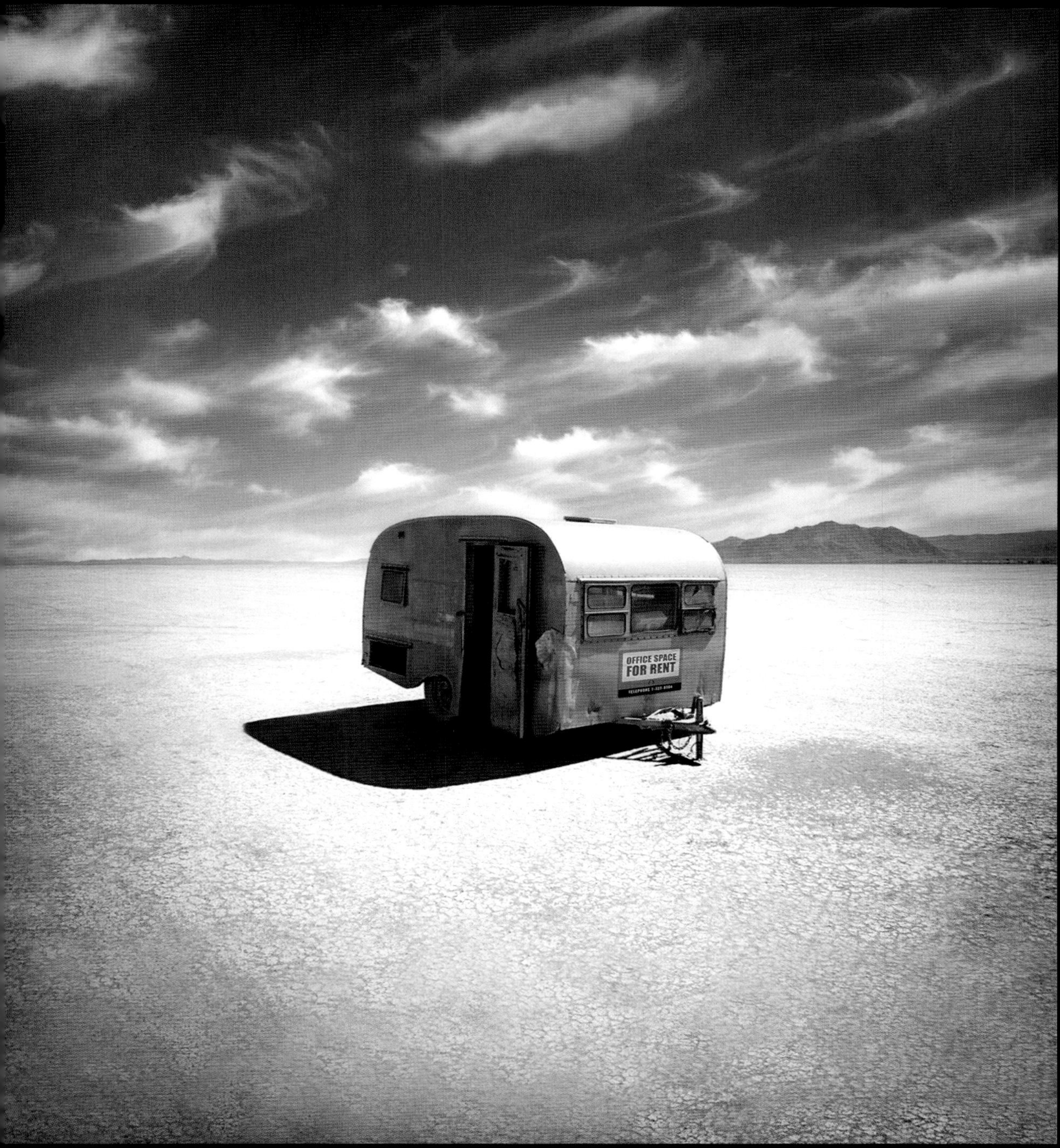

William Huber

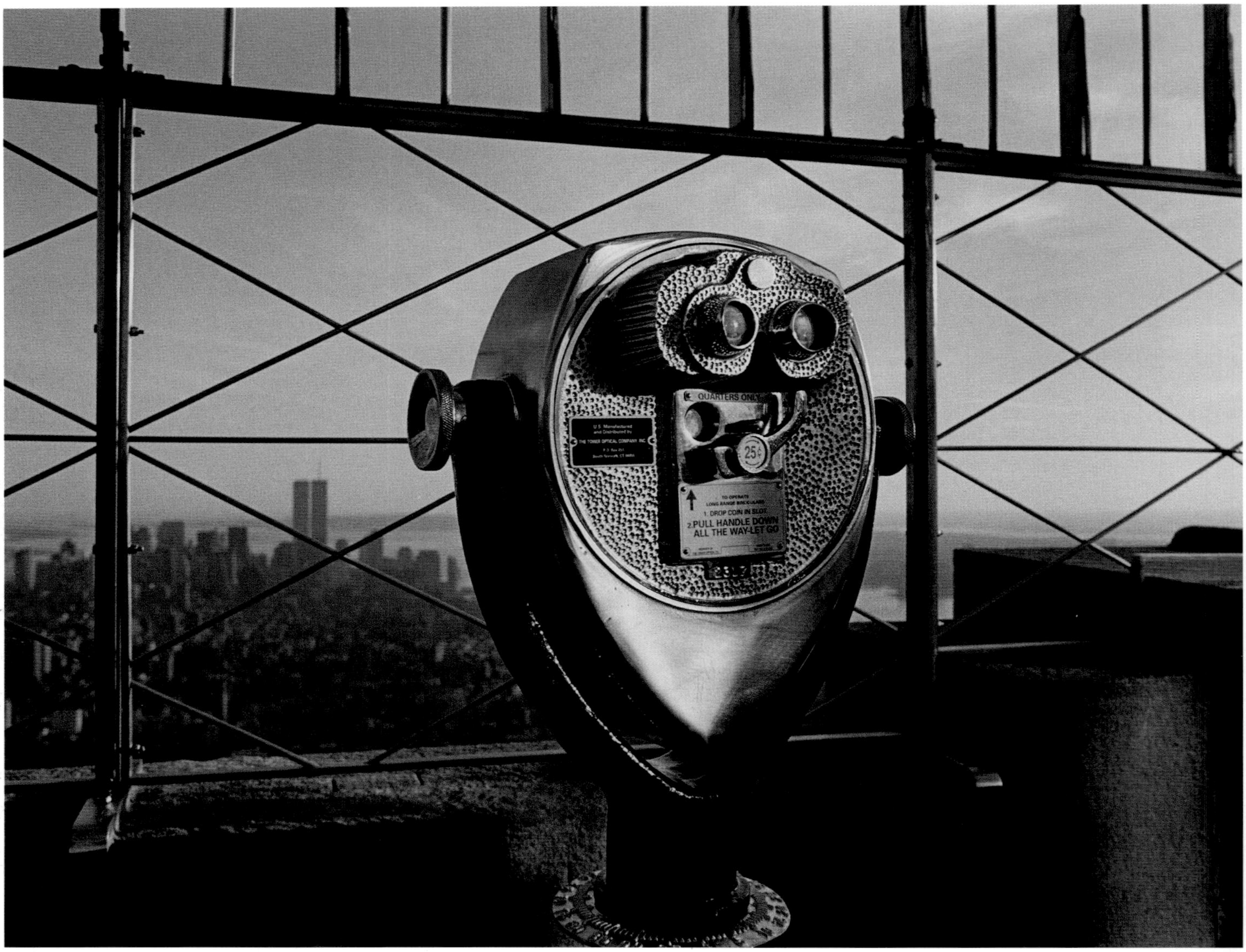

Antonio Bogaert

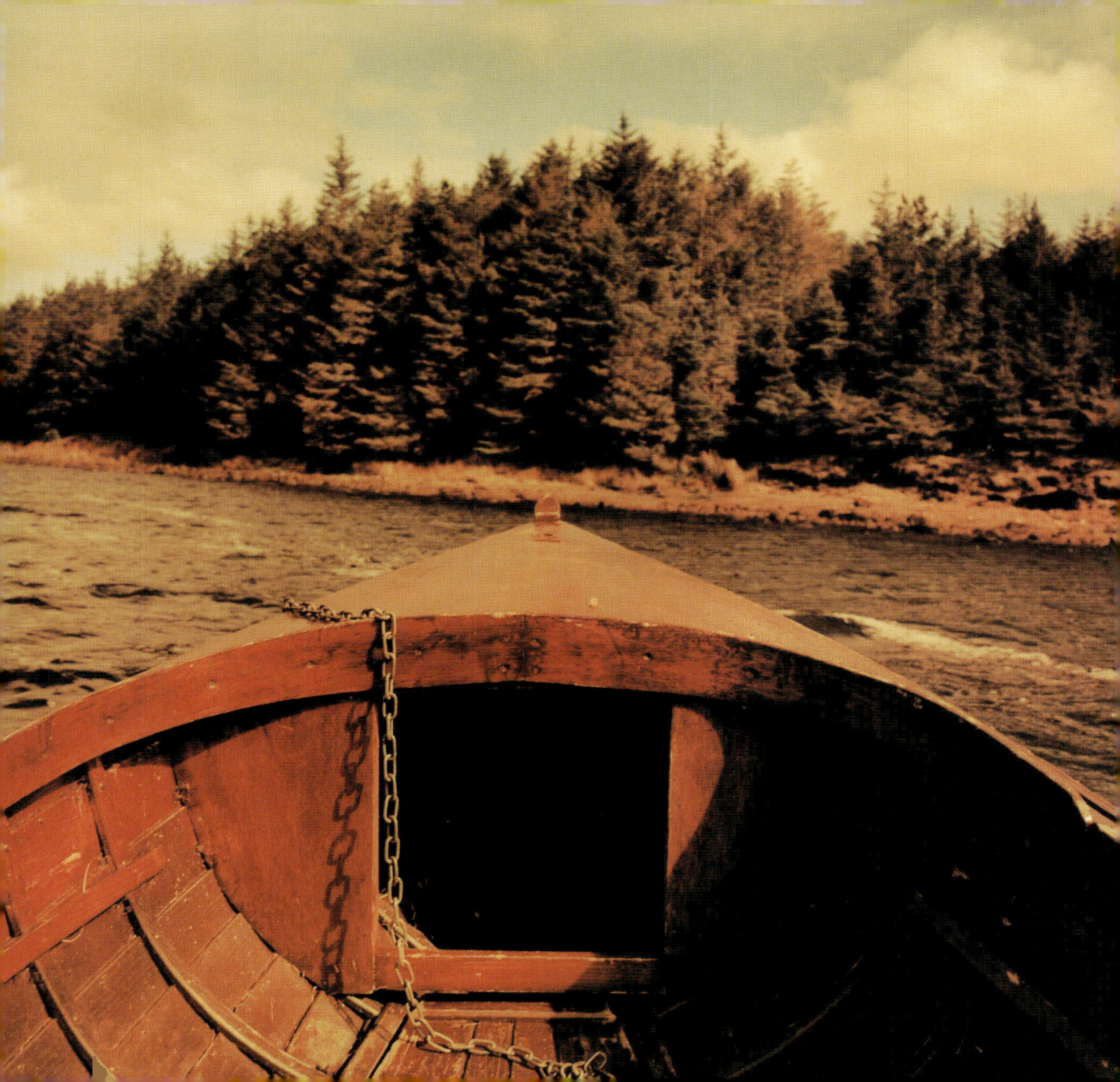

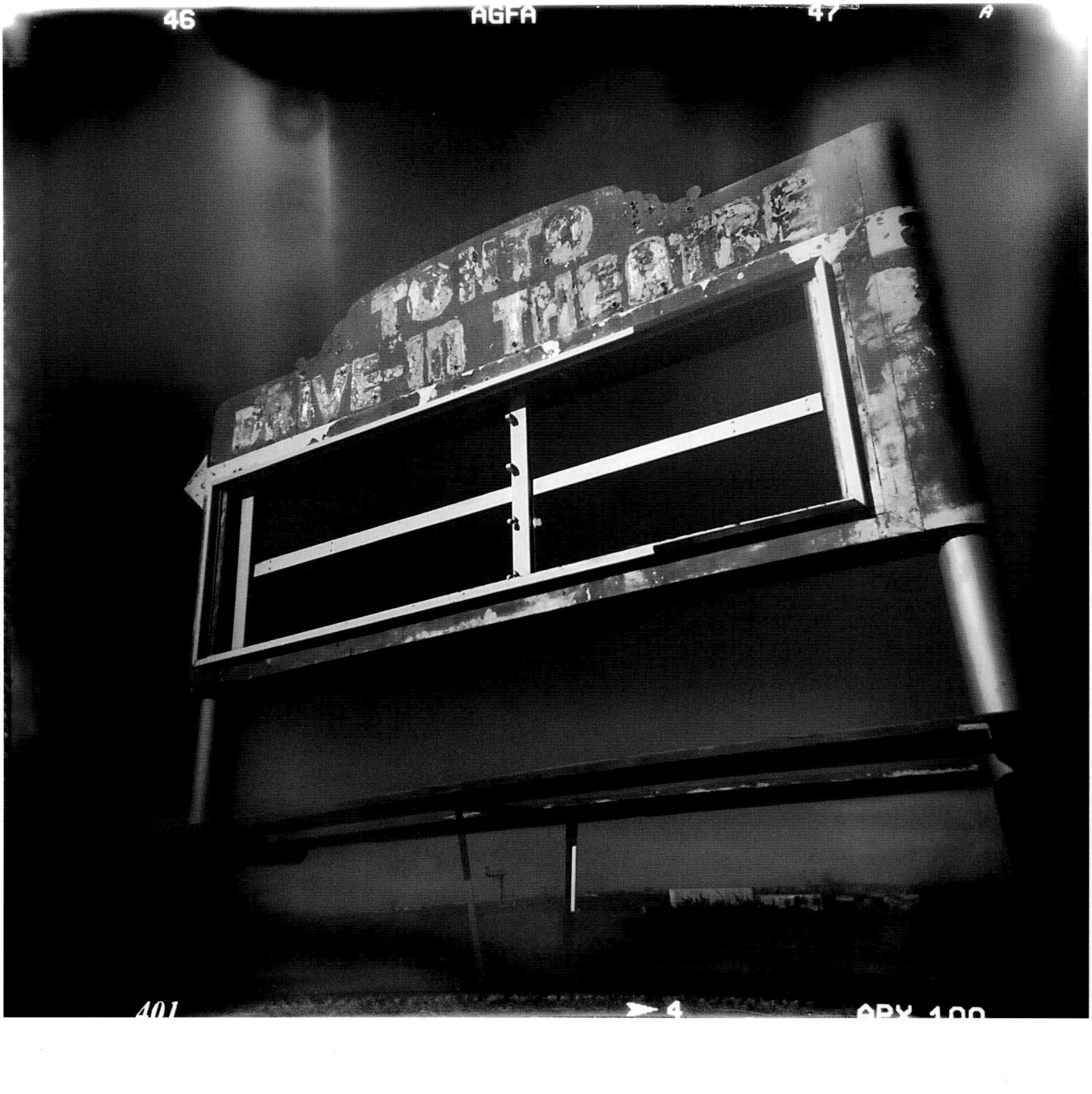

Greg Myhra

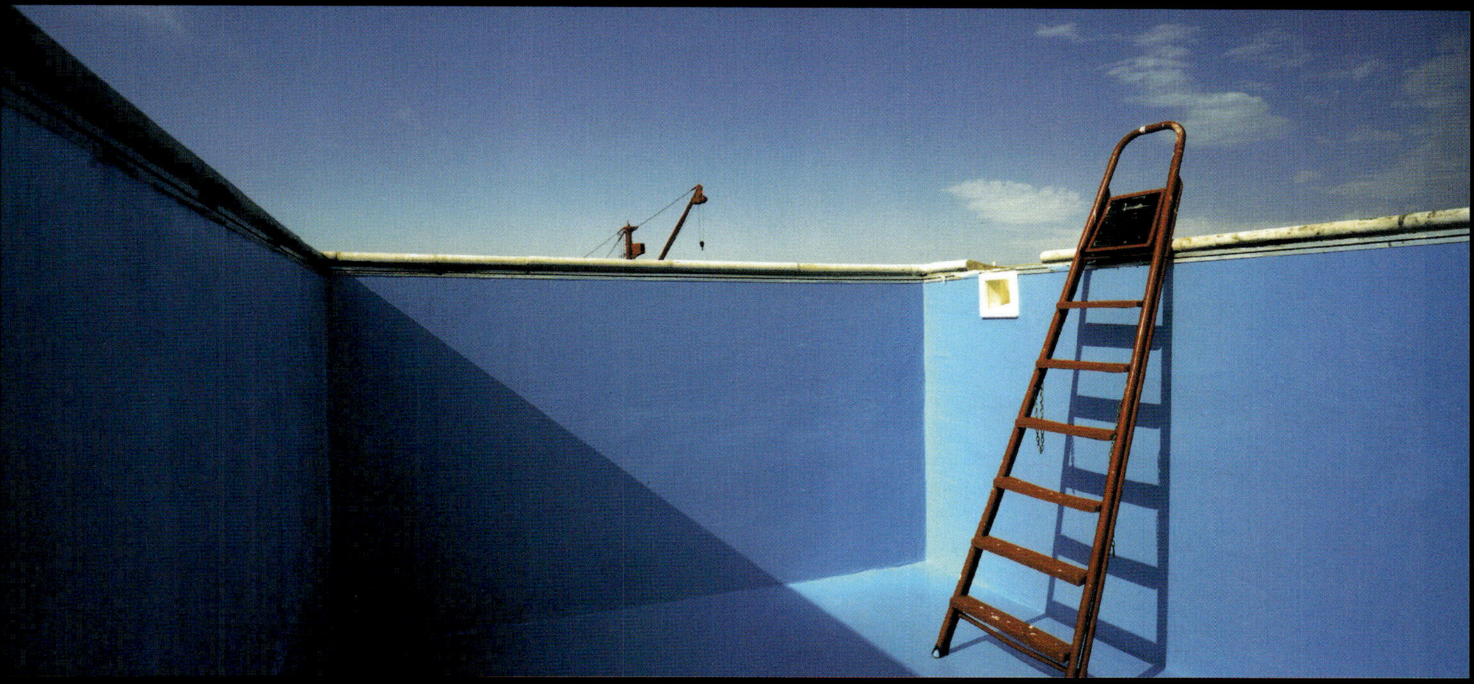

Phil Bekker

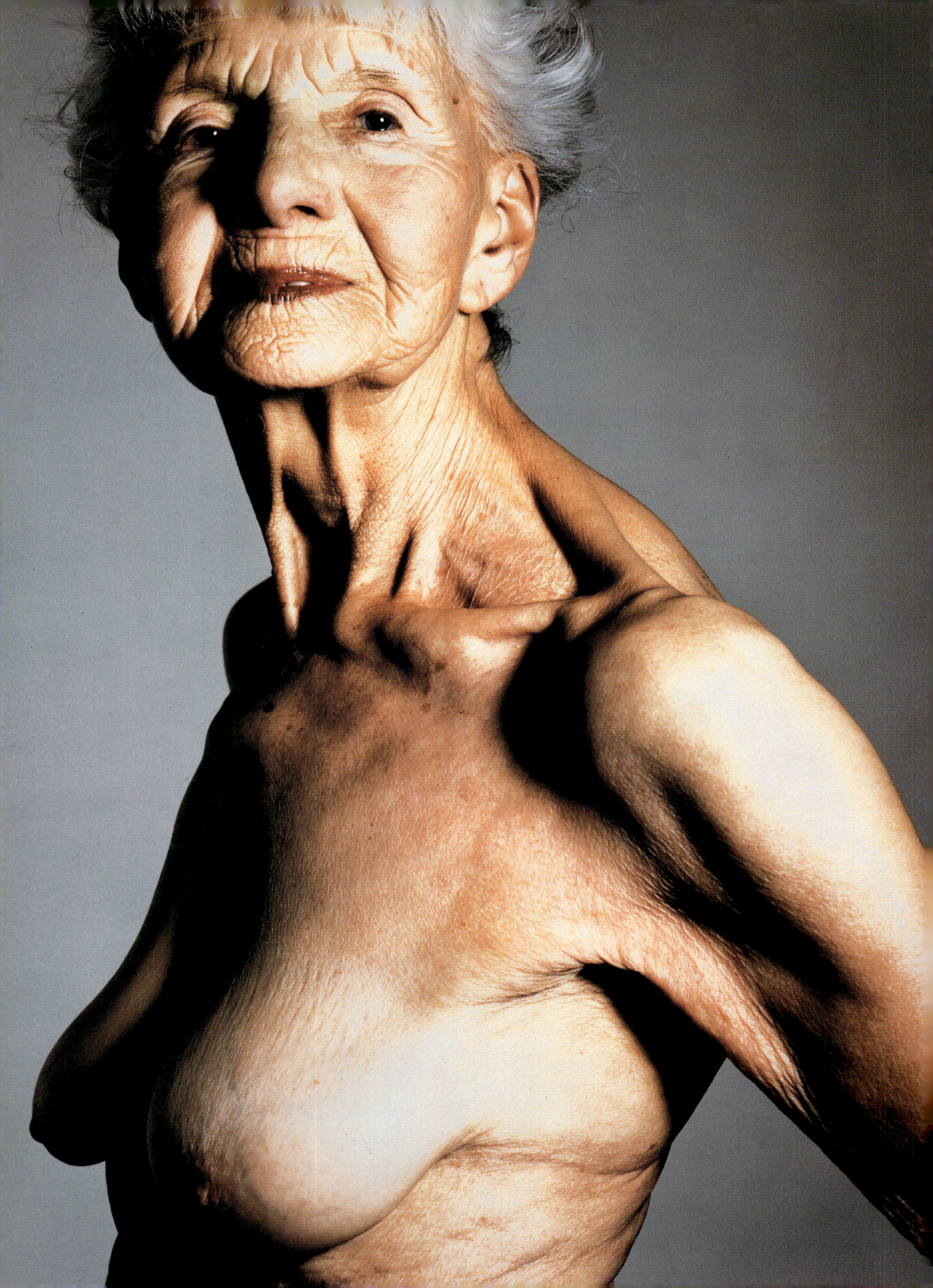

Nudes

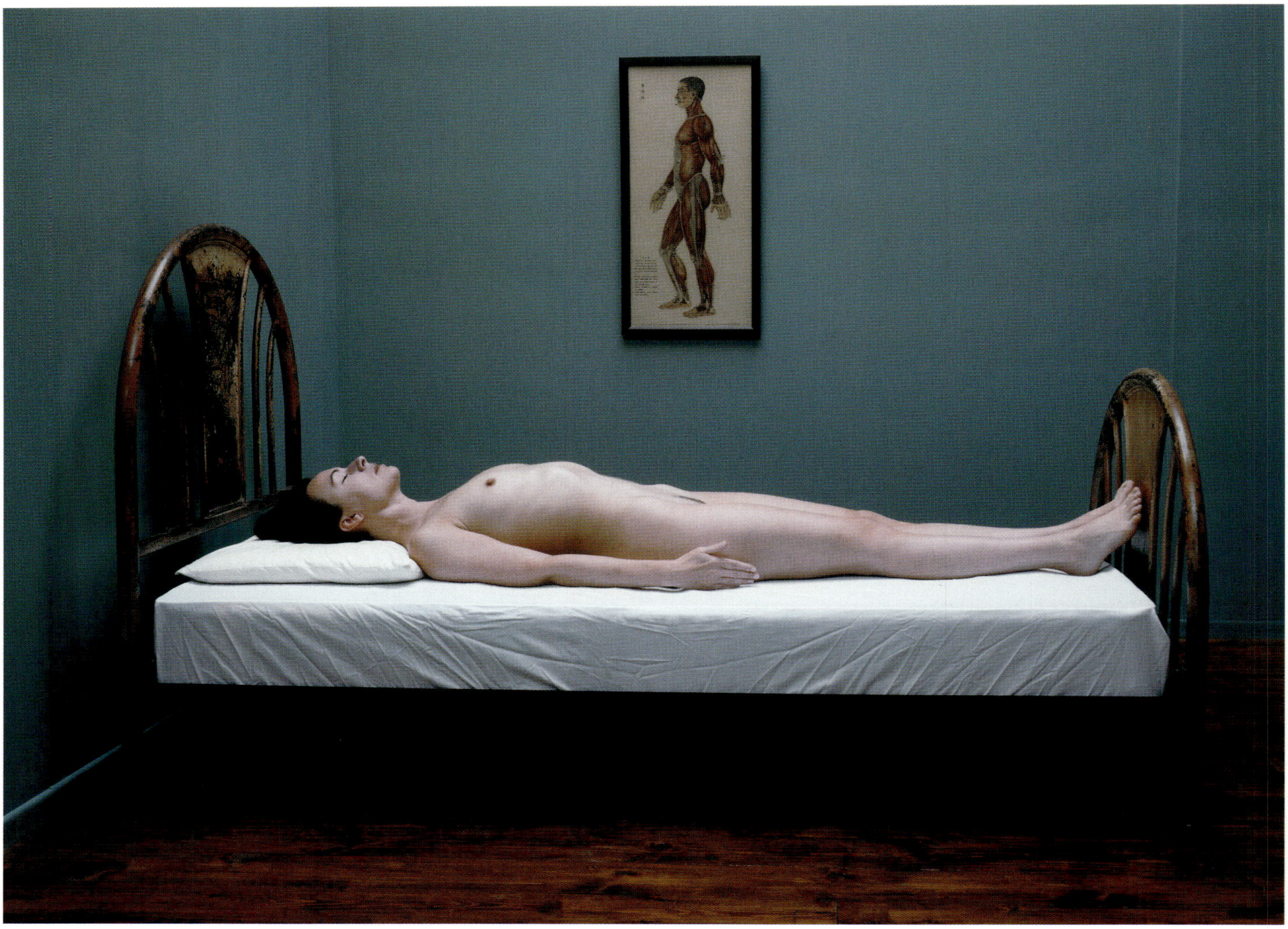

Neal Brown (opening page) Paul Murphy

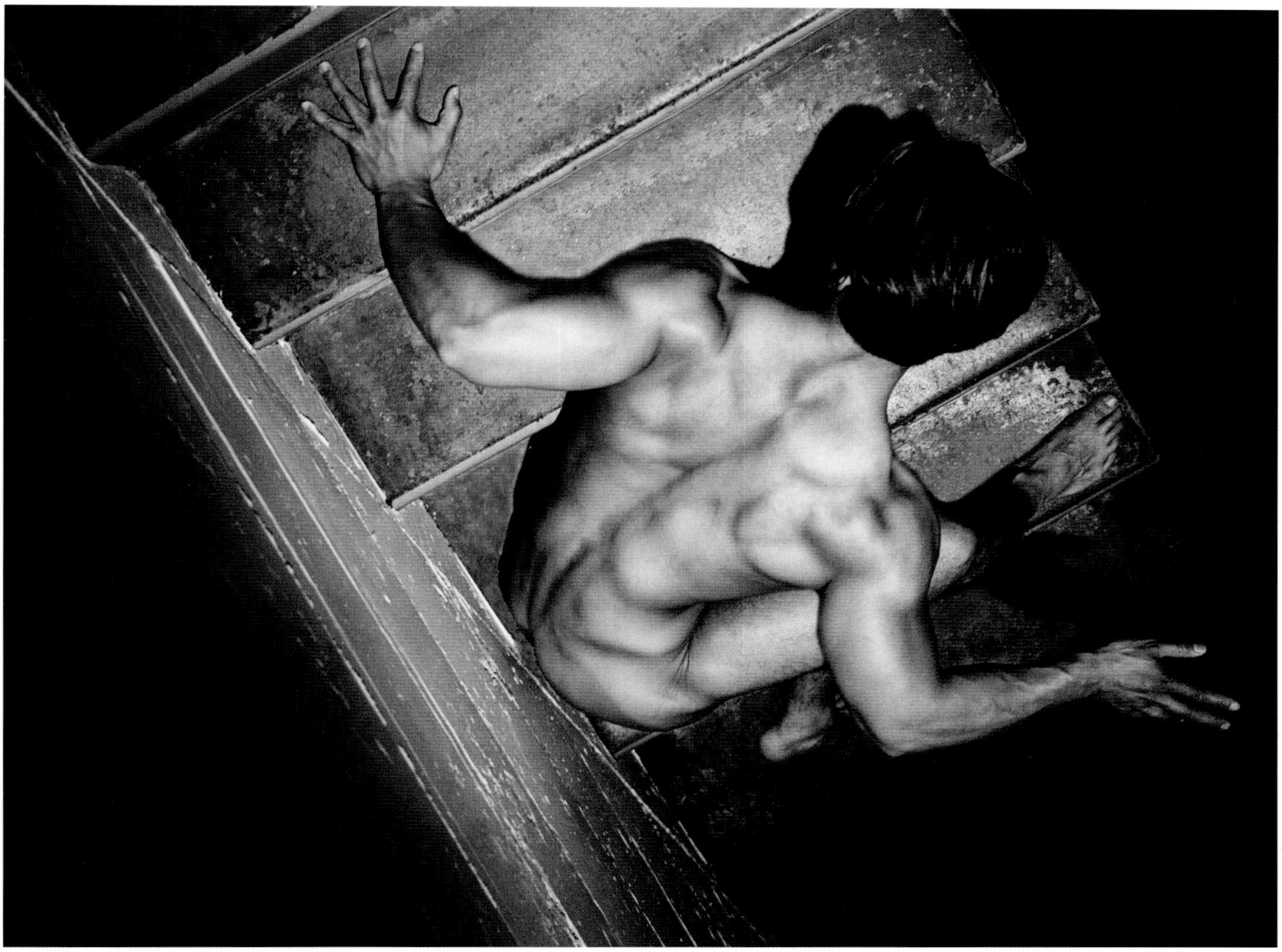

JoSon

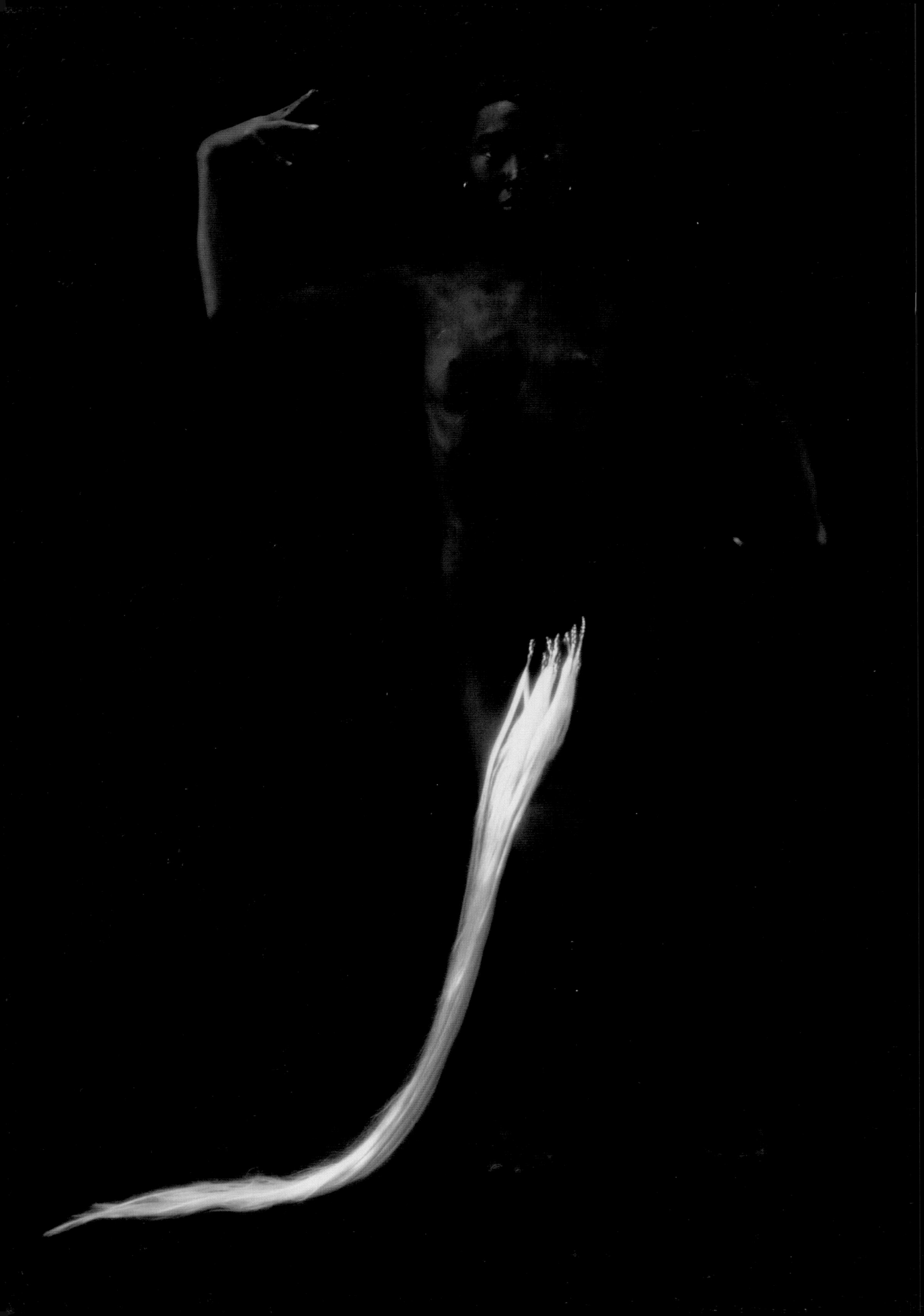

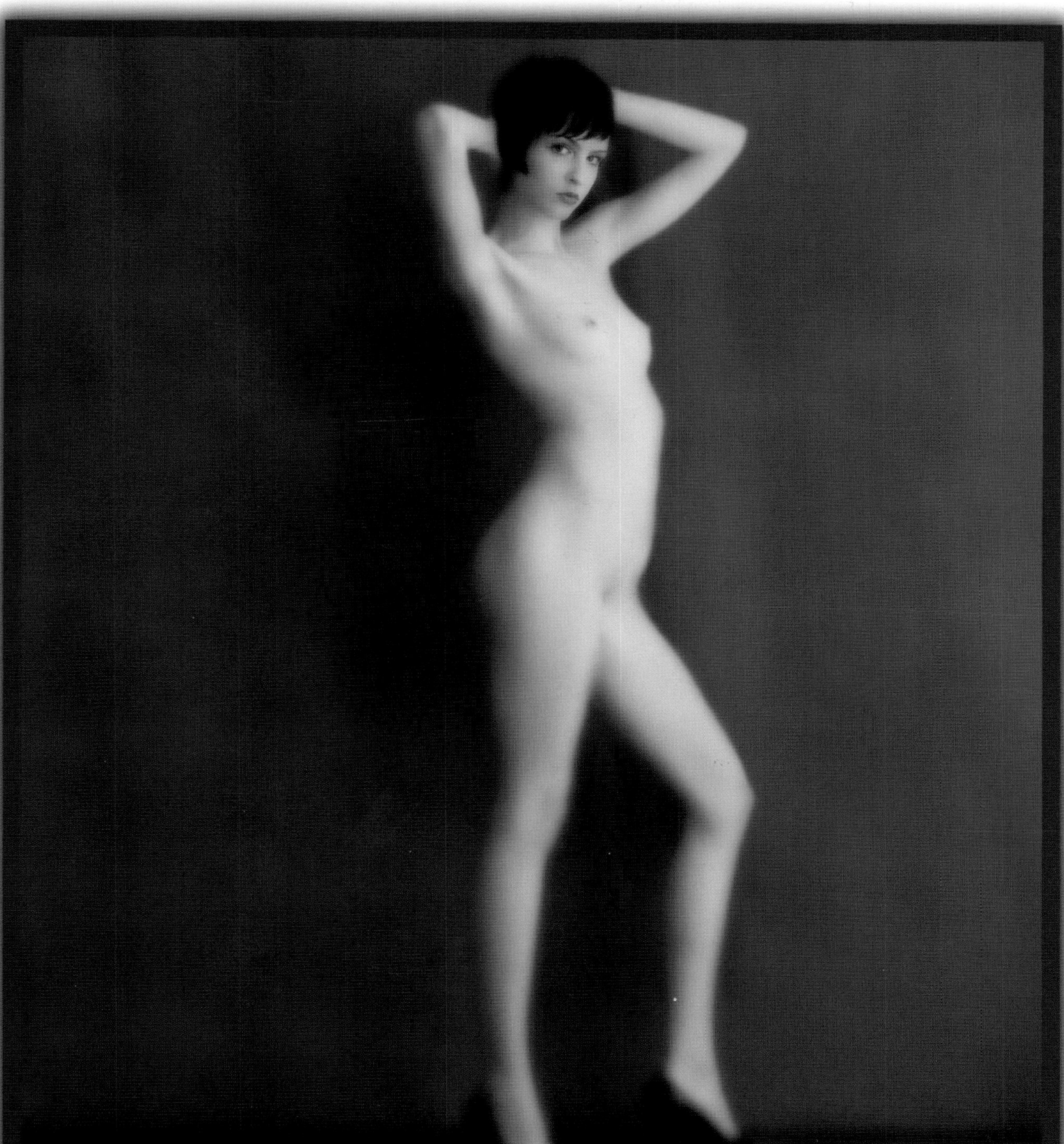

Howard Schatz (opposite) Miro Ito

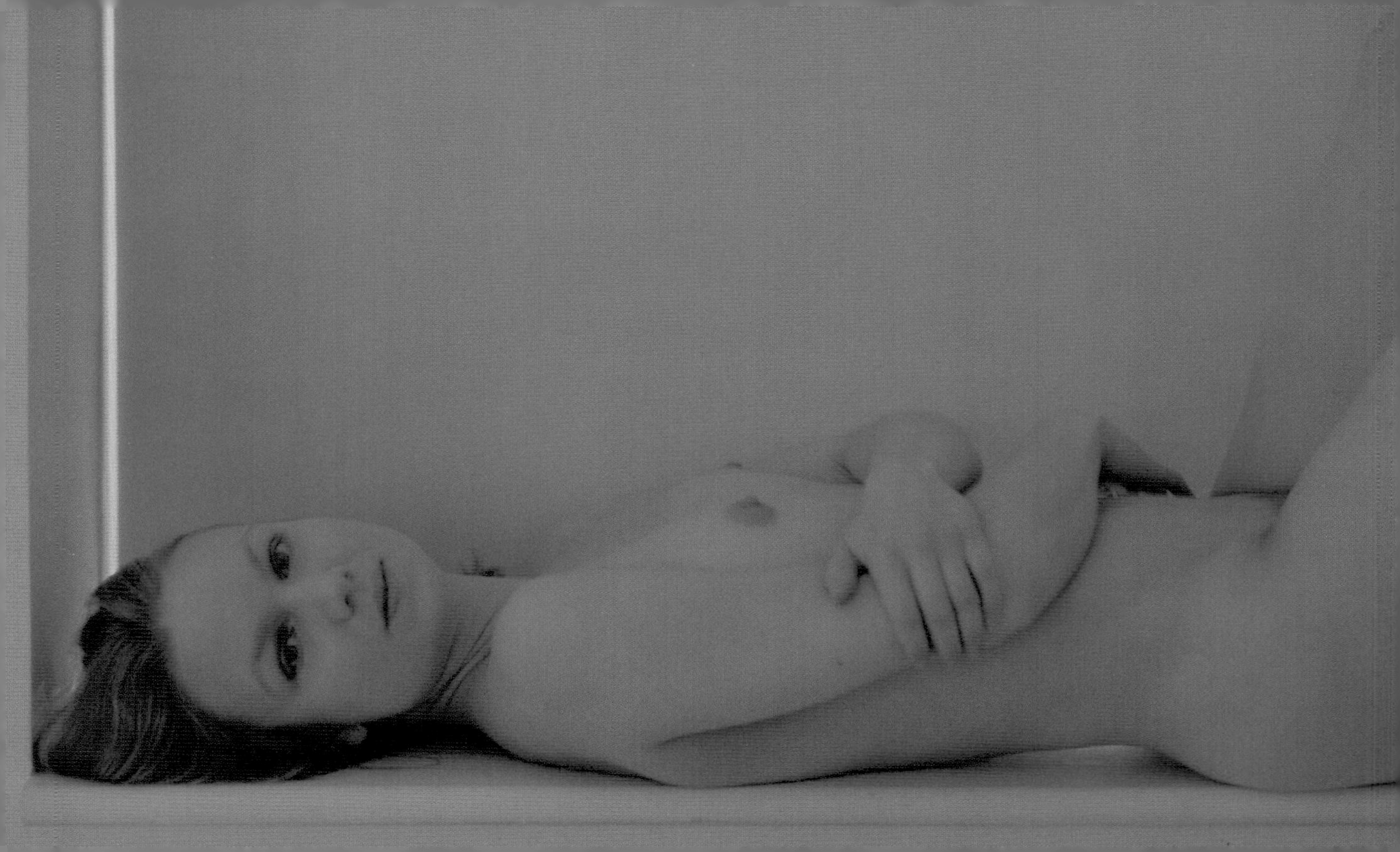

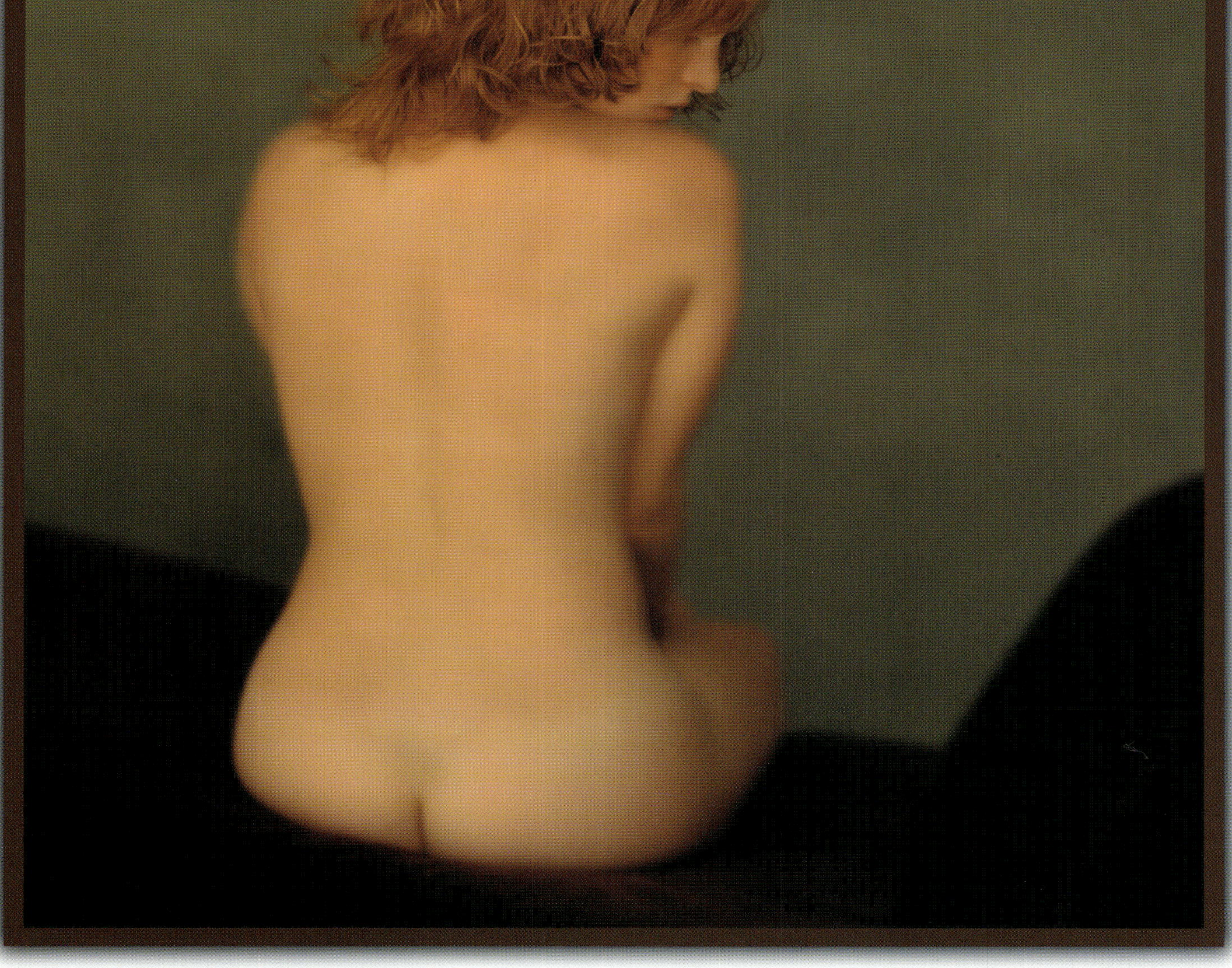

Howard Schatz

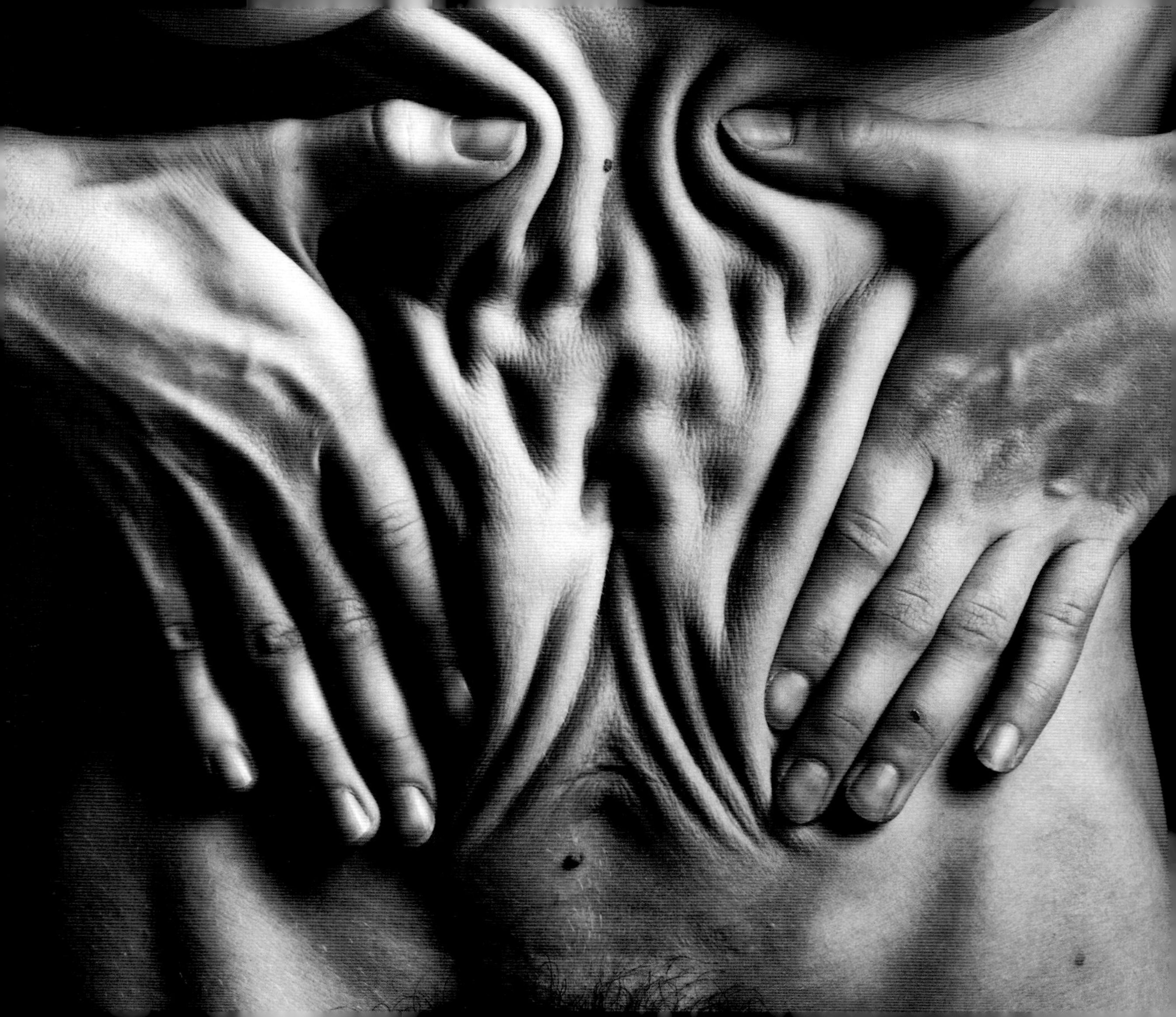

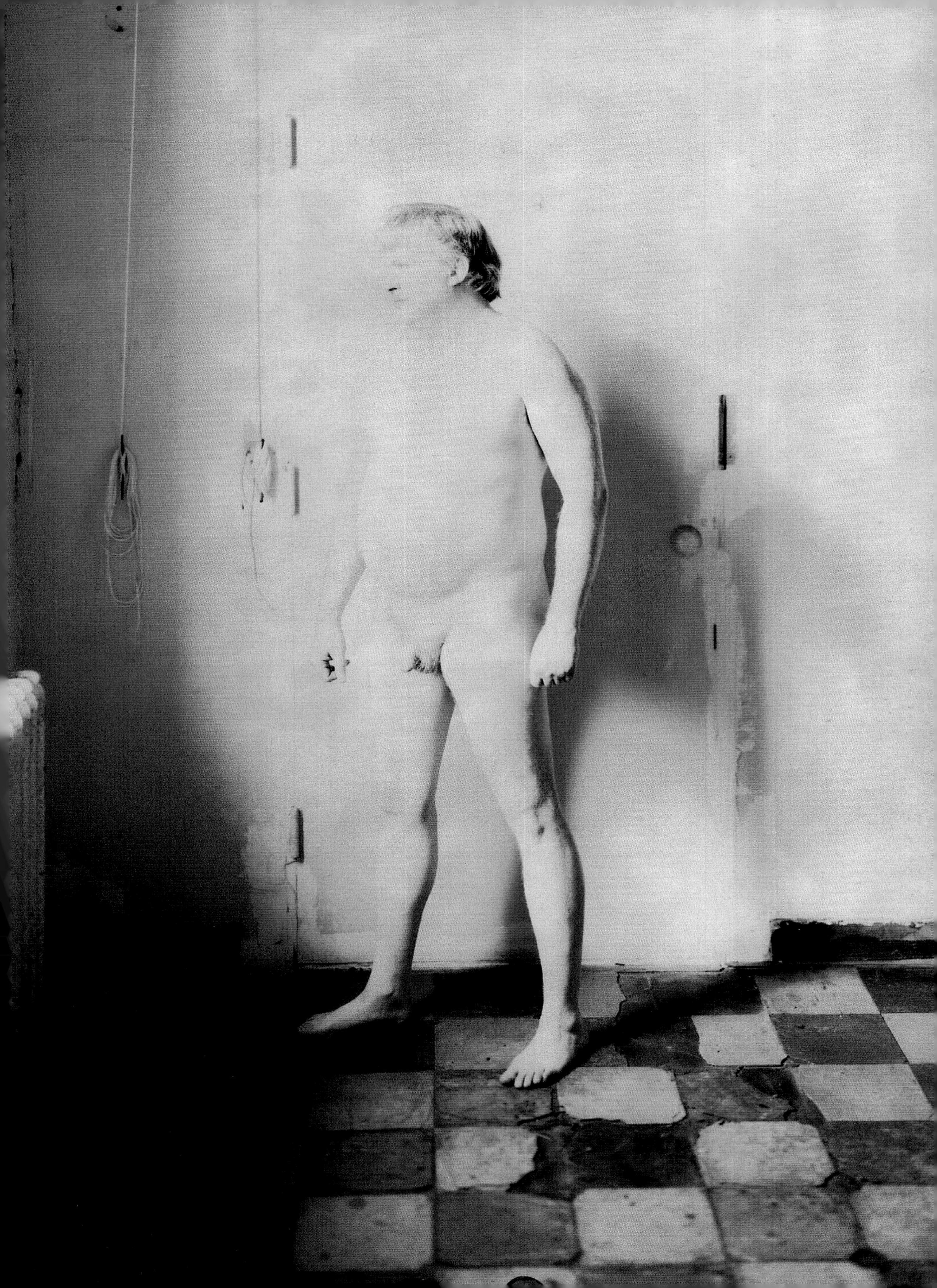

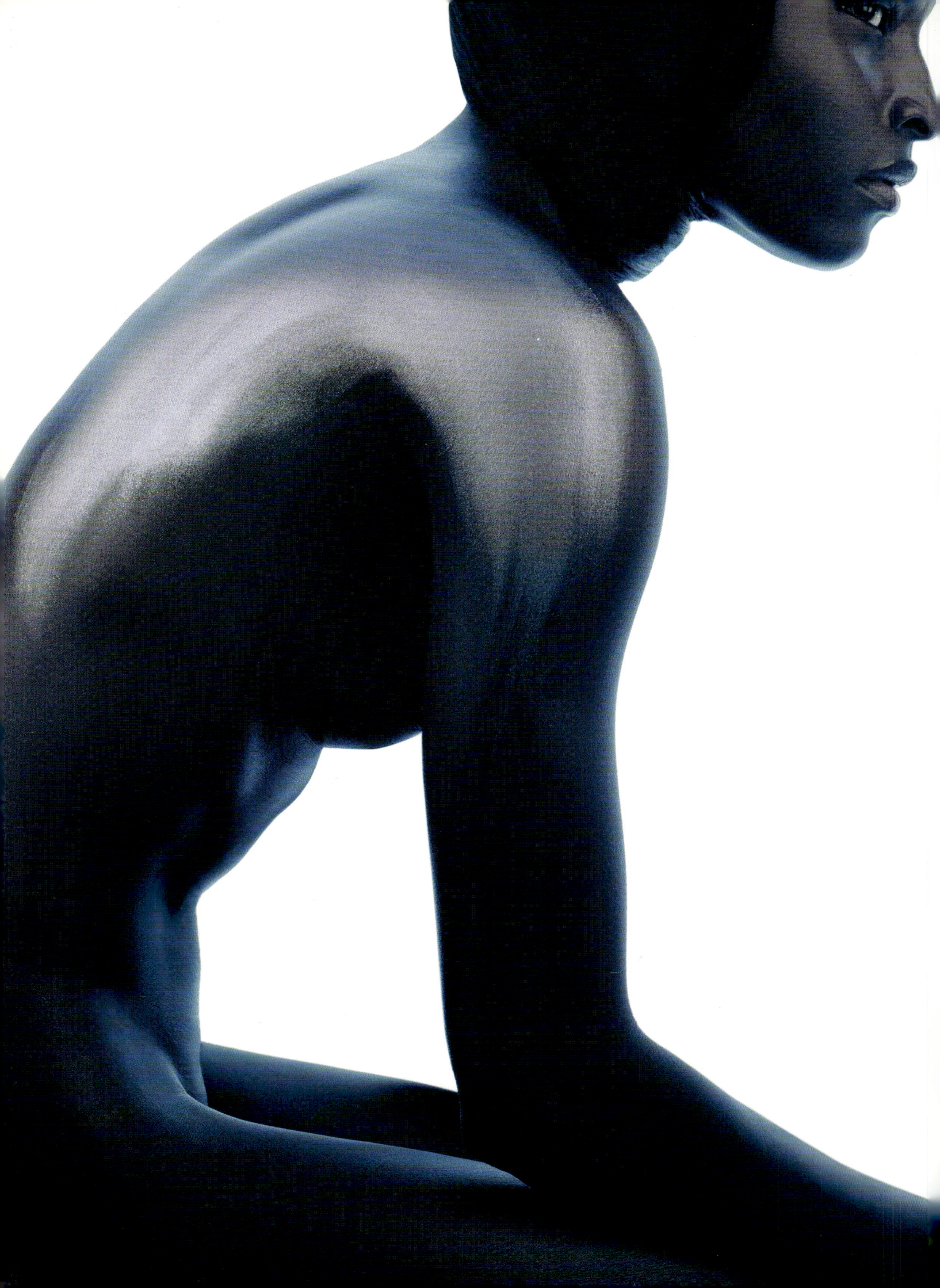

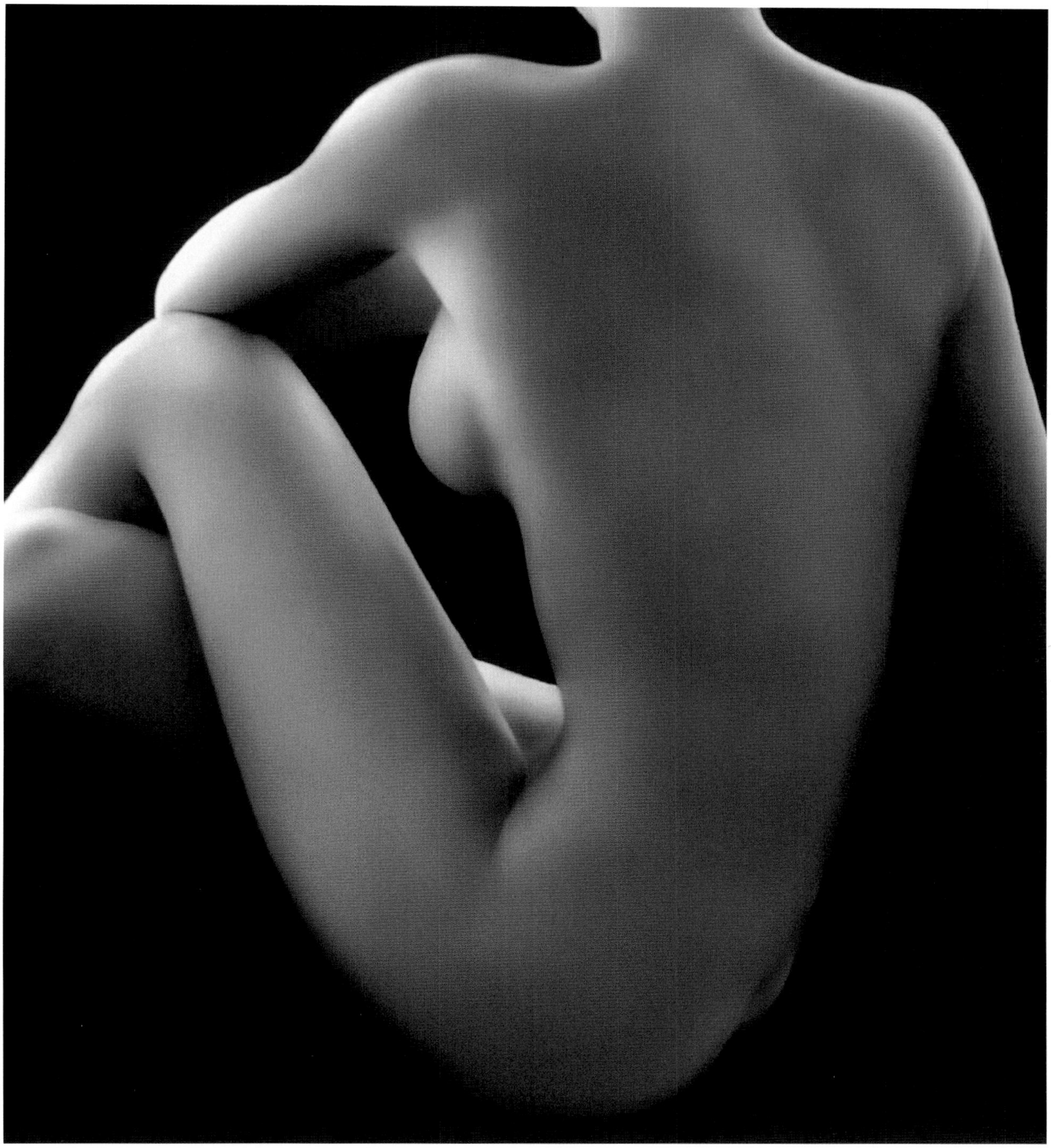

Parish Kohanim (opposite) Eva Mueller

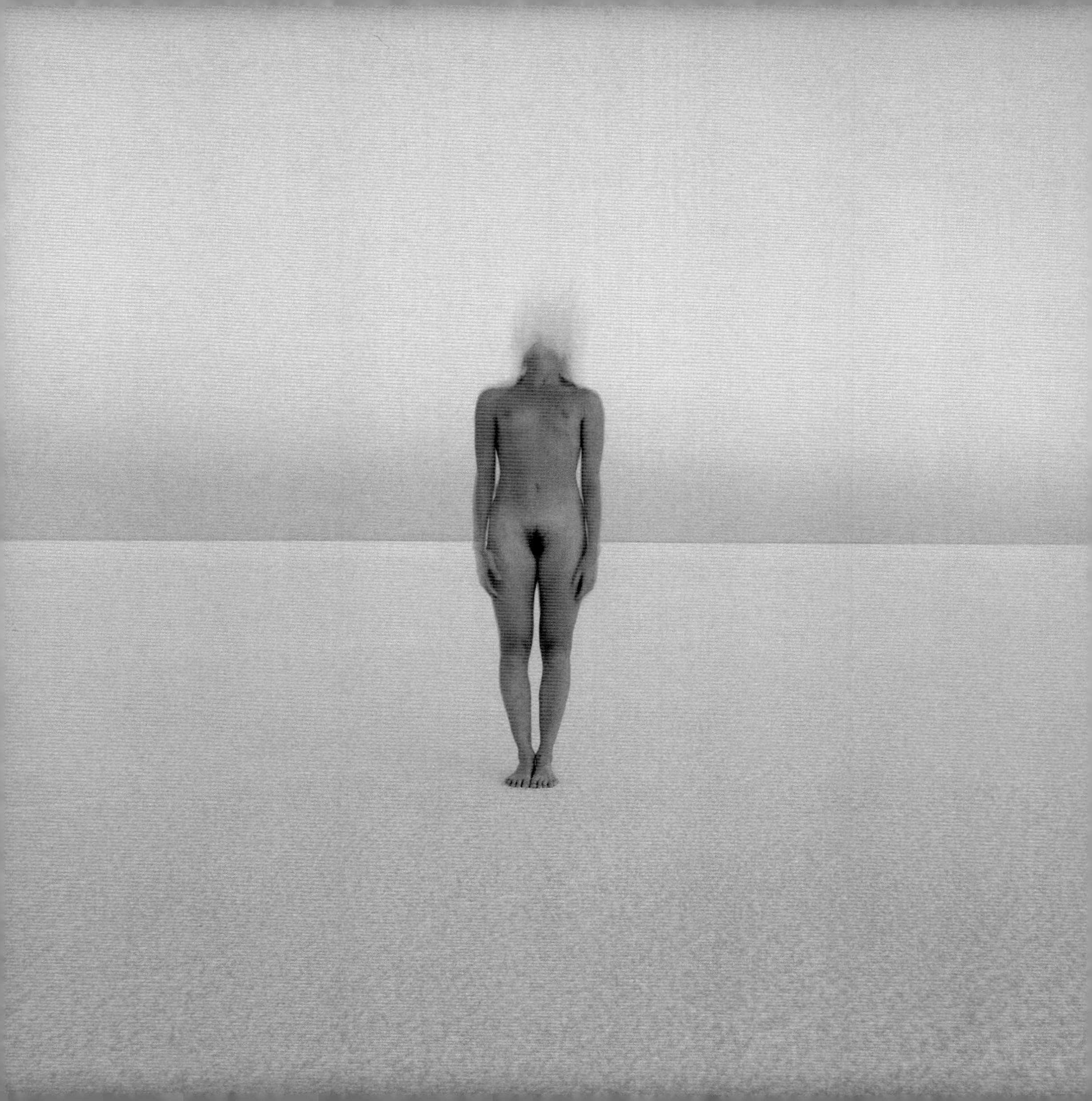

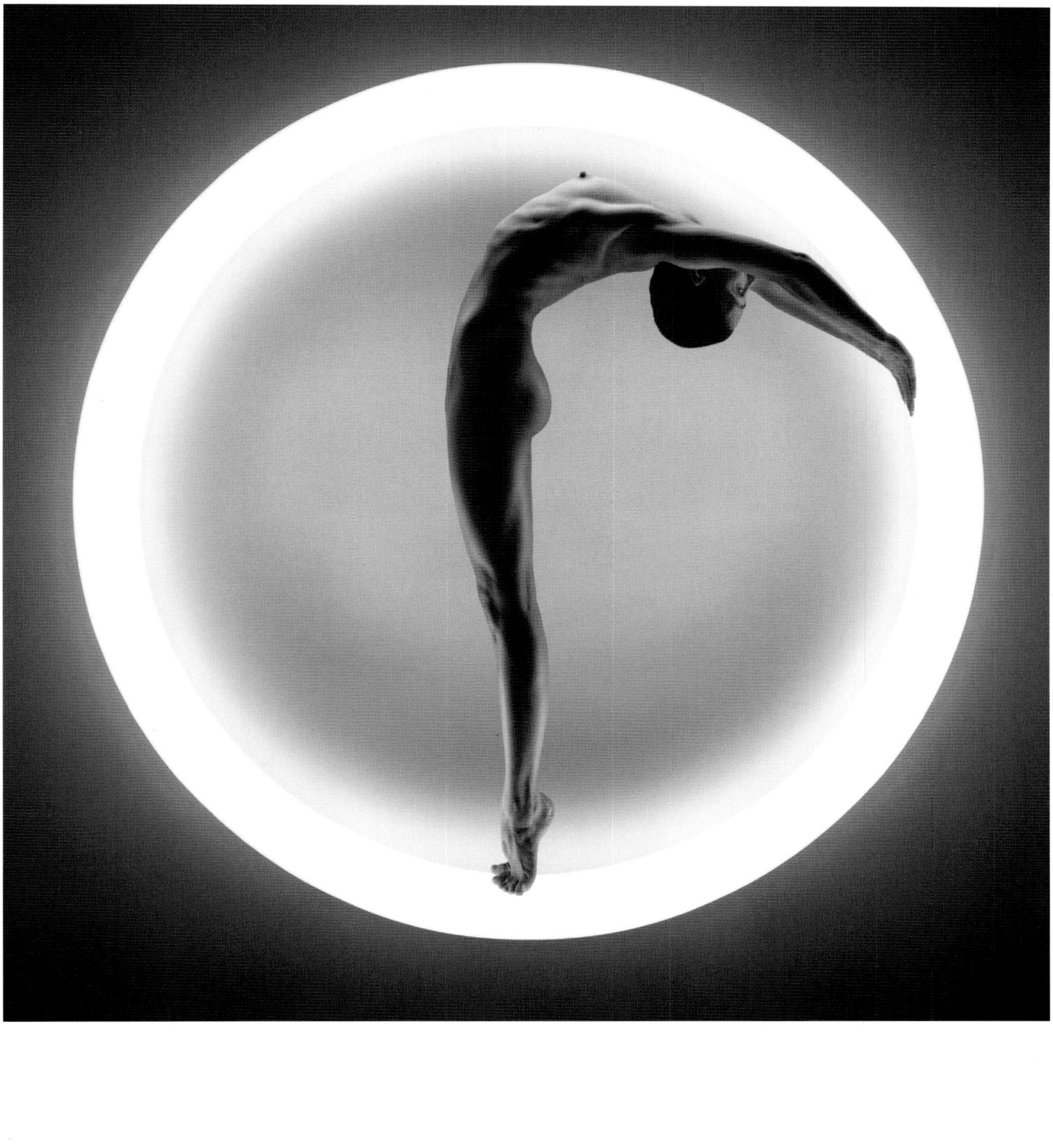

Klaus Kampert

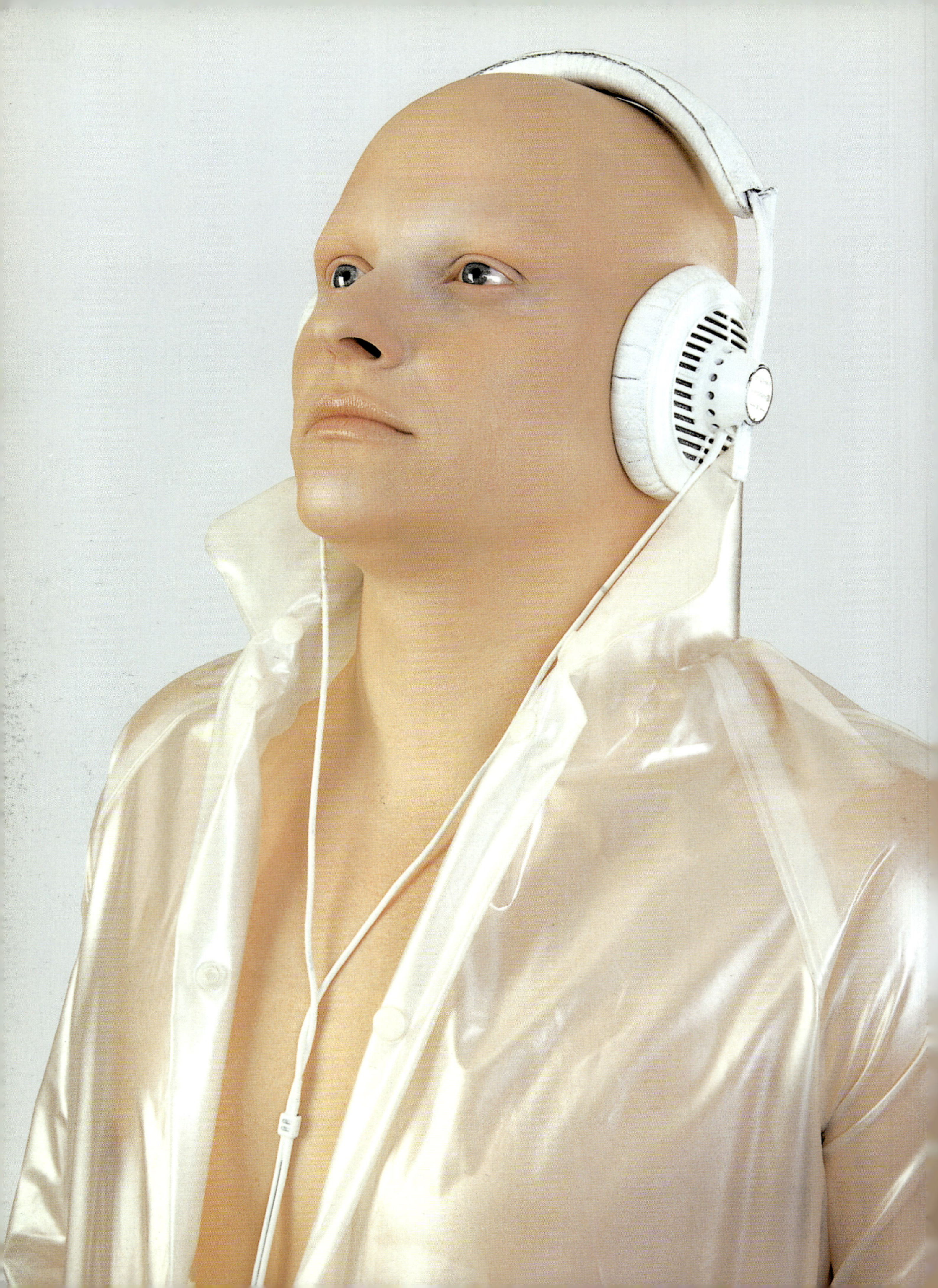

Portraits

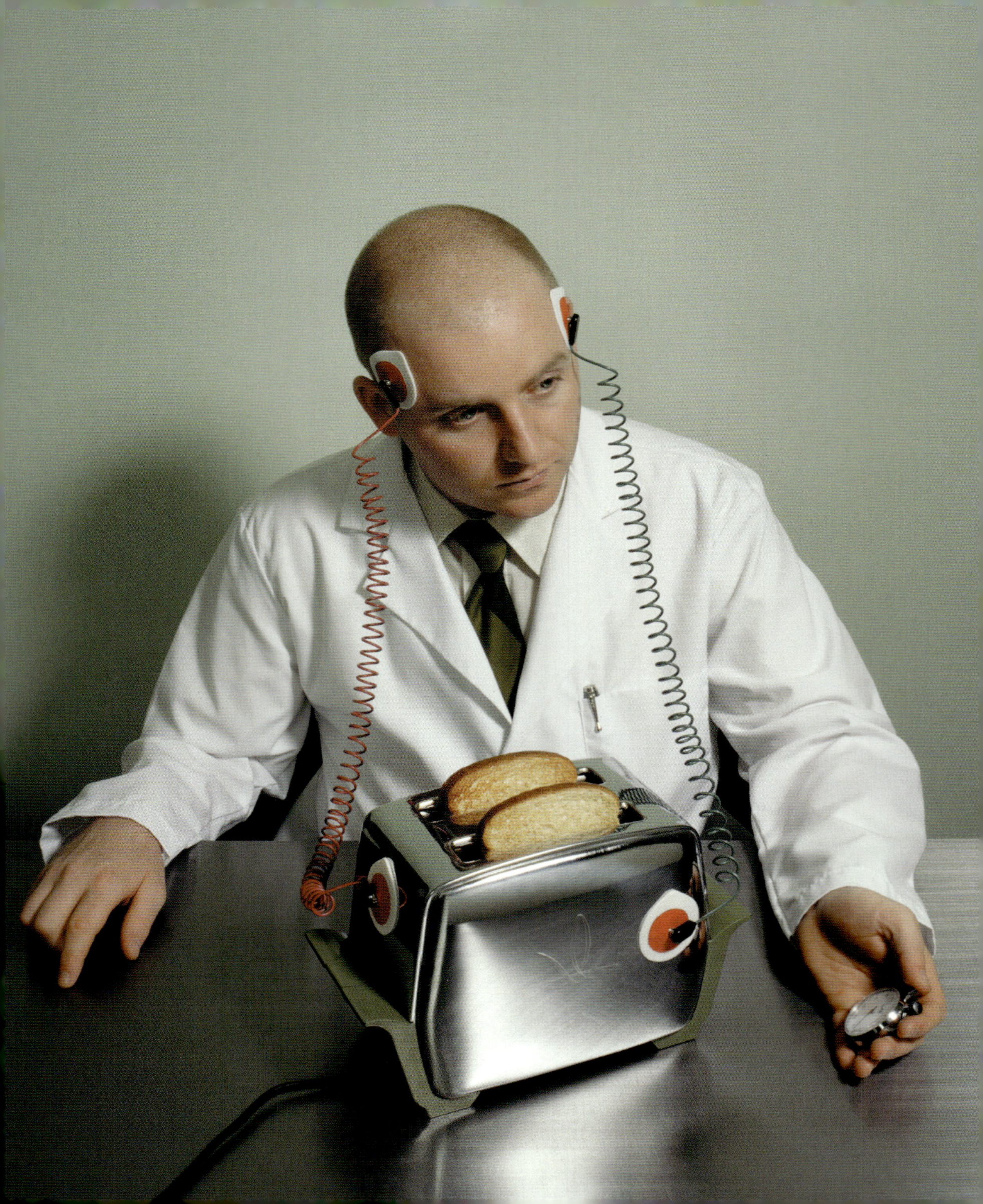

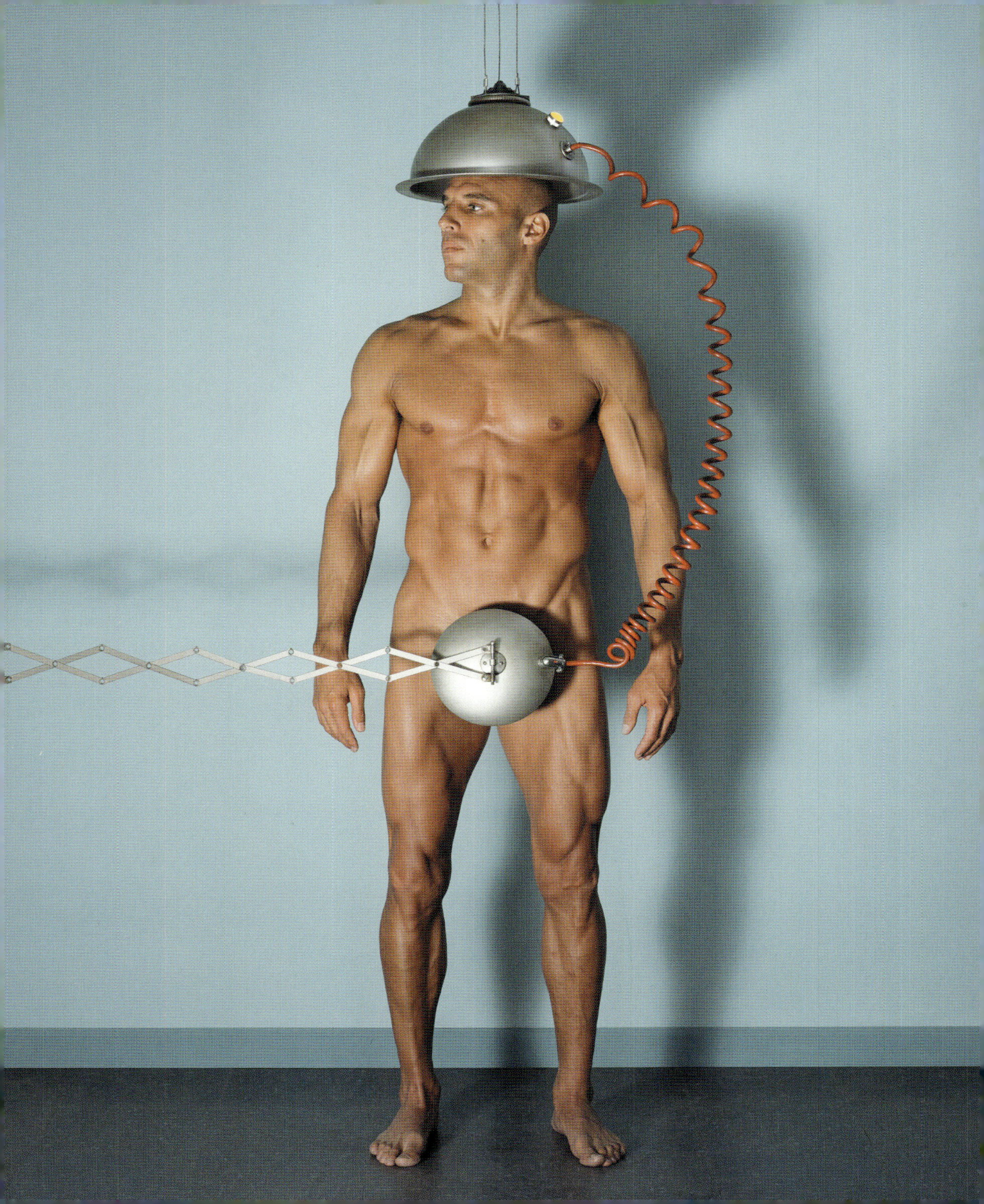

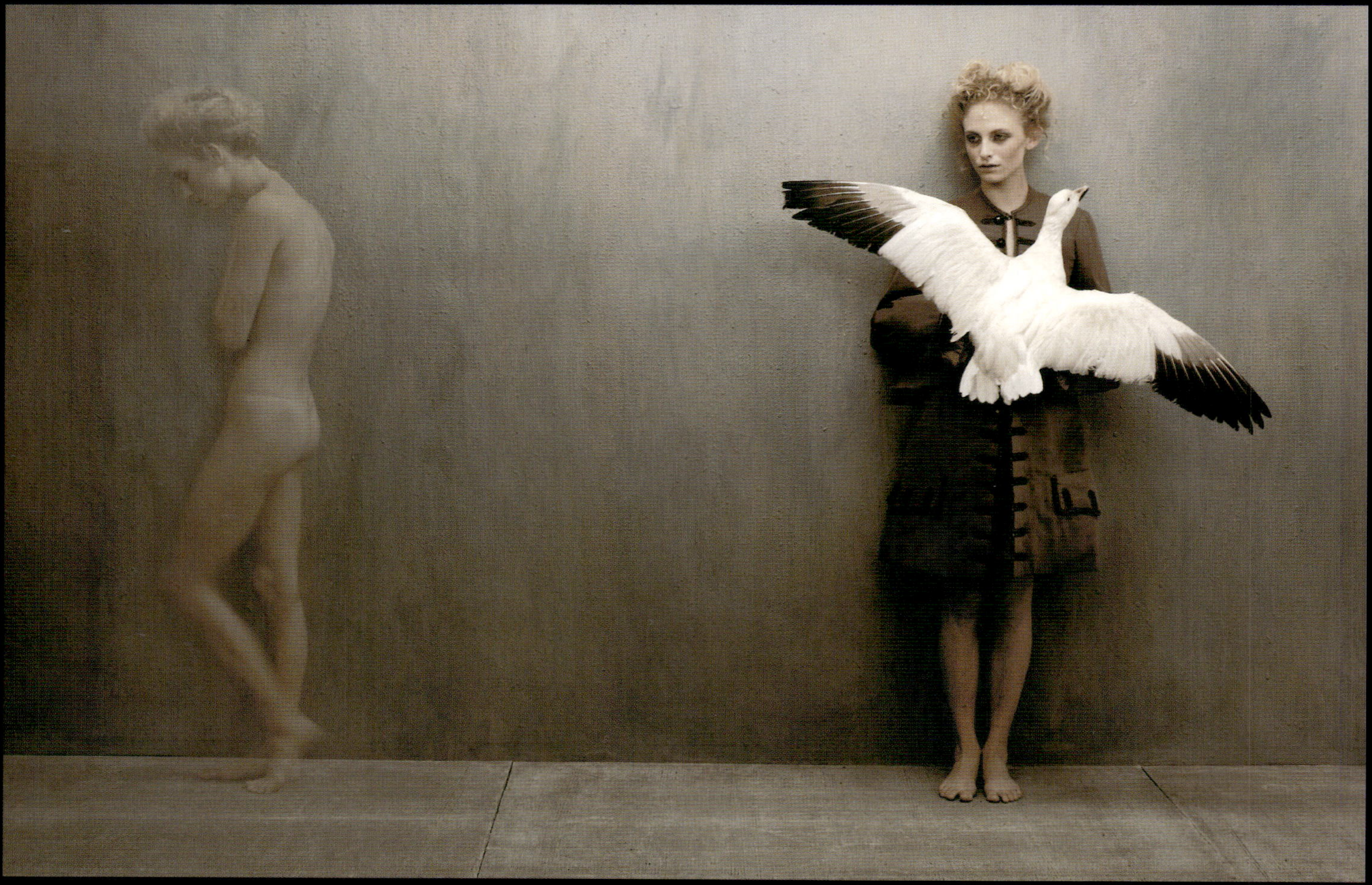

Jeff Stephens

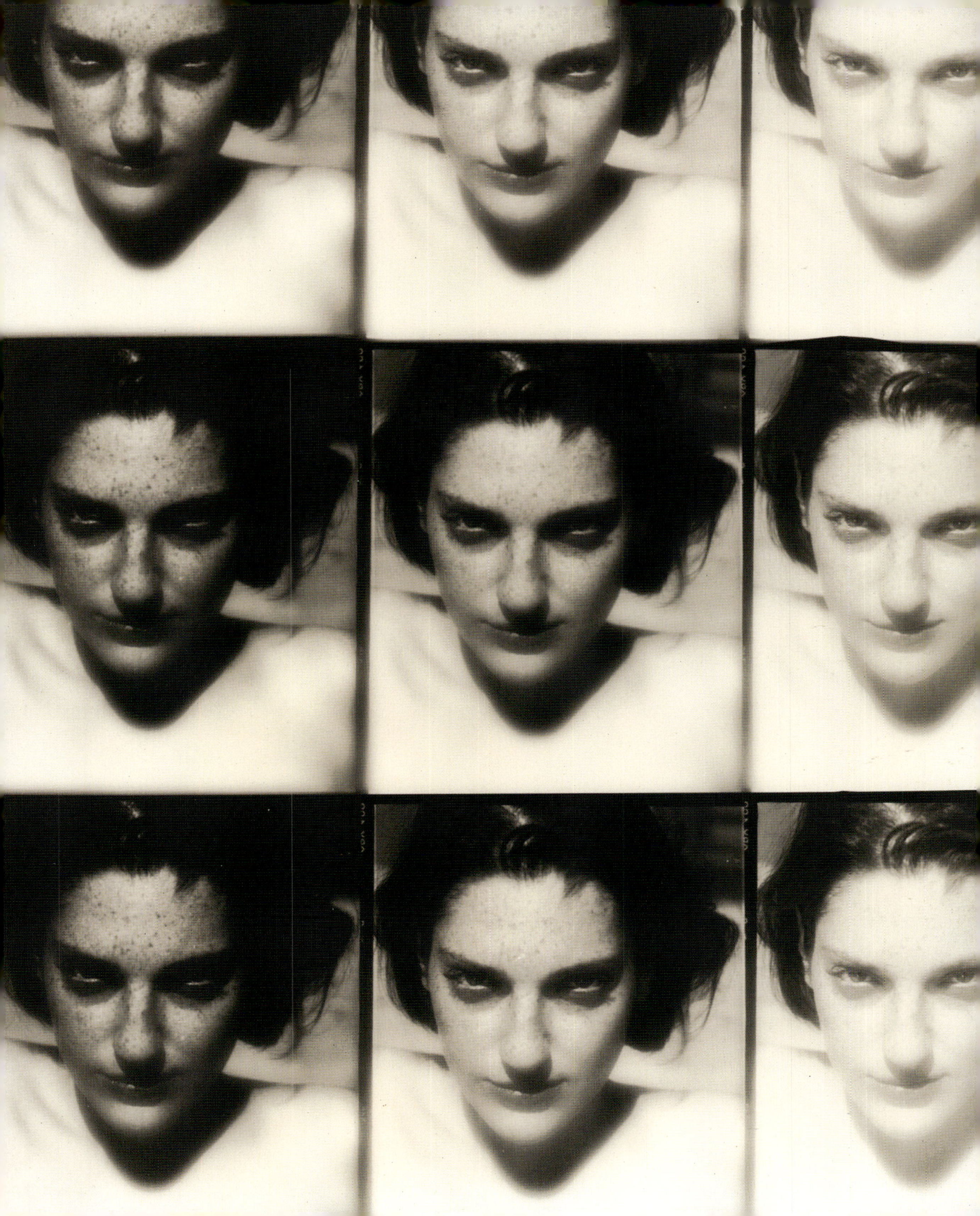

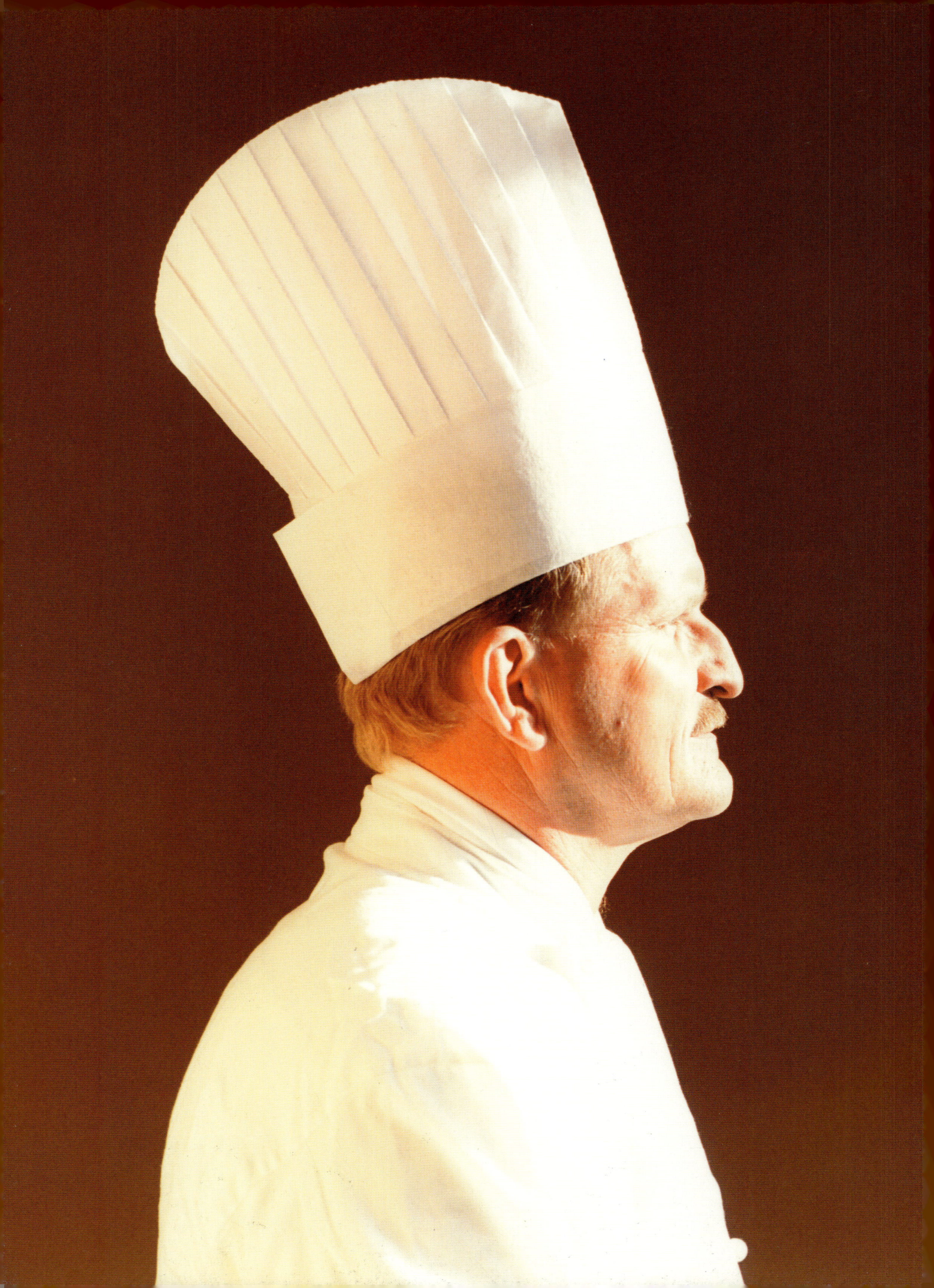

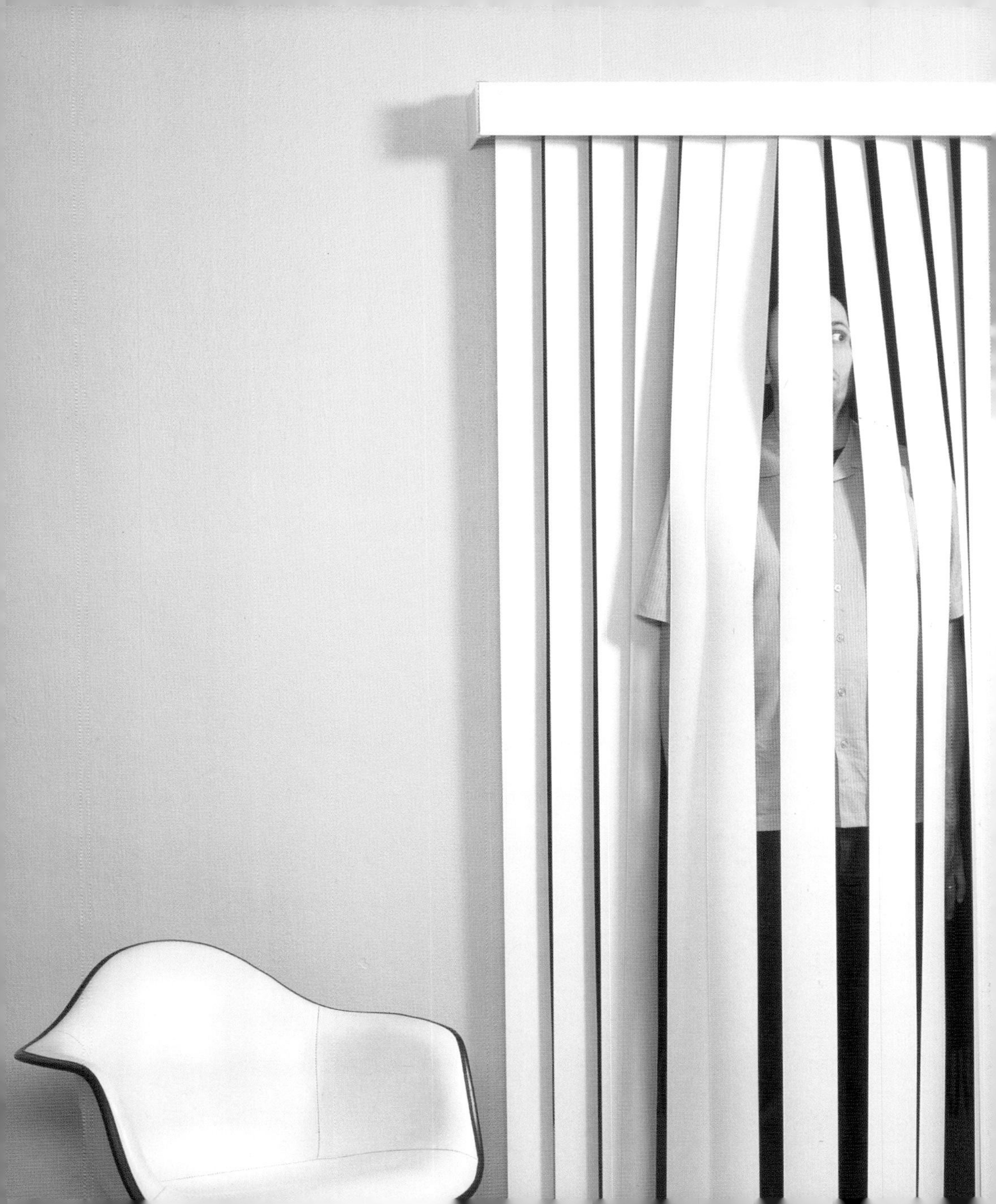

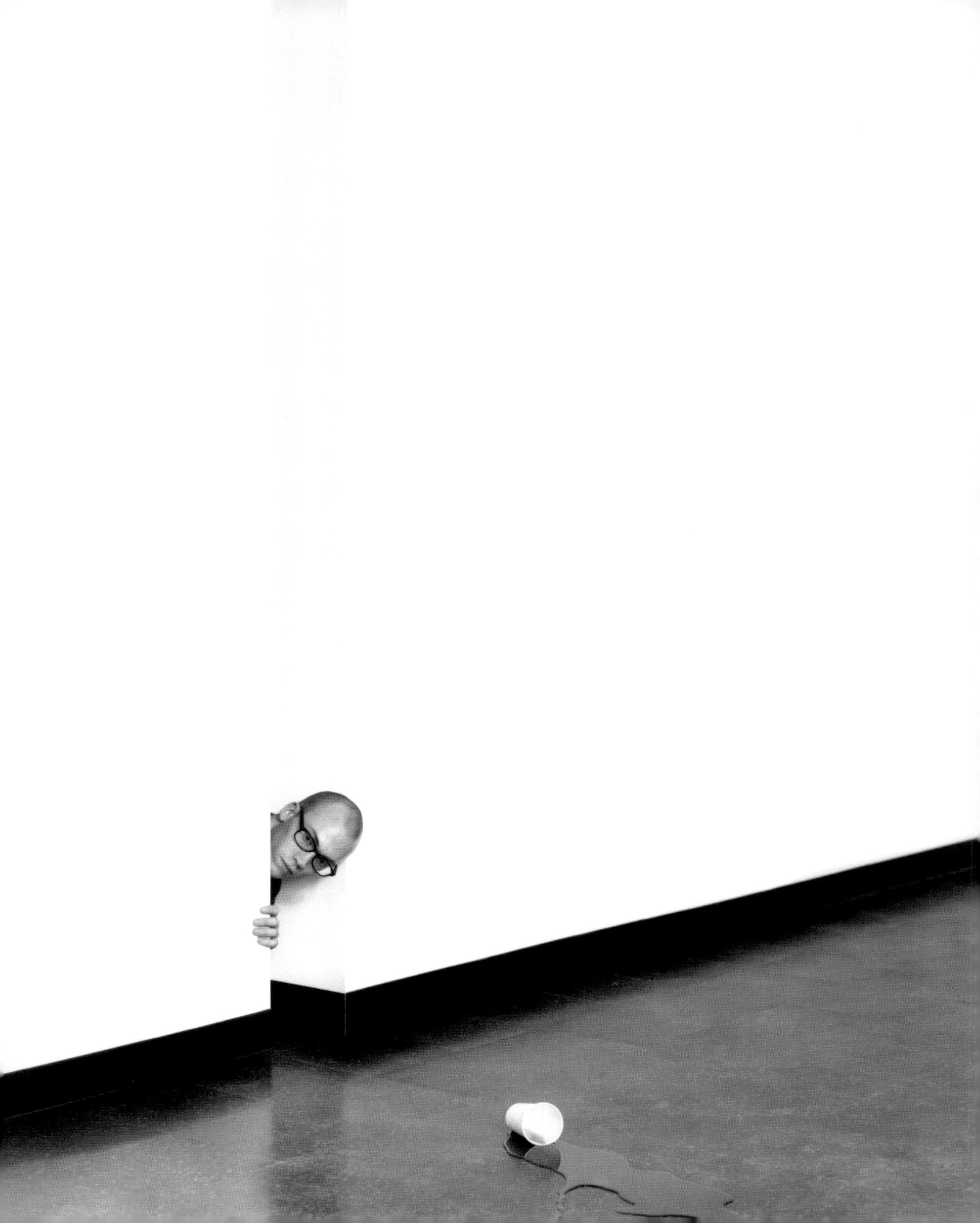

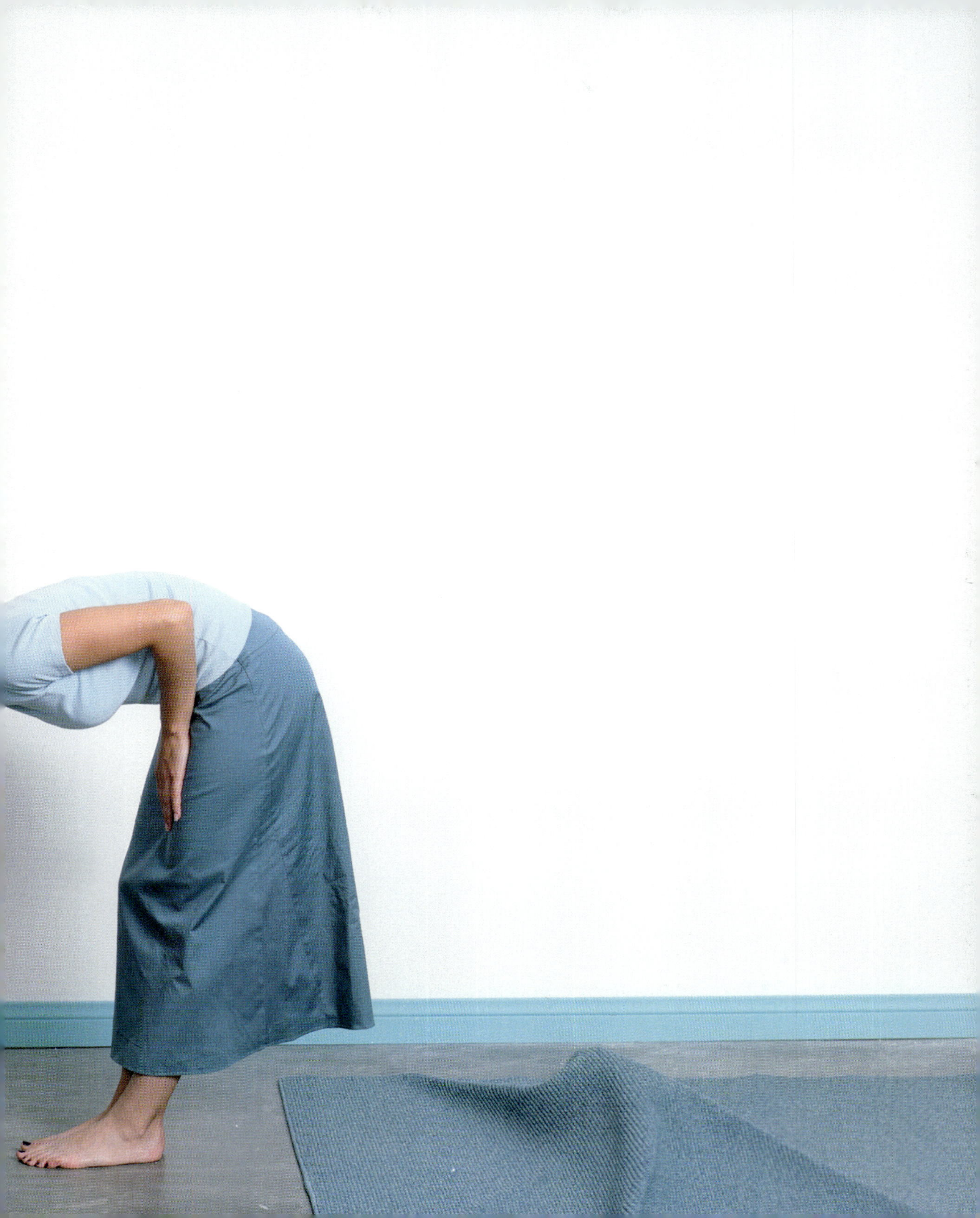

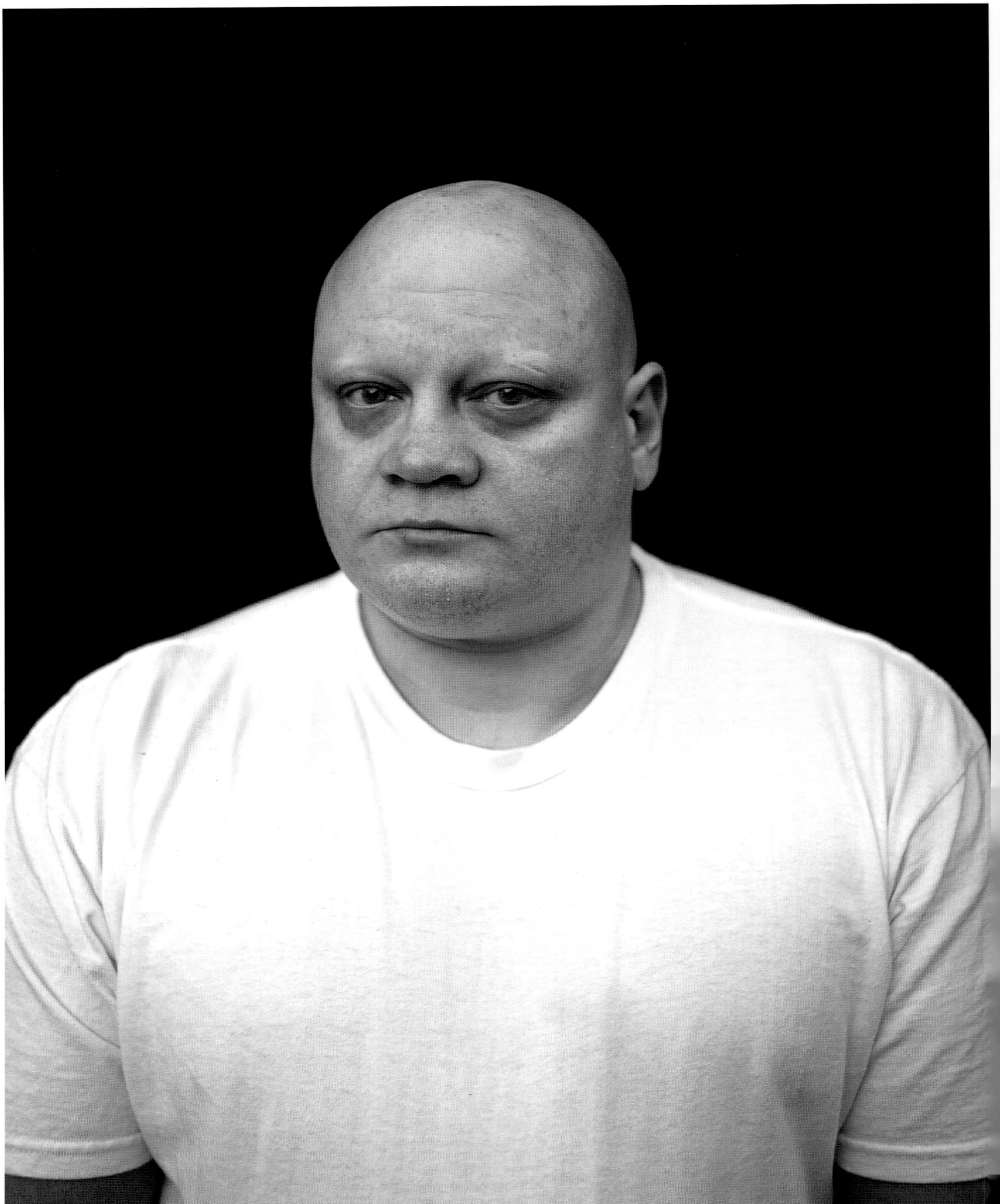

William Huber

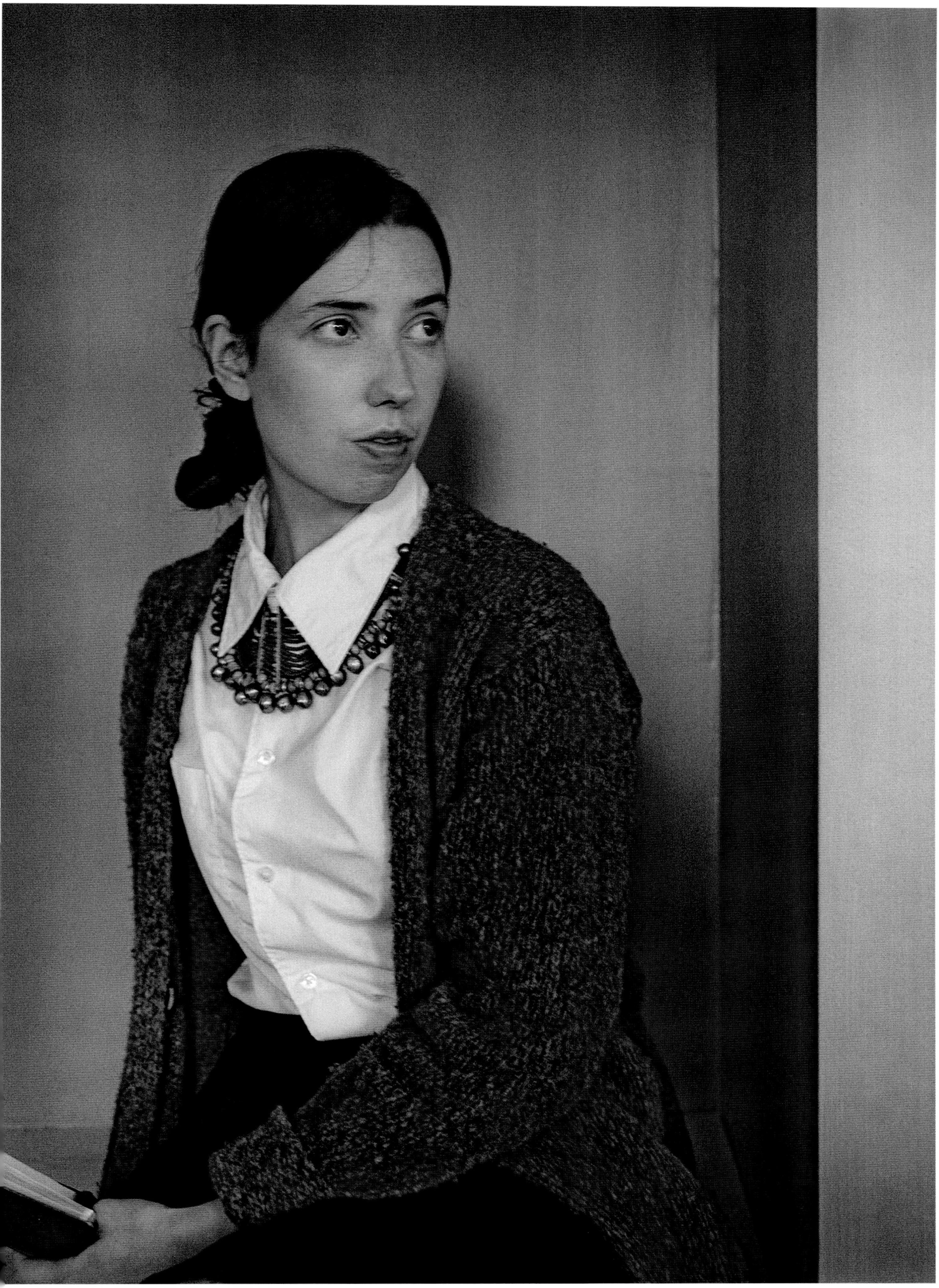

William Huber

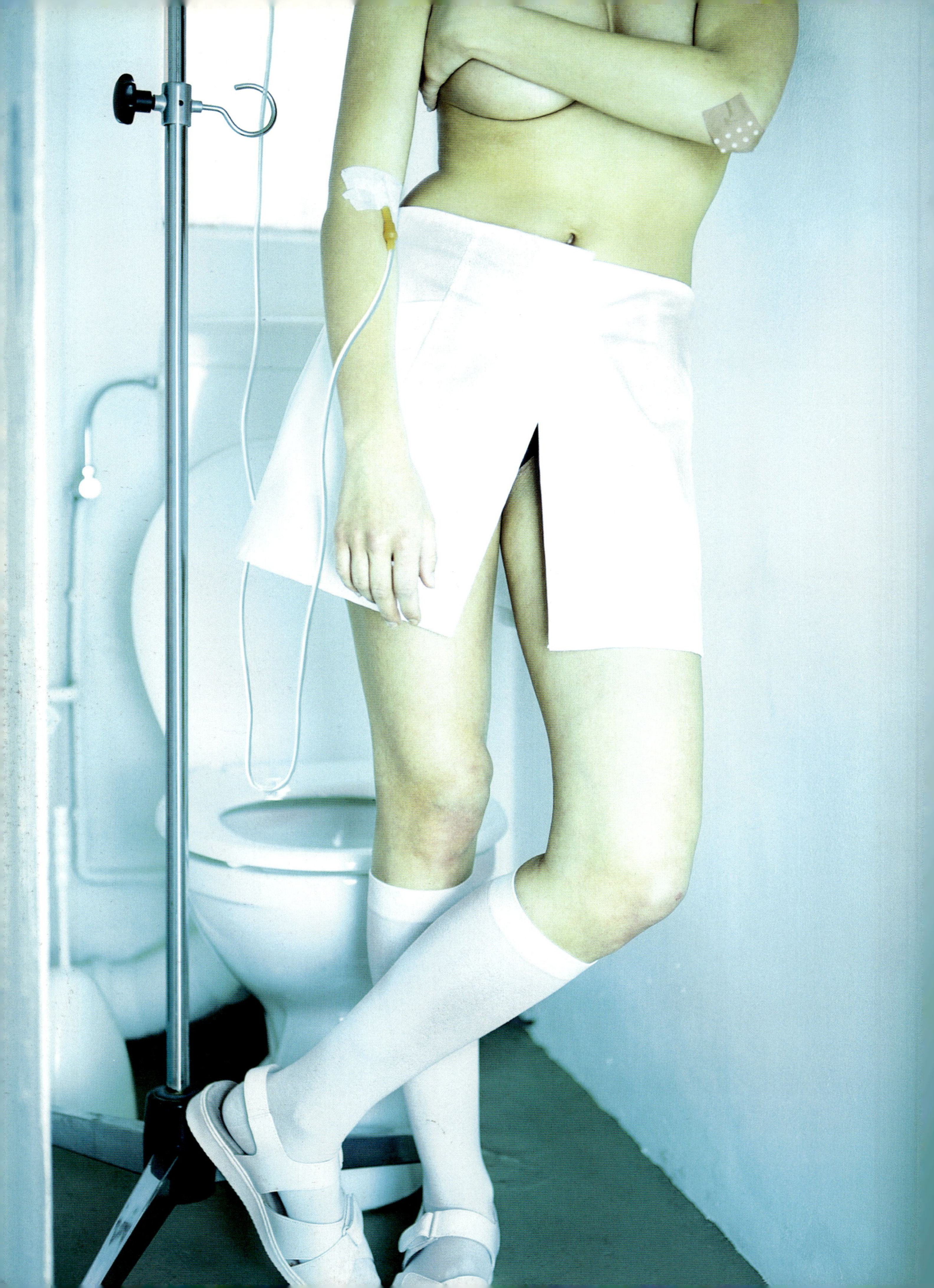

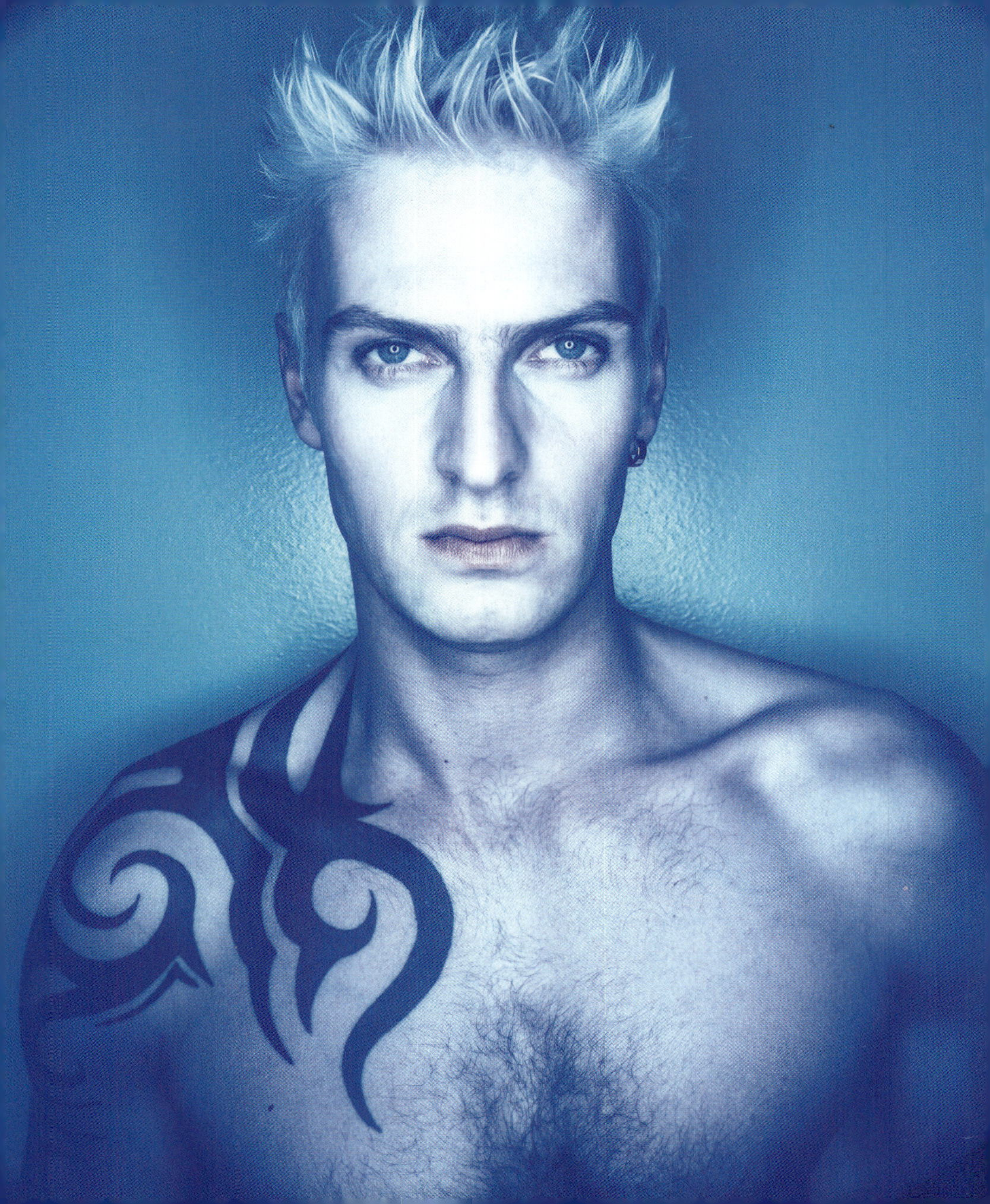

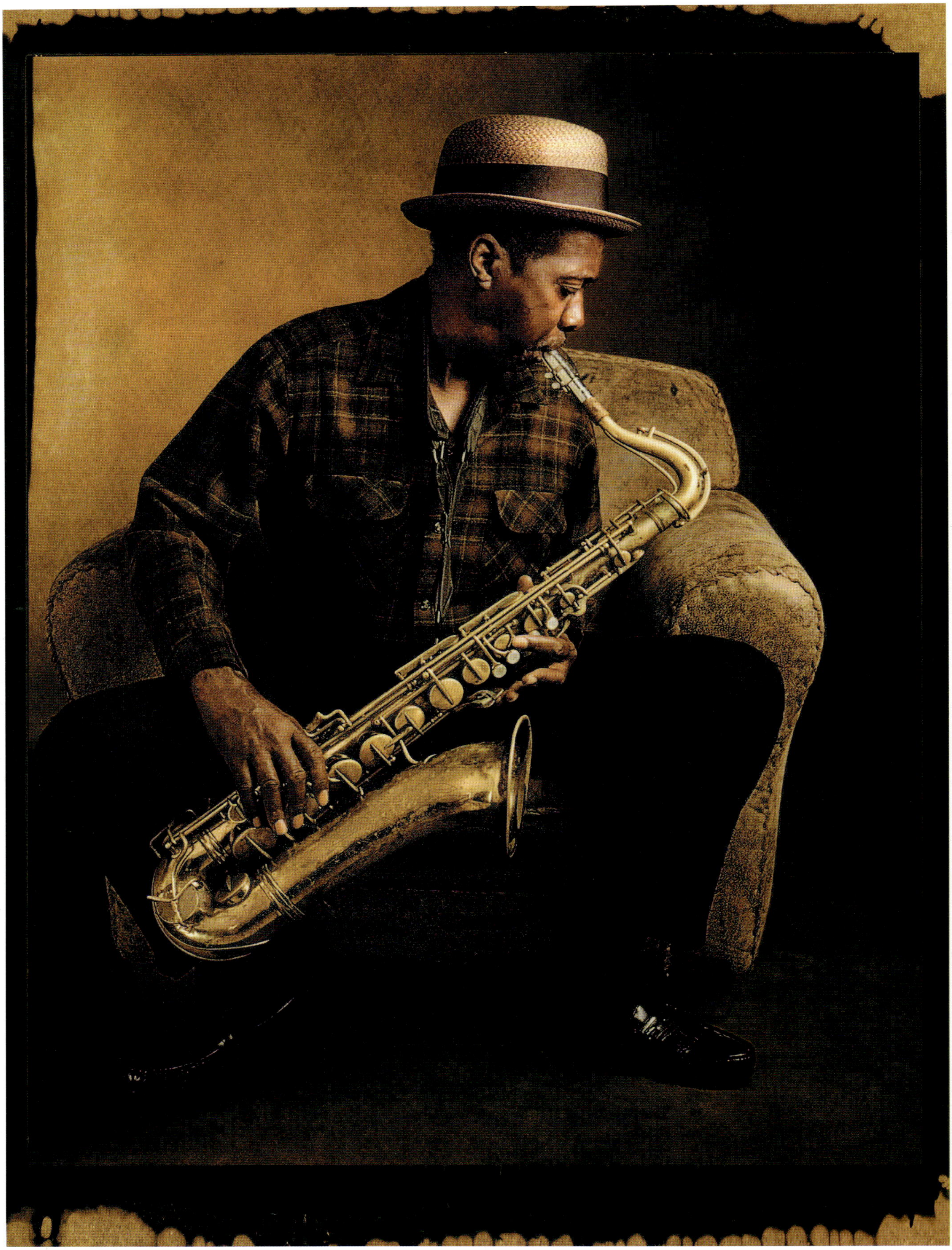

Sue Bennett

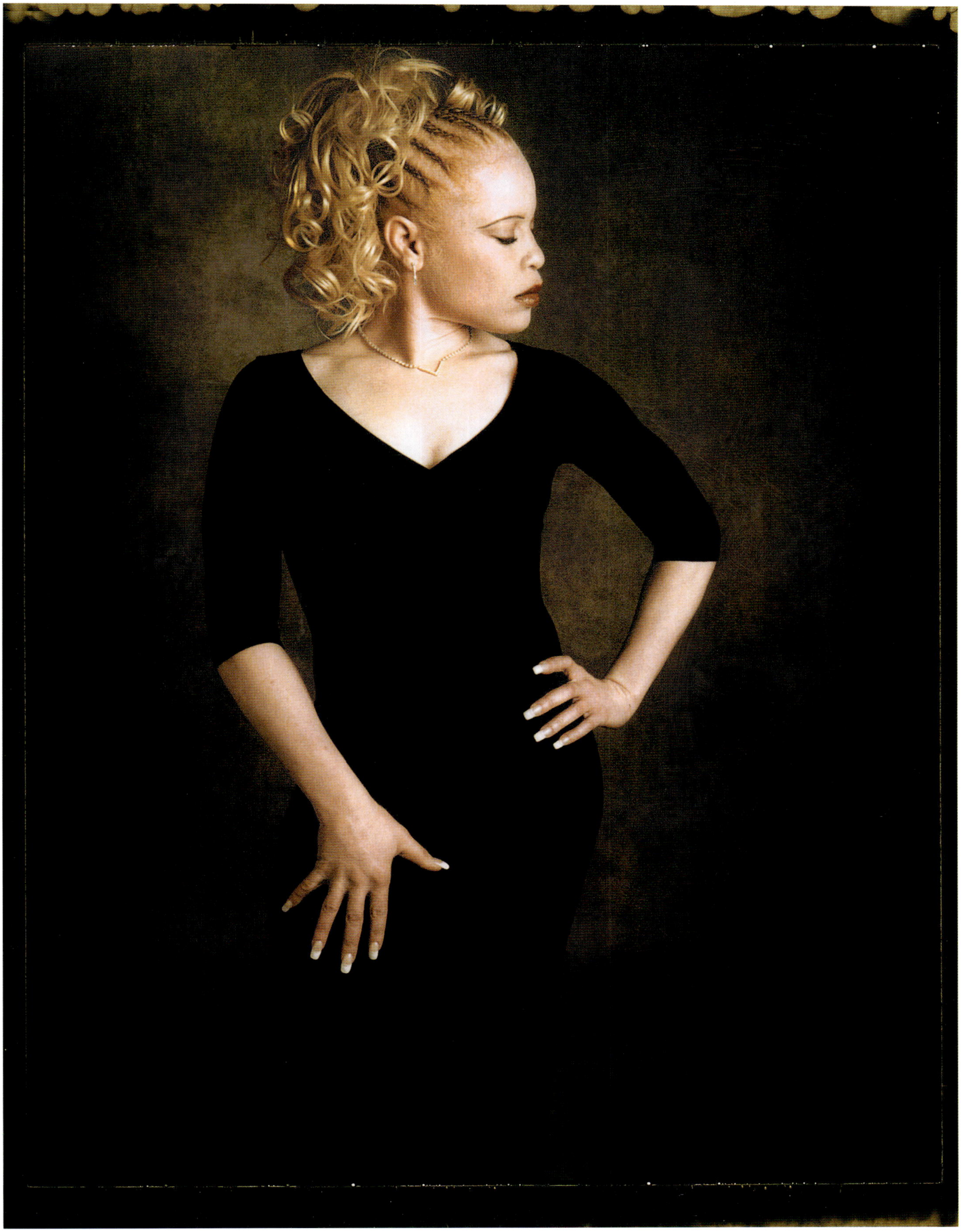

Sue Bennett

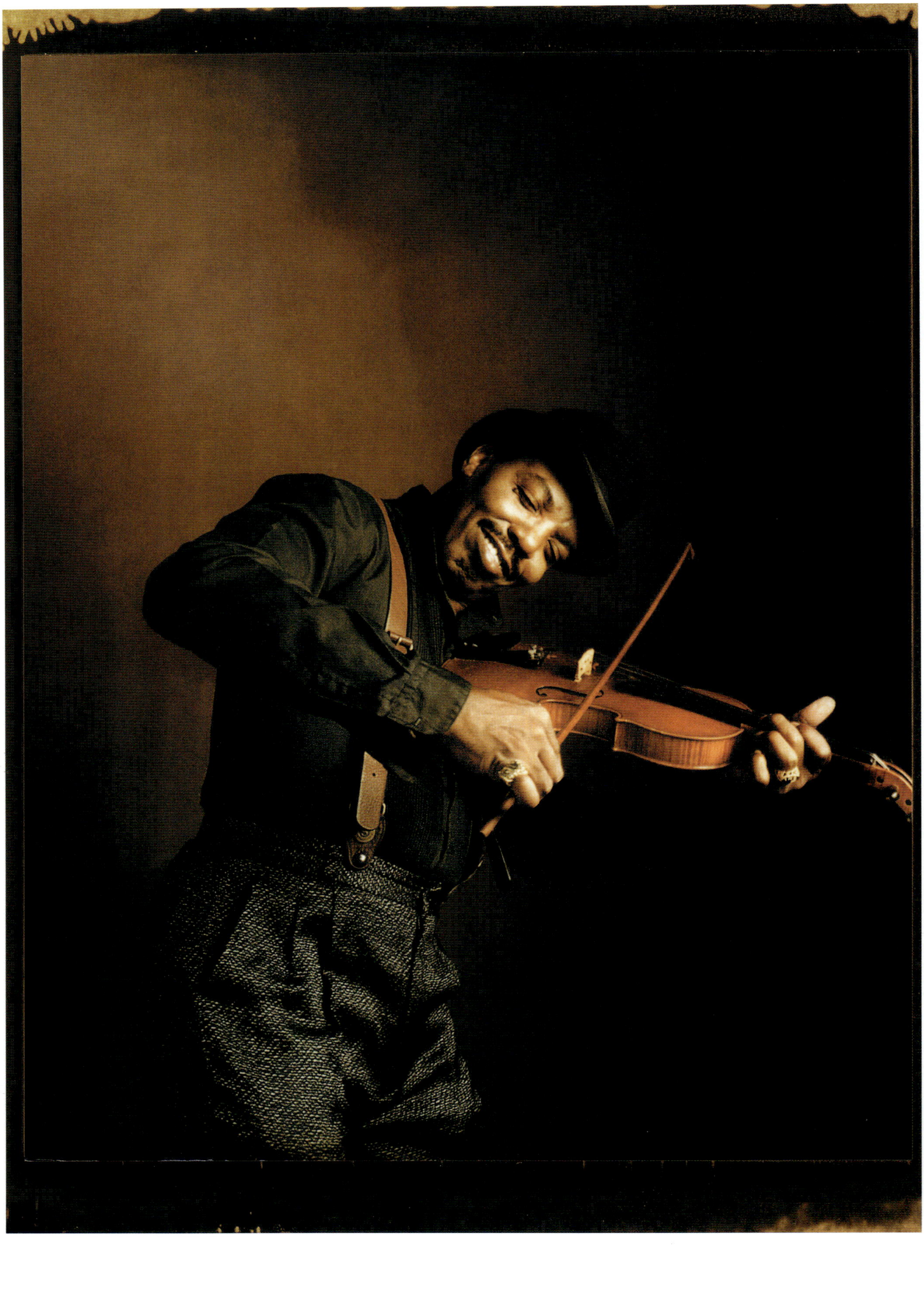

Sue Bennett

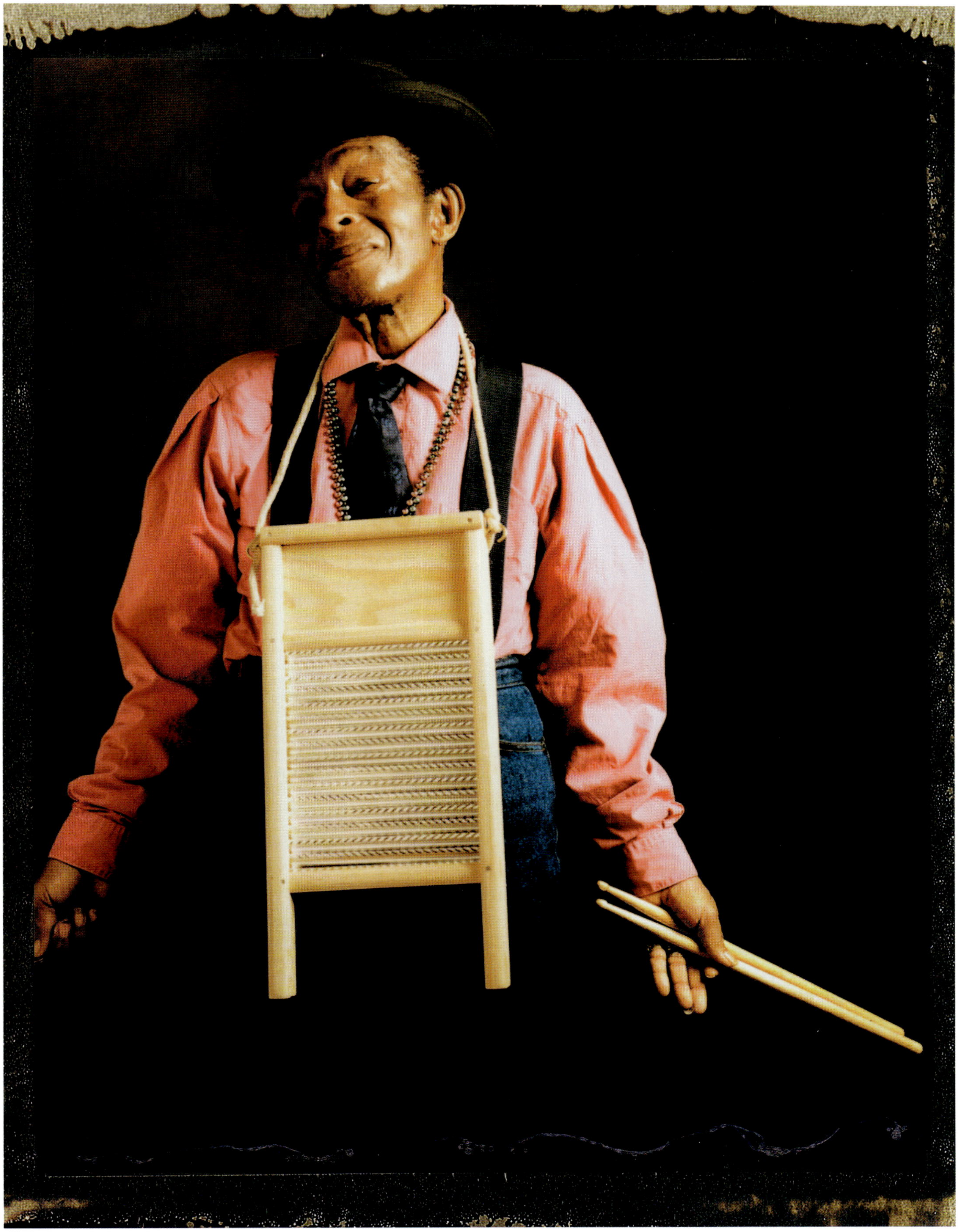

Sue Bennett

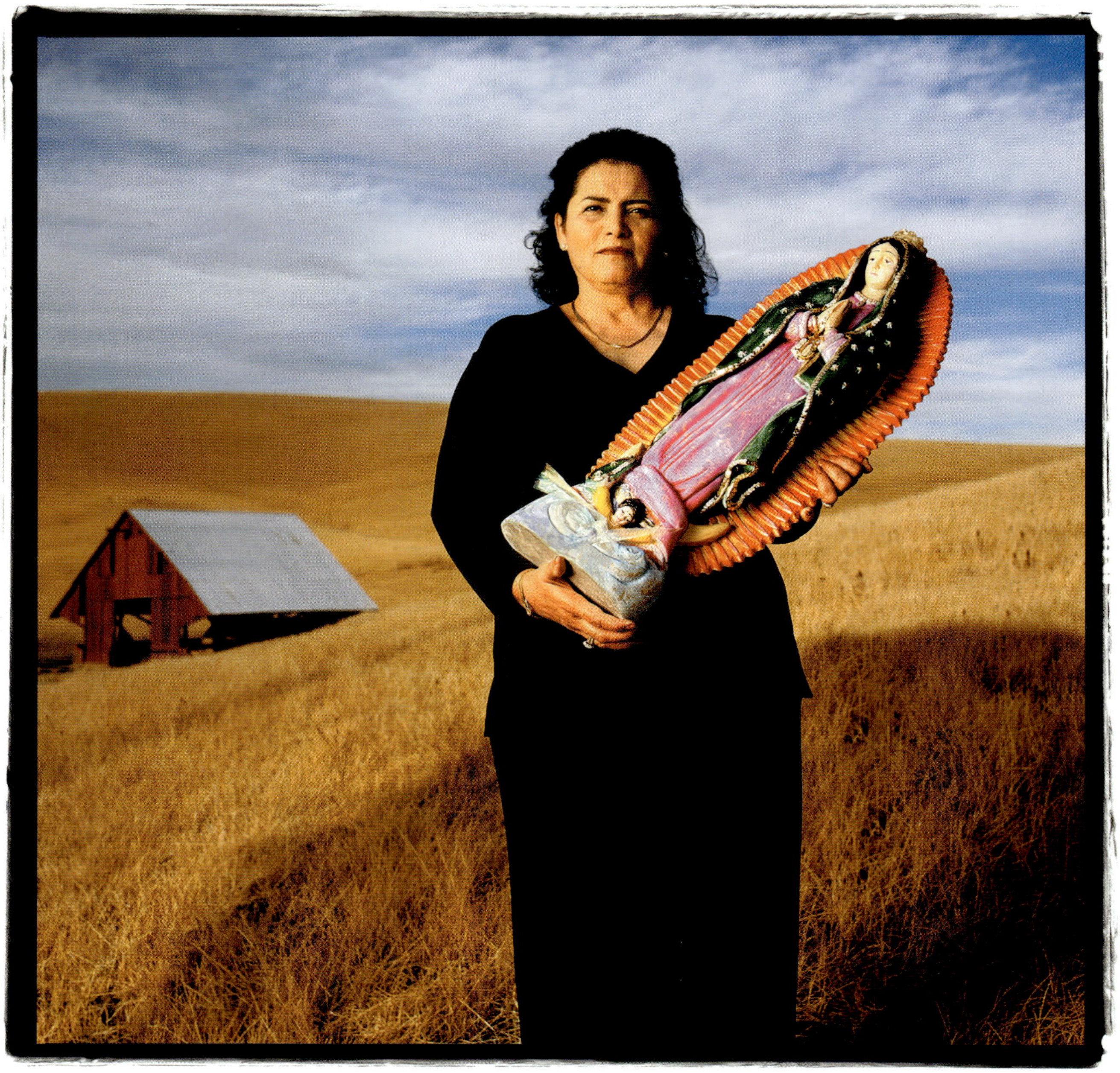

Sue Bennett

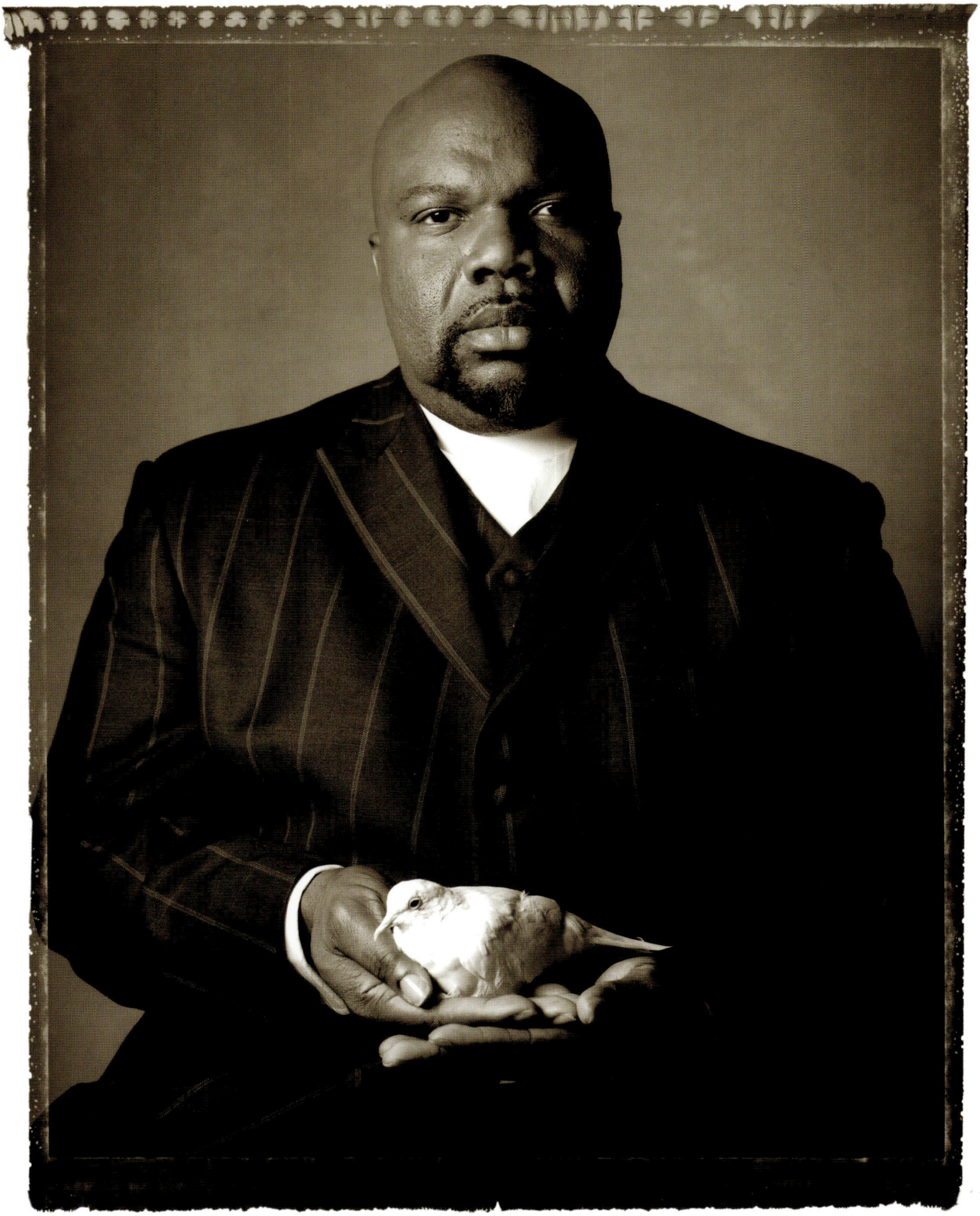

Michael O'Brien

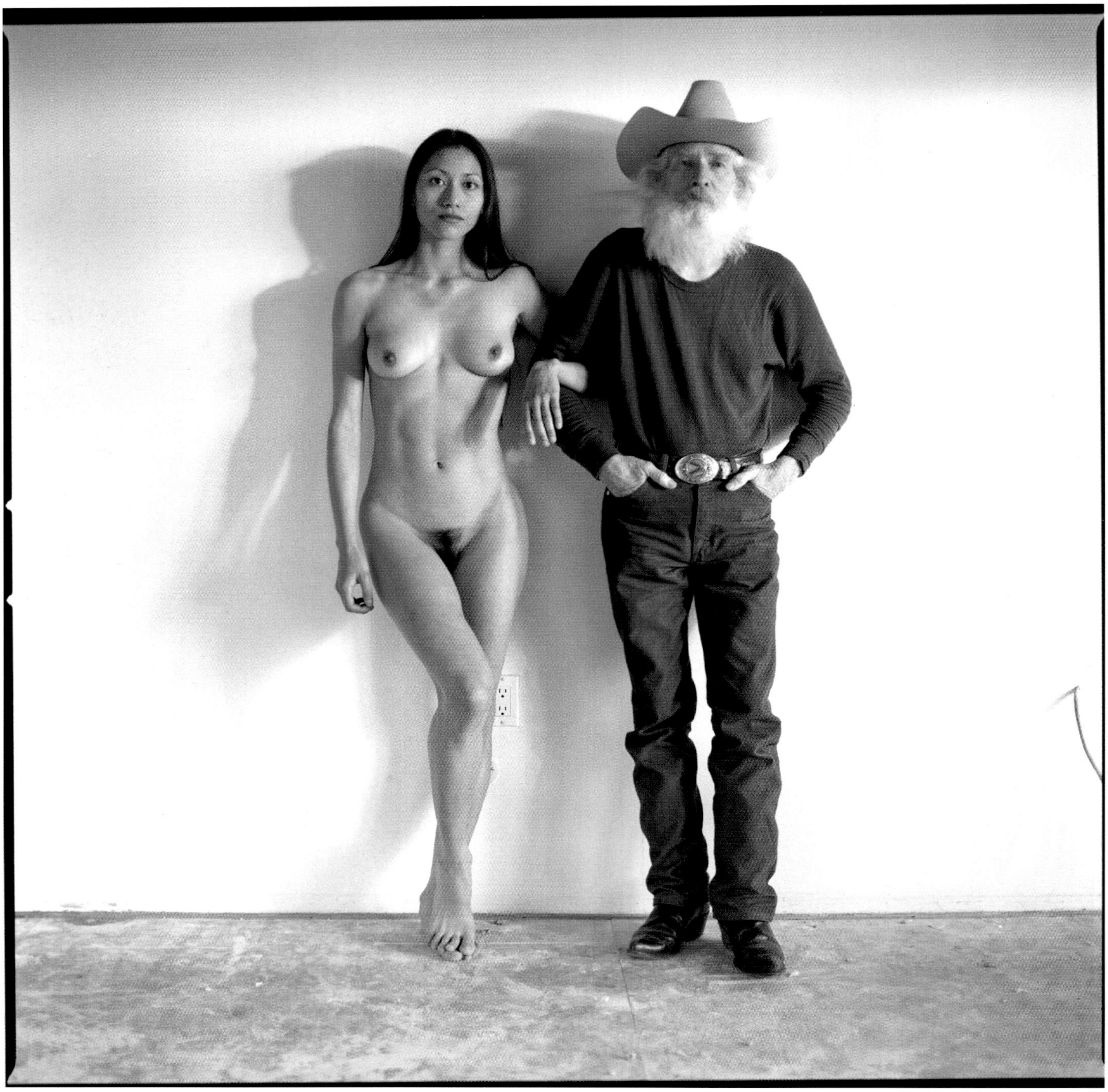

Michael O'Brien (opposite) Stewart Cohen

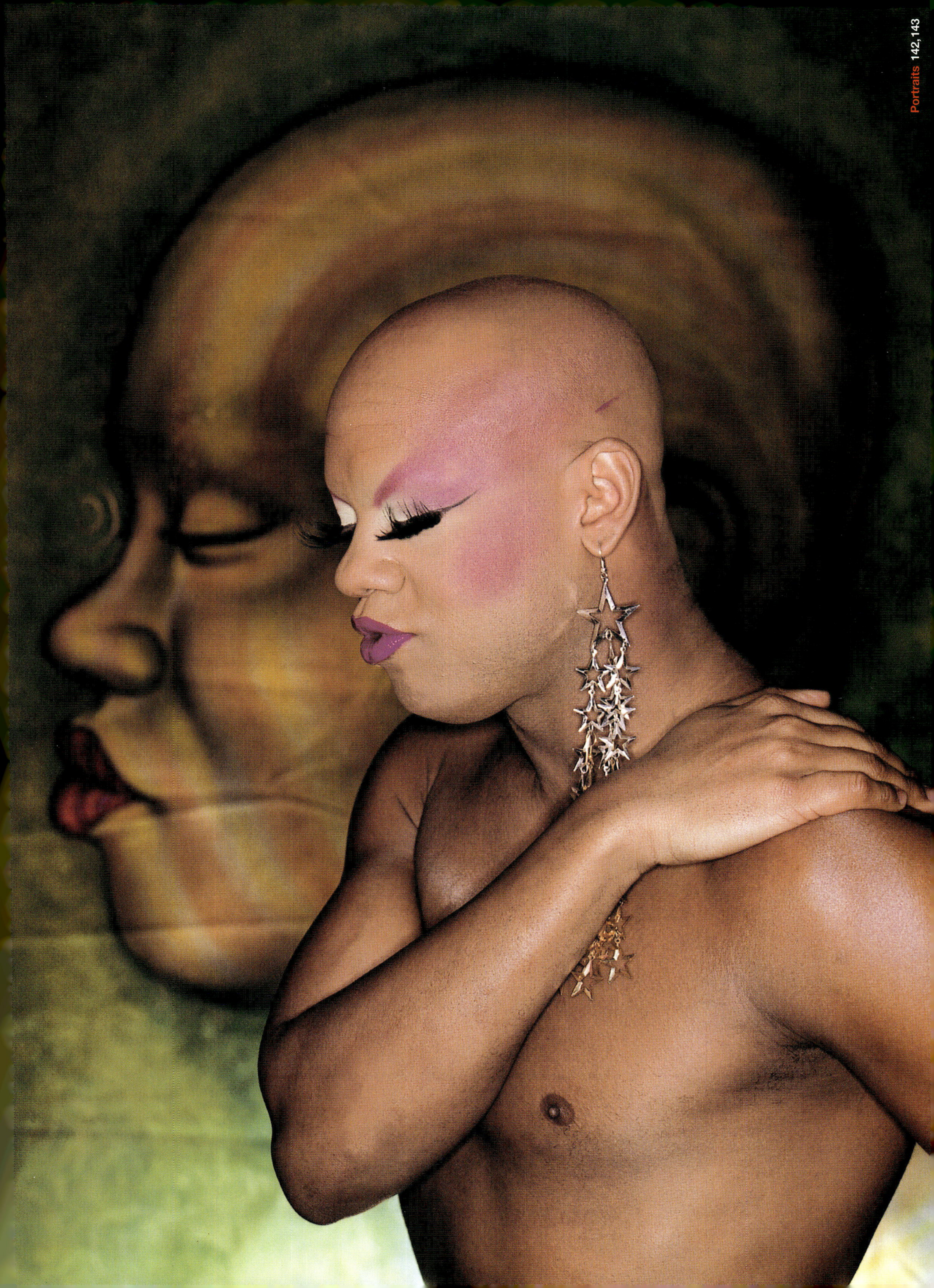

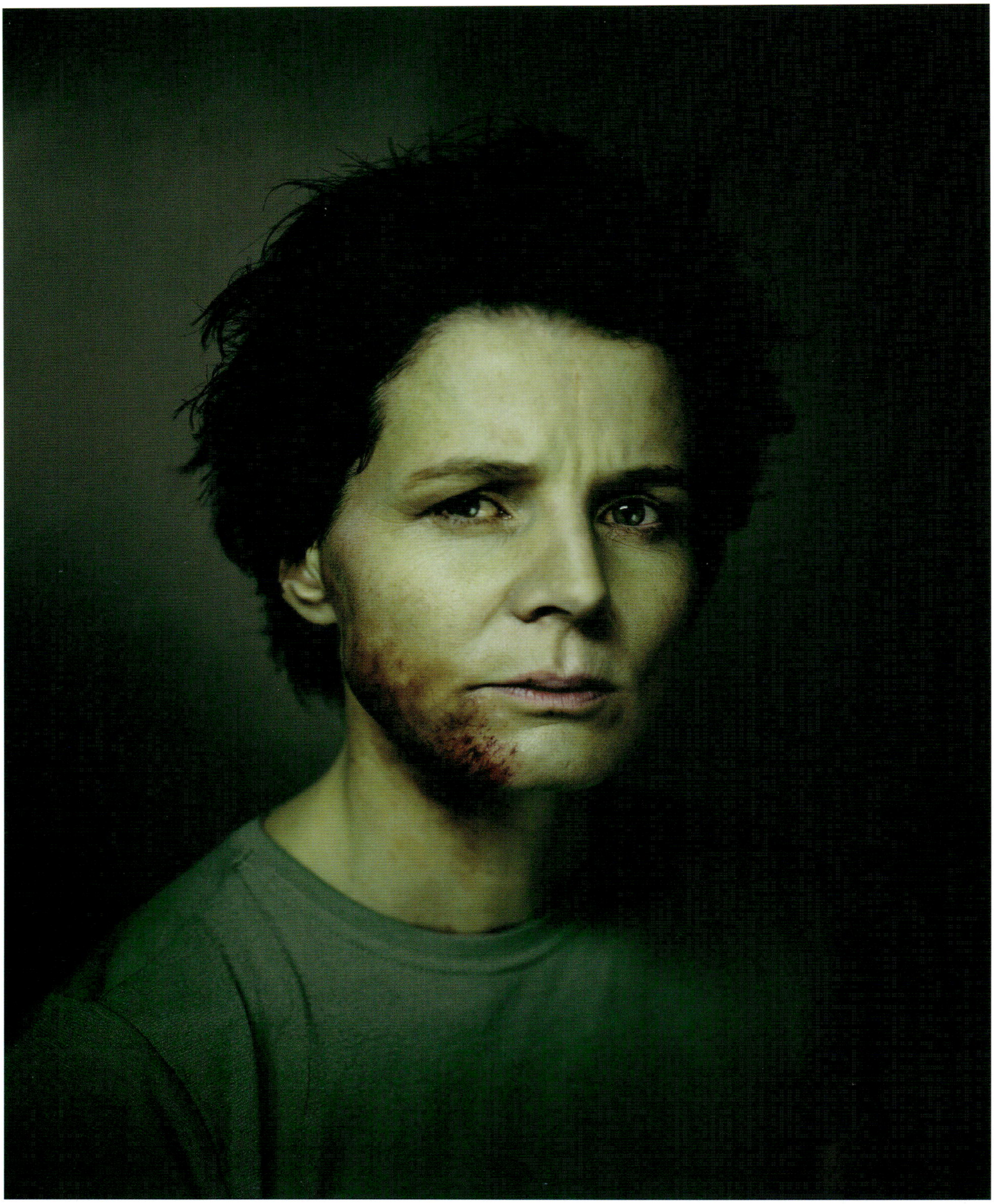

Jono Rotman

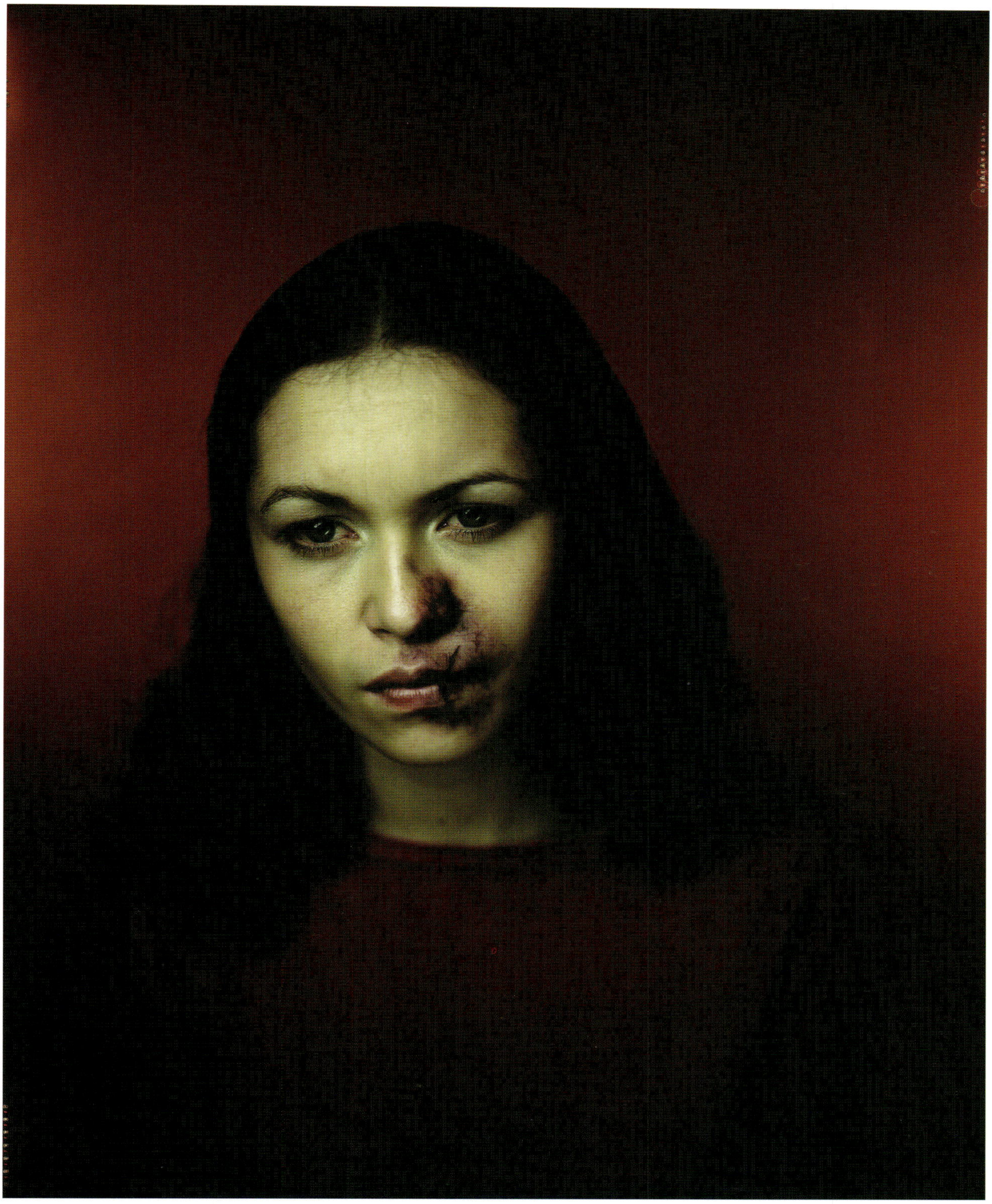

Jono Rotman

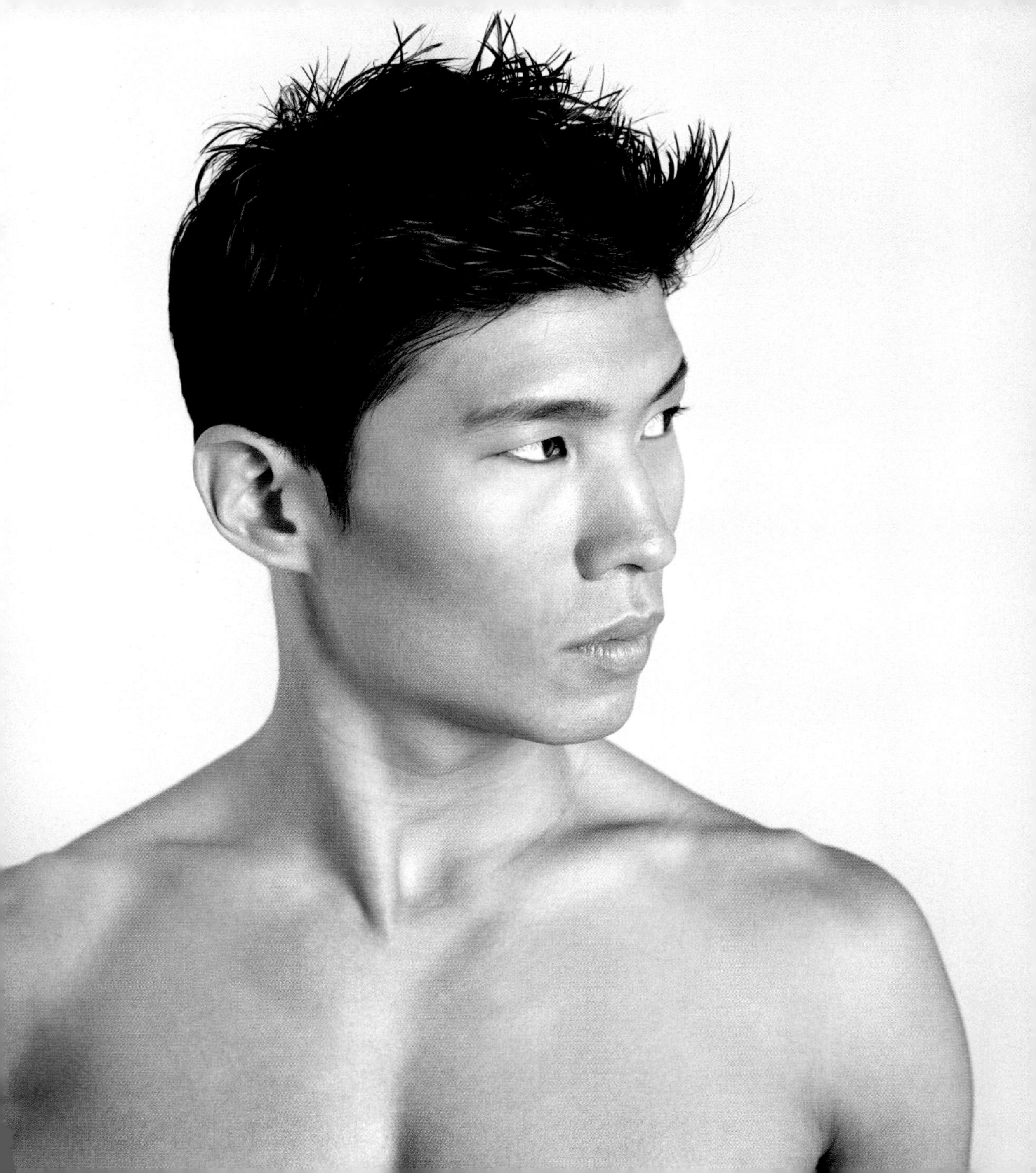

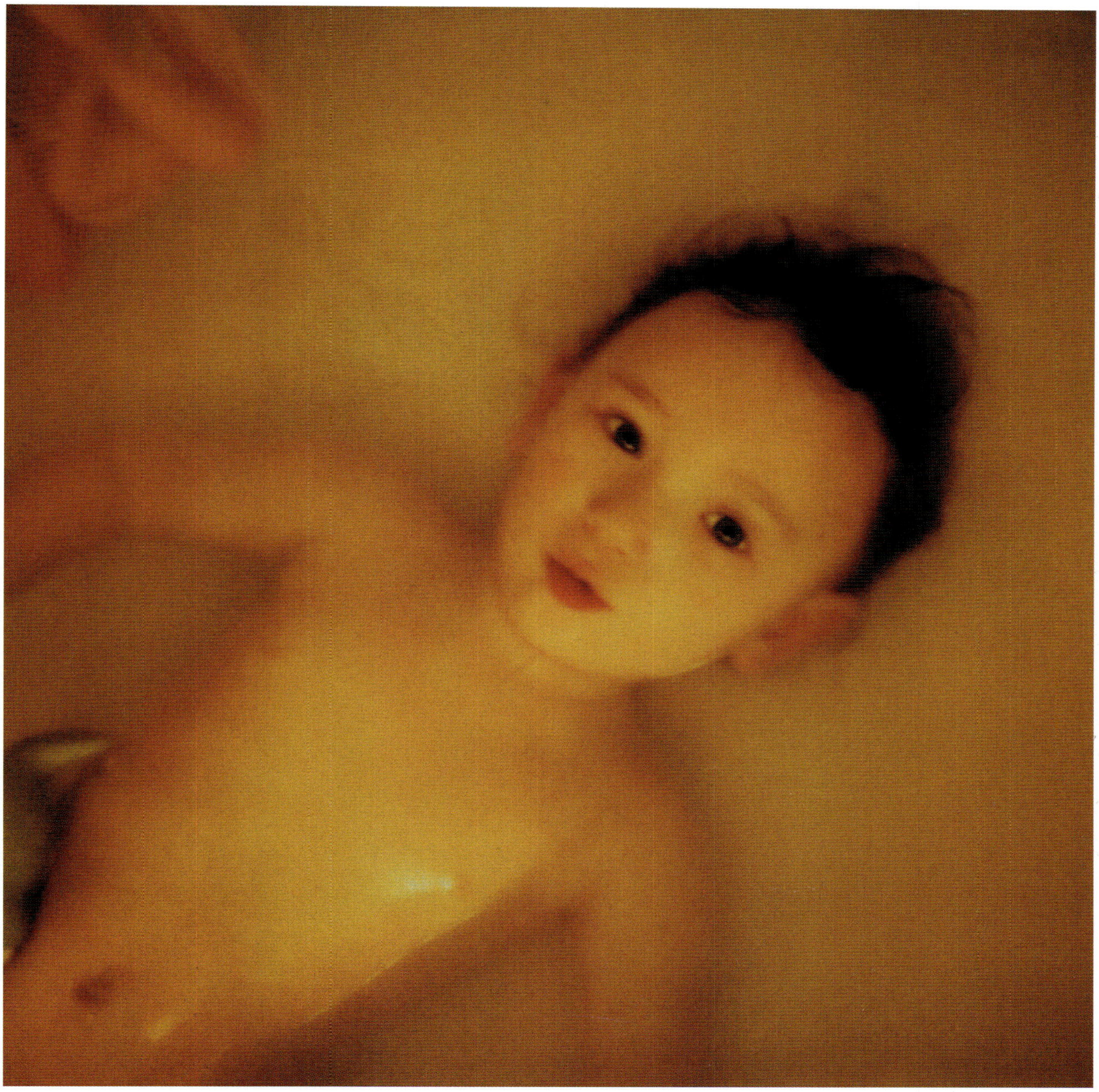

Barry Gnyp

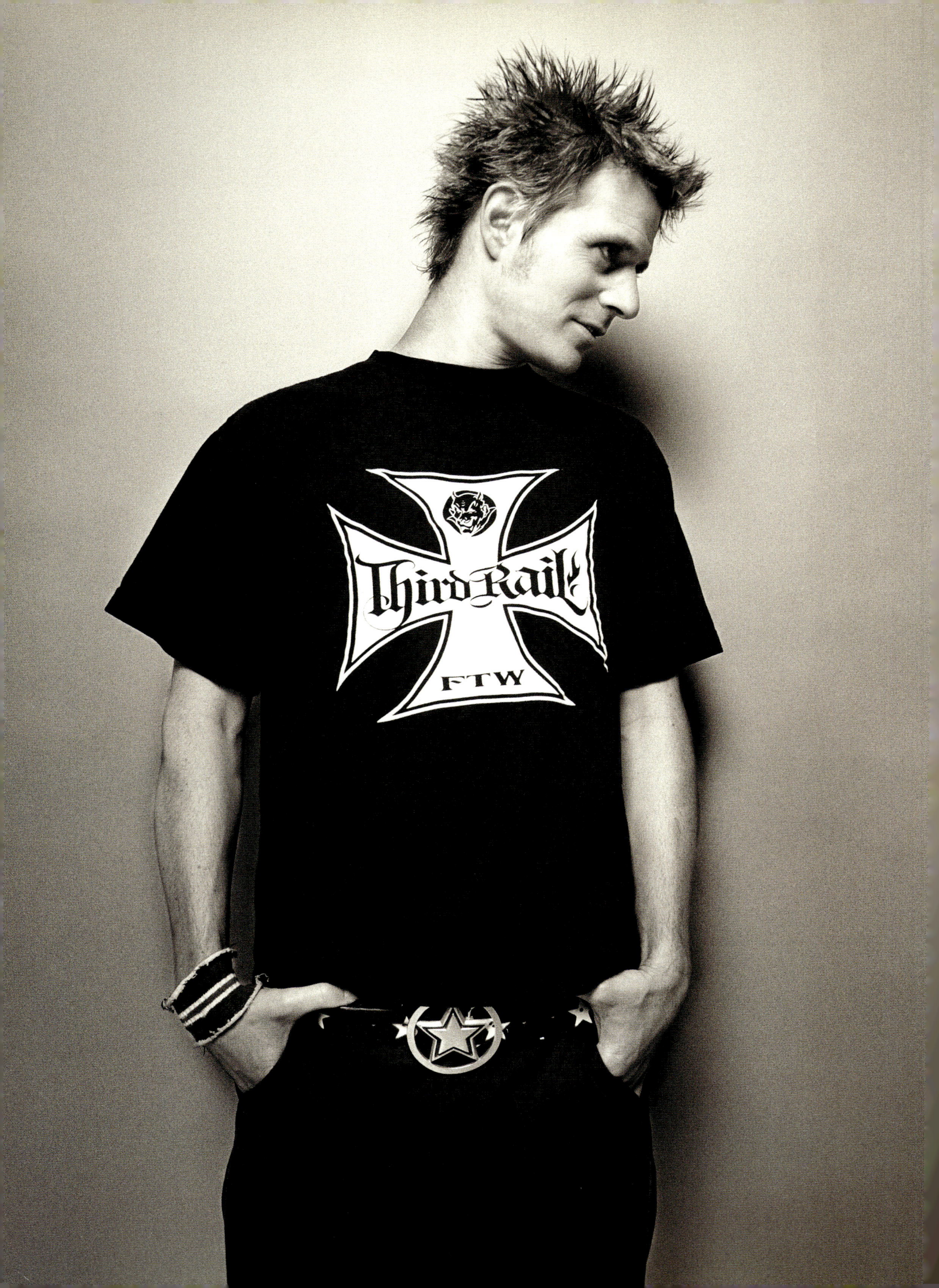
Third Rail
FTW

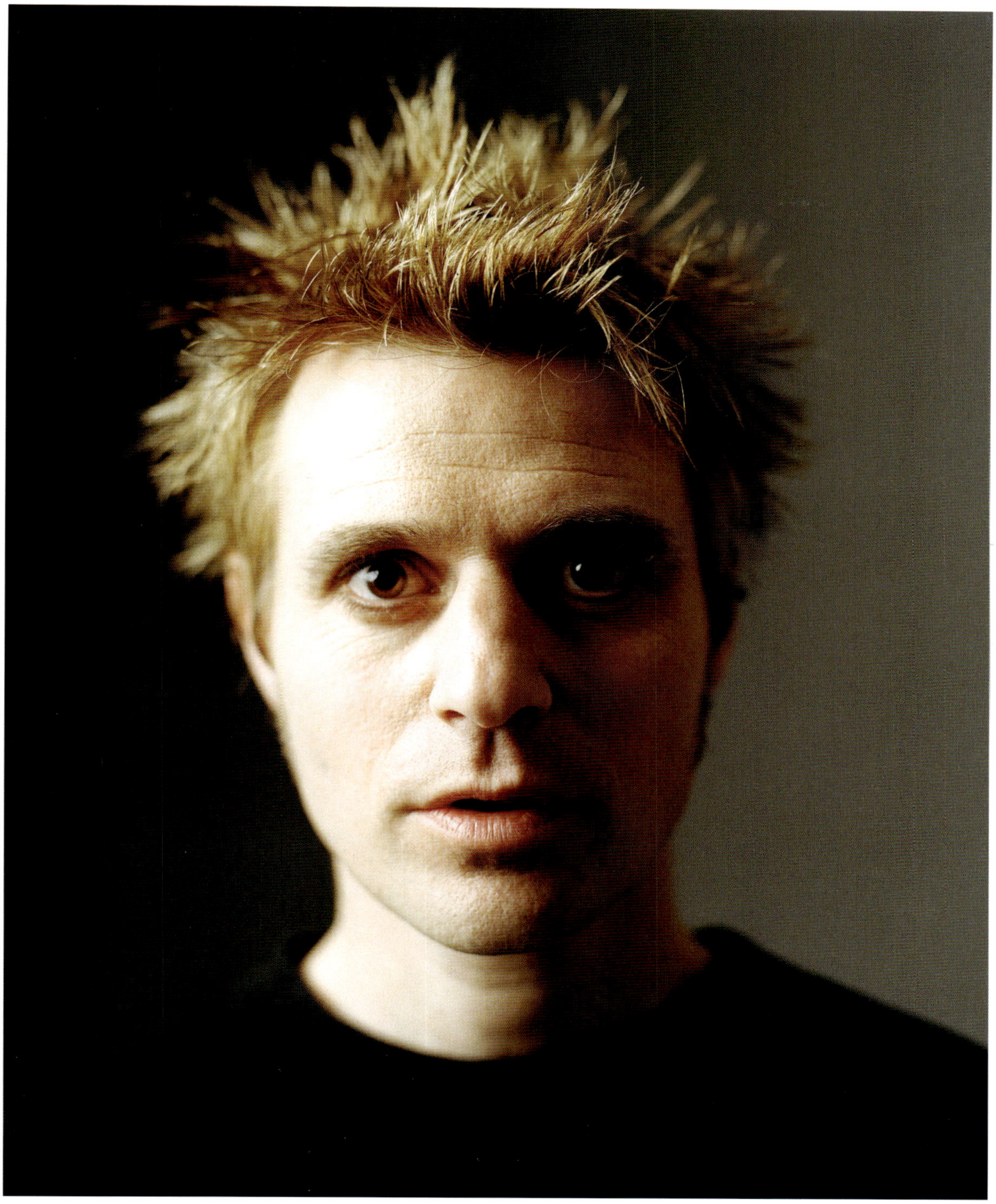

(this spread) K. C. Armstrong

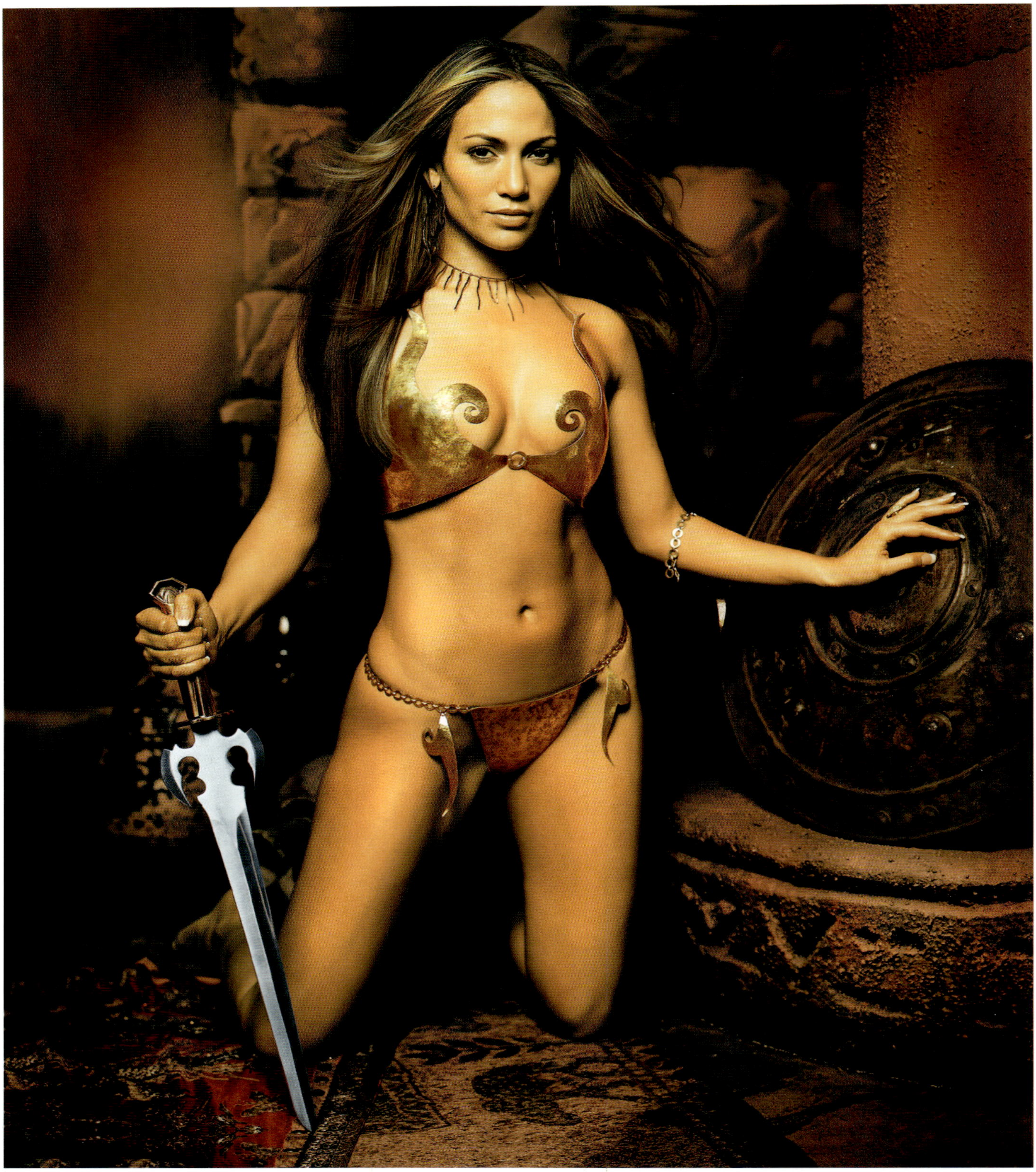

Mark Seliger

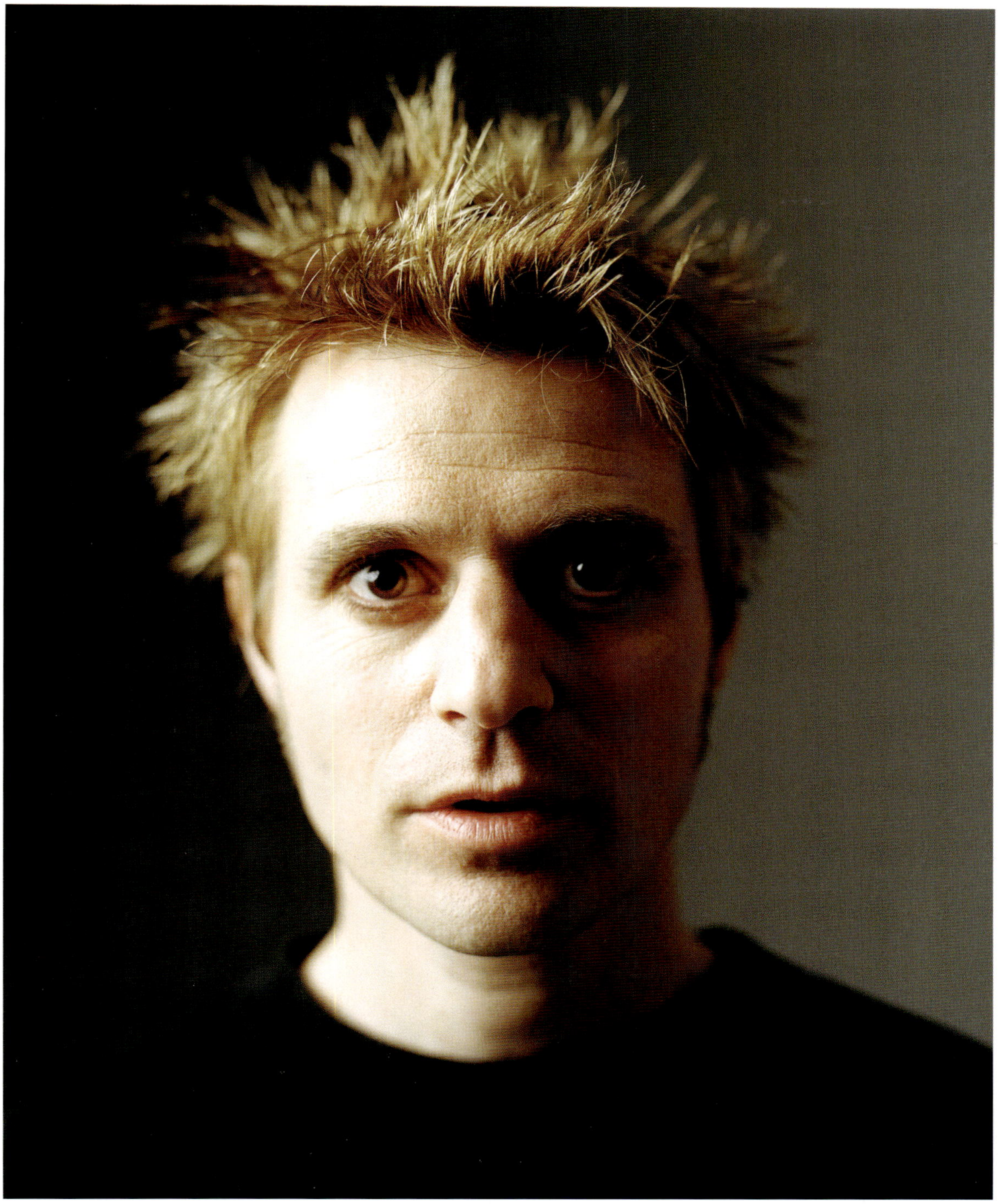

(this spread) K. C. Armstrong

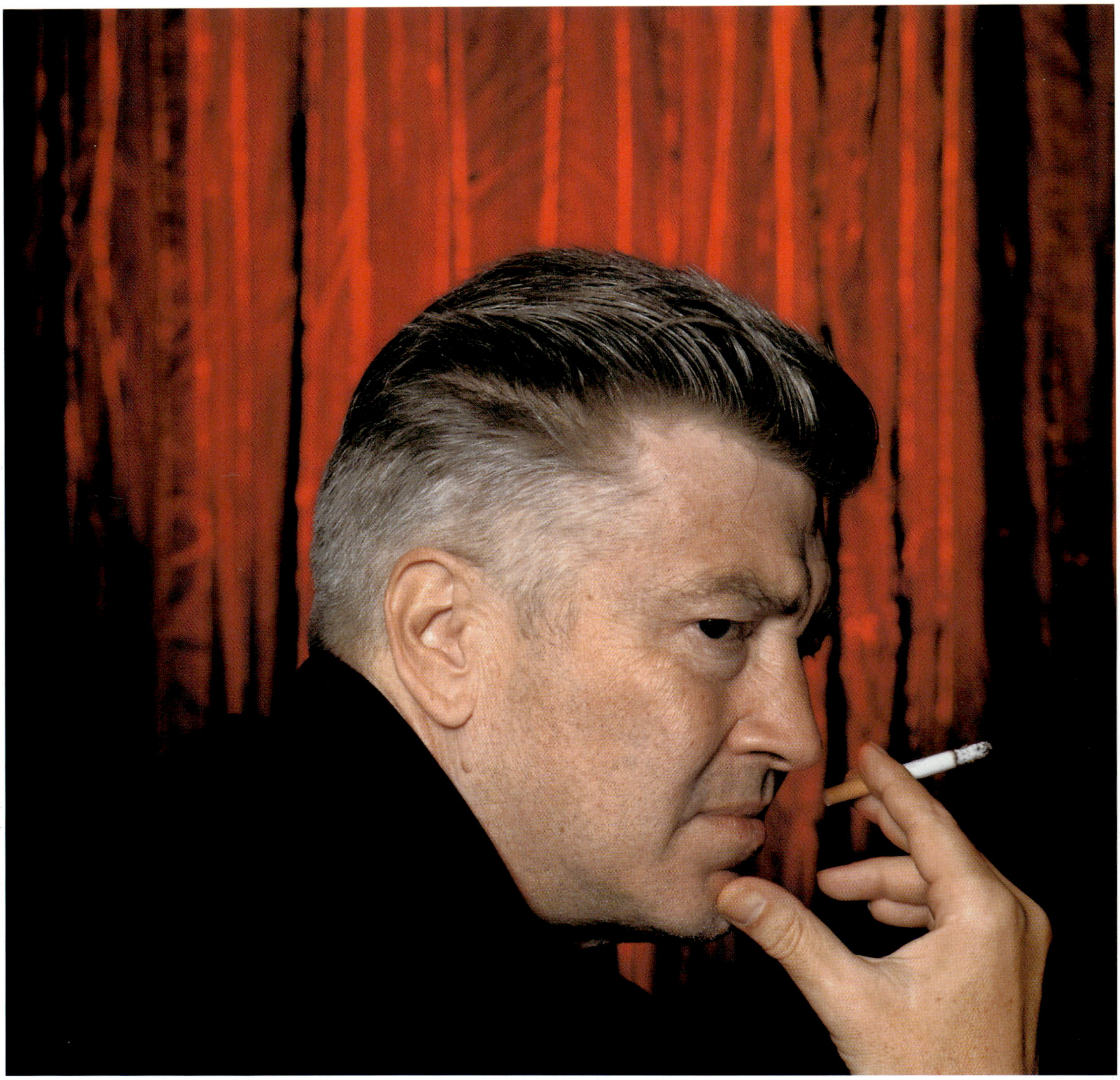

Robin Holland

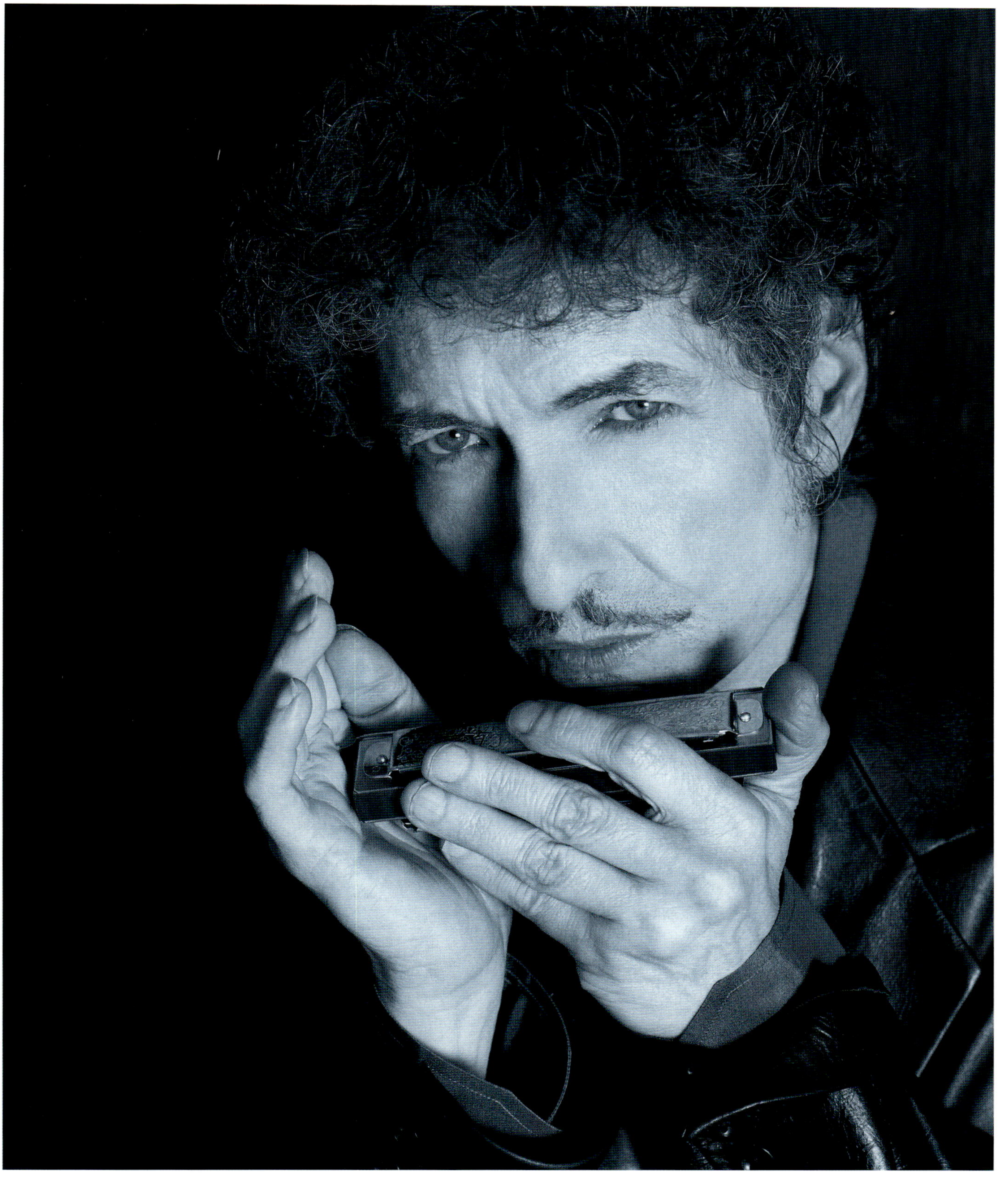

Herb Ritts

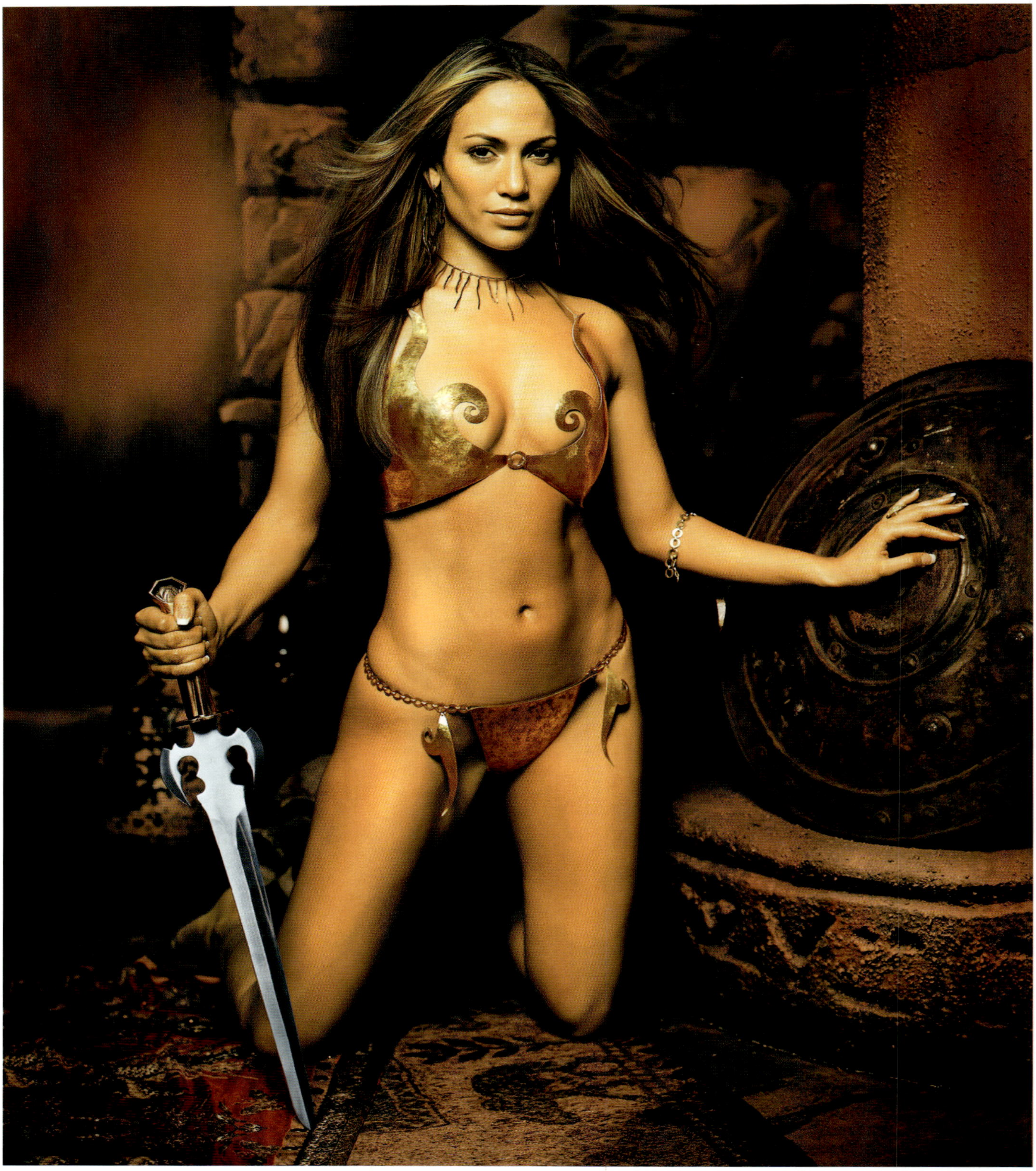

Mark Seliger

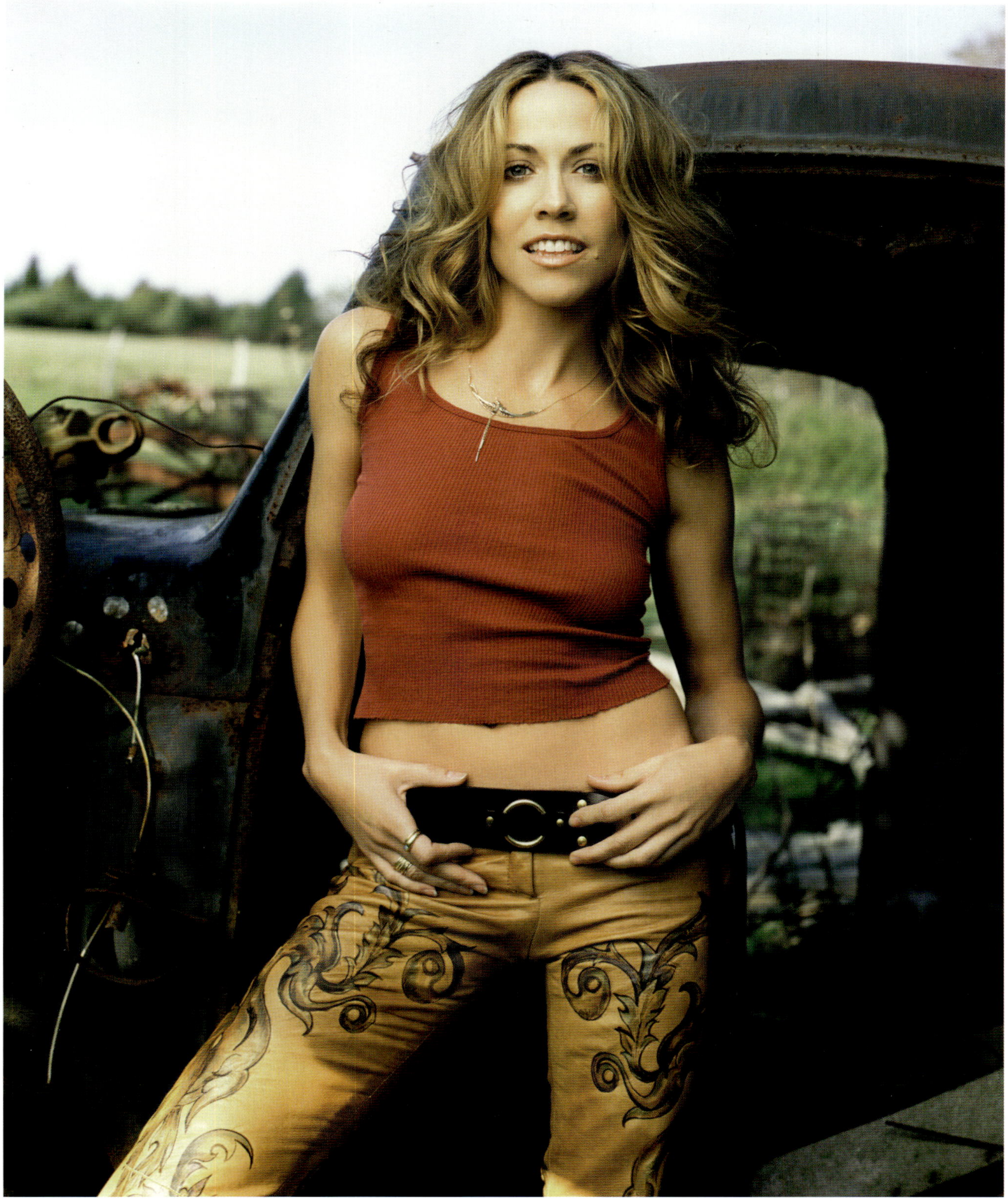

Mark Seliger

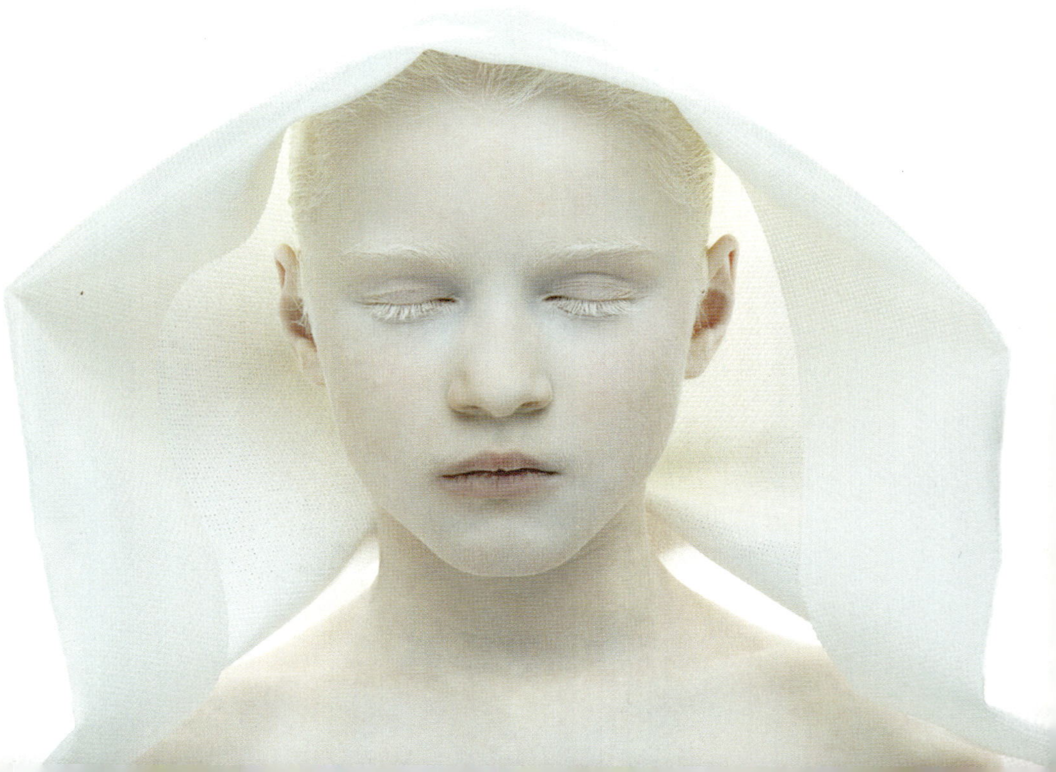

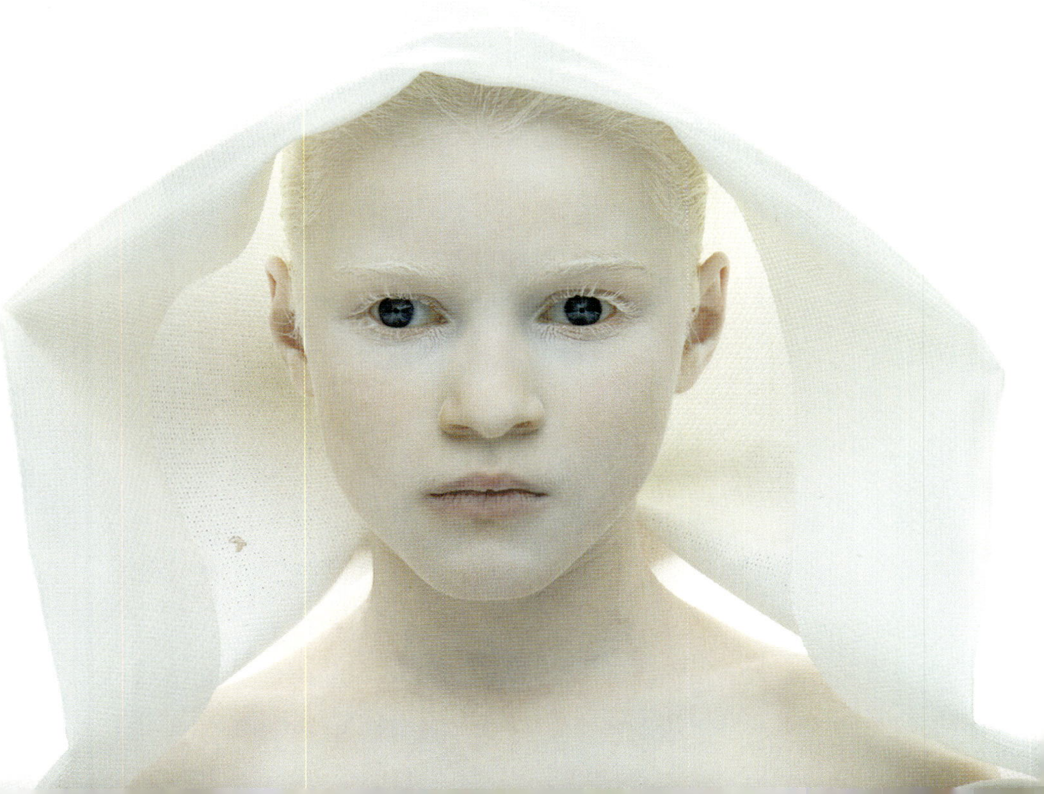

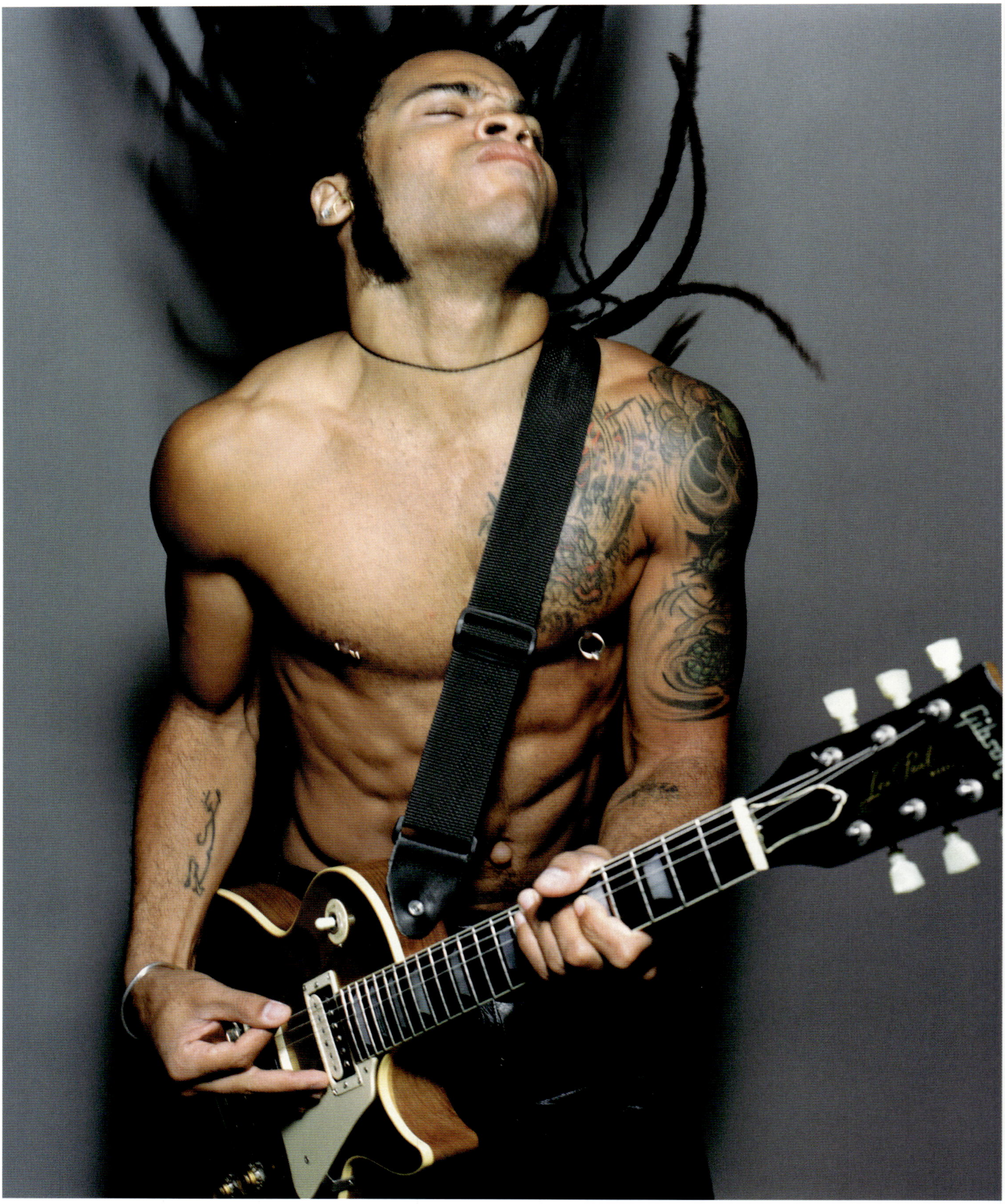

Mark Seliger

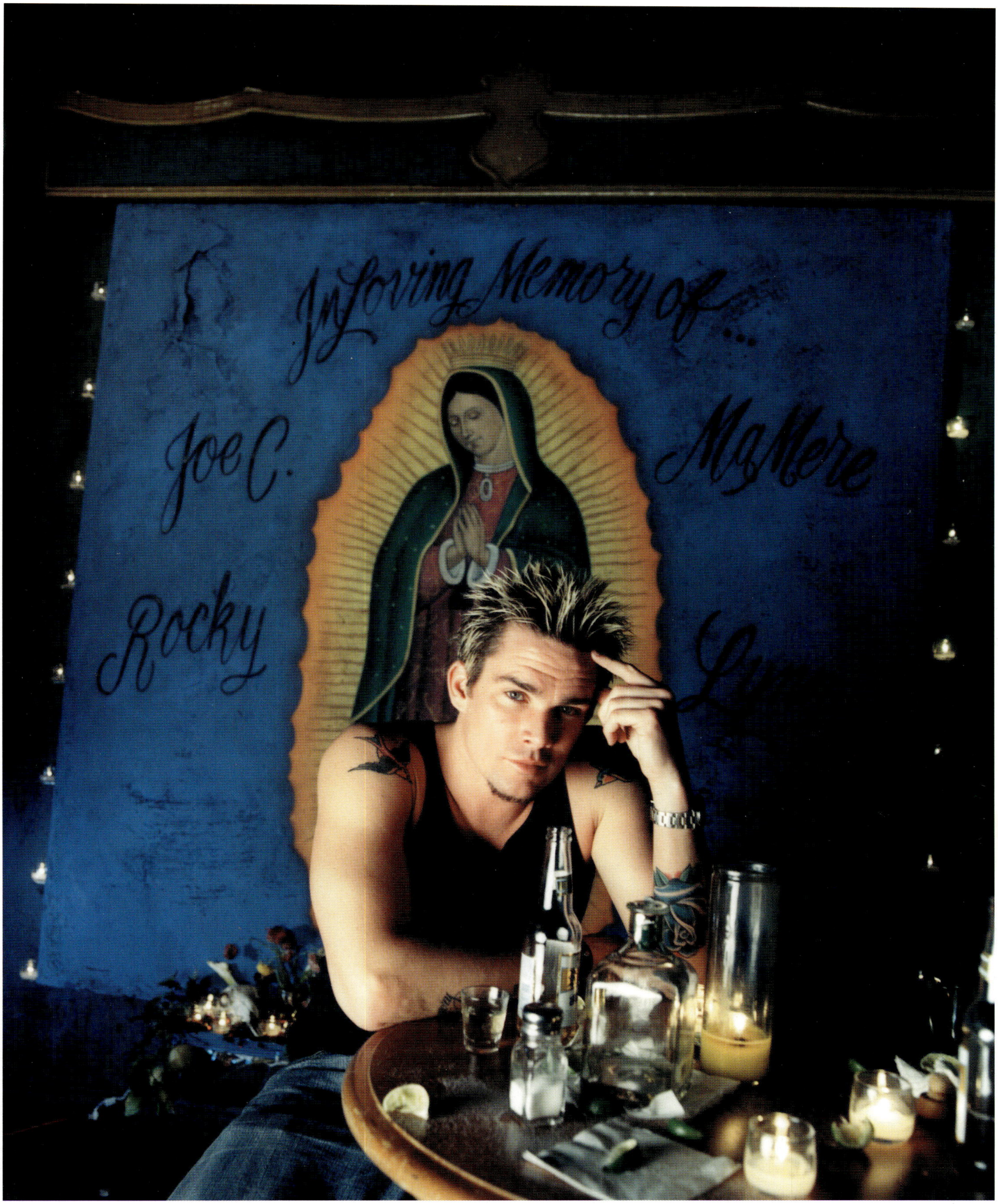

Mark Seliger

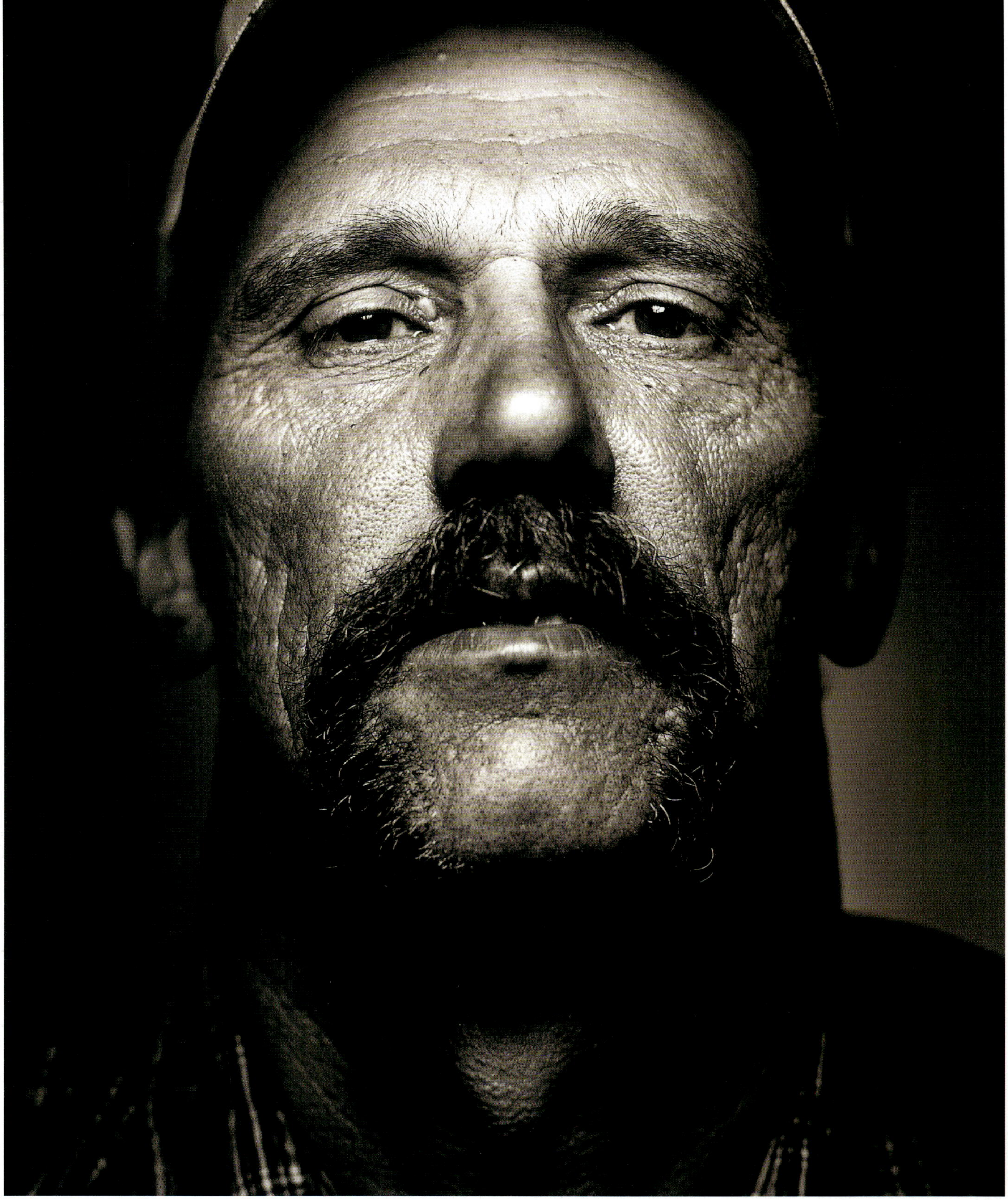

Paul Murphy

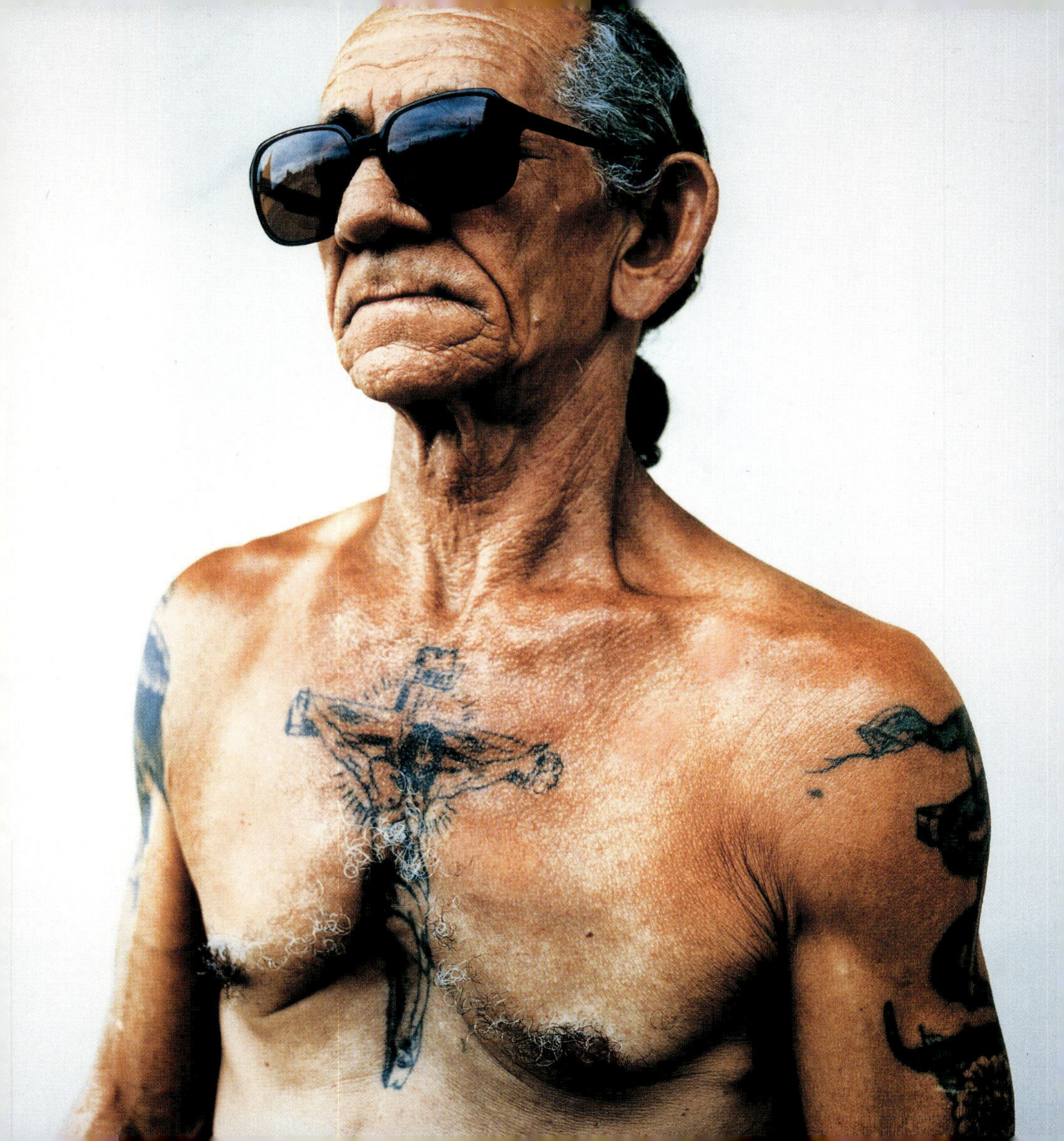

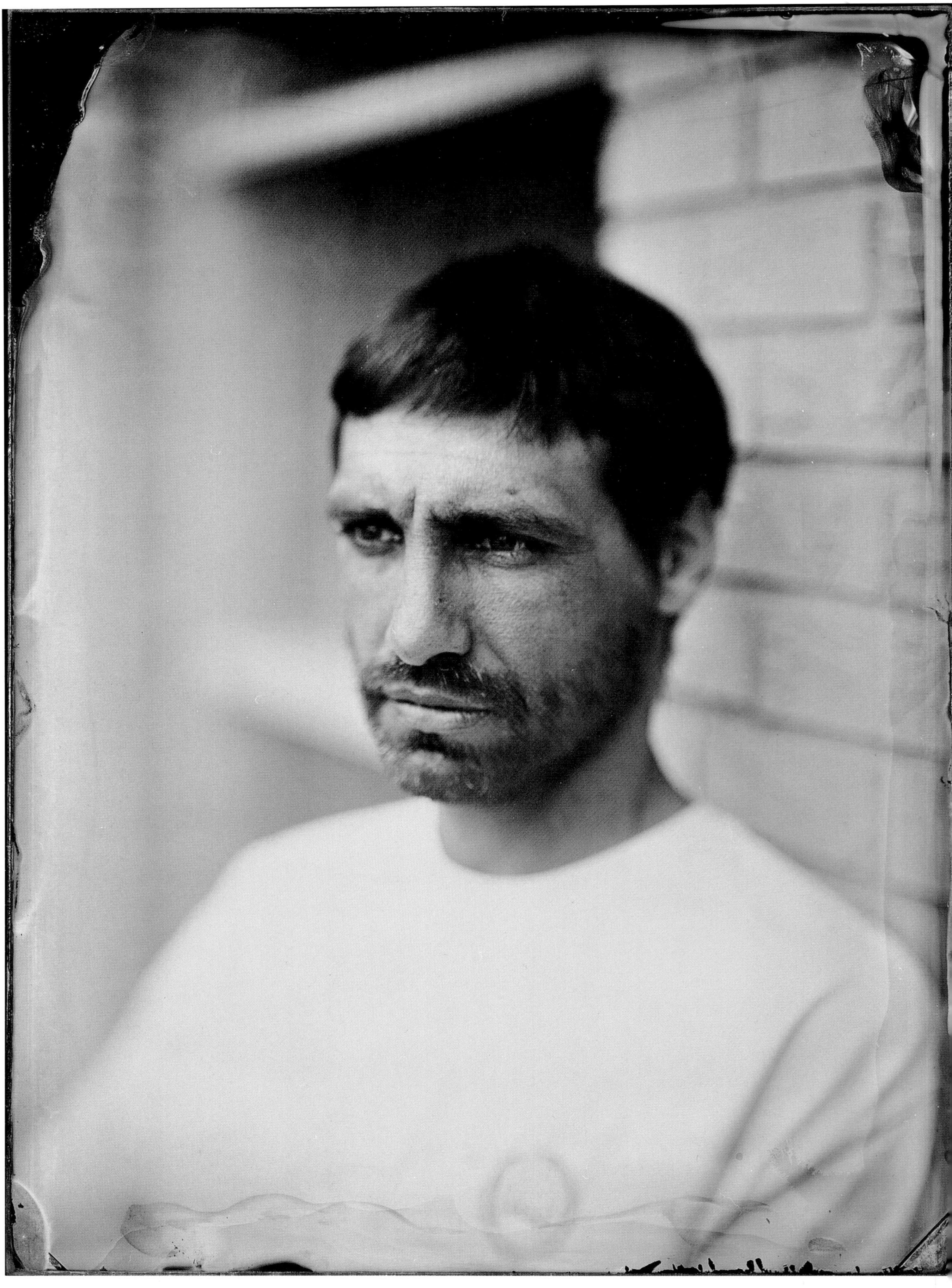

Dale Bernstein

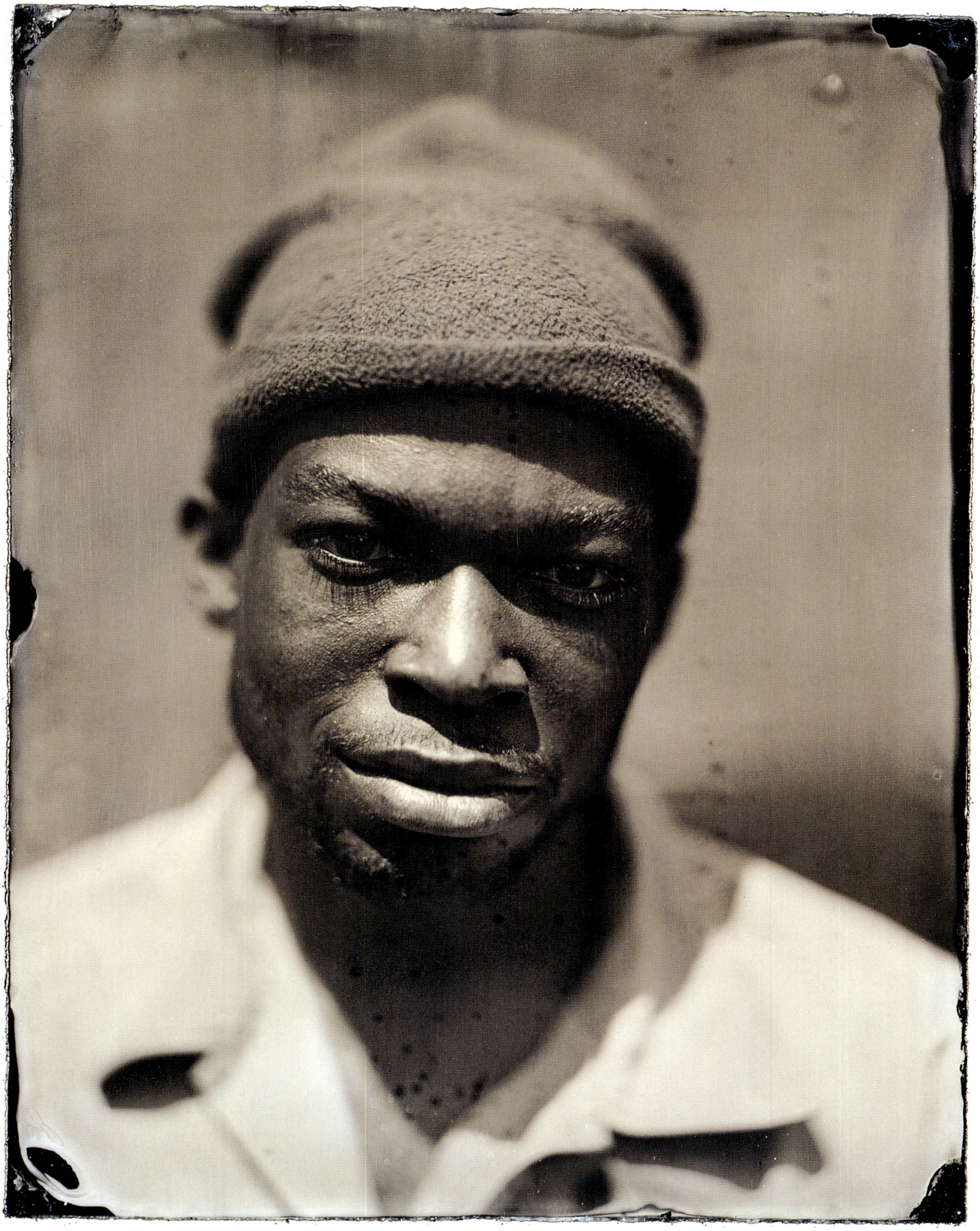

Dale Bernstein

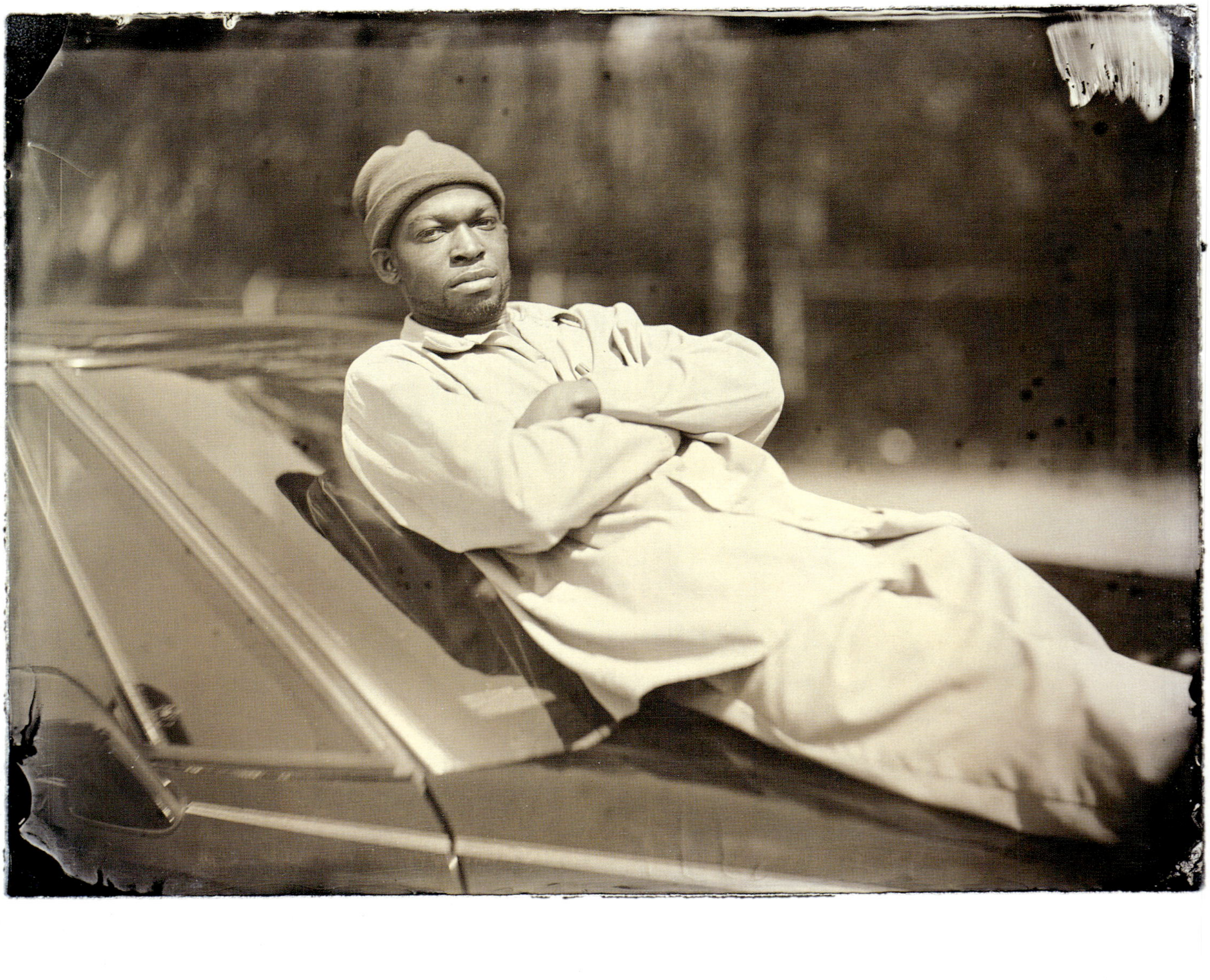

Dale Bernstein

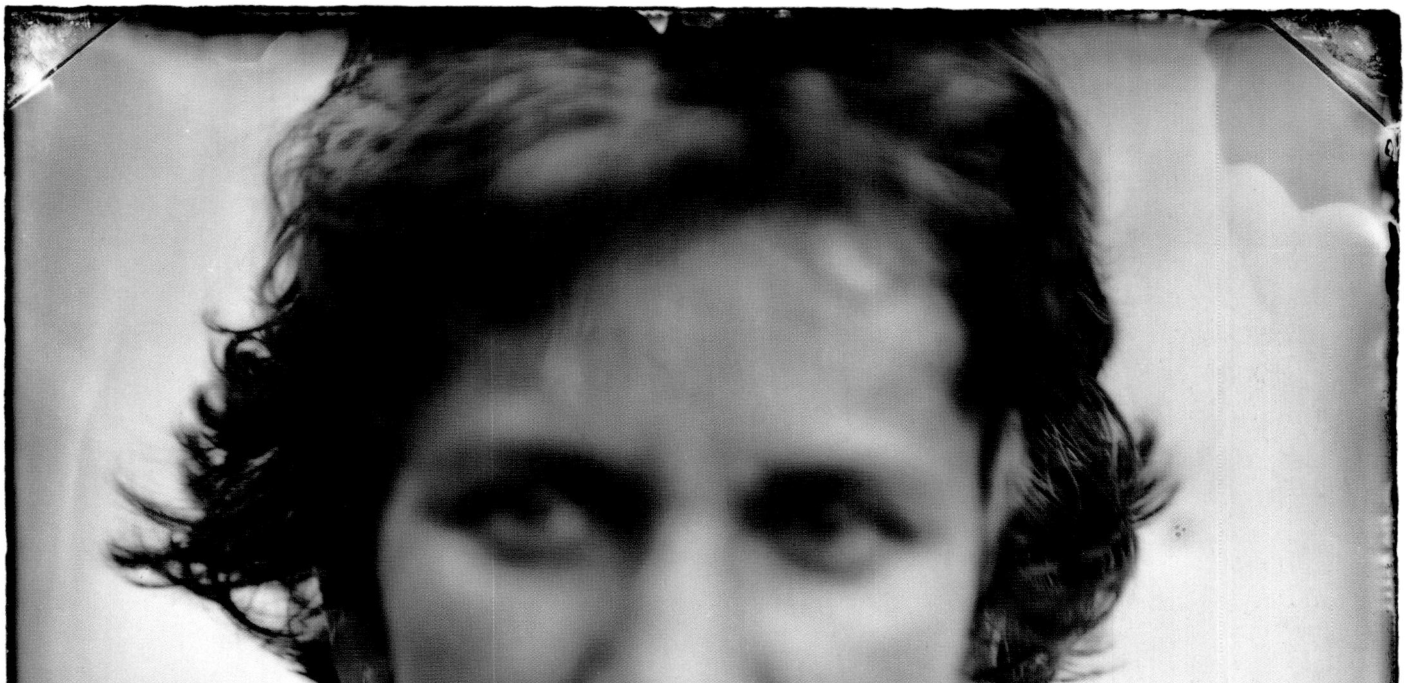

Dale Bernstein

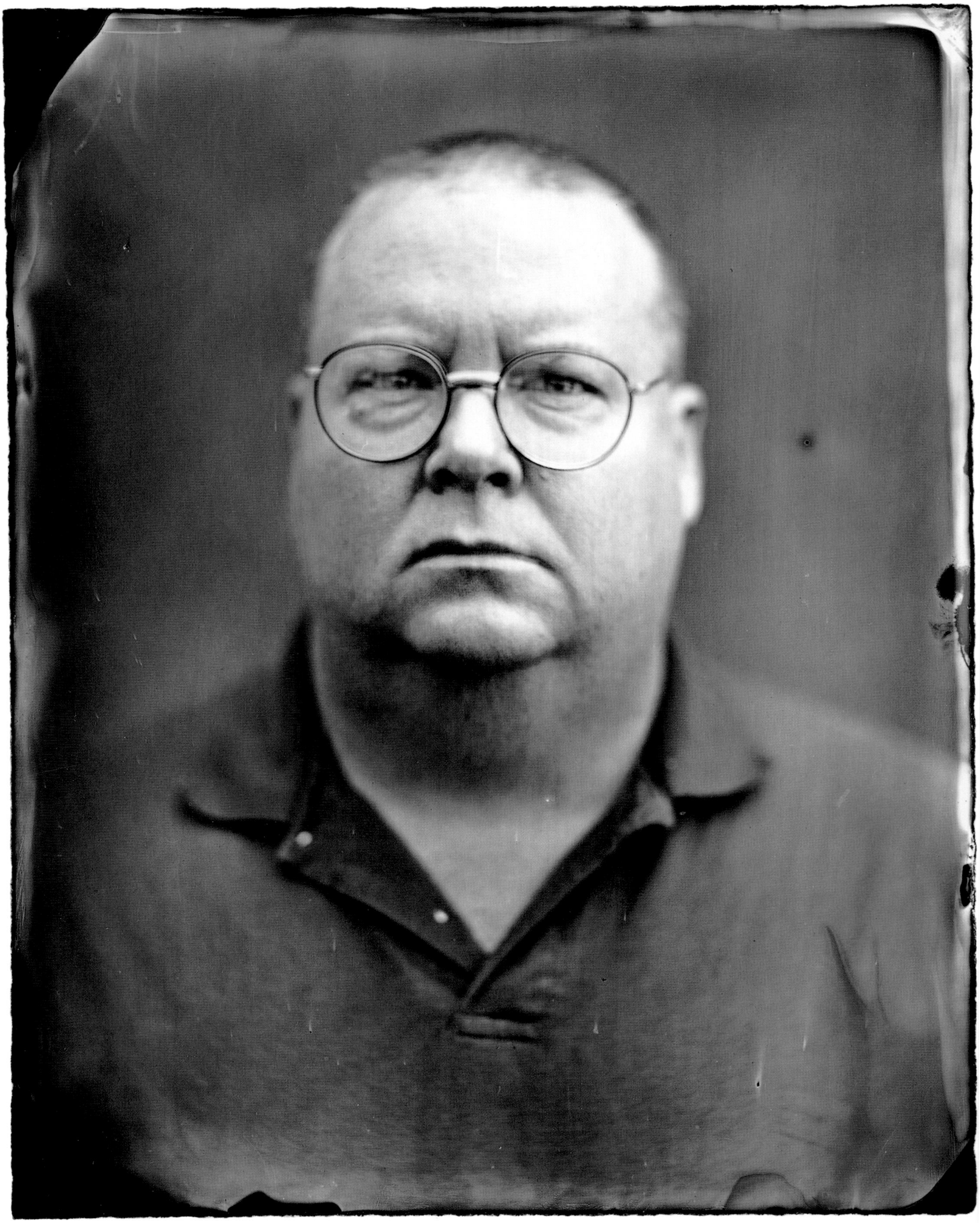

Dale Bernstein

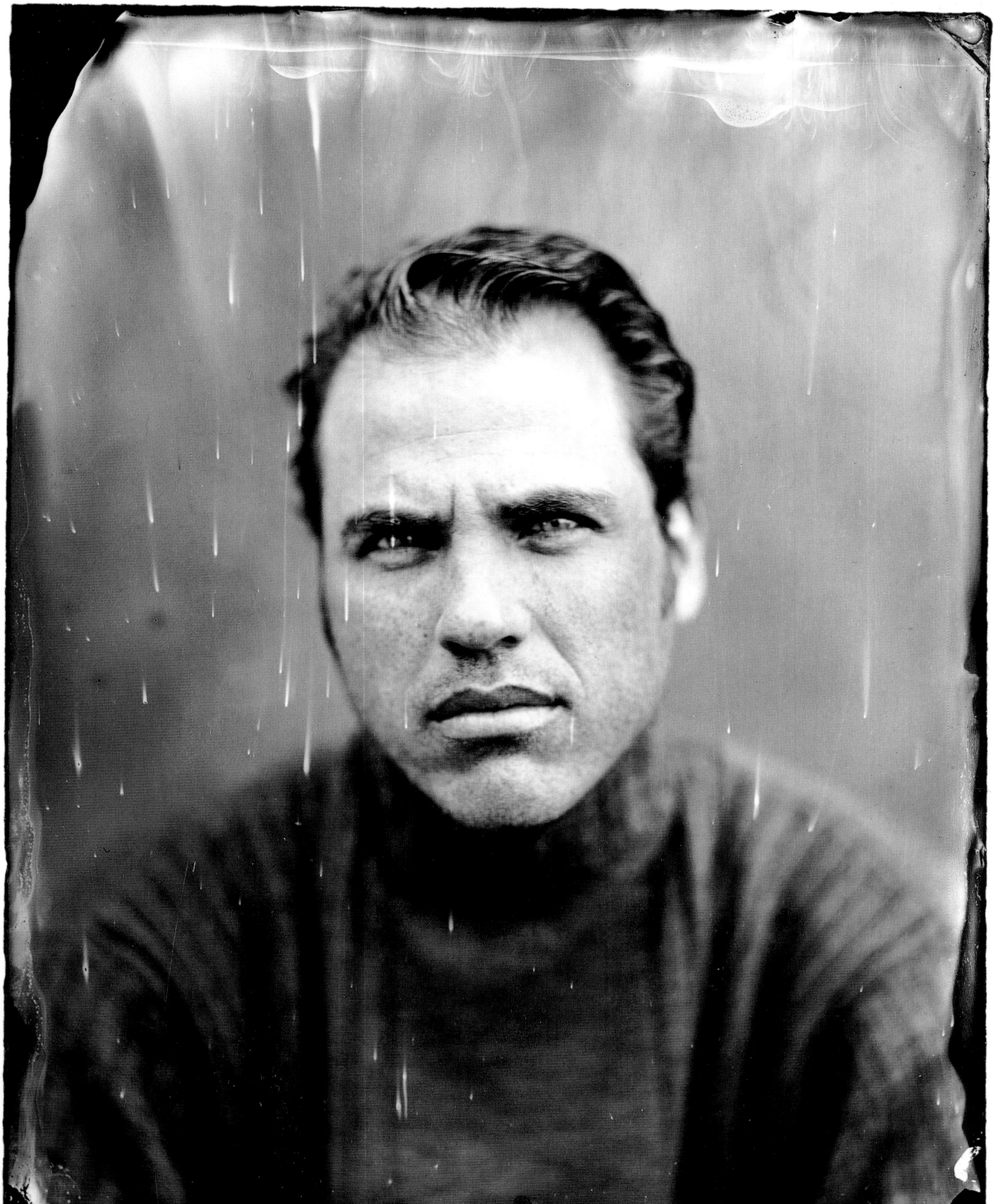

Dale Bernstein

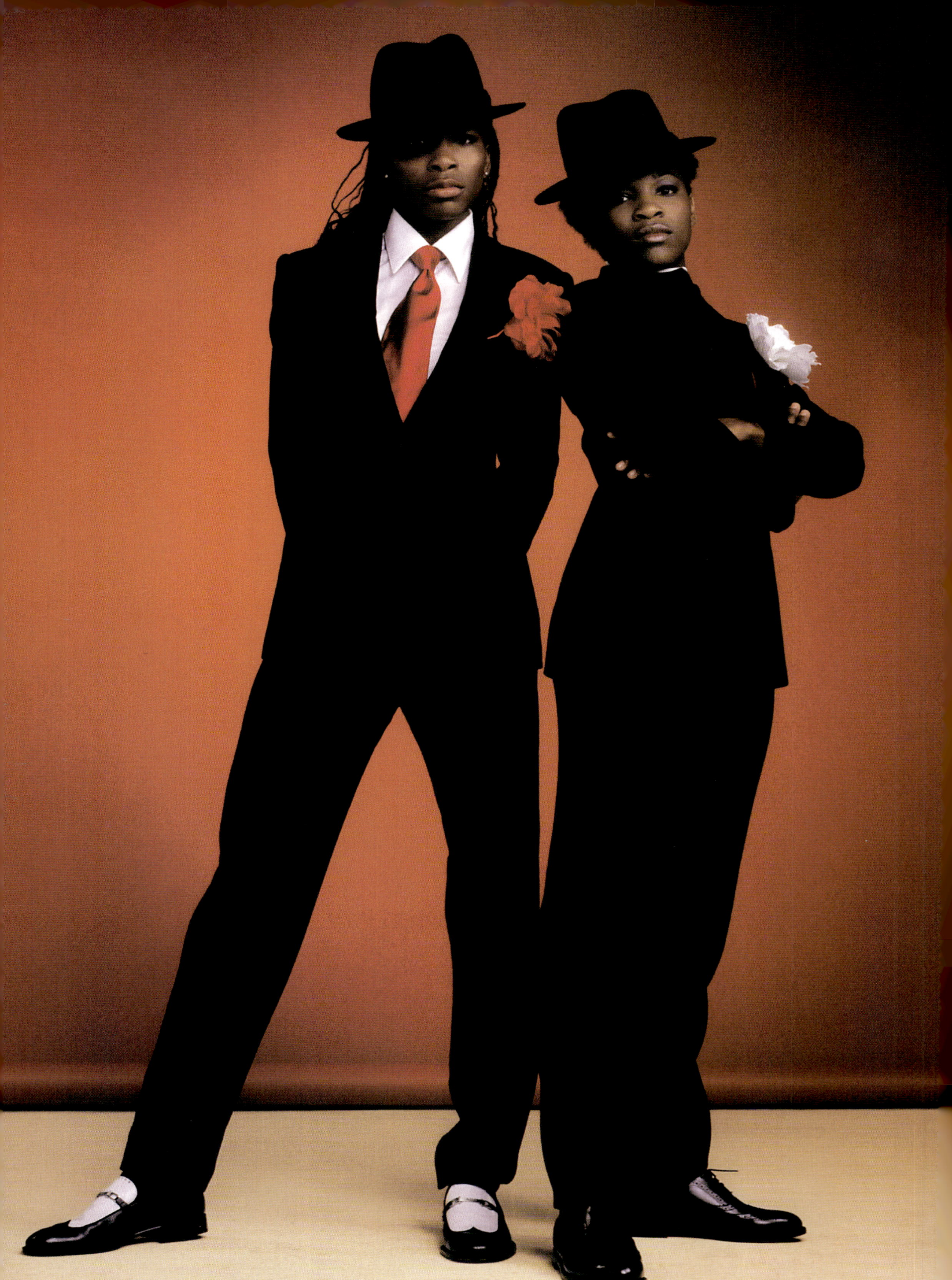

Howard Schatz

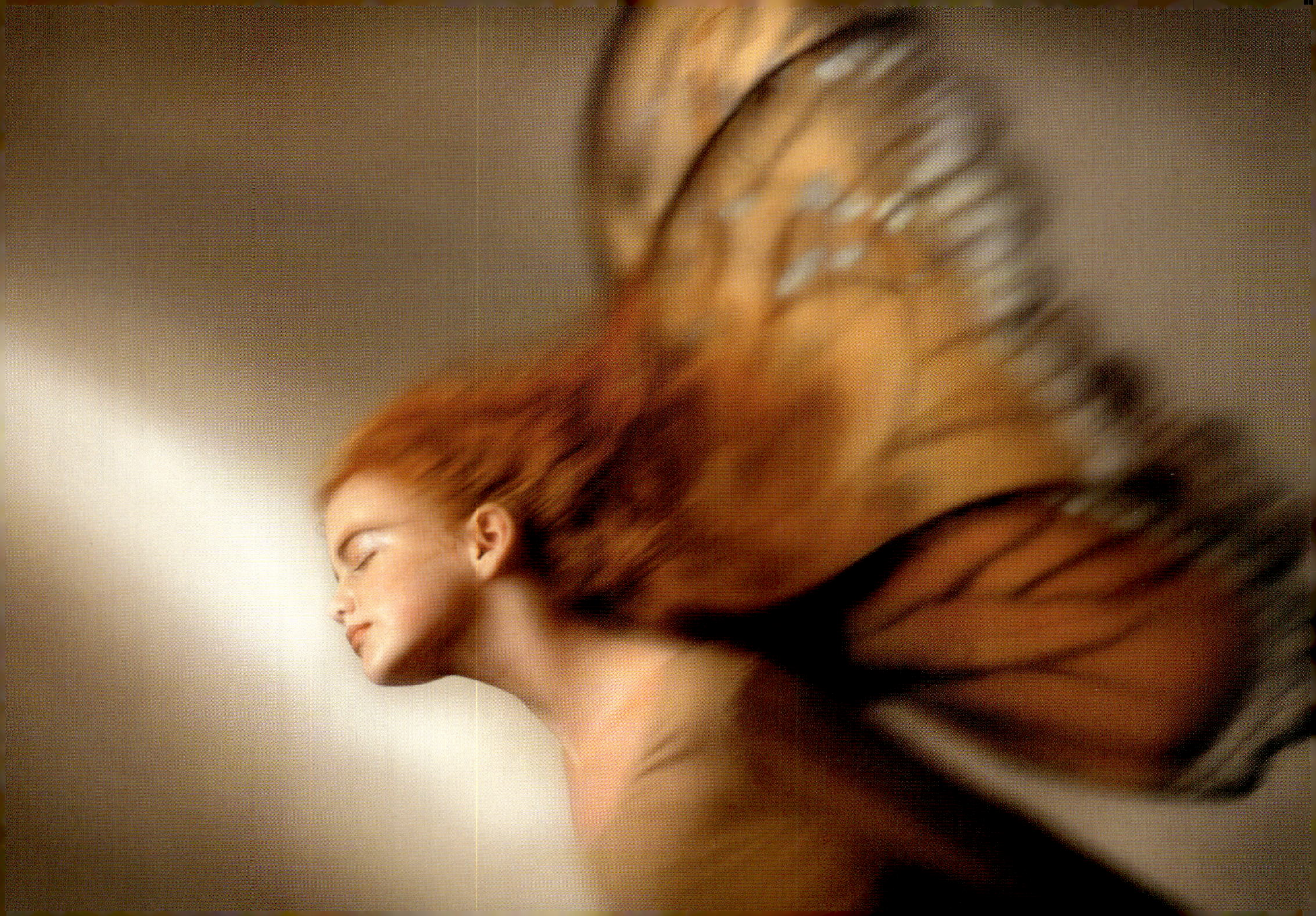

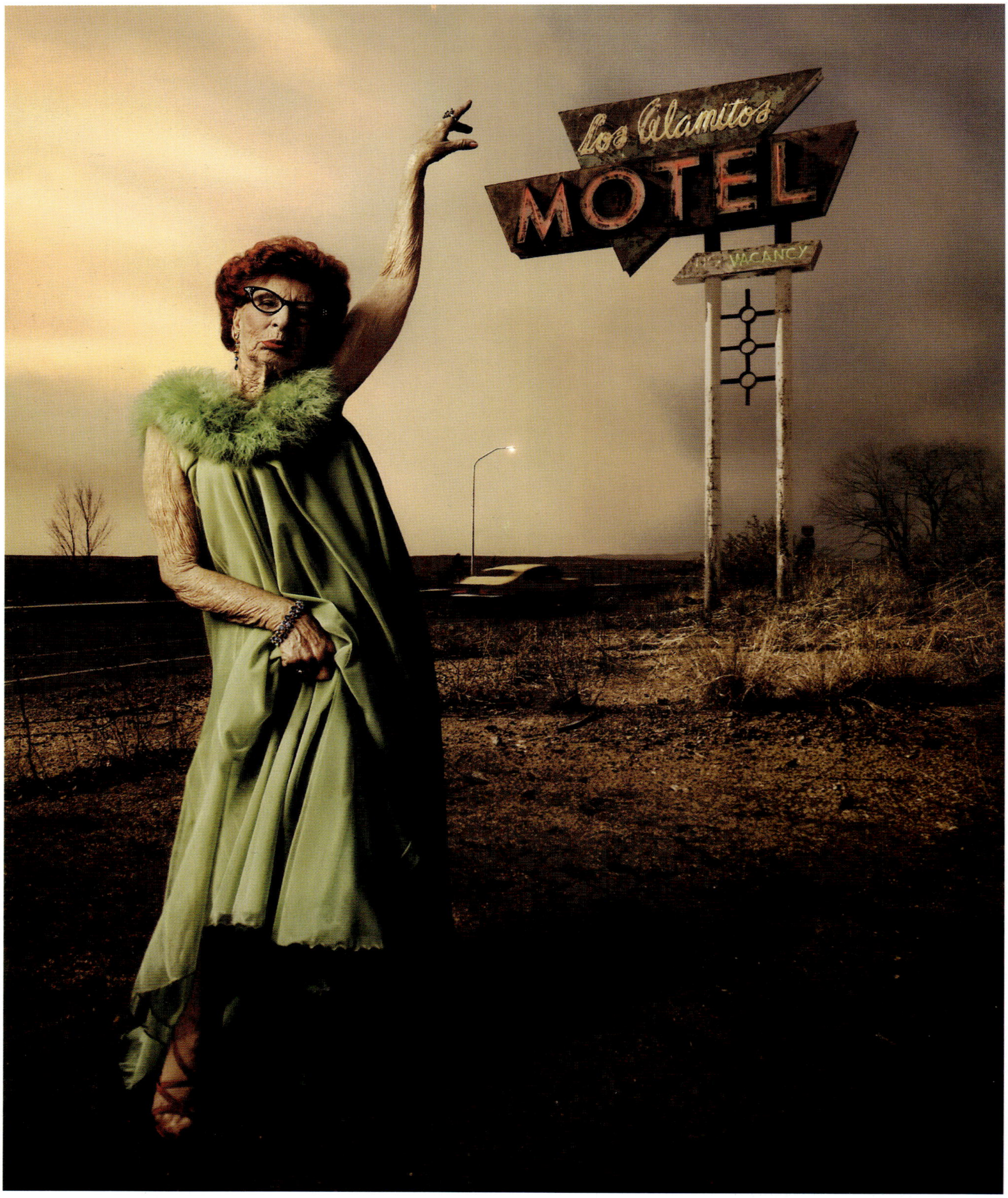

Jim Fiscus (opposite) Cindy James

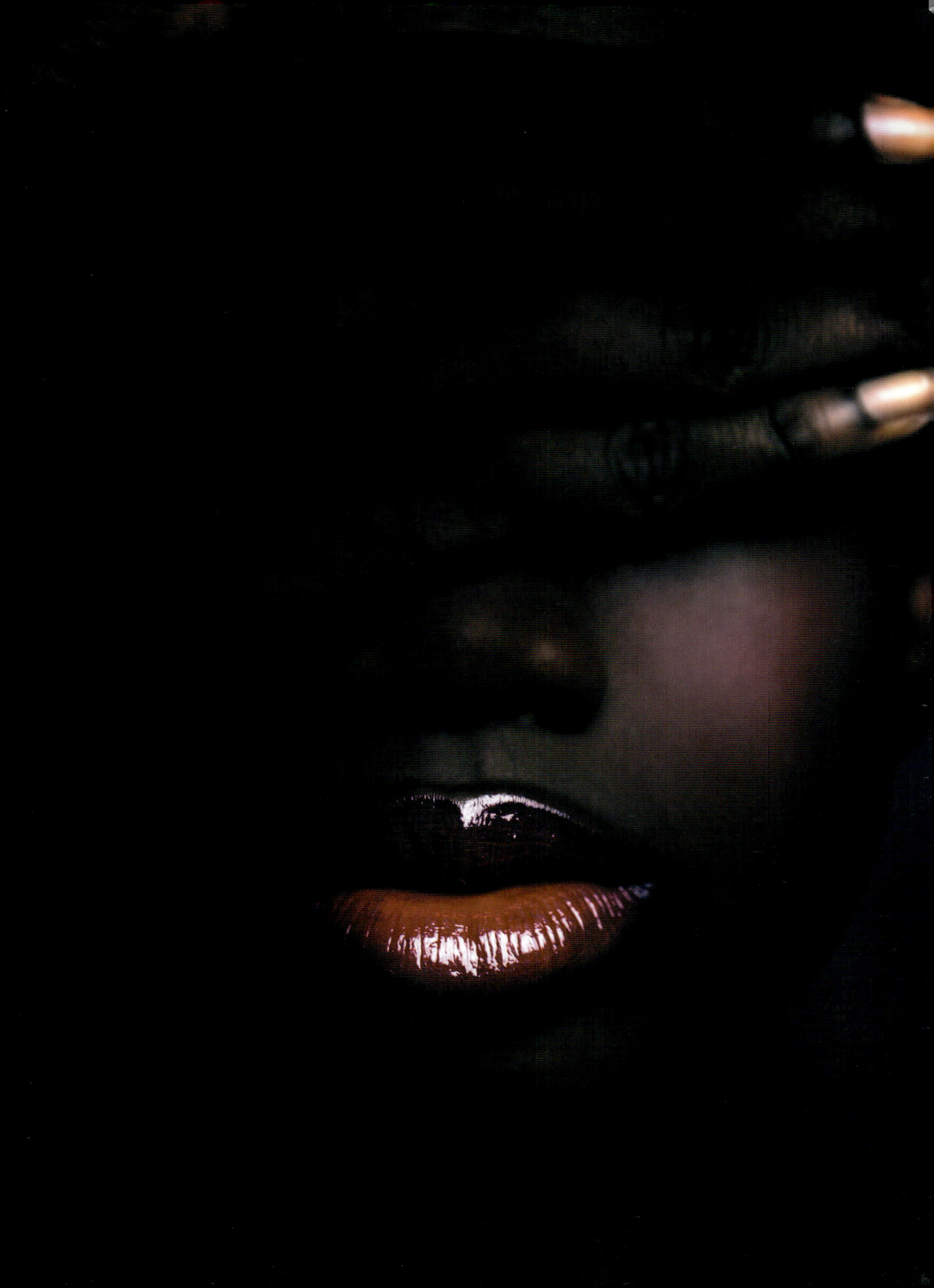

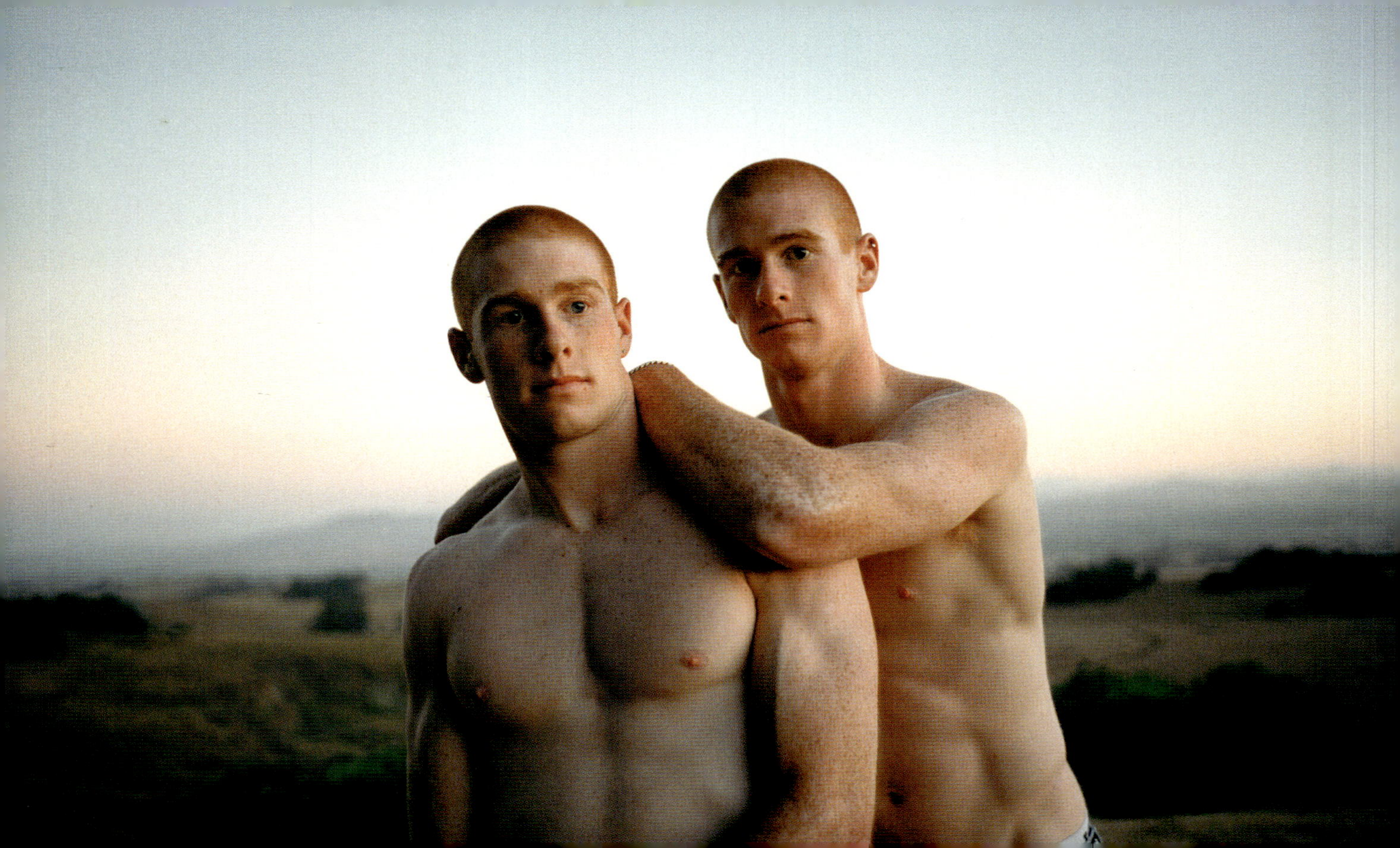

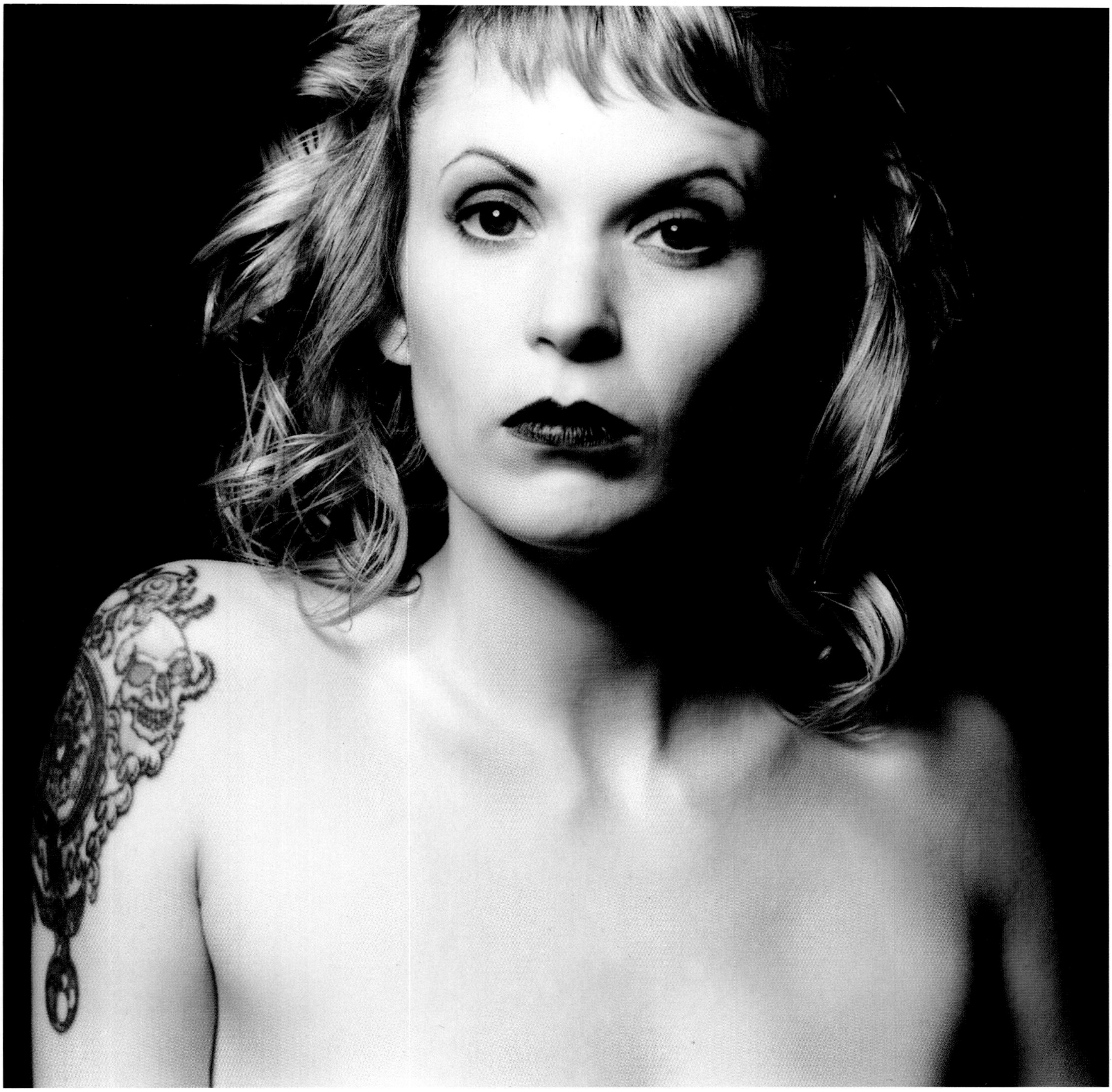

Ken Villeneuve

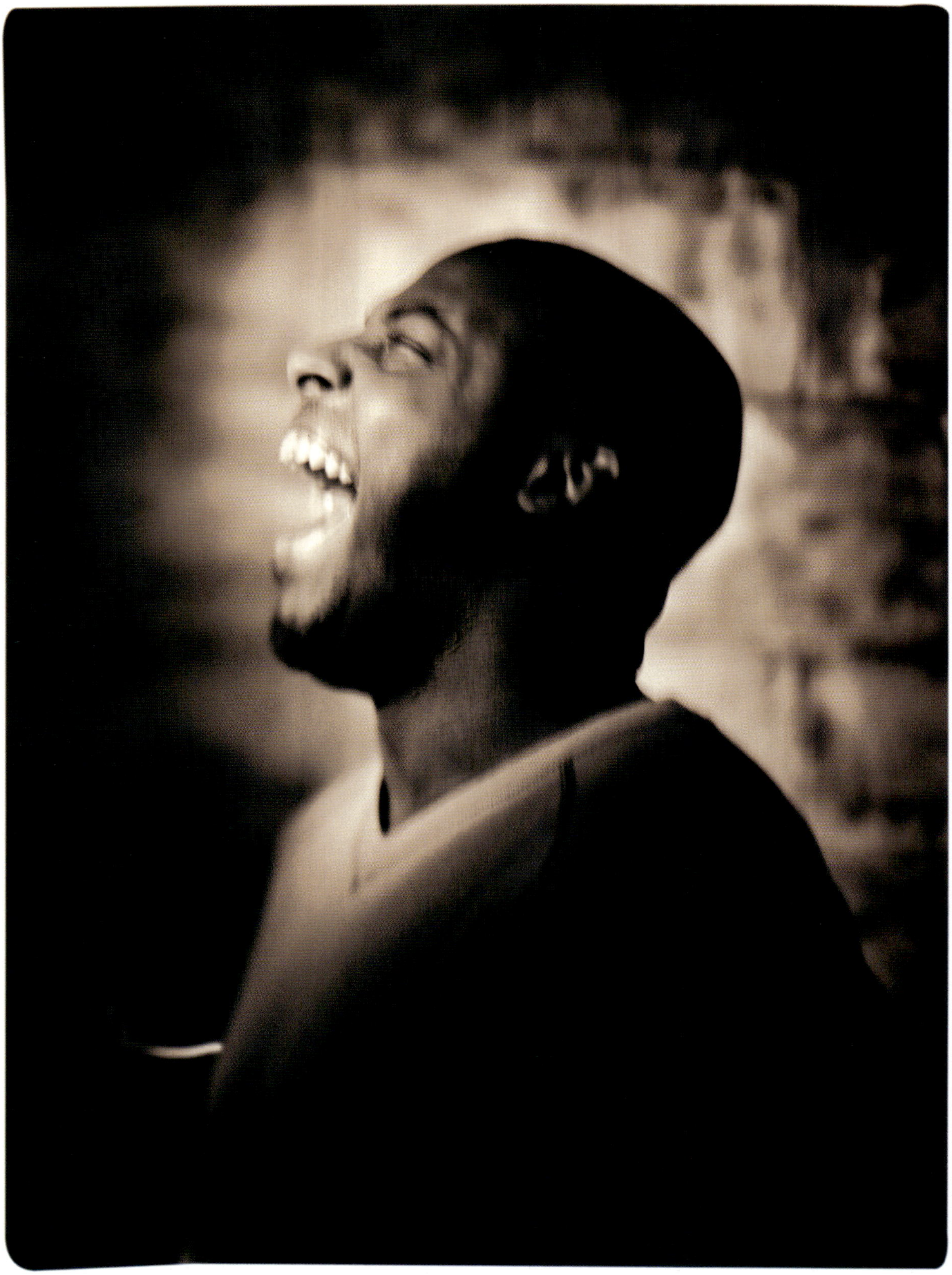

Lars Topelmann (opposite) Sean W. Hennessy

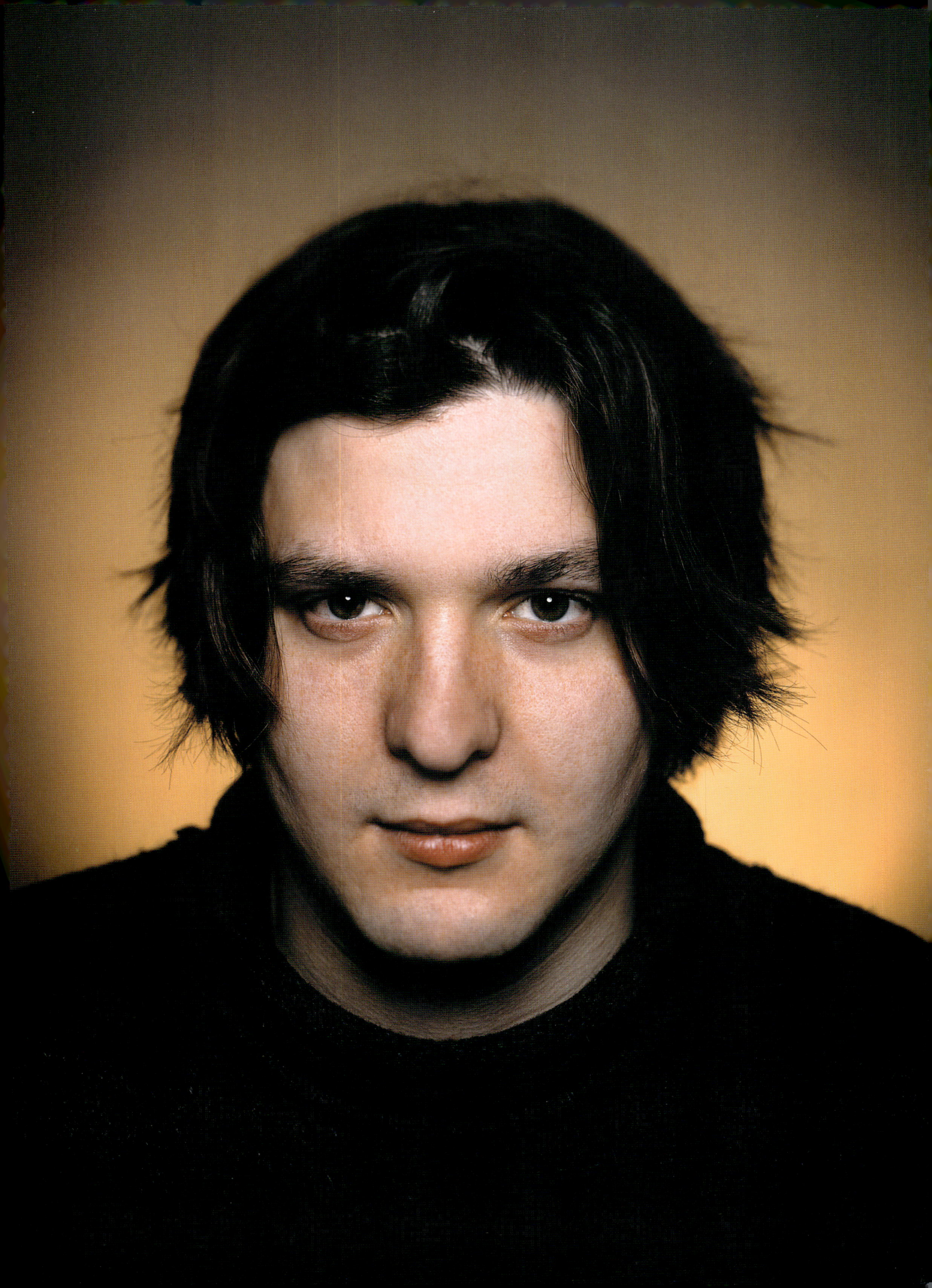

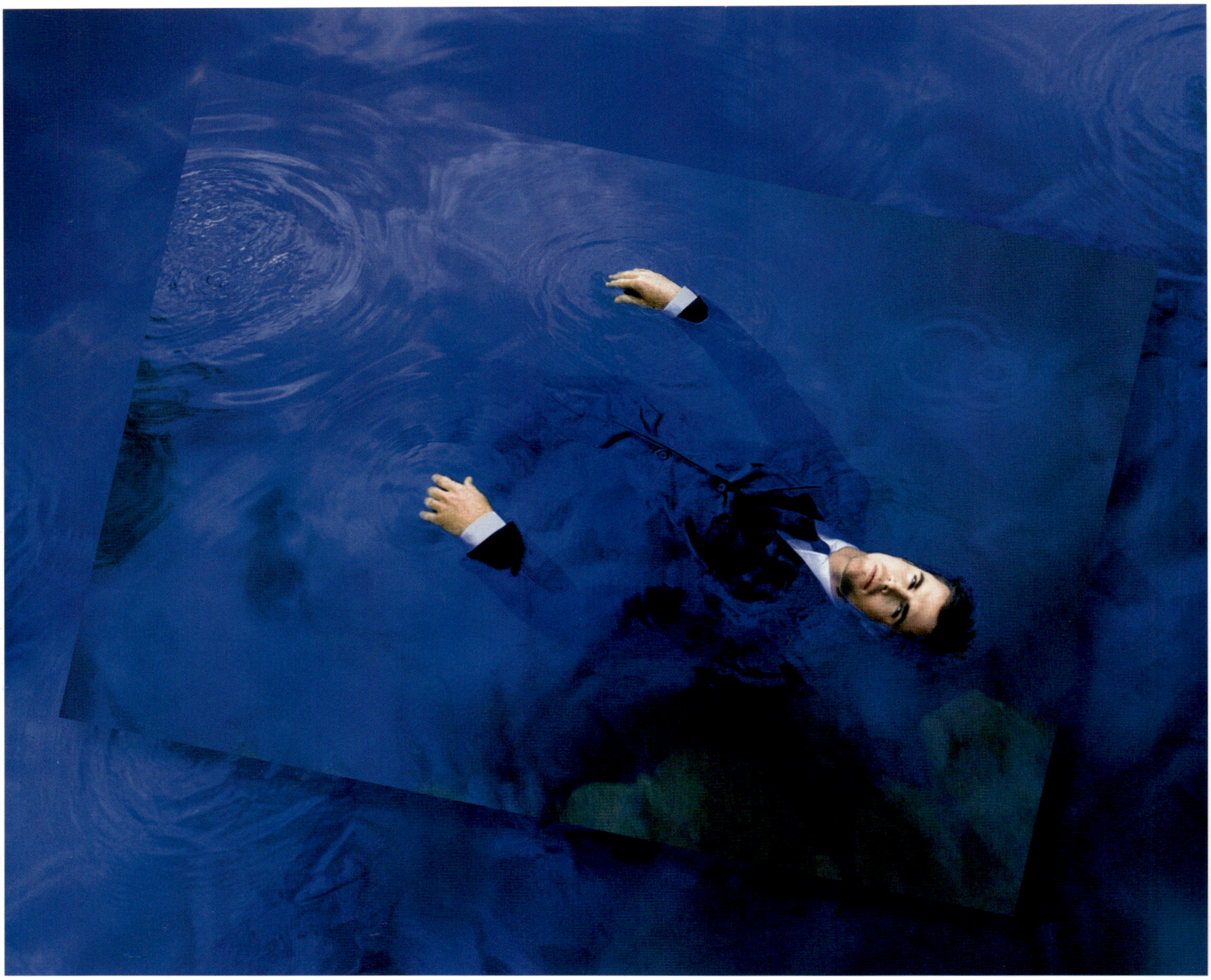

Parish Kohanim

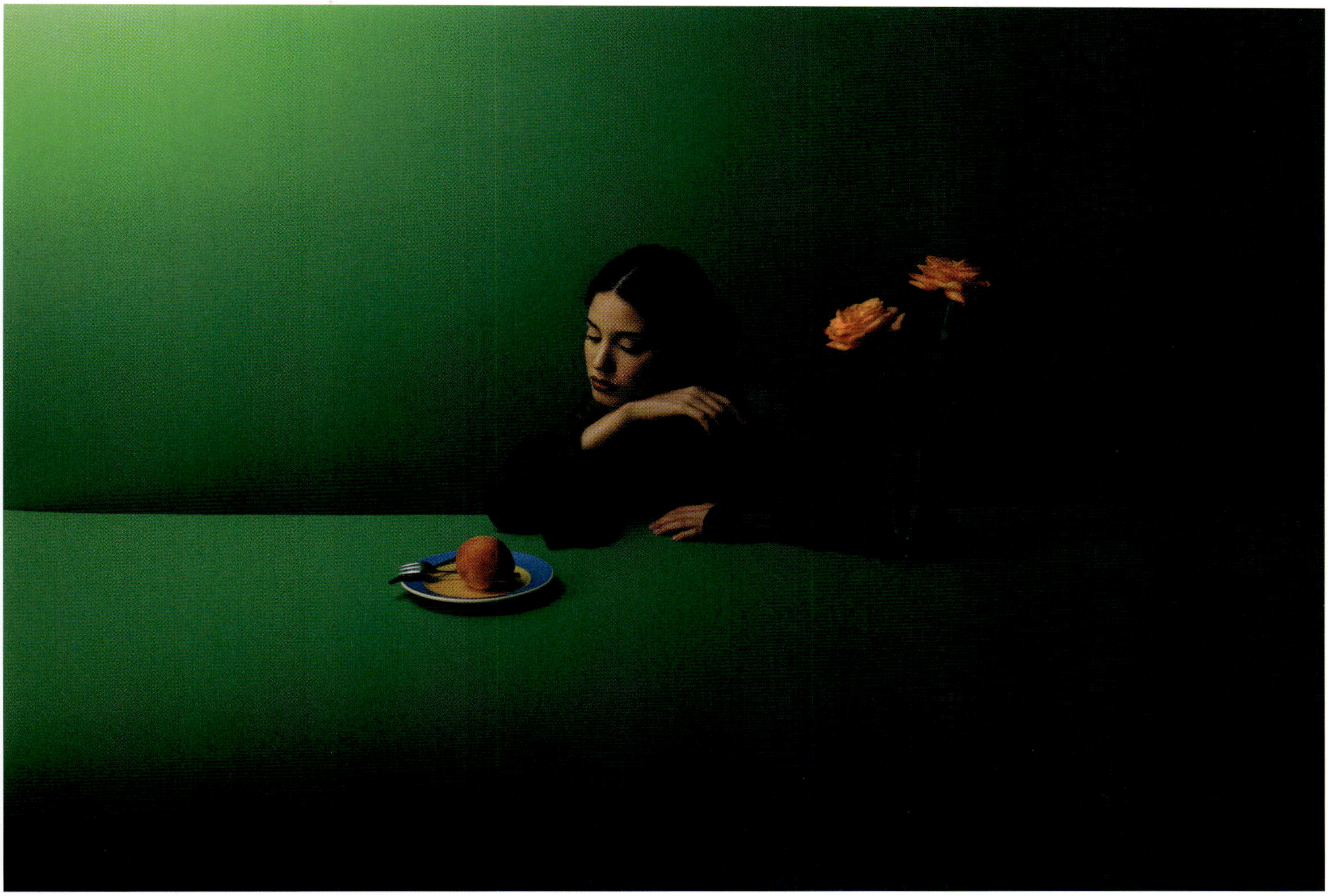

Parish Kohanim

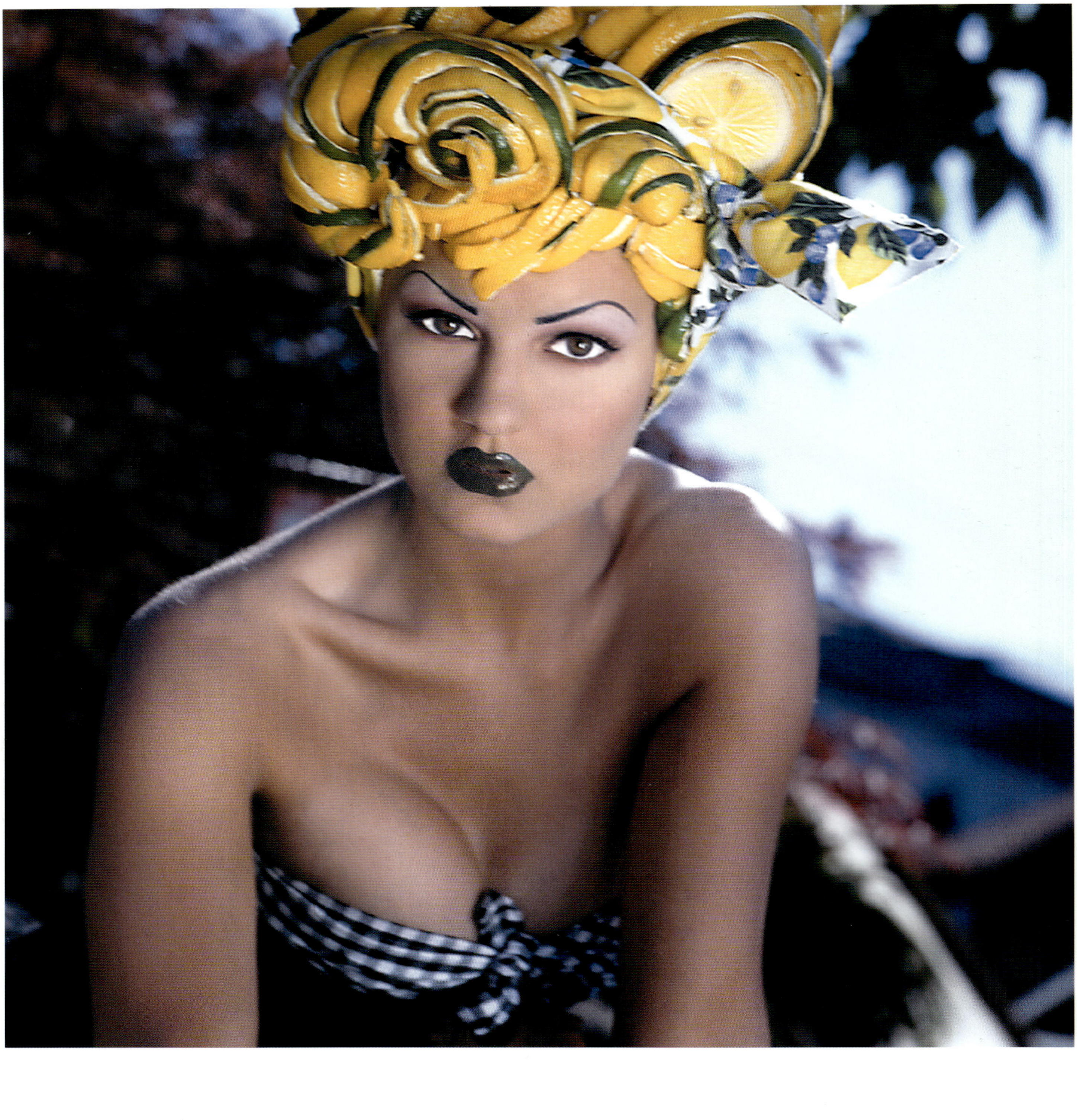

Danelle Dalpra

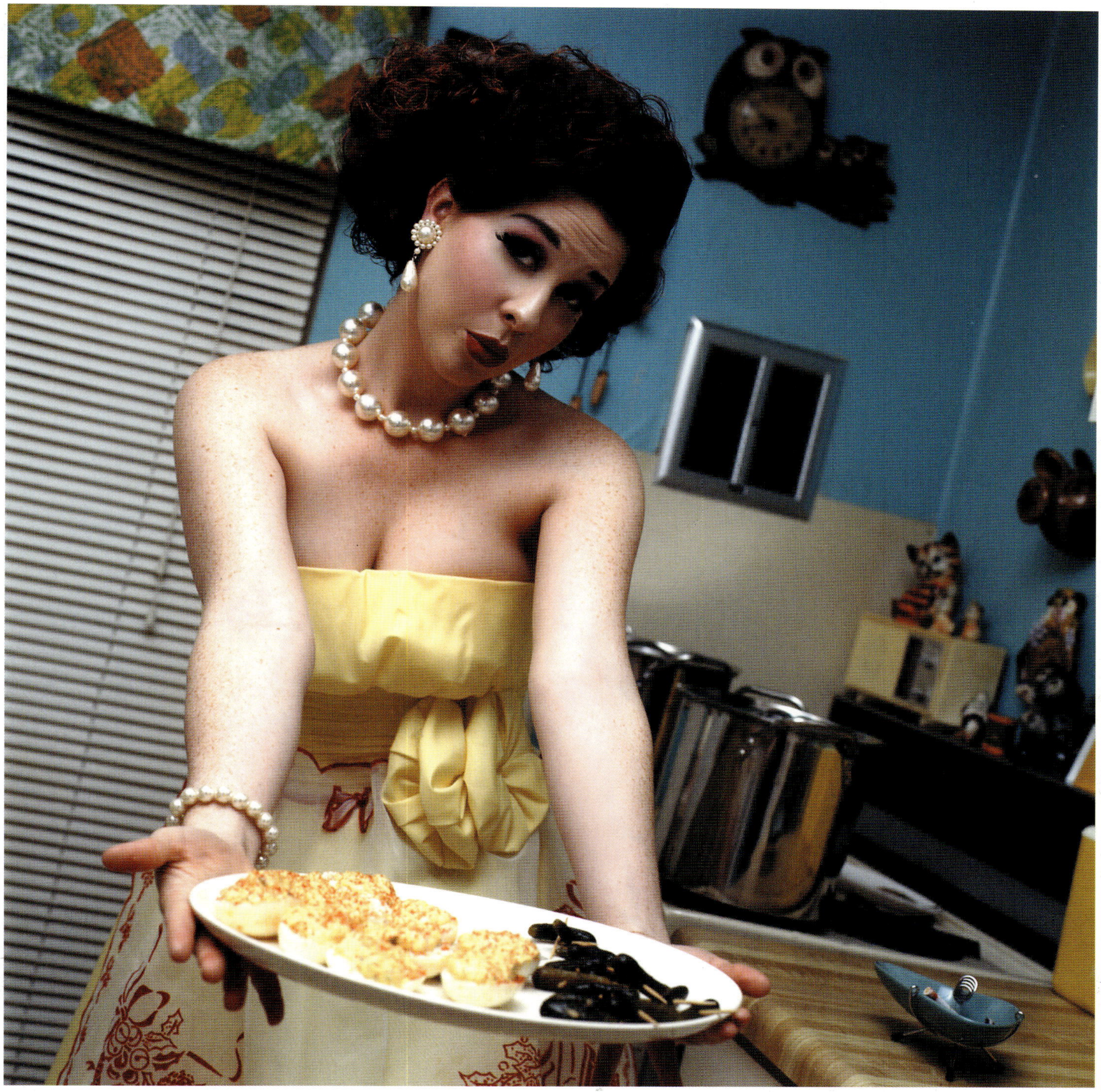

Danelle Dalpra

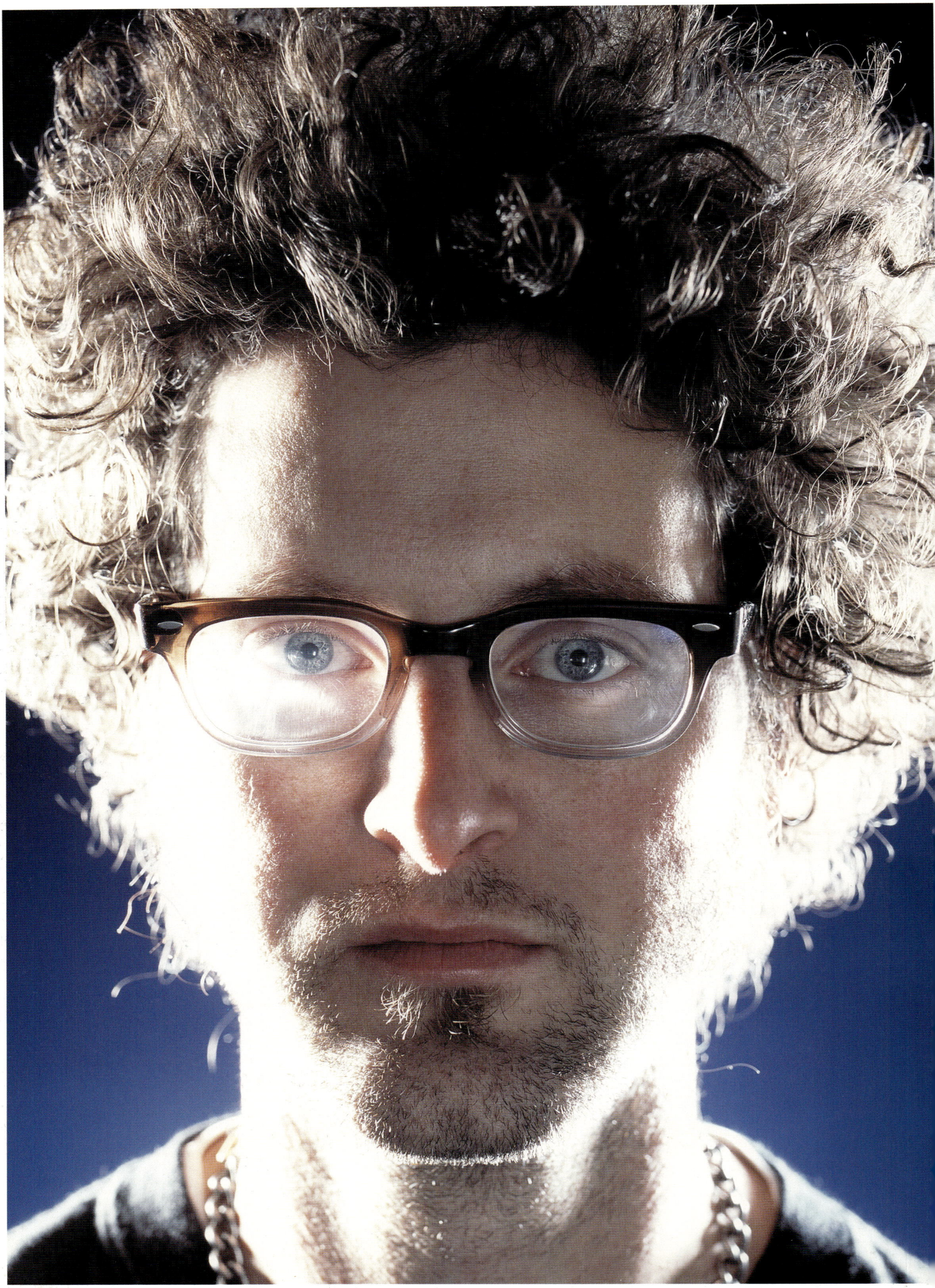

Rob Stephen

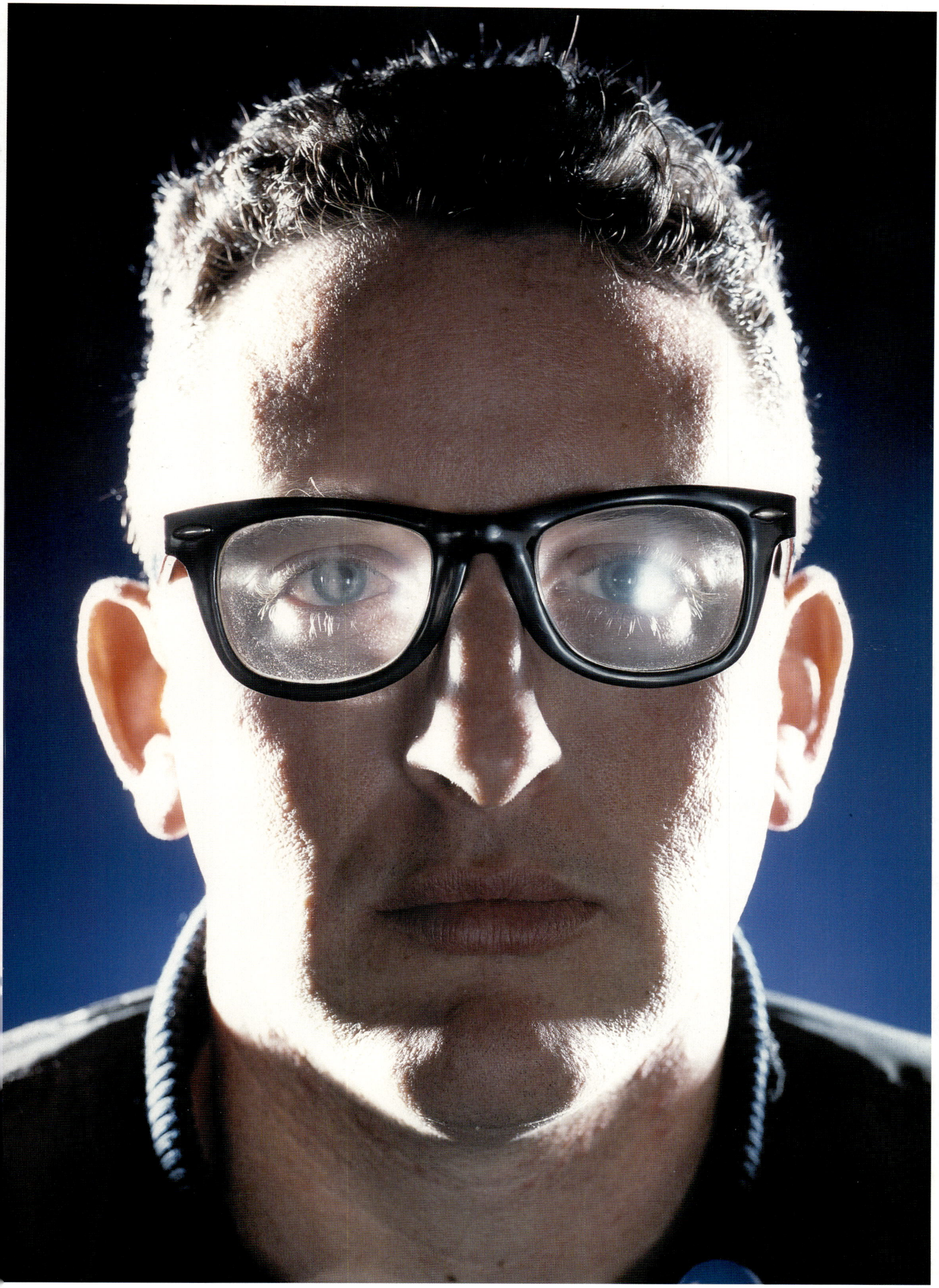

Rob Stephen

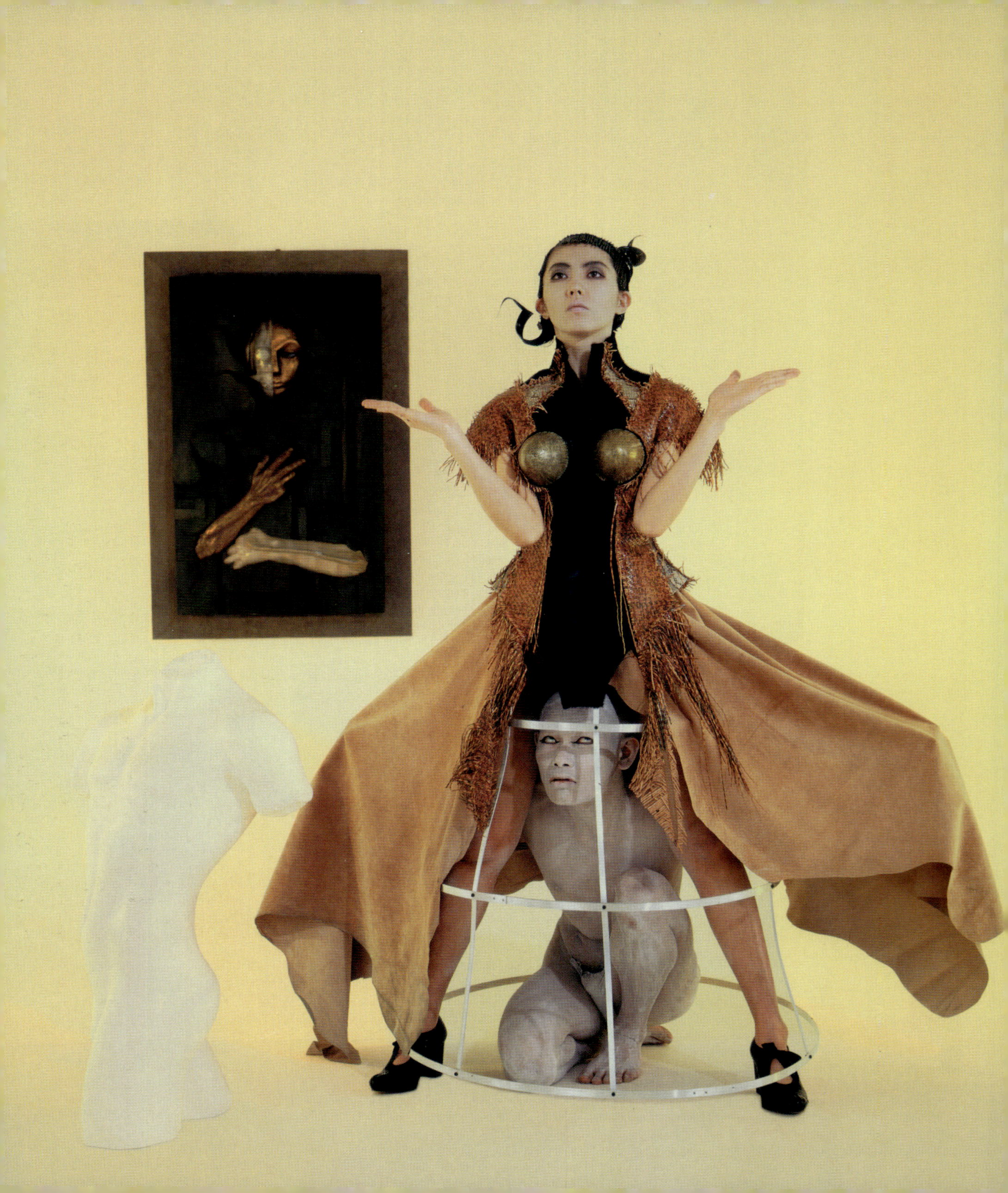

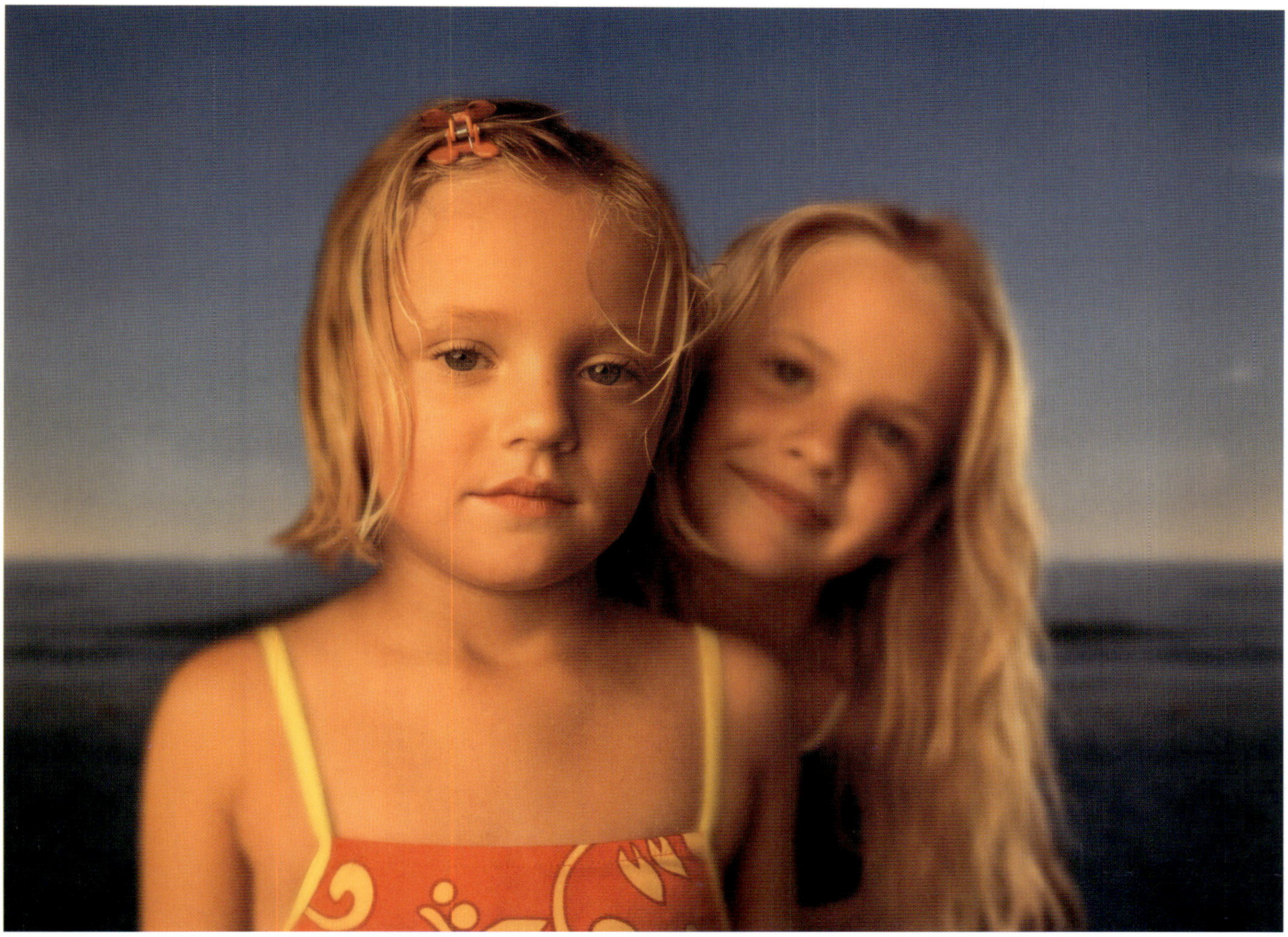

Jimmy Williams

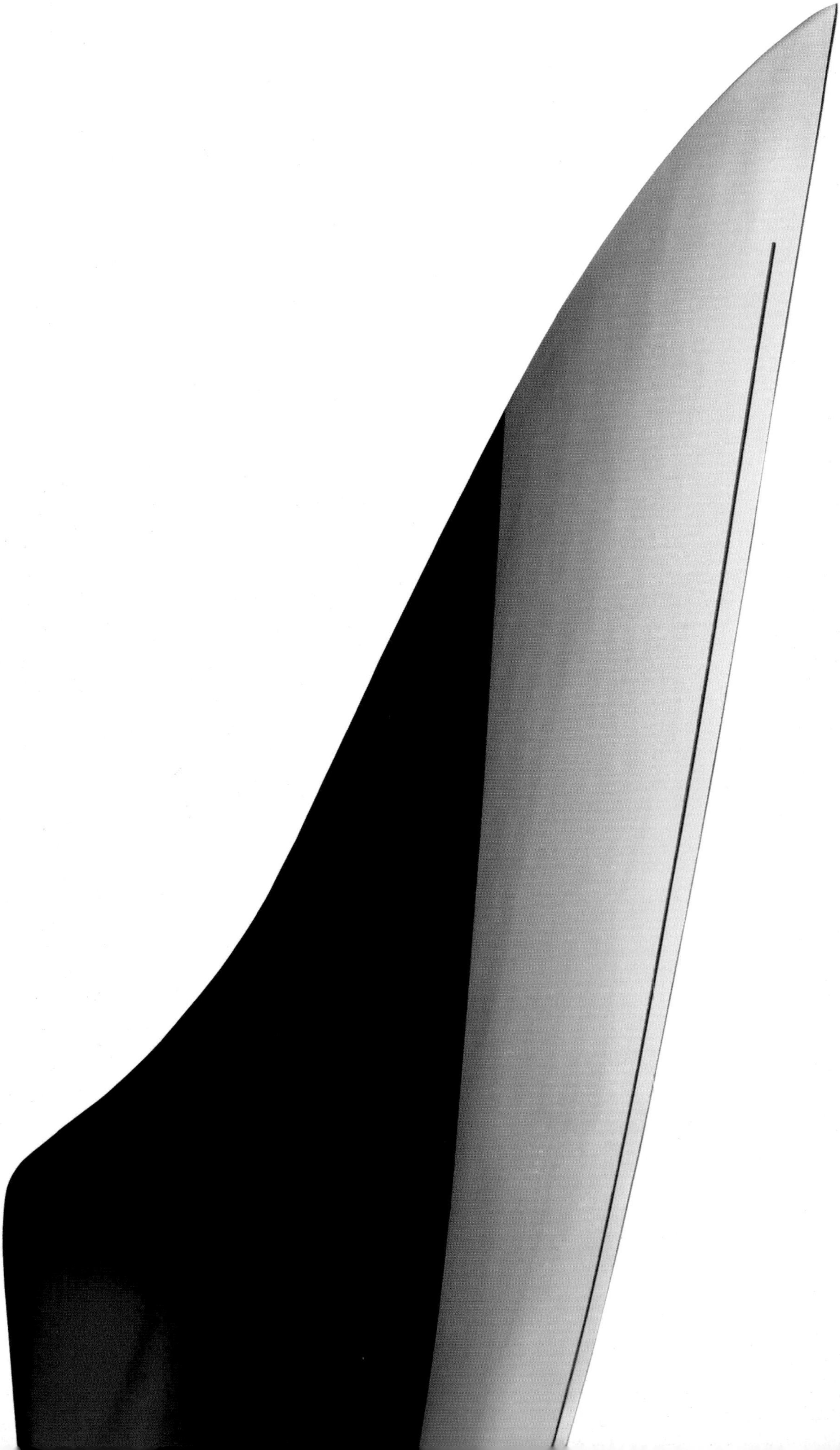

Products

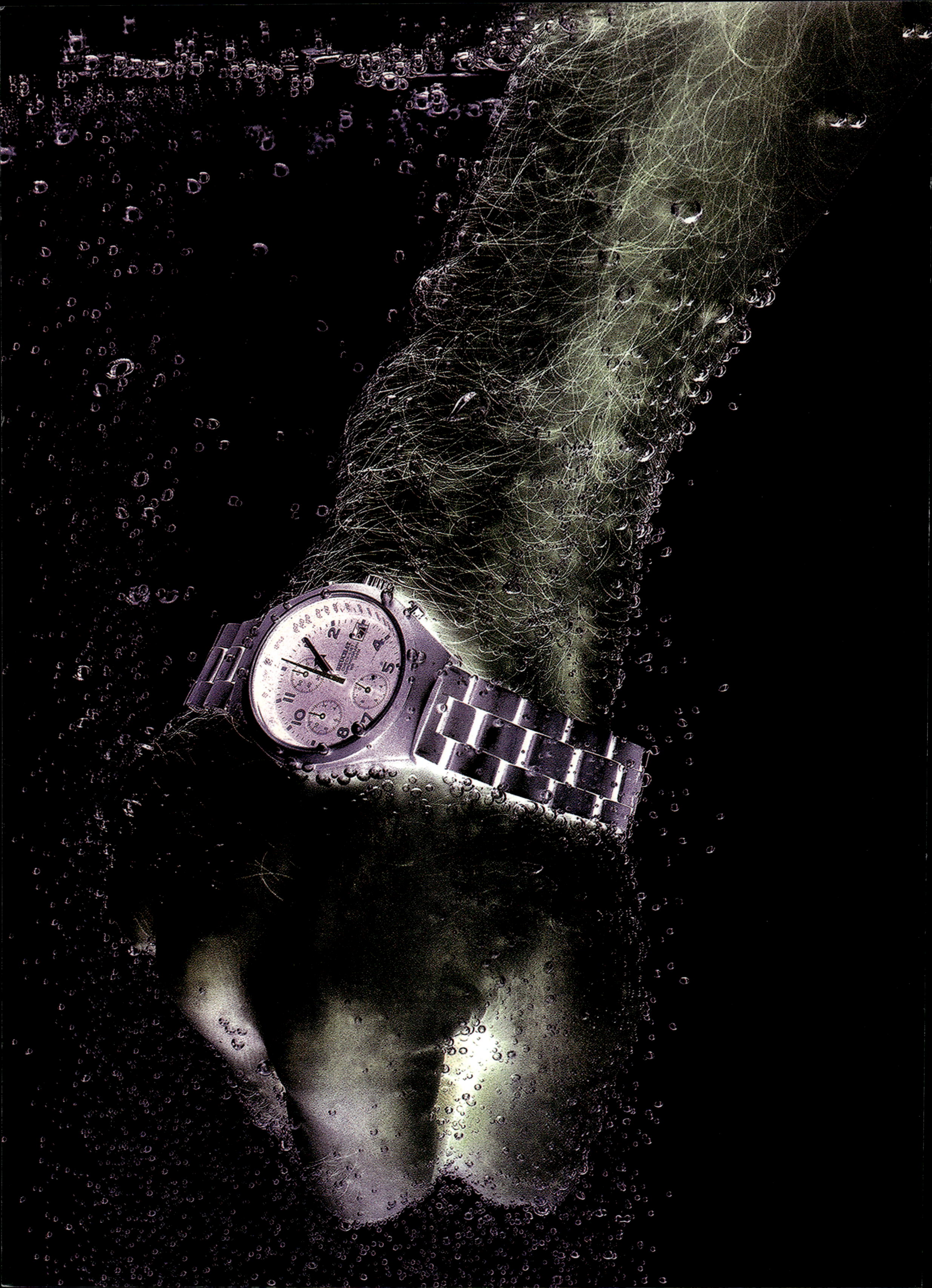

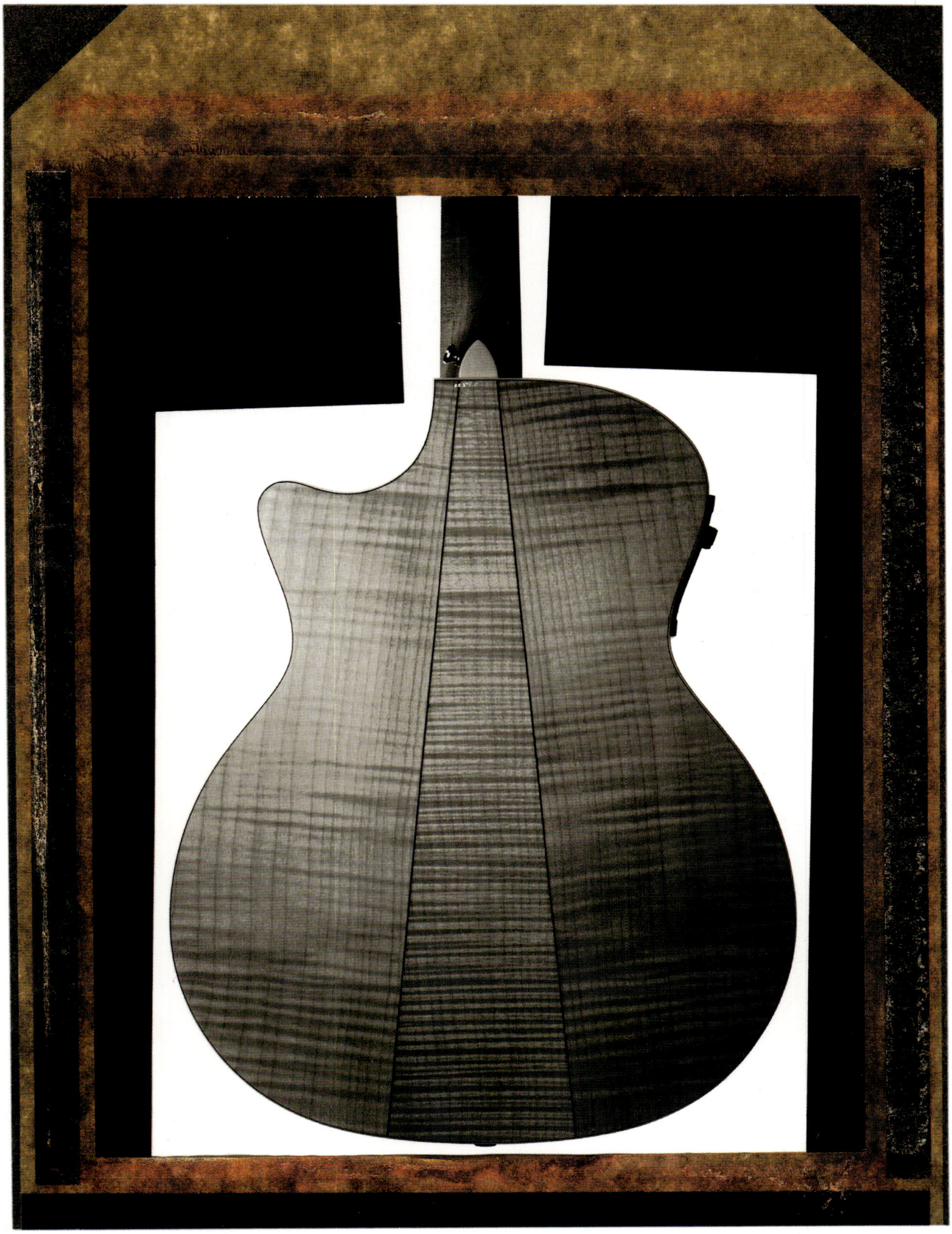

Marshall Harrington (opening page) Fabrizio Ferri (opposite) Eric Bottero

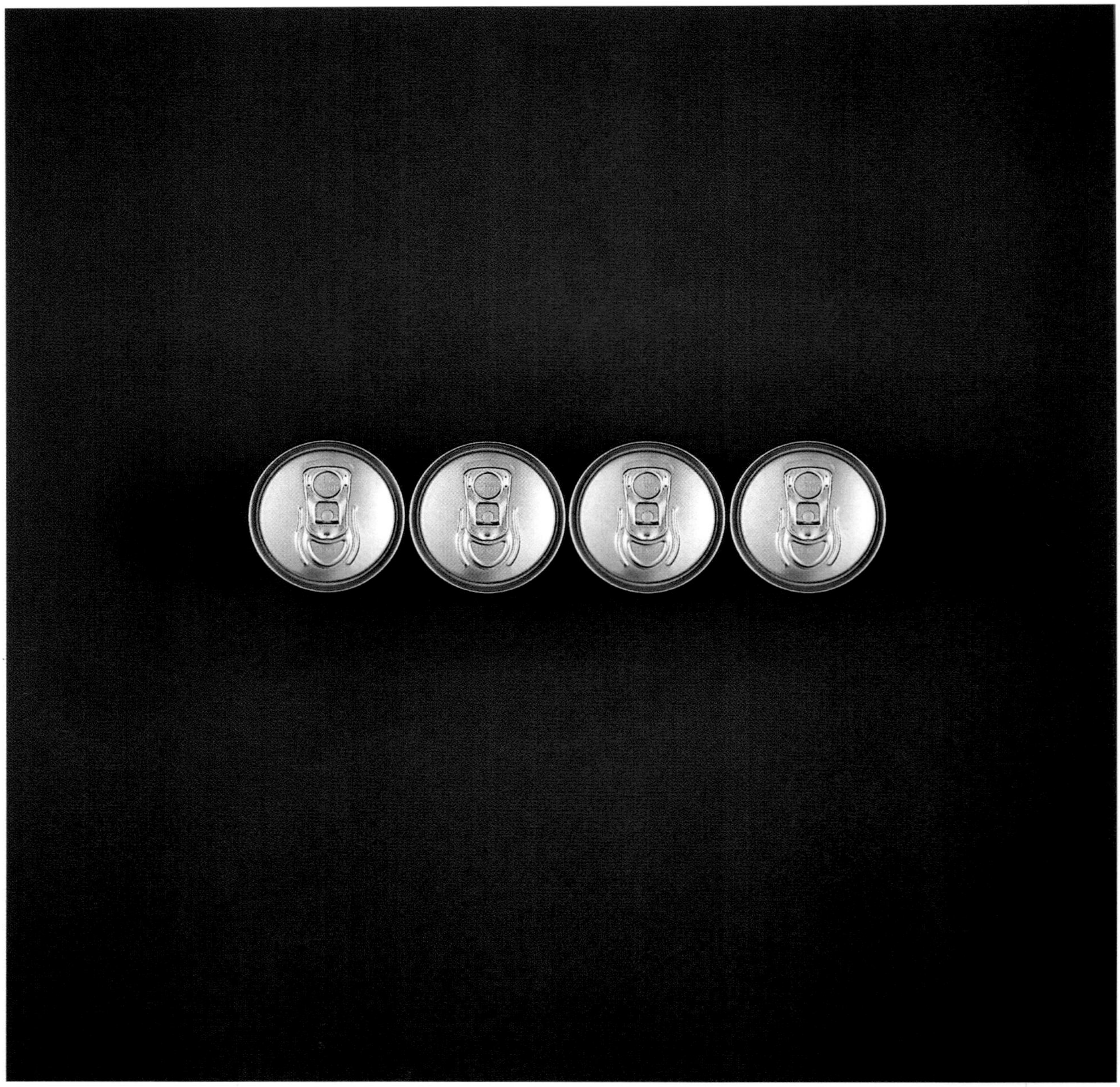

Felix Holzer

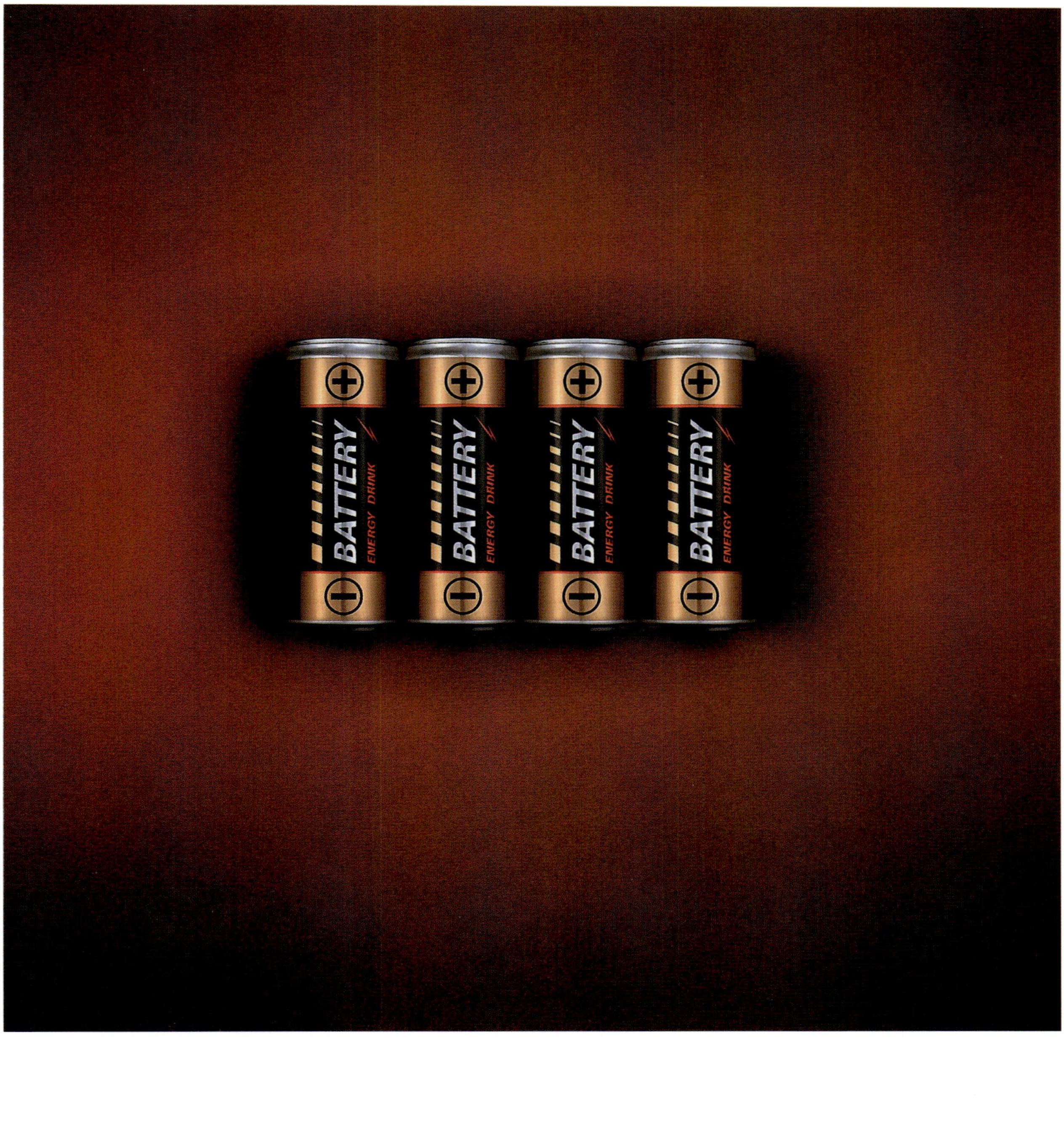

Felix Holzer

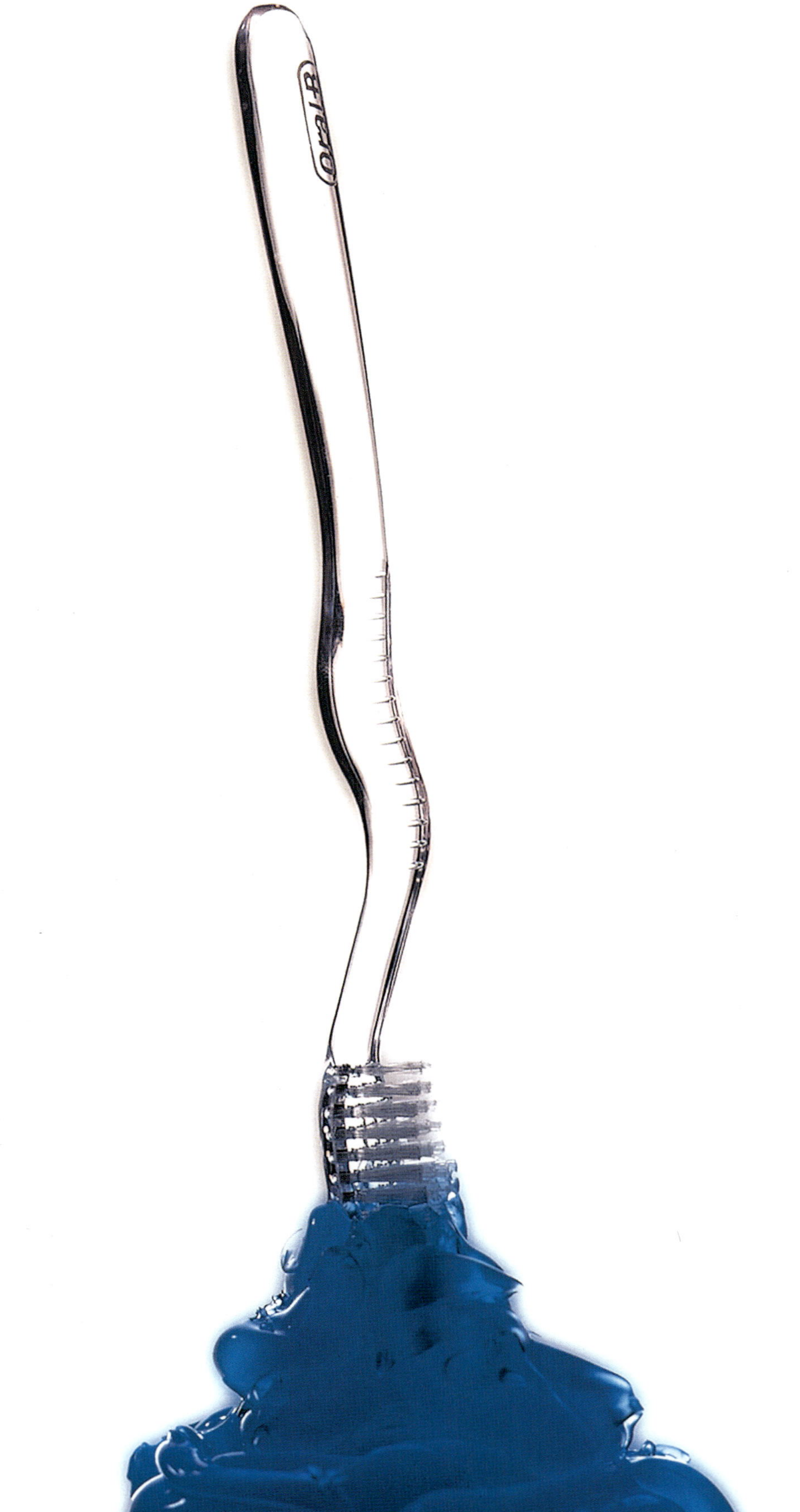
Oral-B

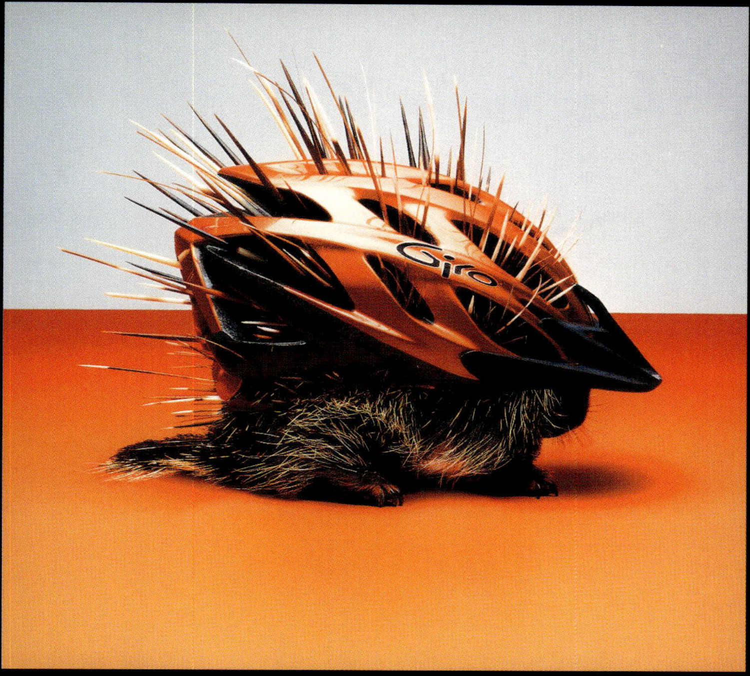

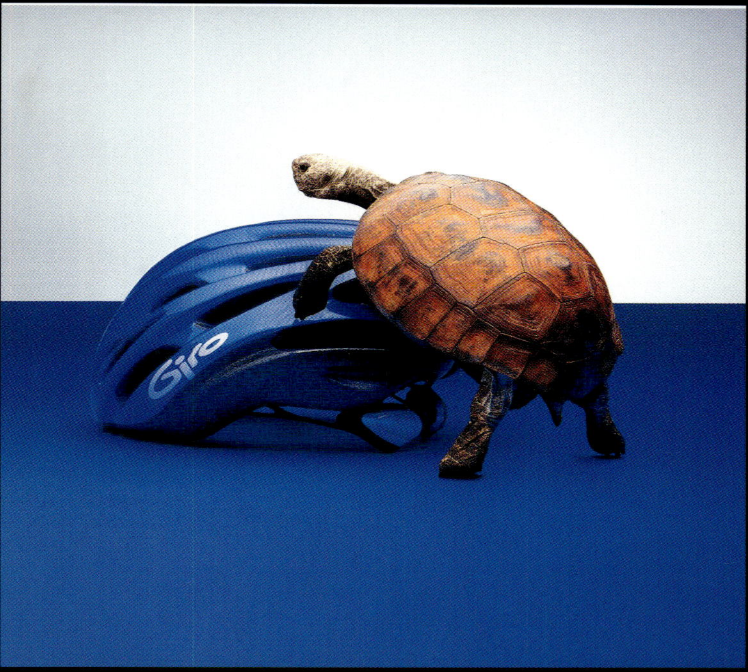

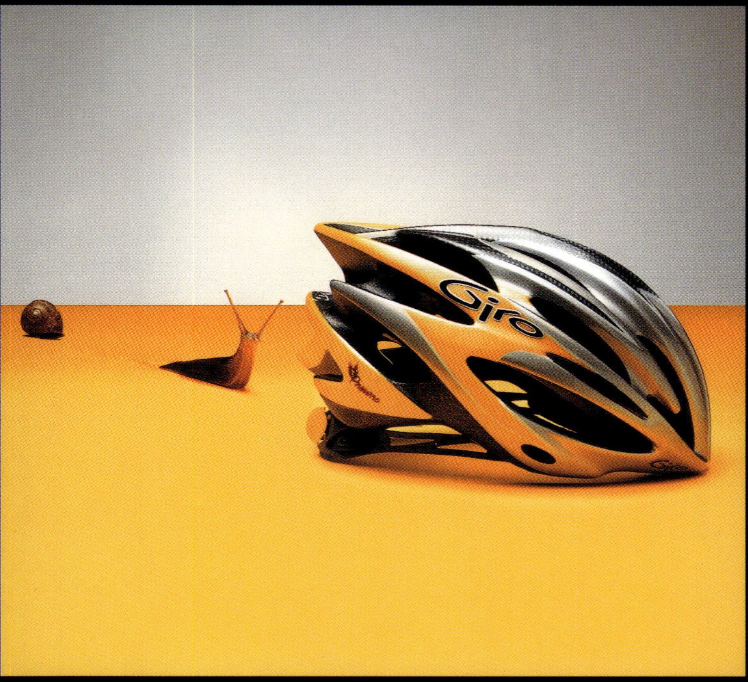

Mark Laita (opposite) Steven Moeder

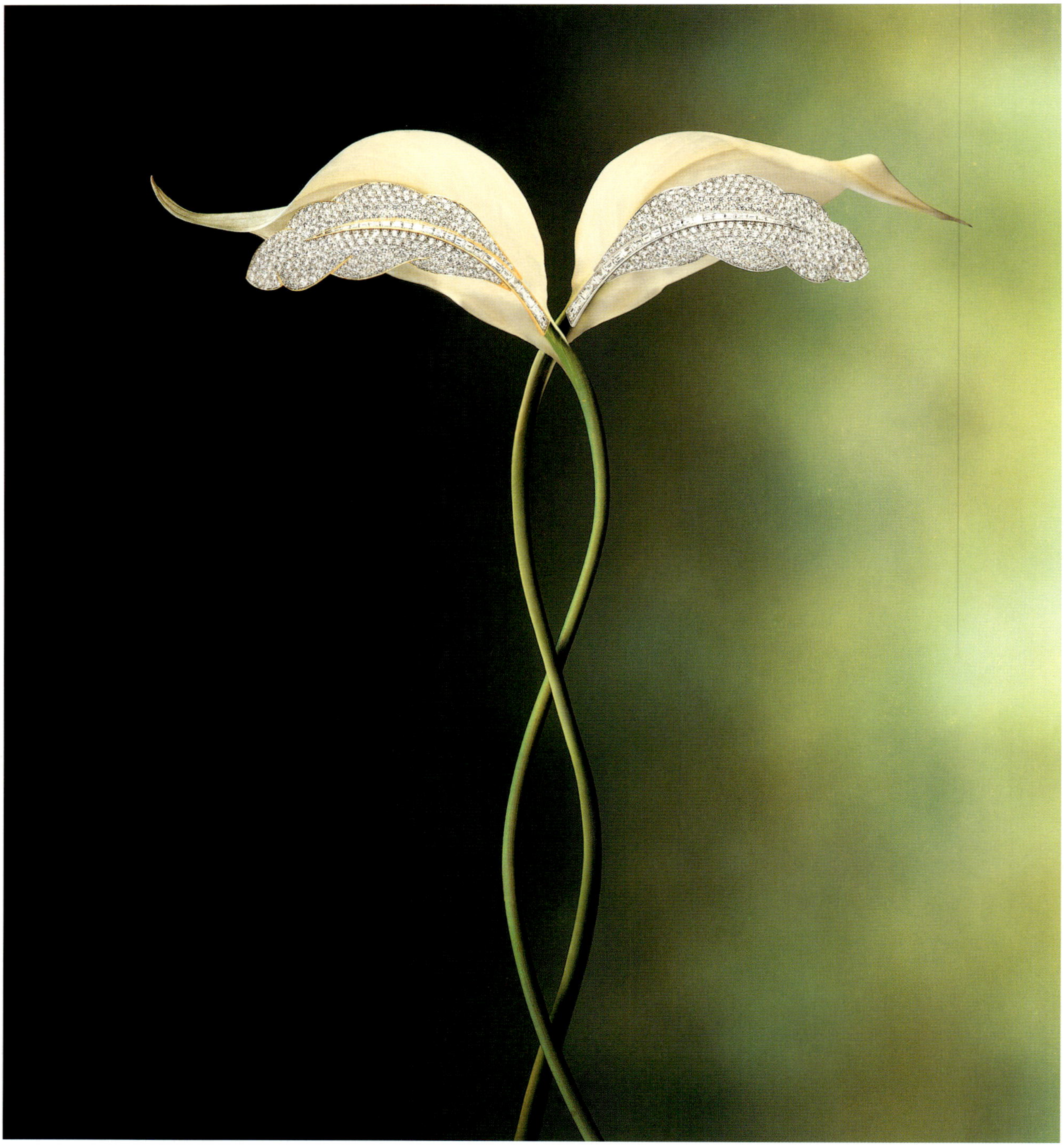

(this spread) Mark Laita

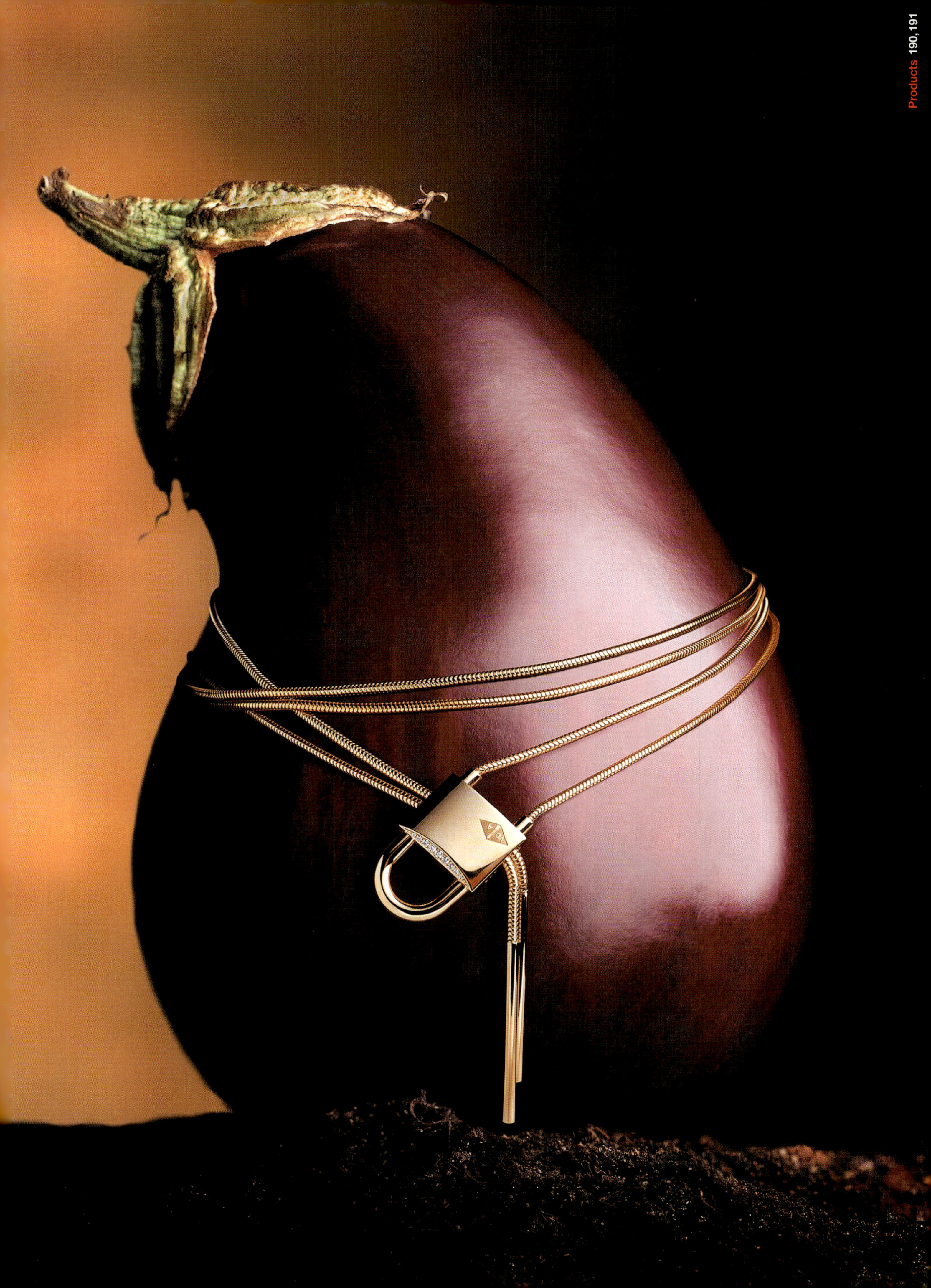

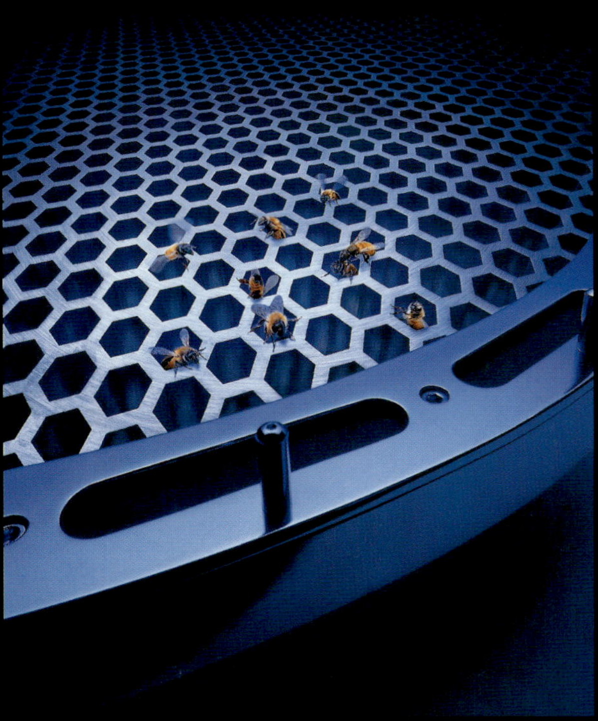
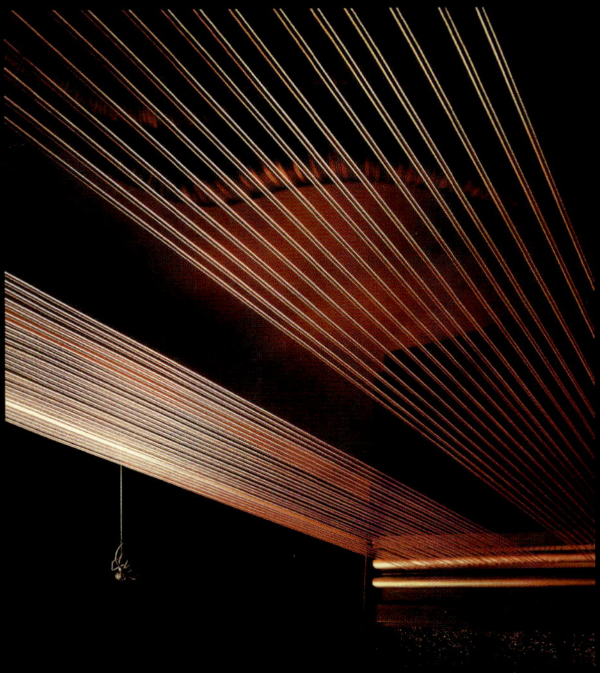
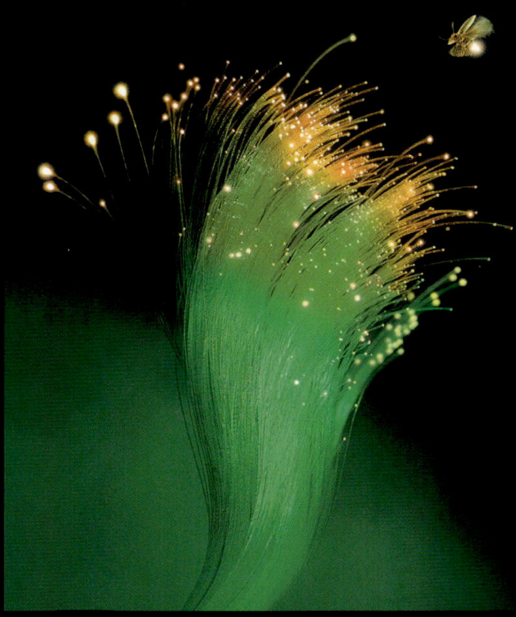
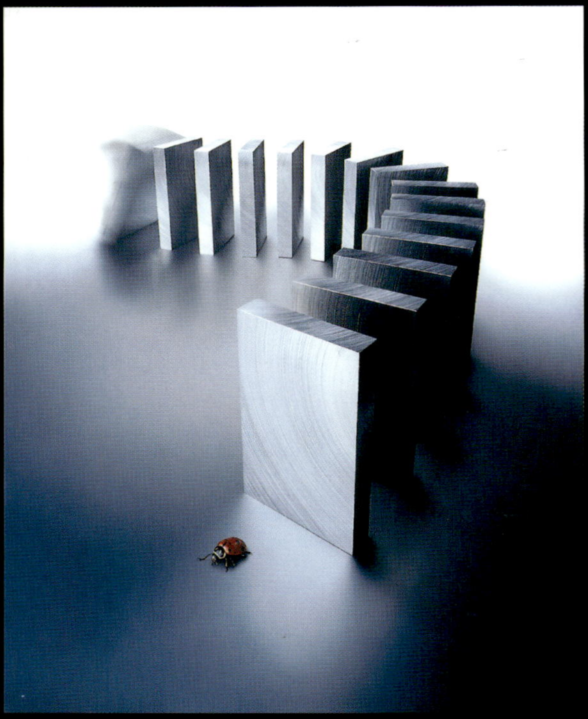

Mark Laita

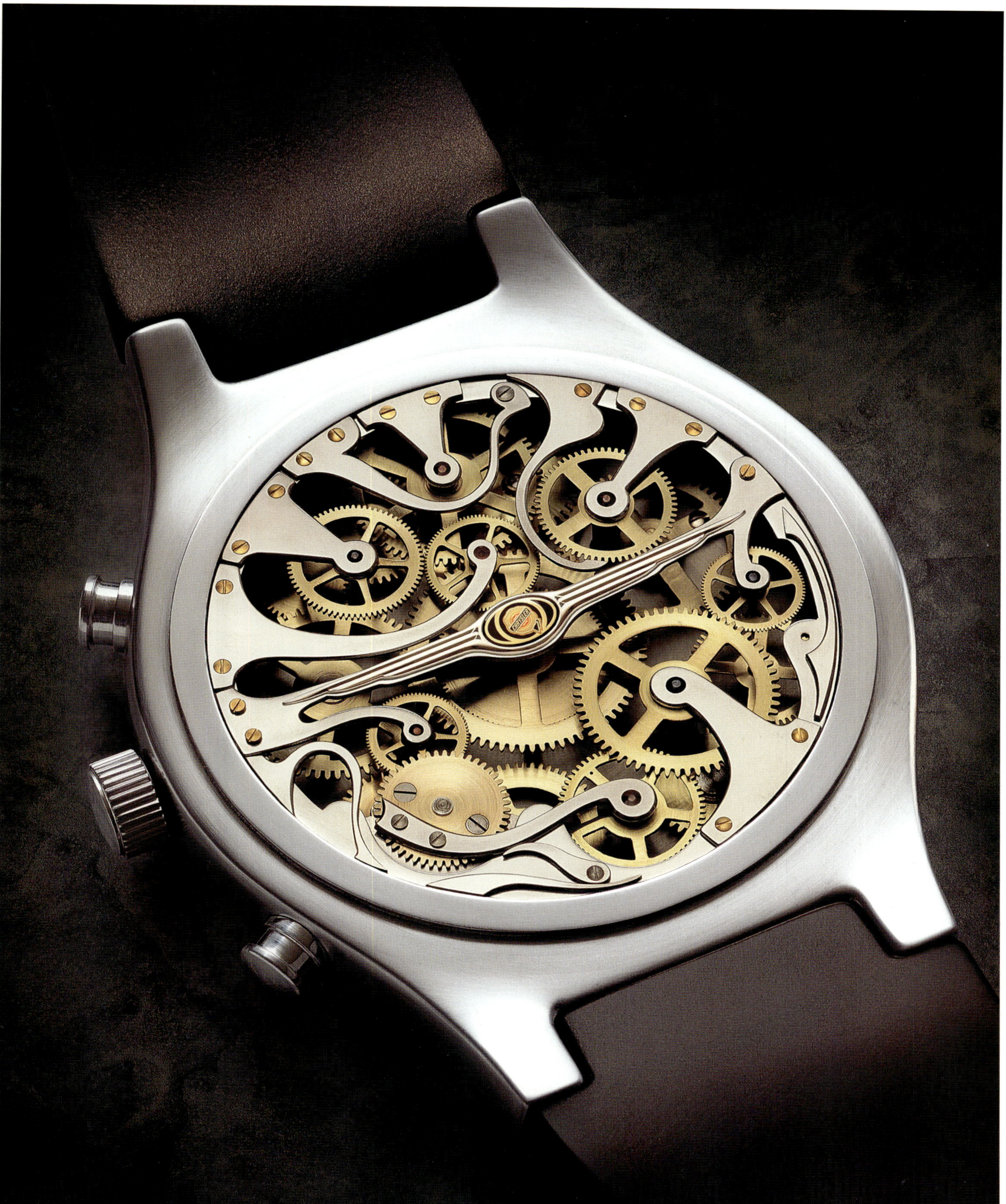

Markku Lahdesmaku

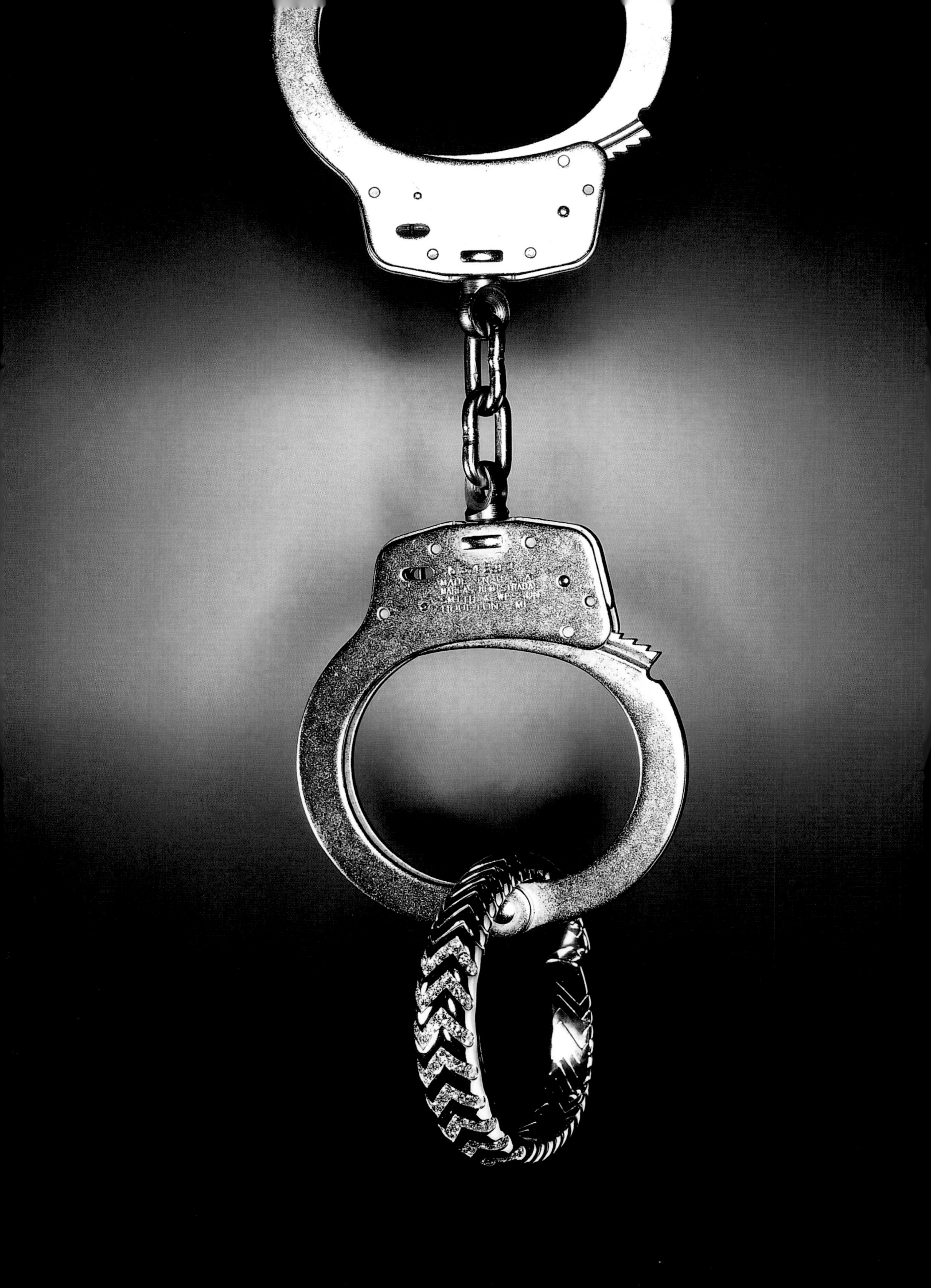

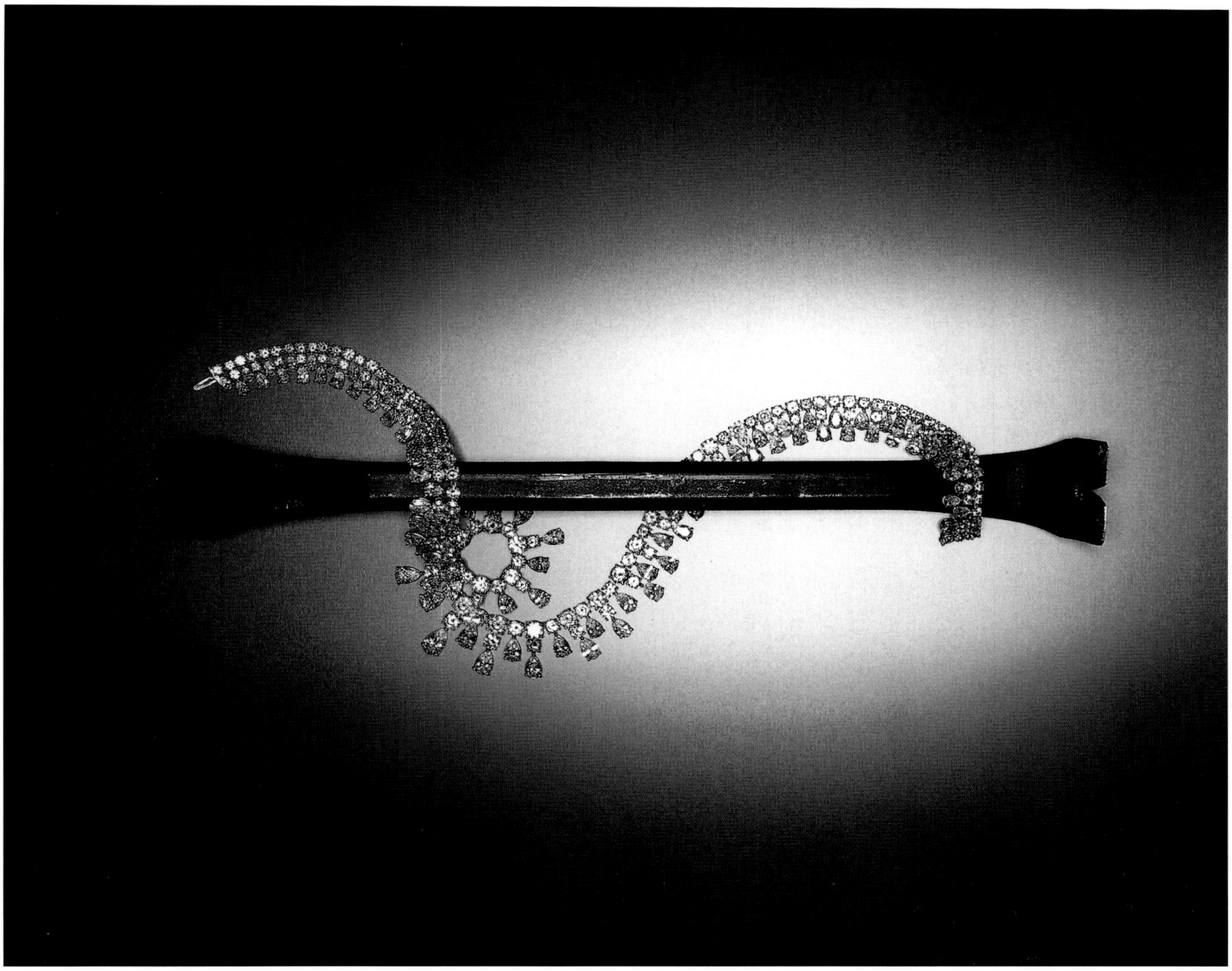

(this spread) Craig Cutler

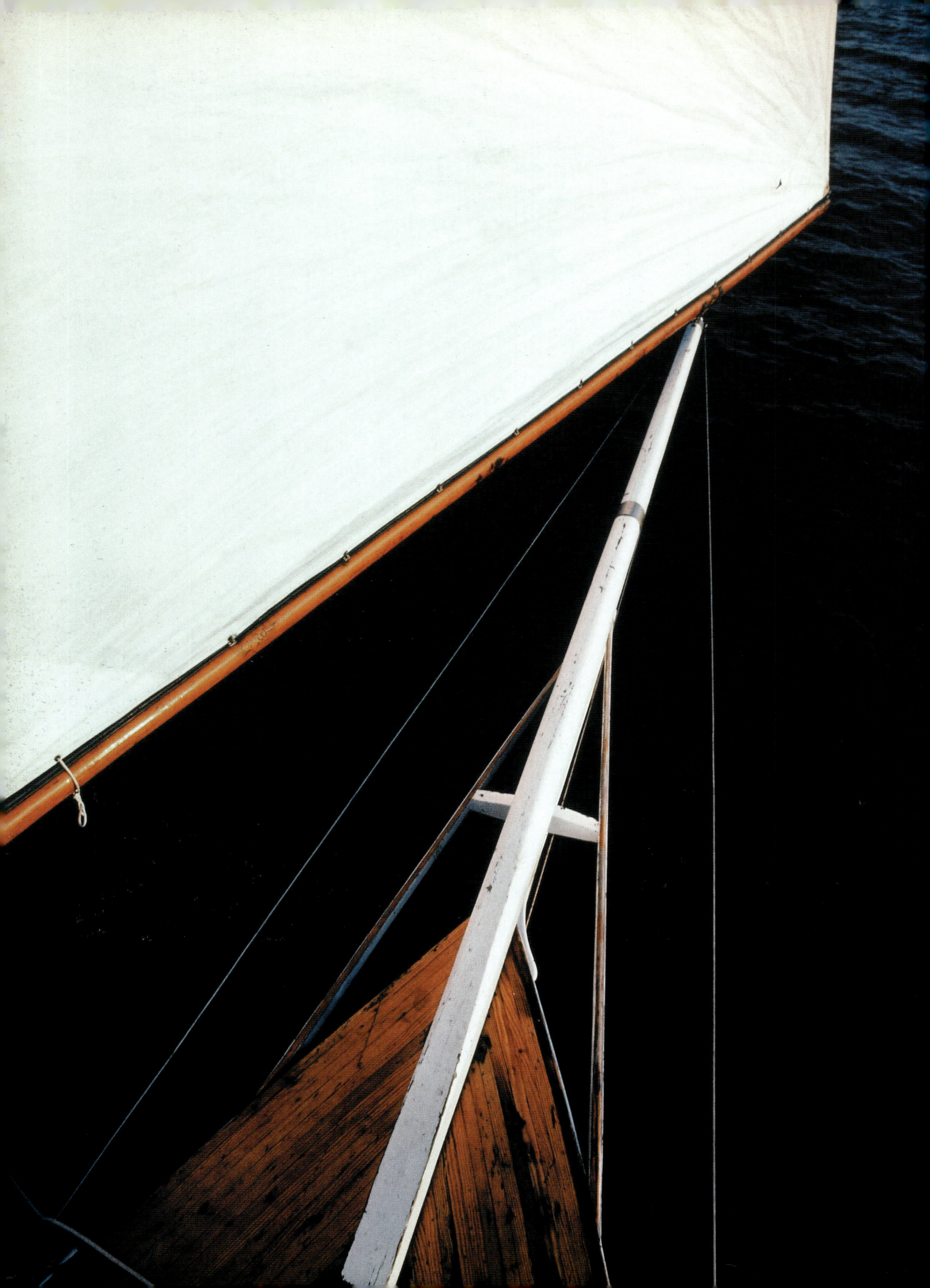

Sports

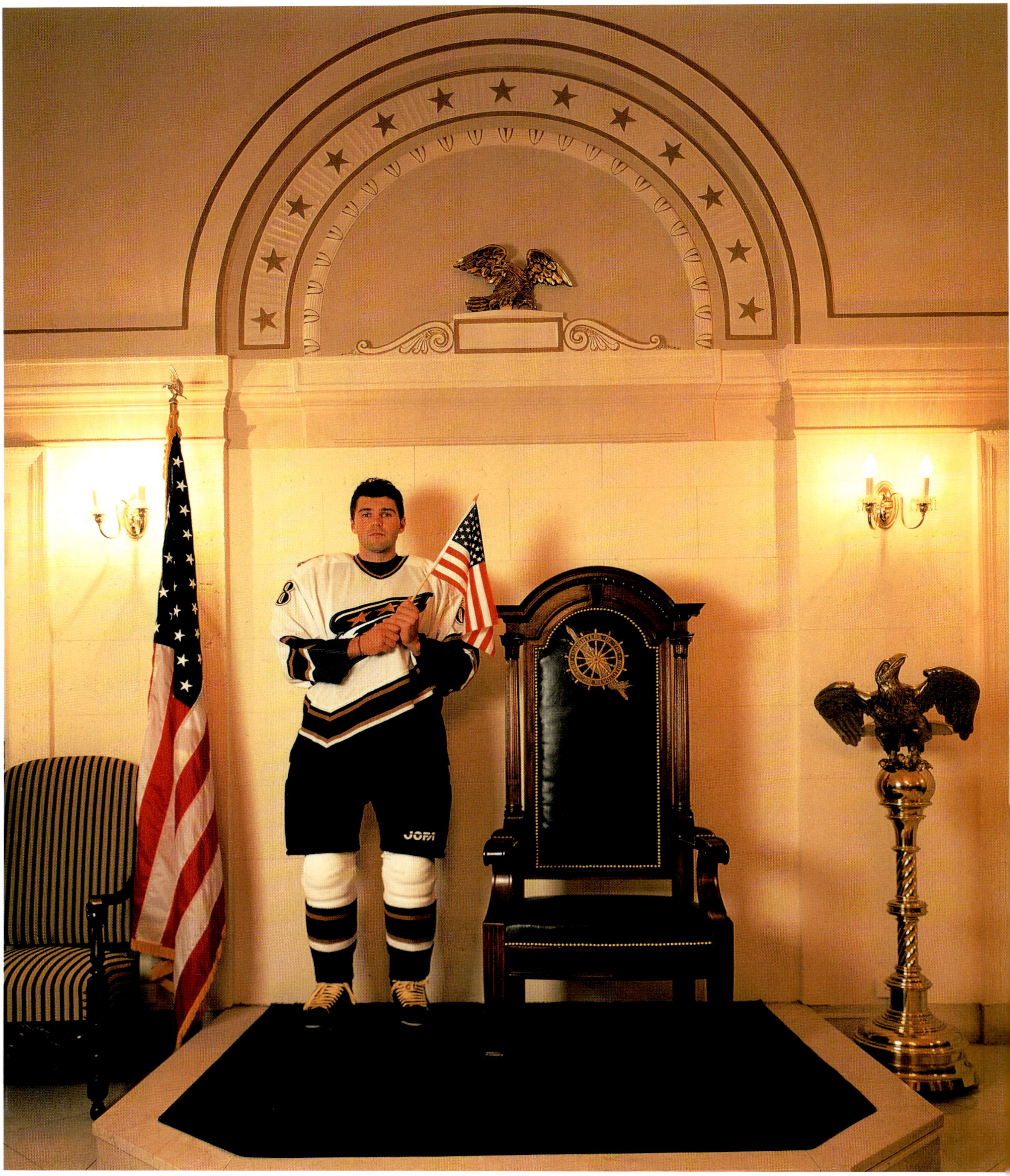

(this spread) Michael O'Brien (opening page) Eric Poggenpohl

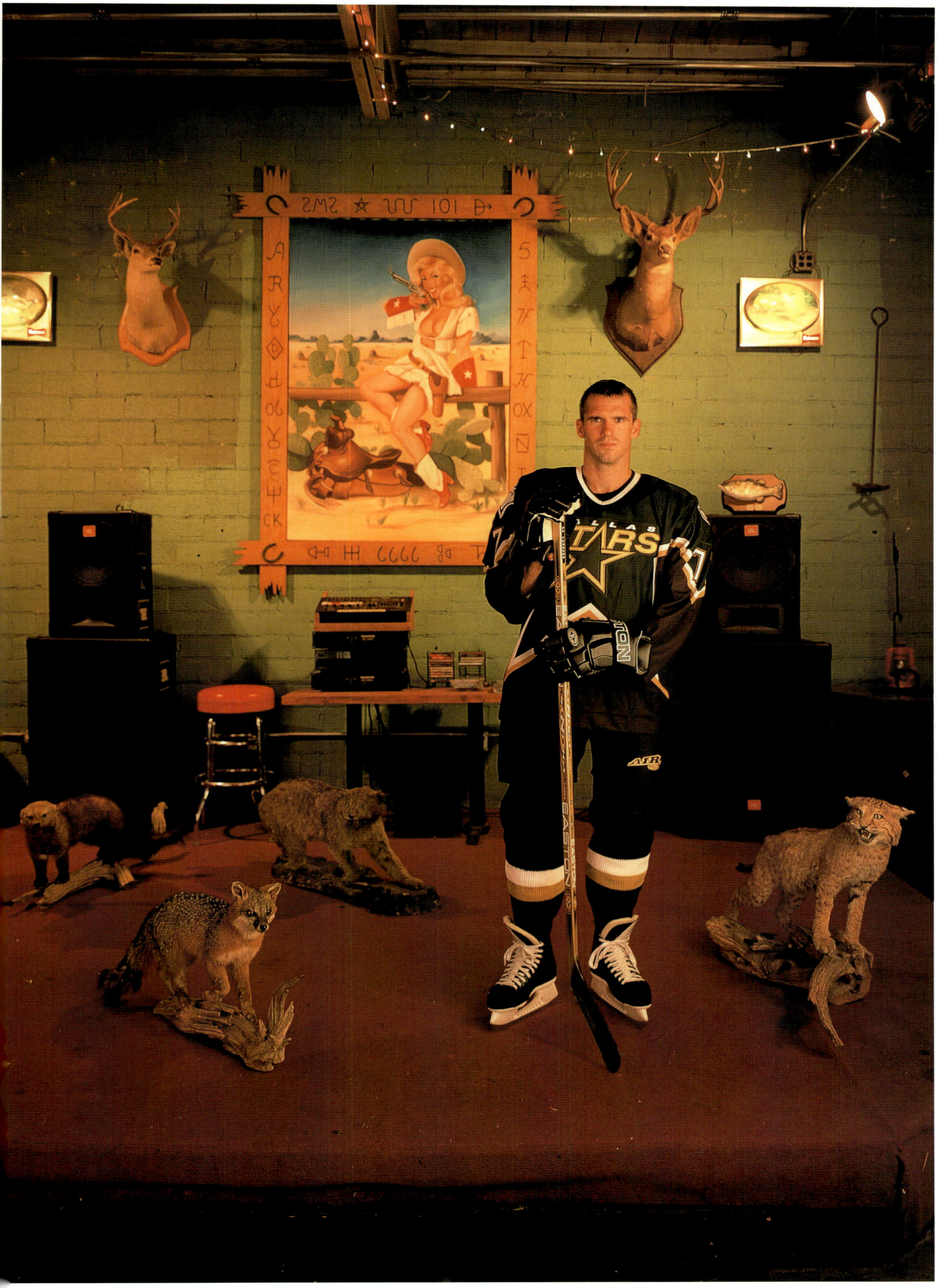
TARS

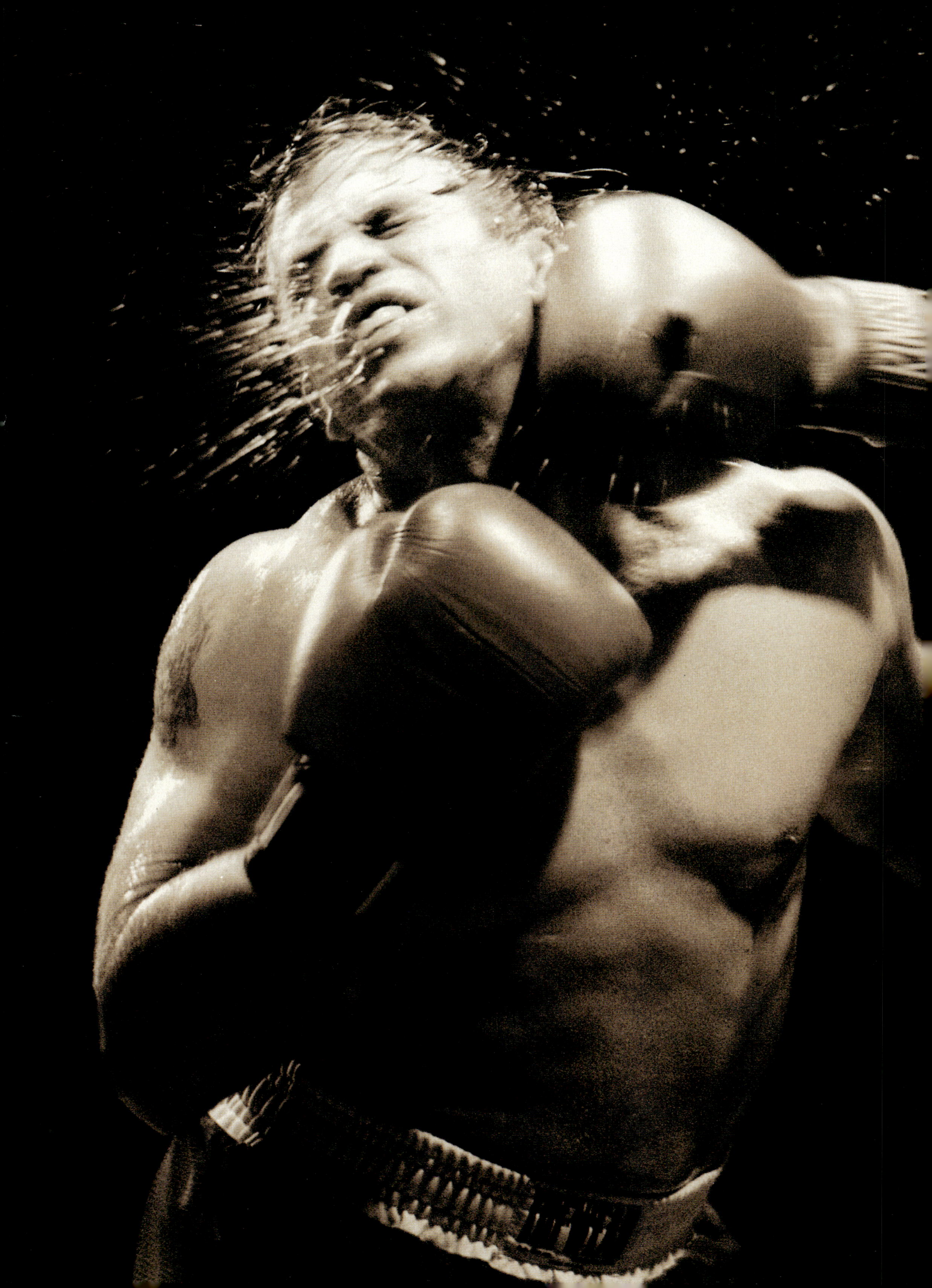

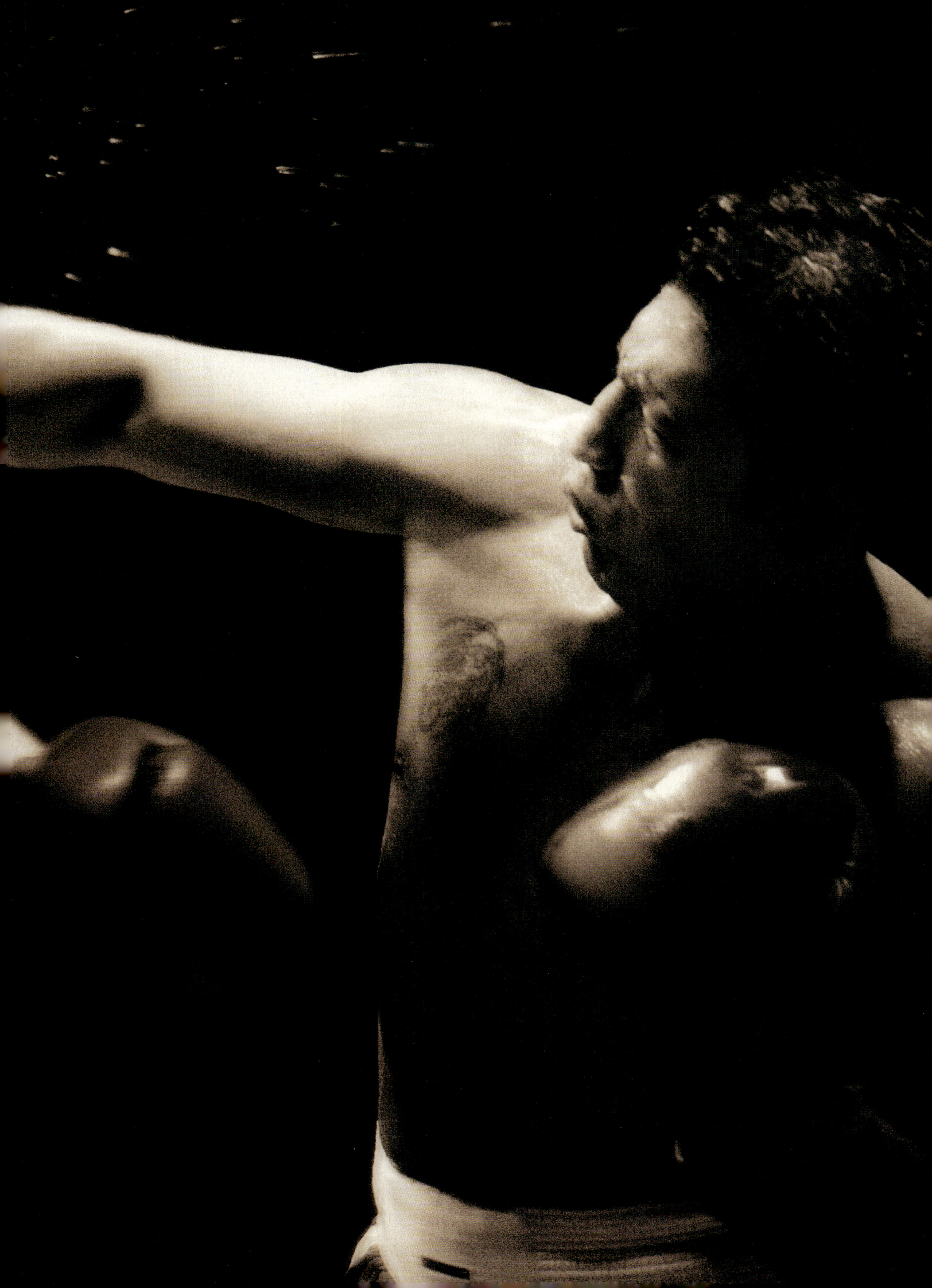

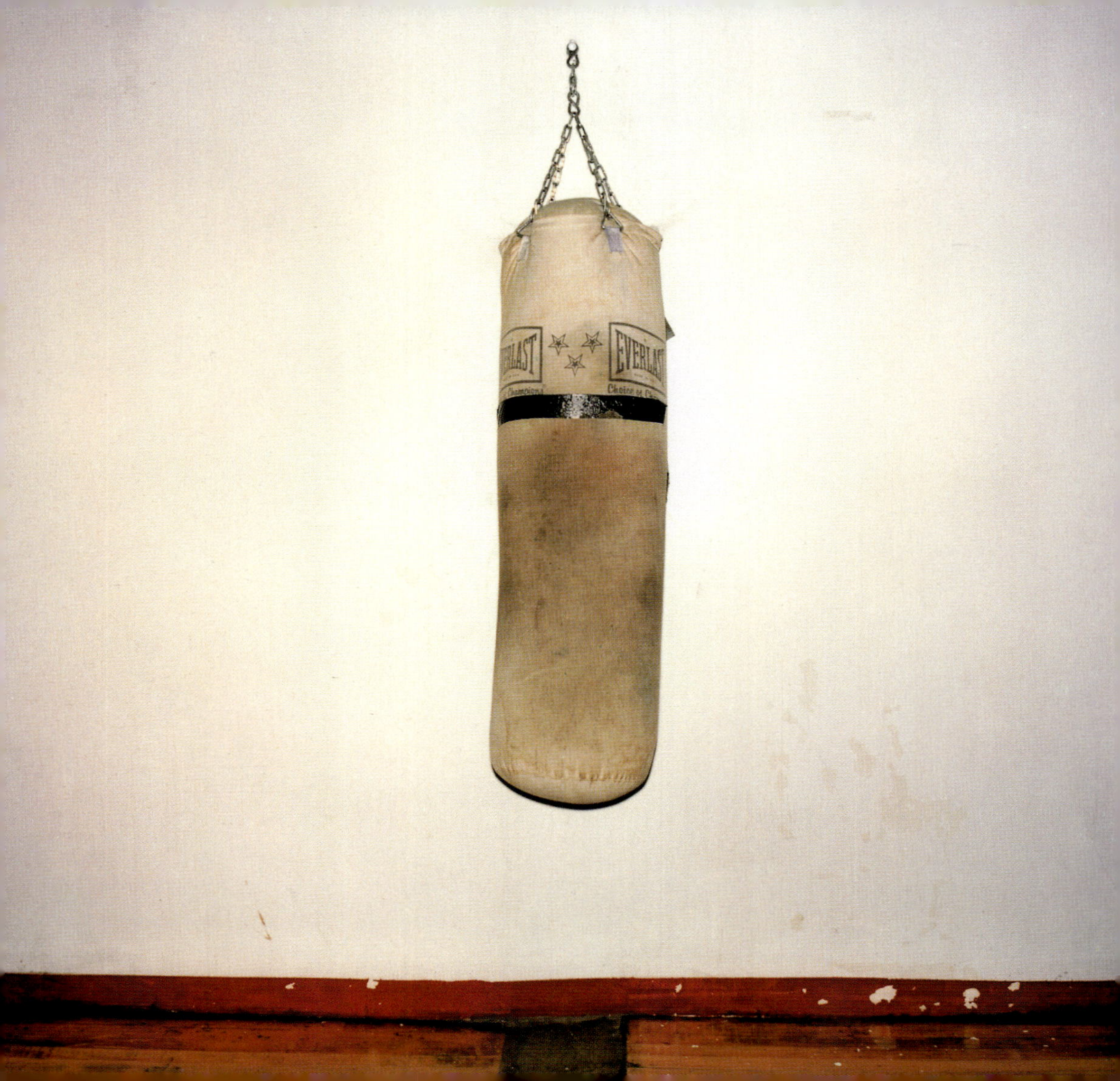
EVERLAST

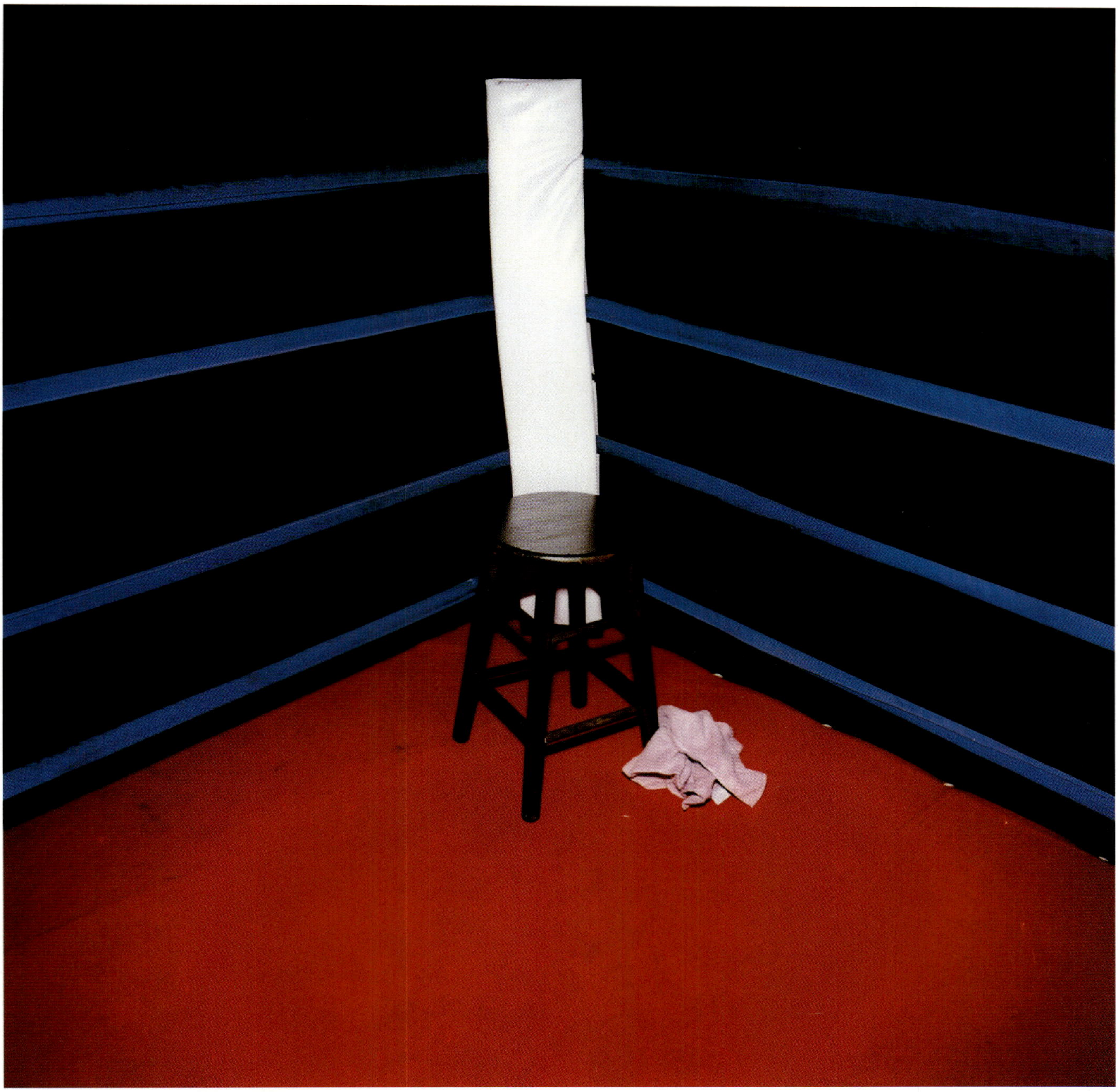

(this spread) Craig Cutler

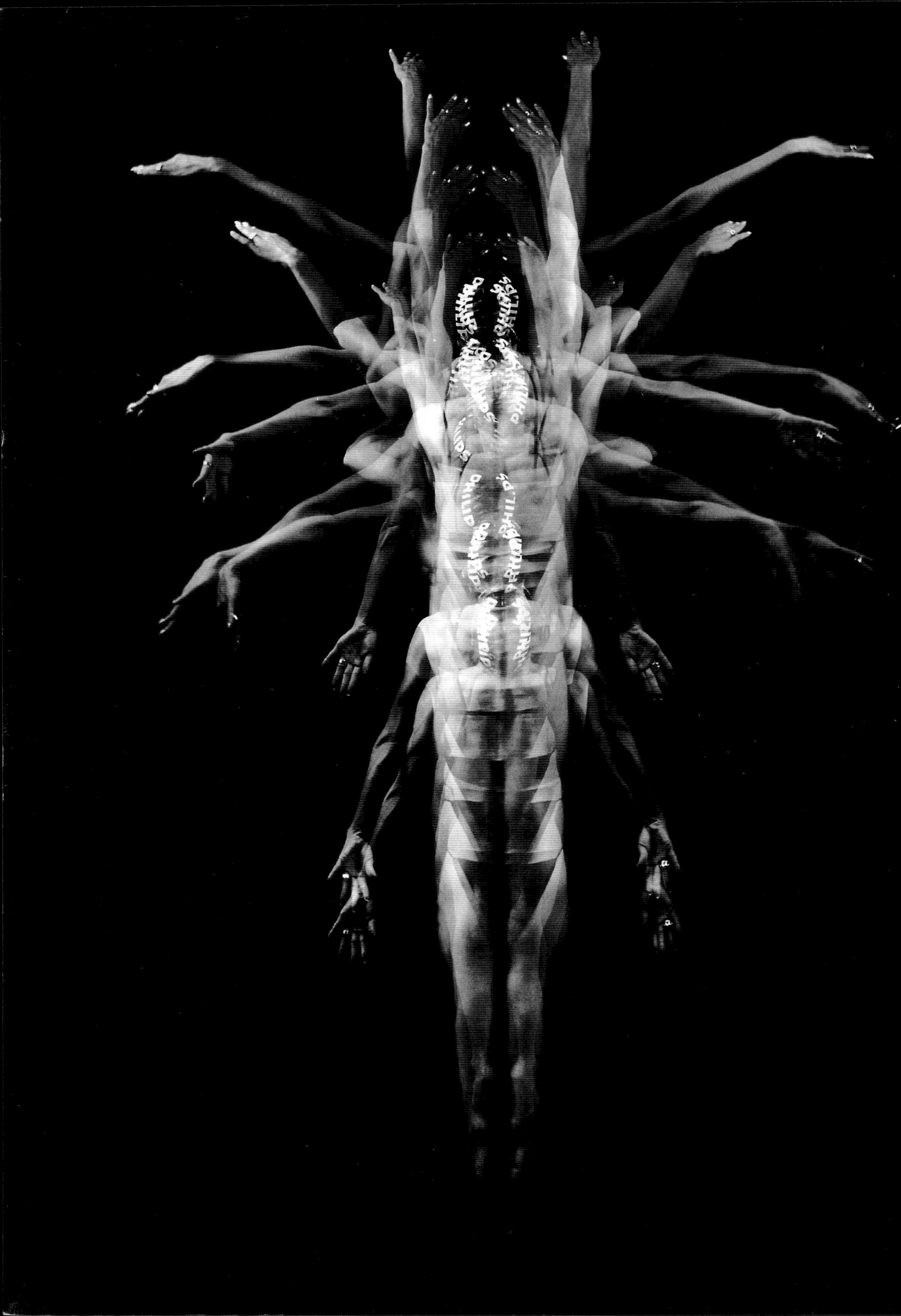
PHILIPS

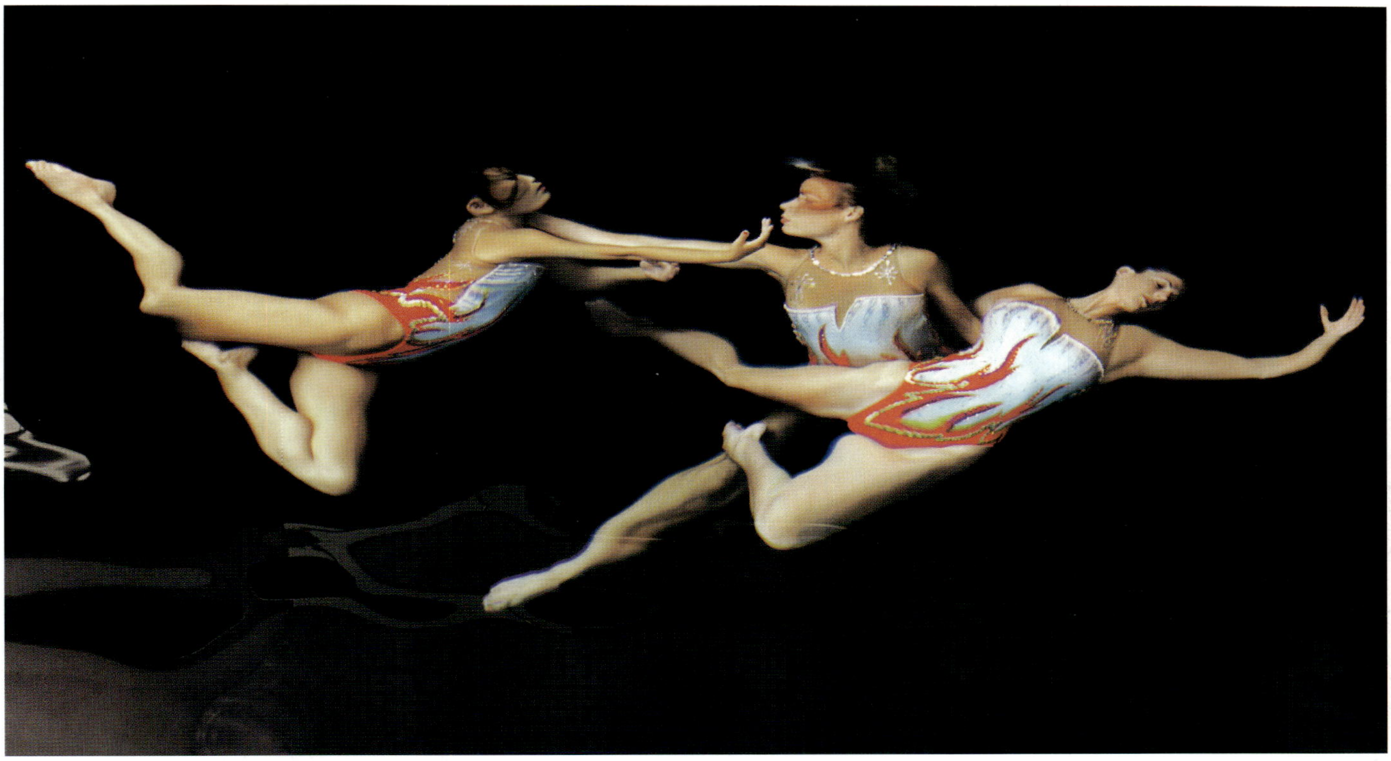

(this spread) Howard Schatz

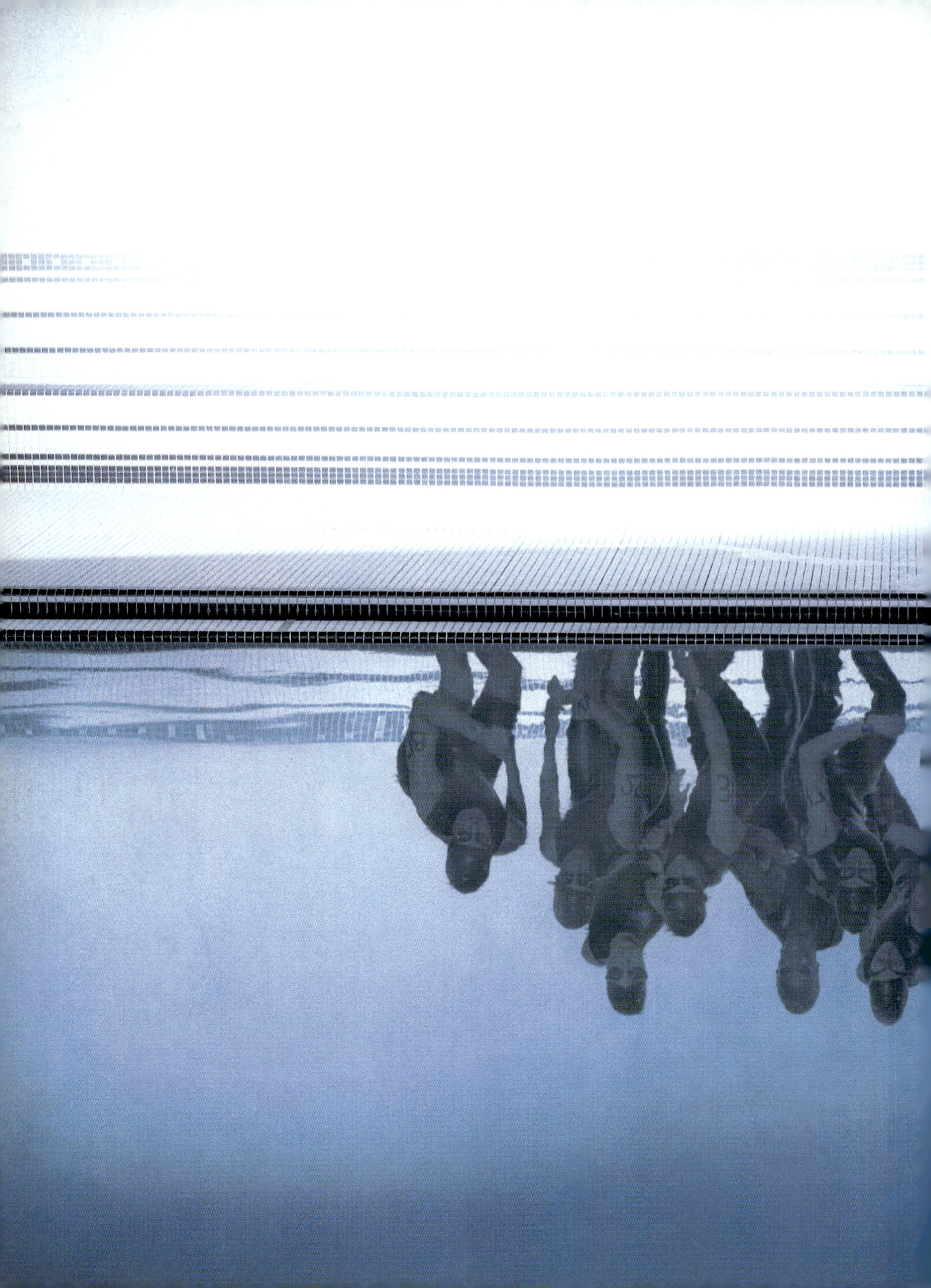

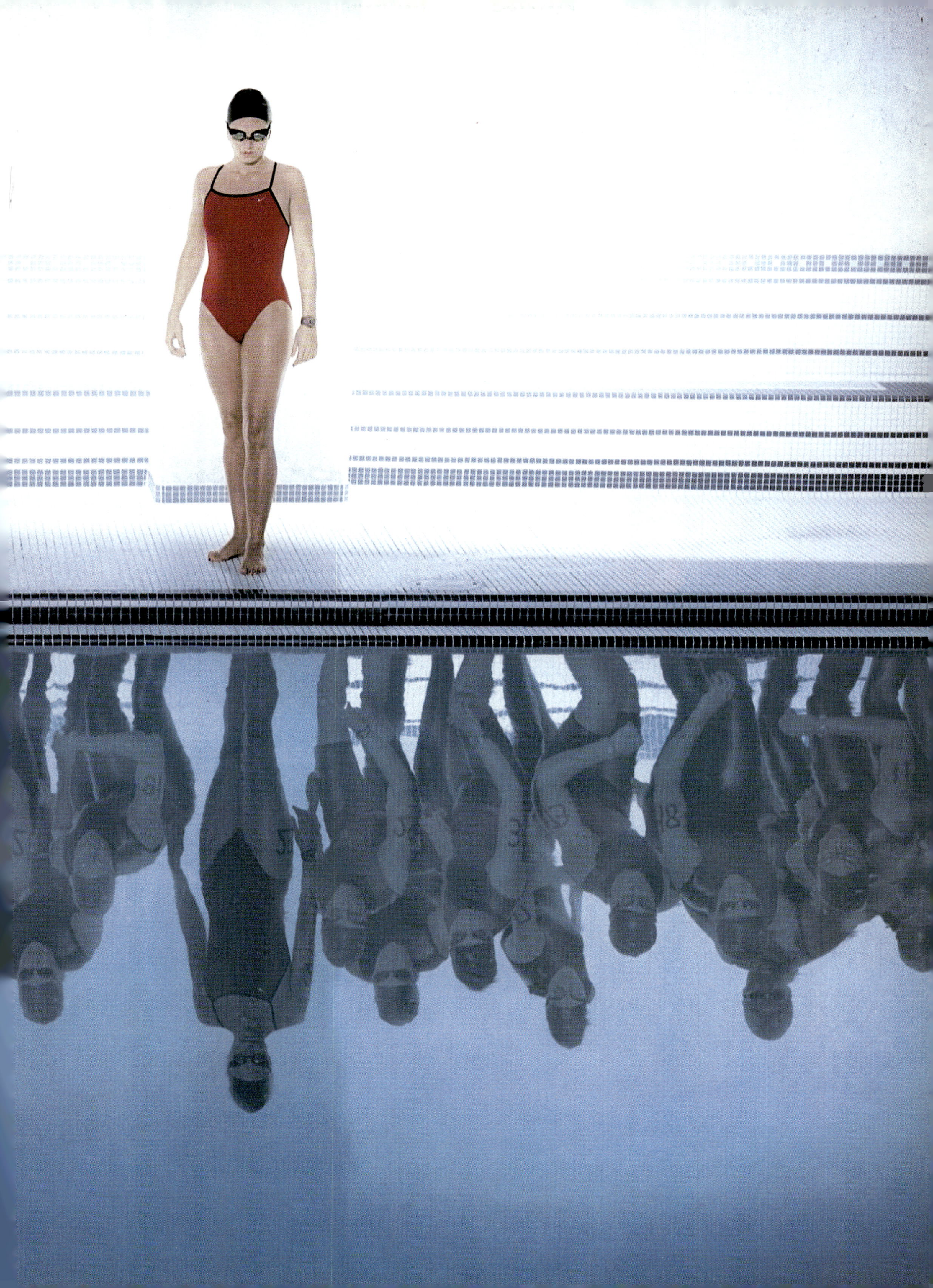

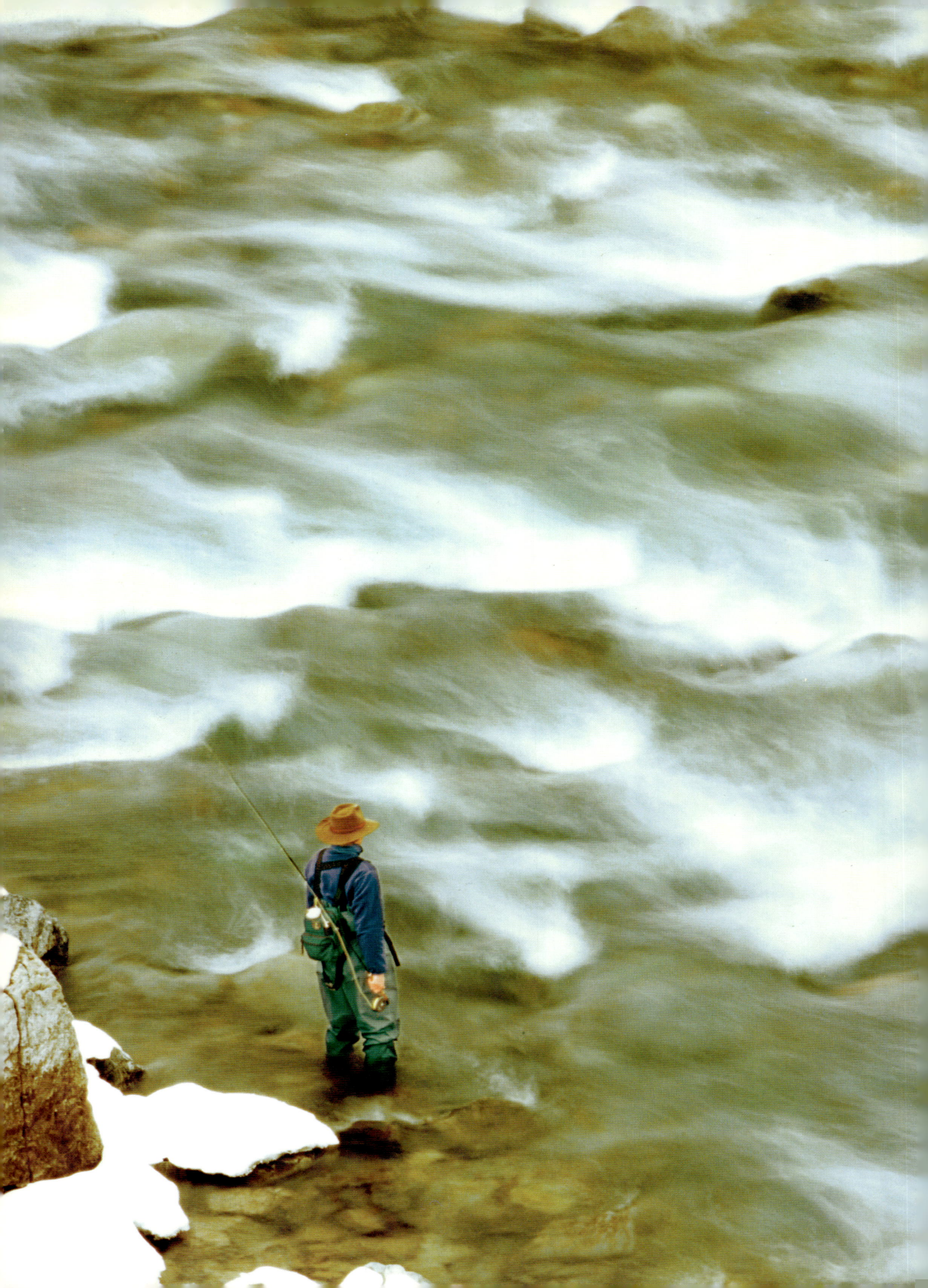

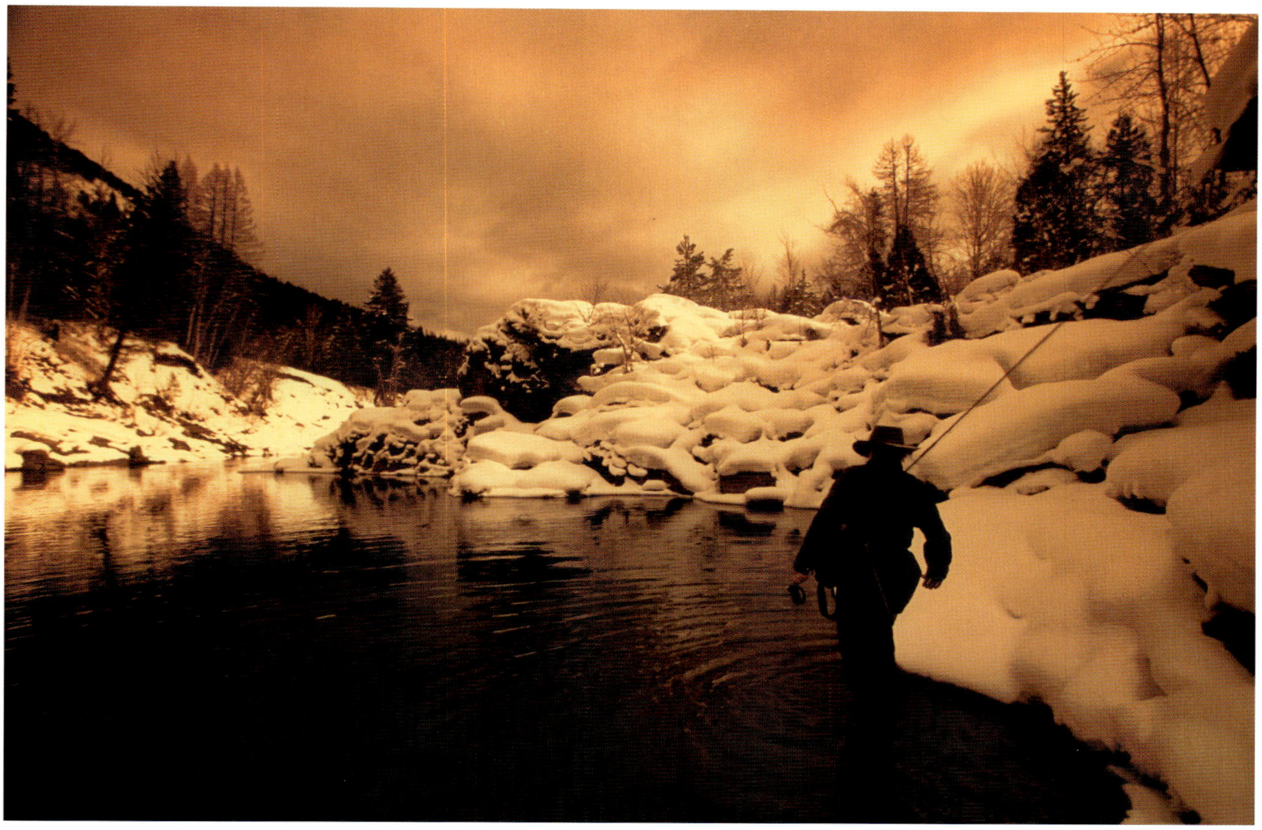

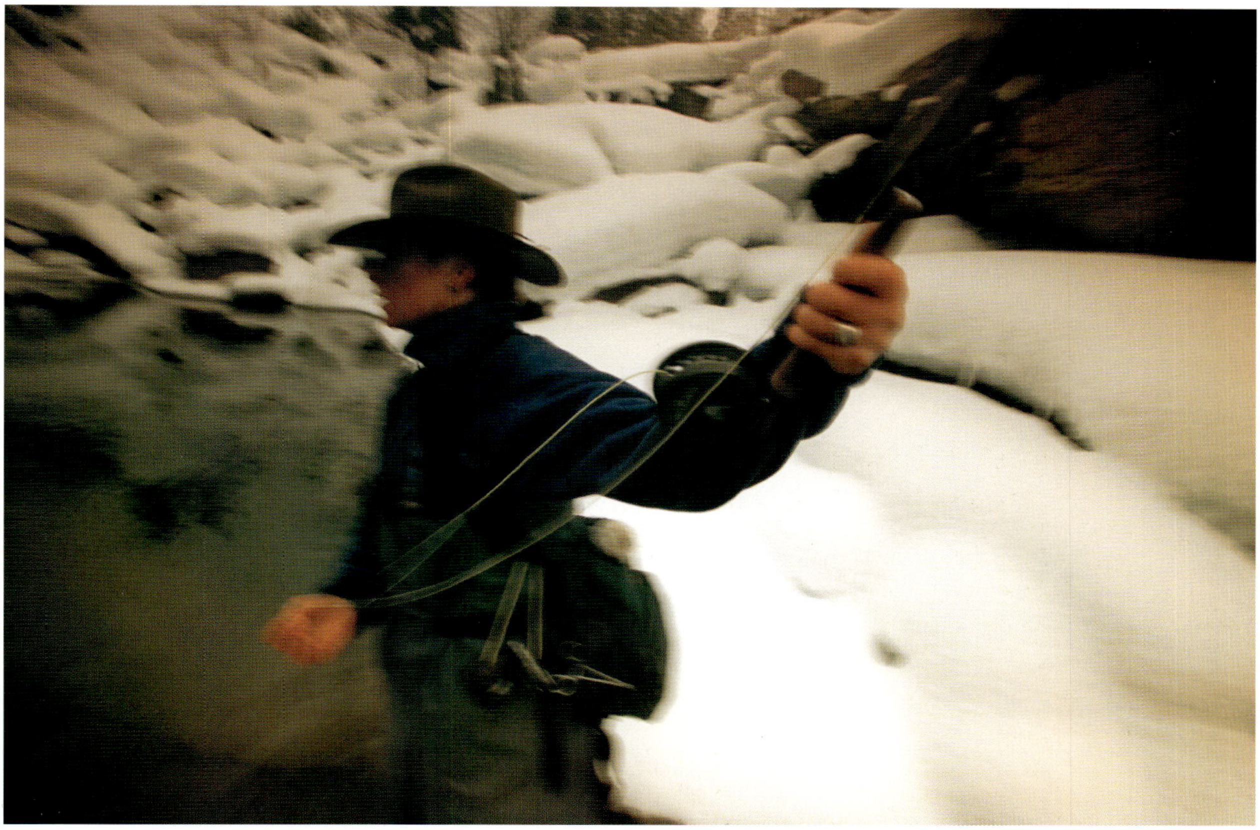

(previous spread) Chris Gordaneer (this spread) Scott Spiker

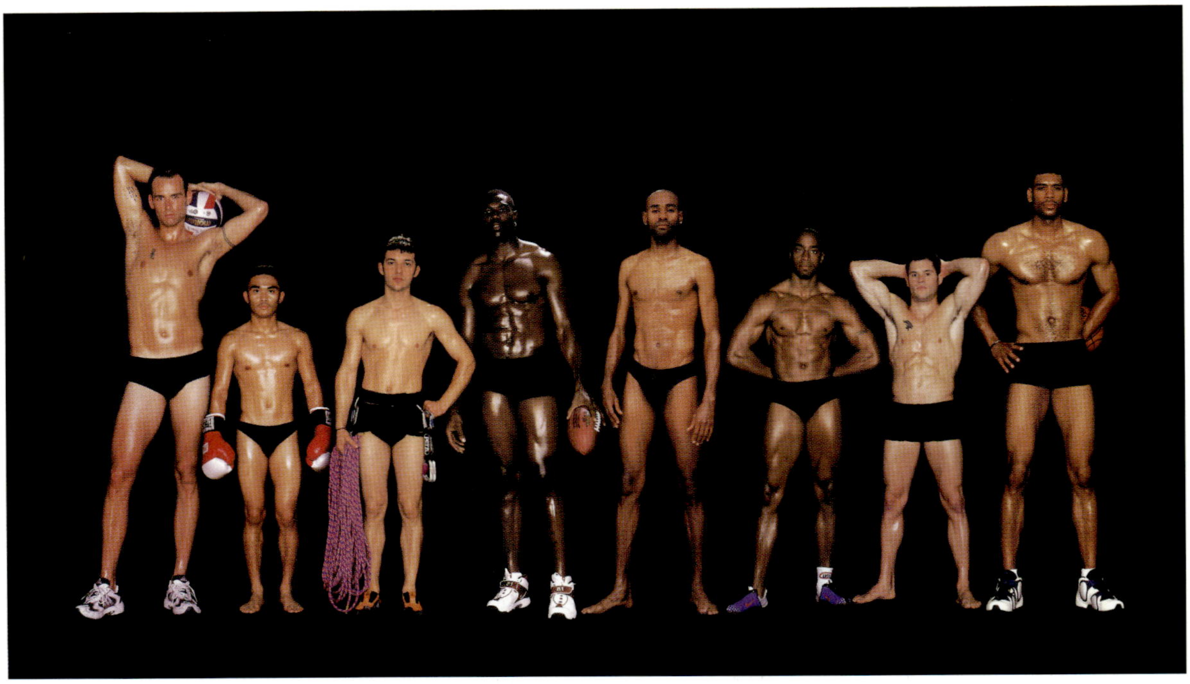

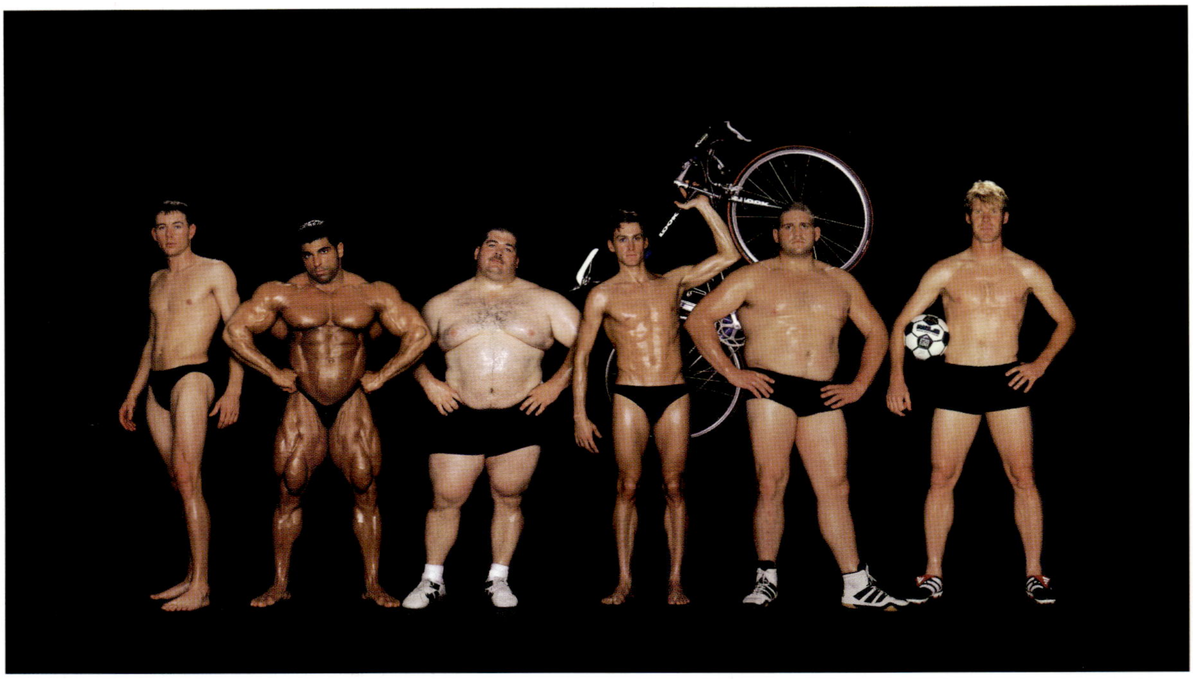

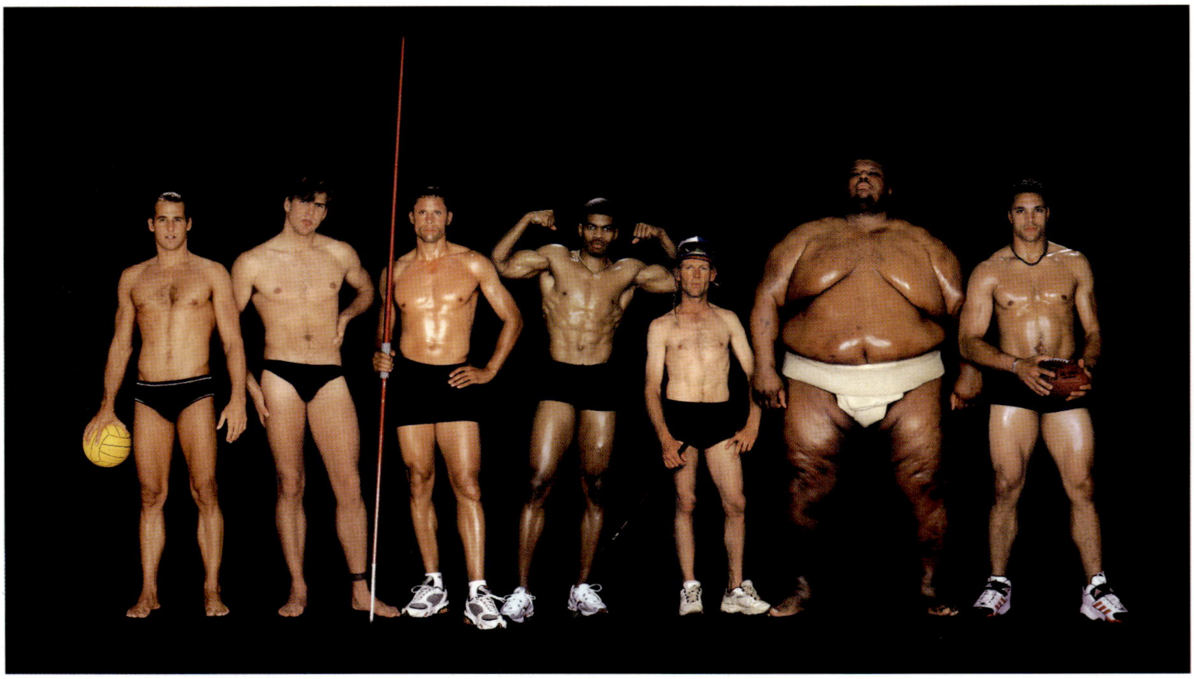

Howard Schatz

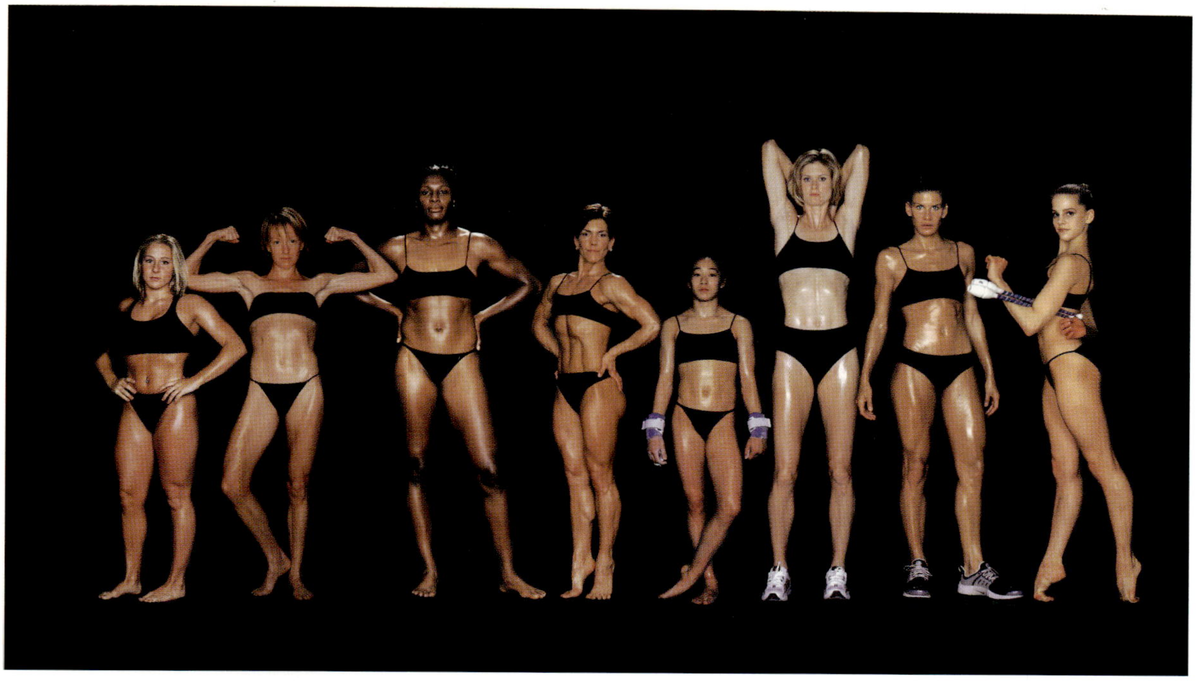

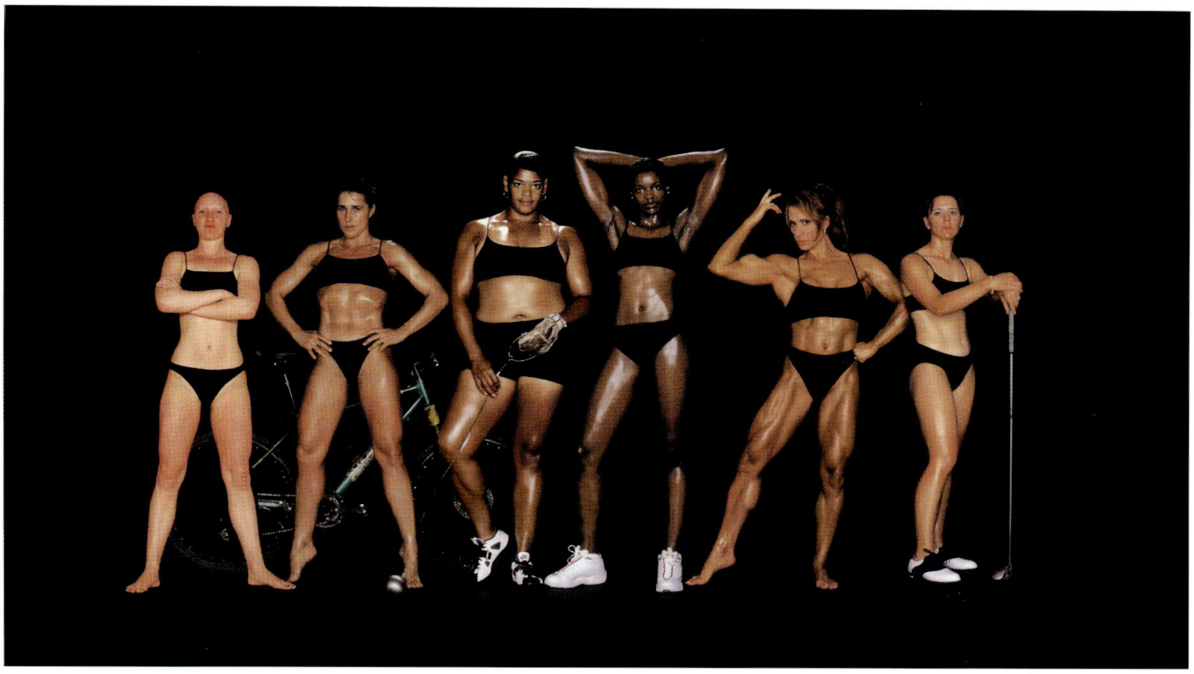

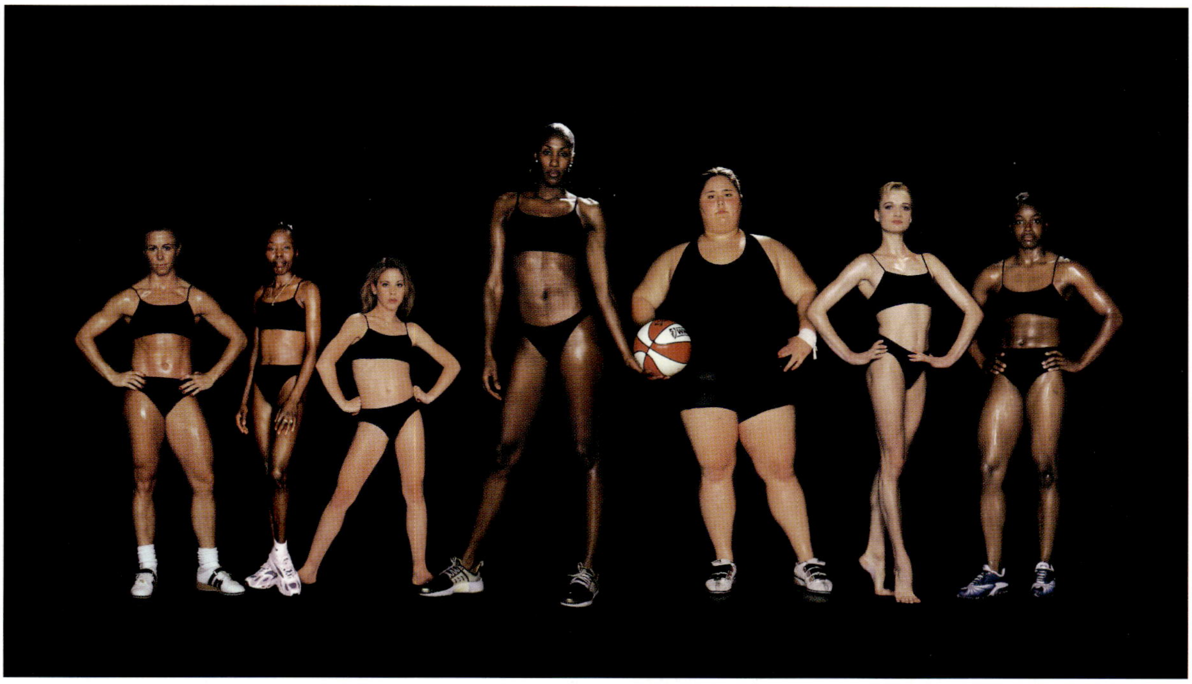

Howard Schatz

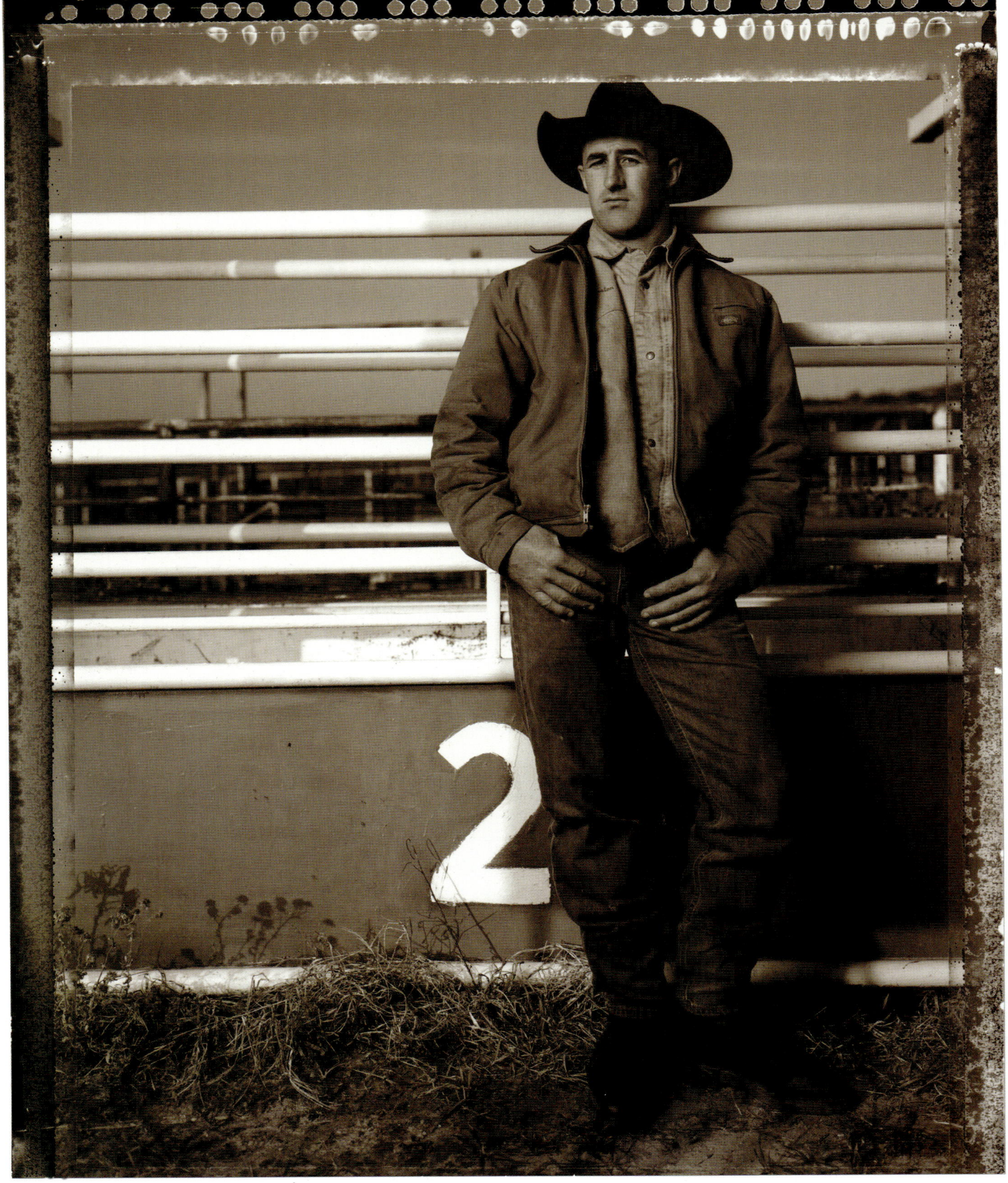

Michael O'Brien

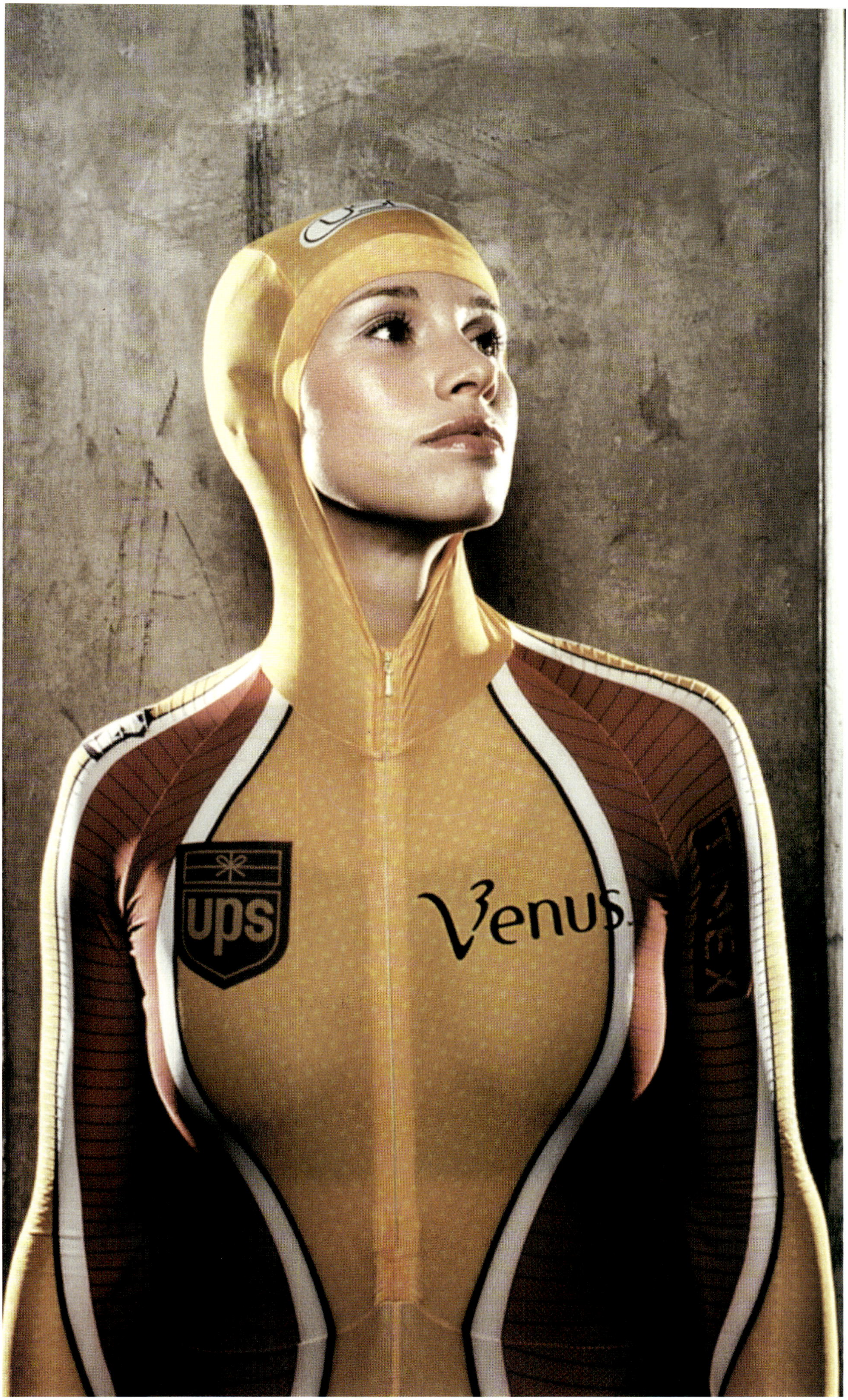

Mark Zibert

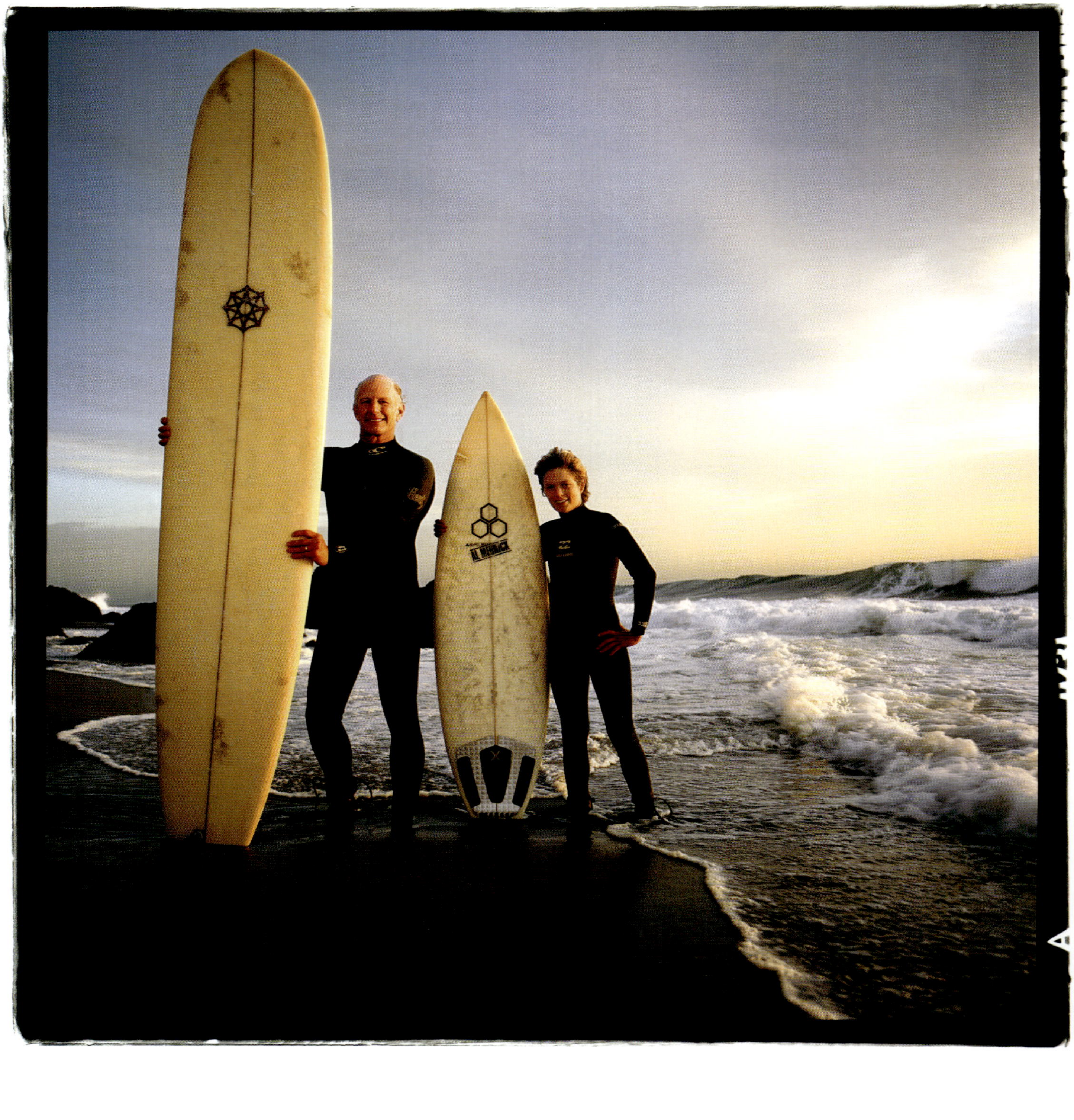

Sue Bennett

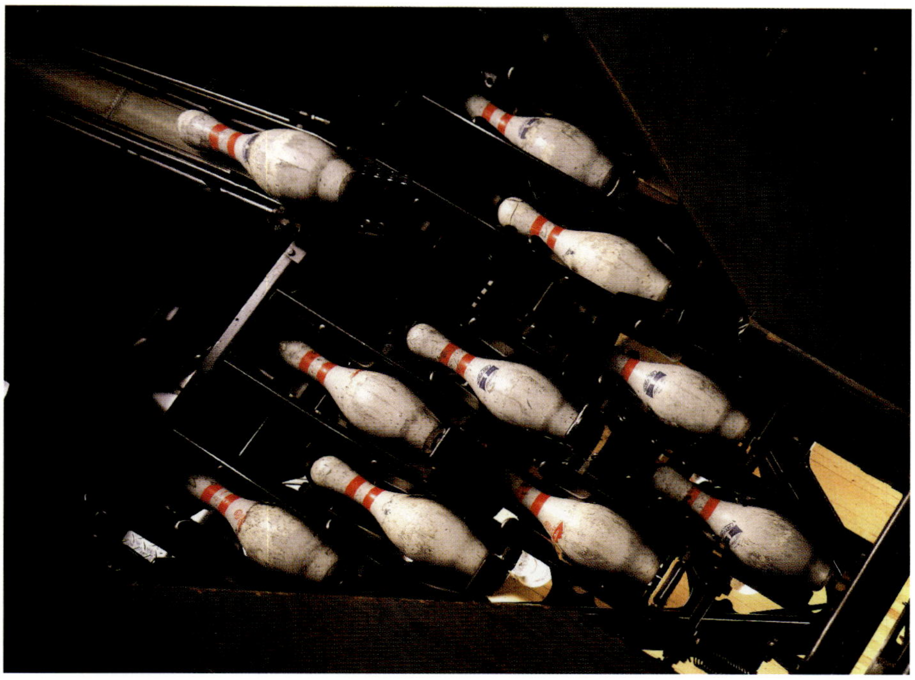

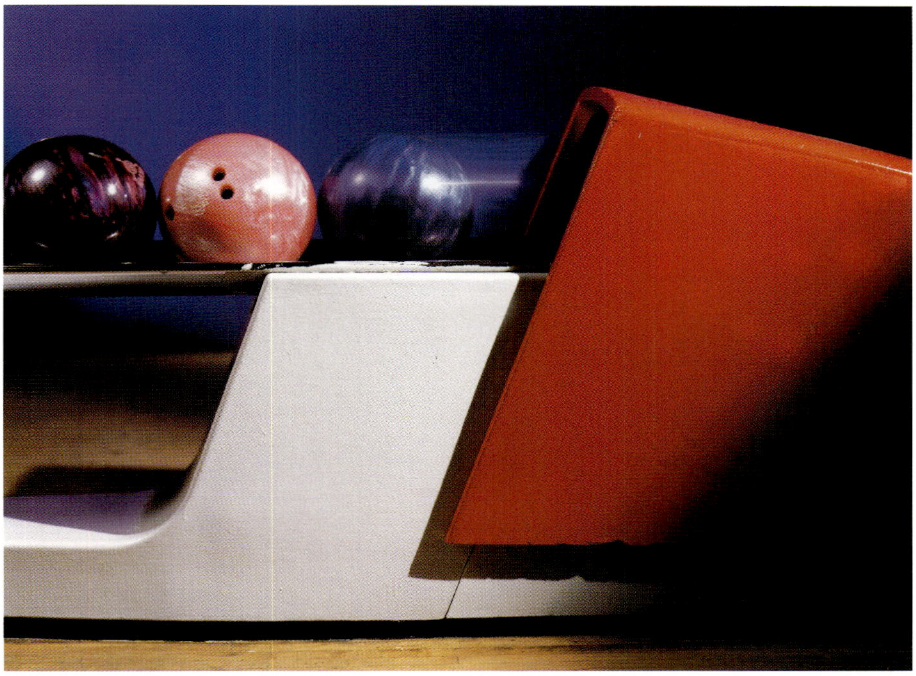

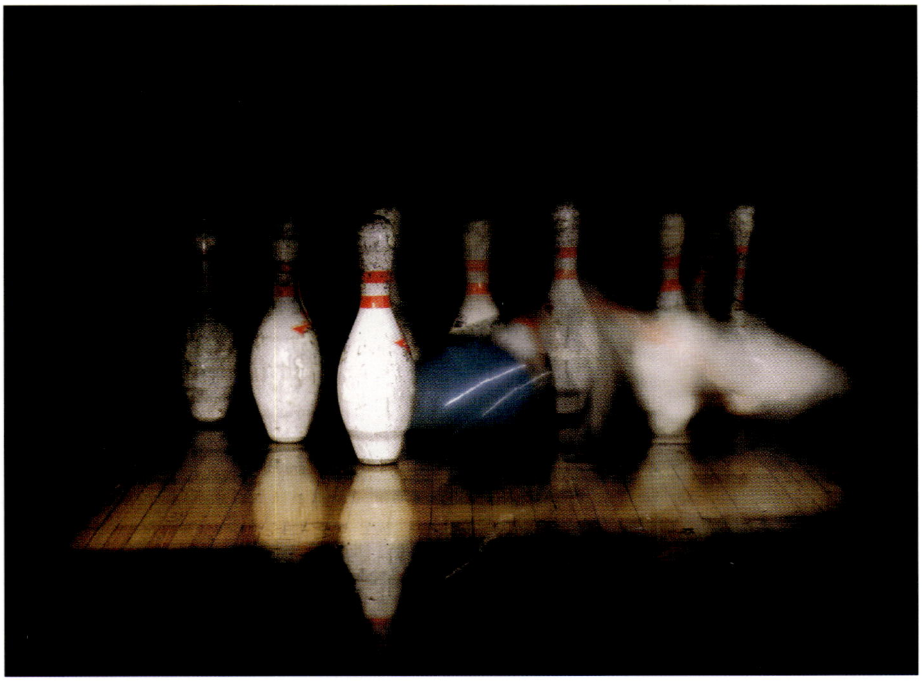

Bret Wills

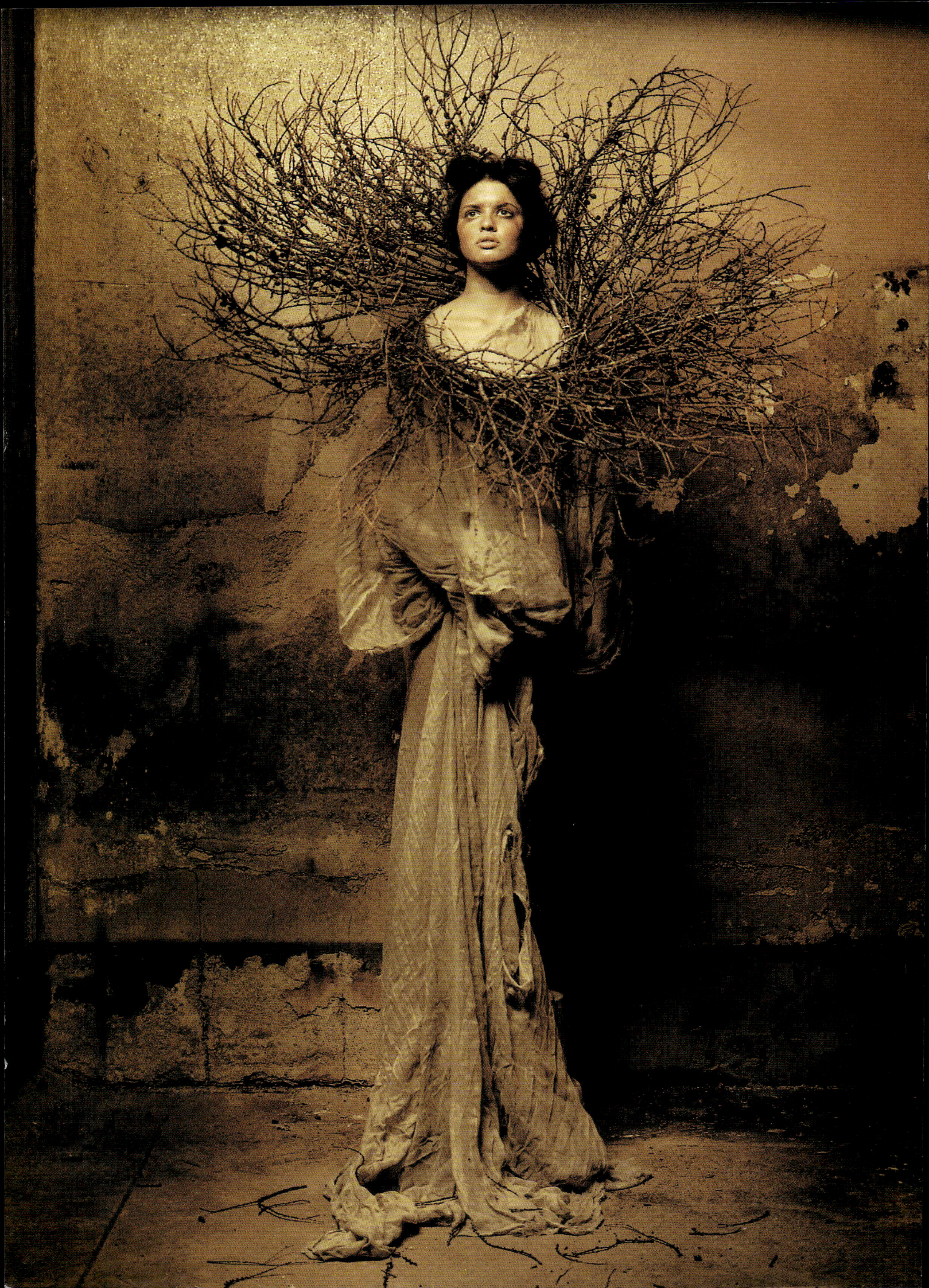

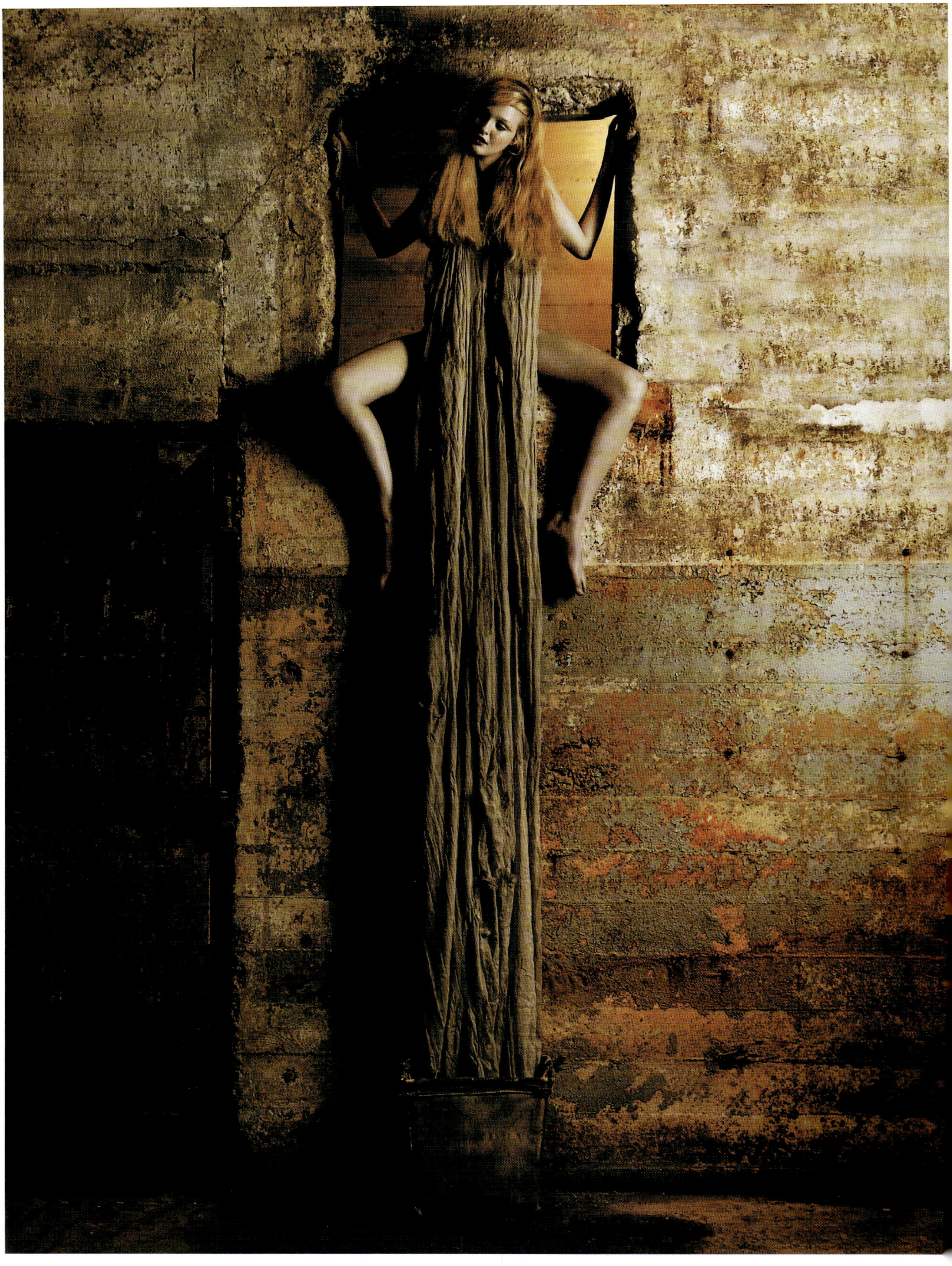

(this and opening page) Jeff Stephens

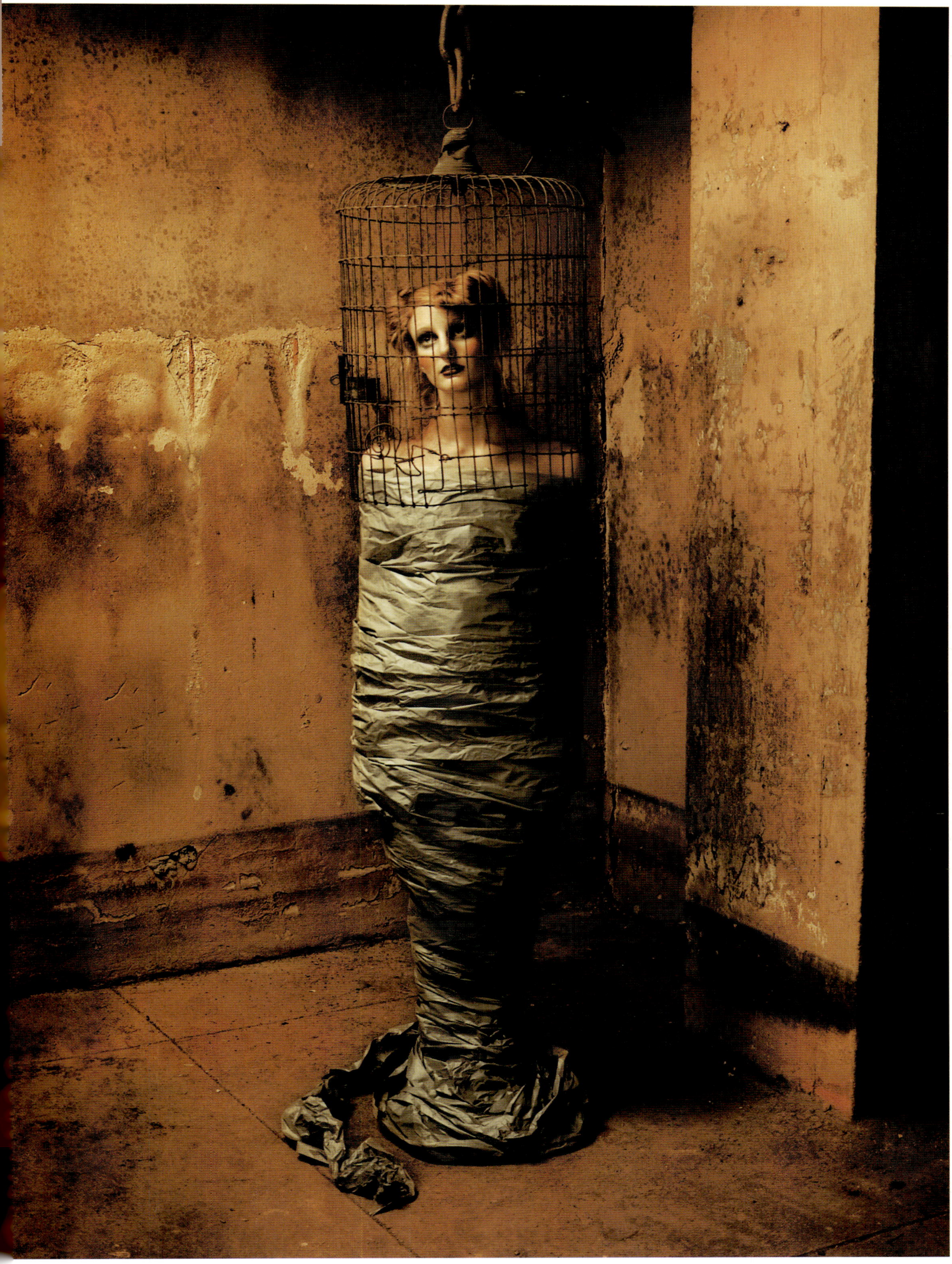

Jeff Stephens

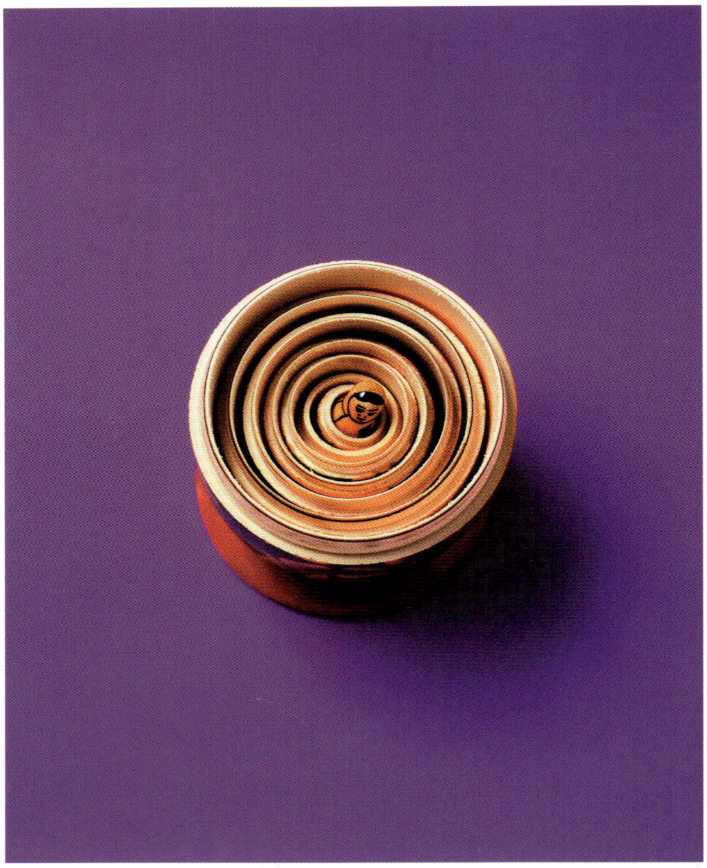 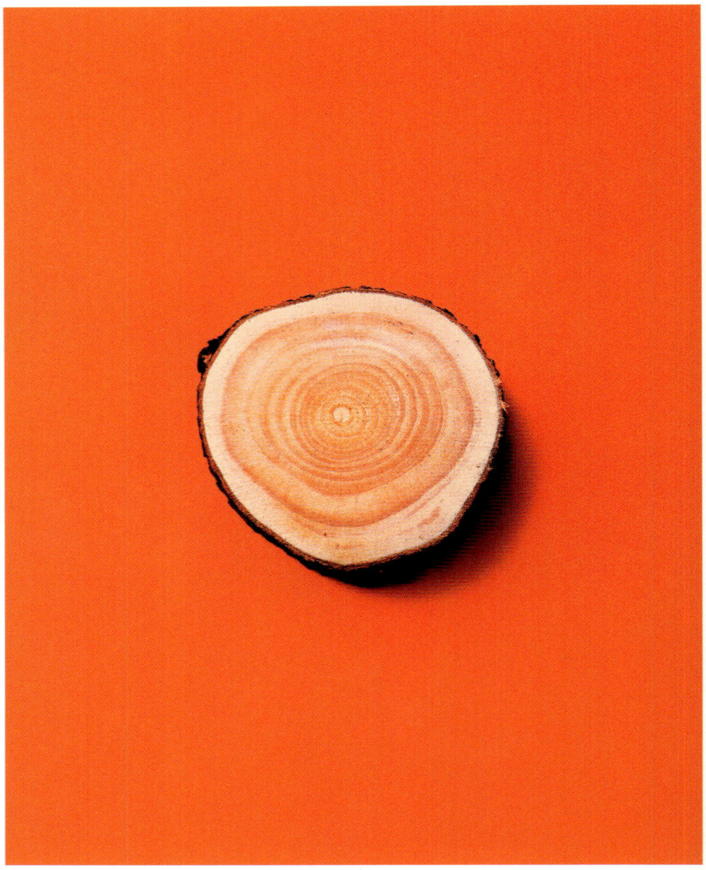

(this spread) Mark Weiss

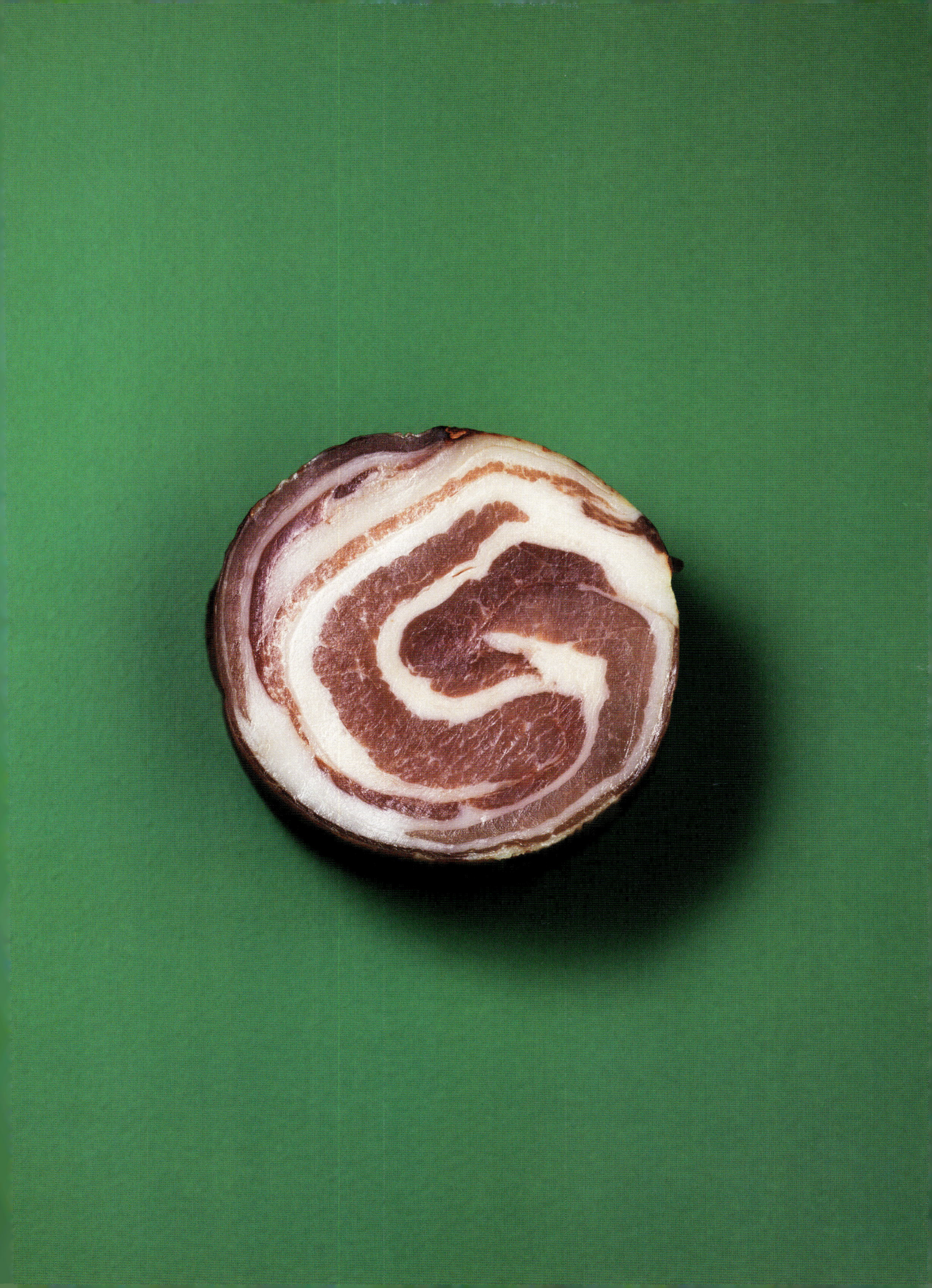

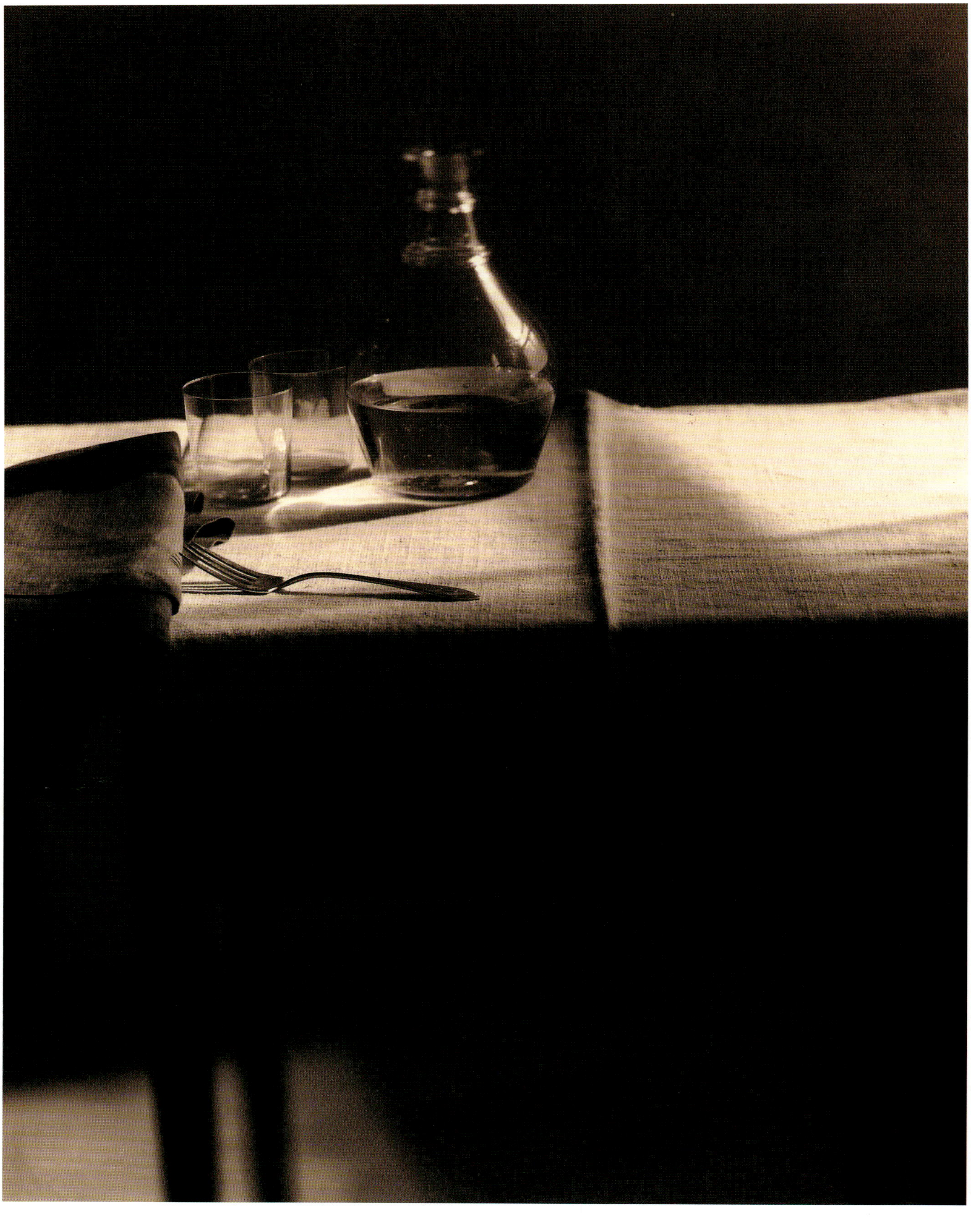

Maria Robledo

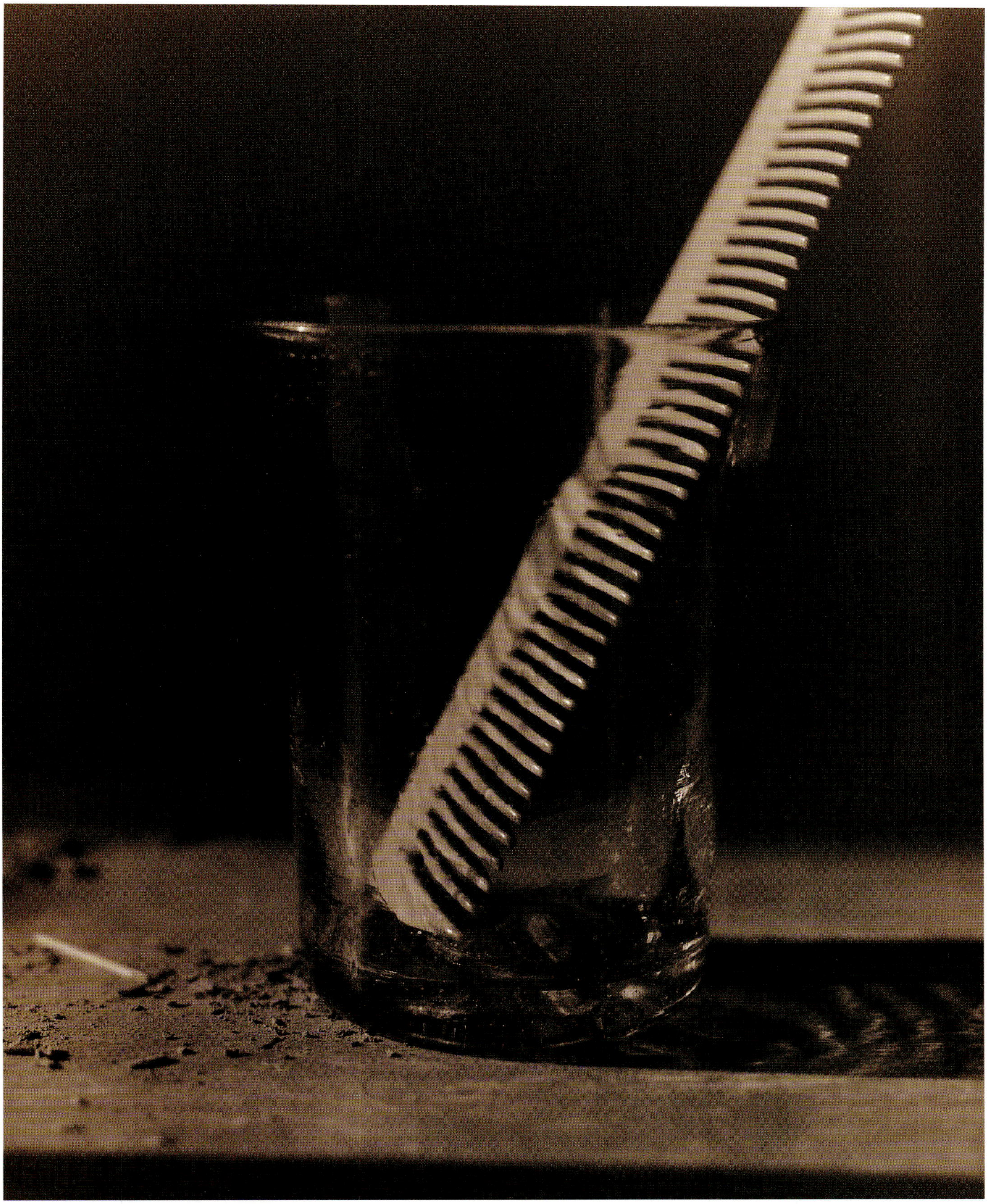

Maria Robledo

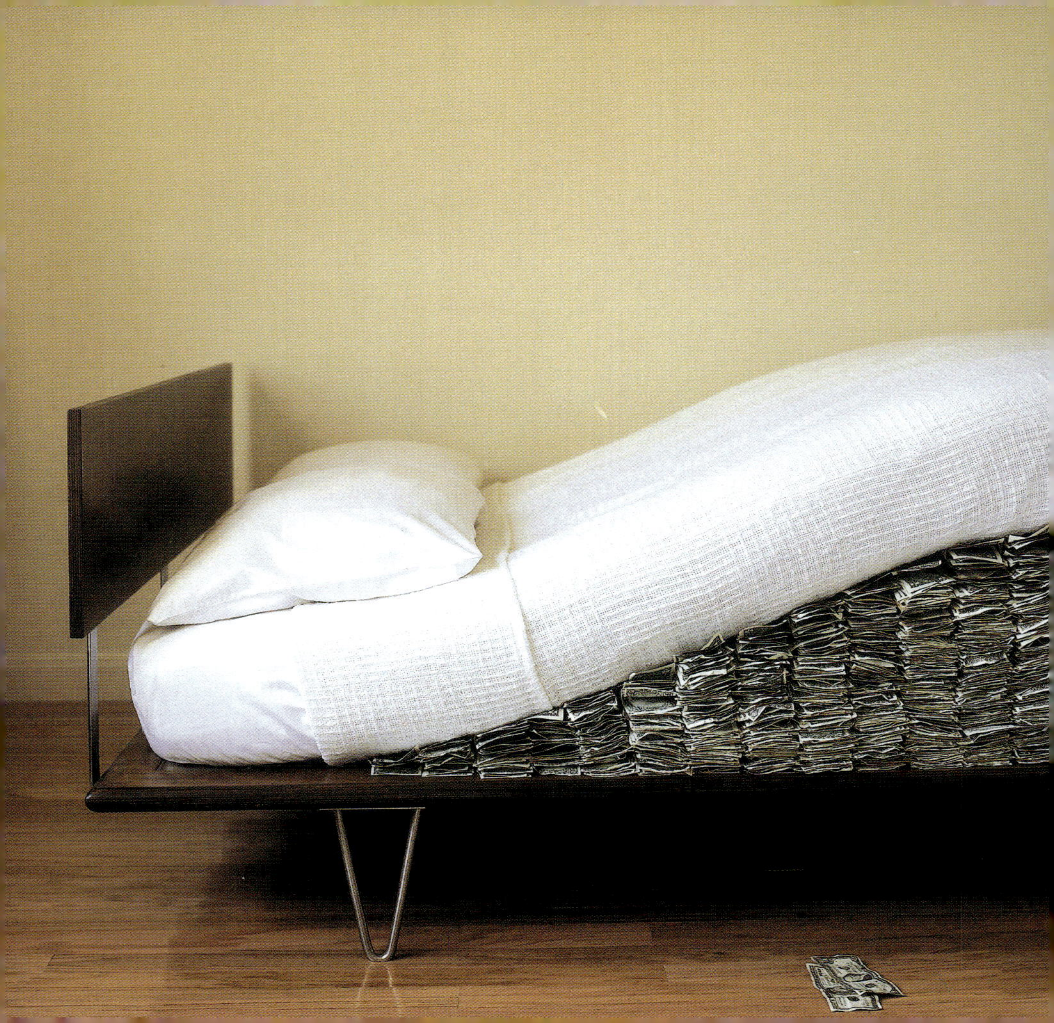

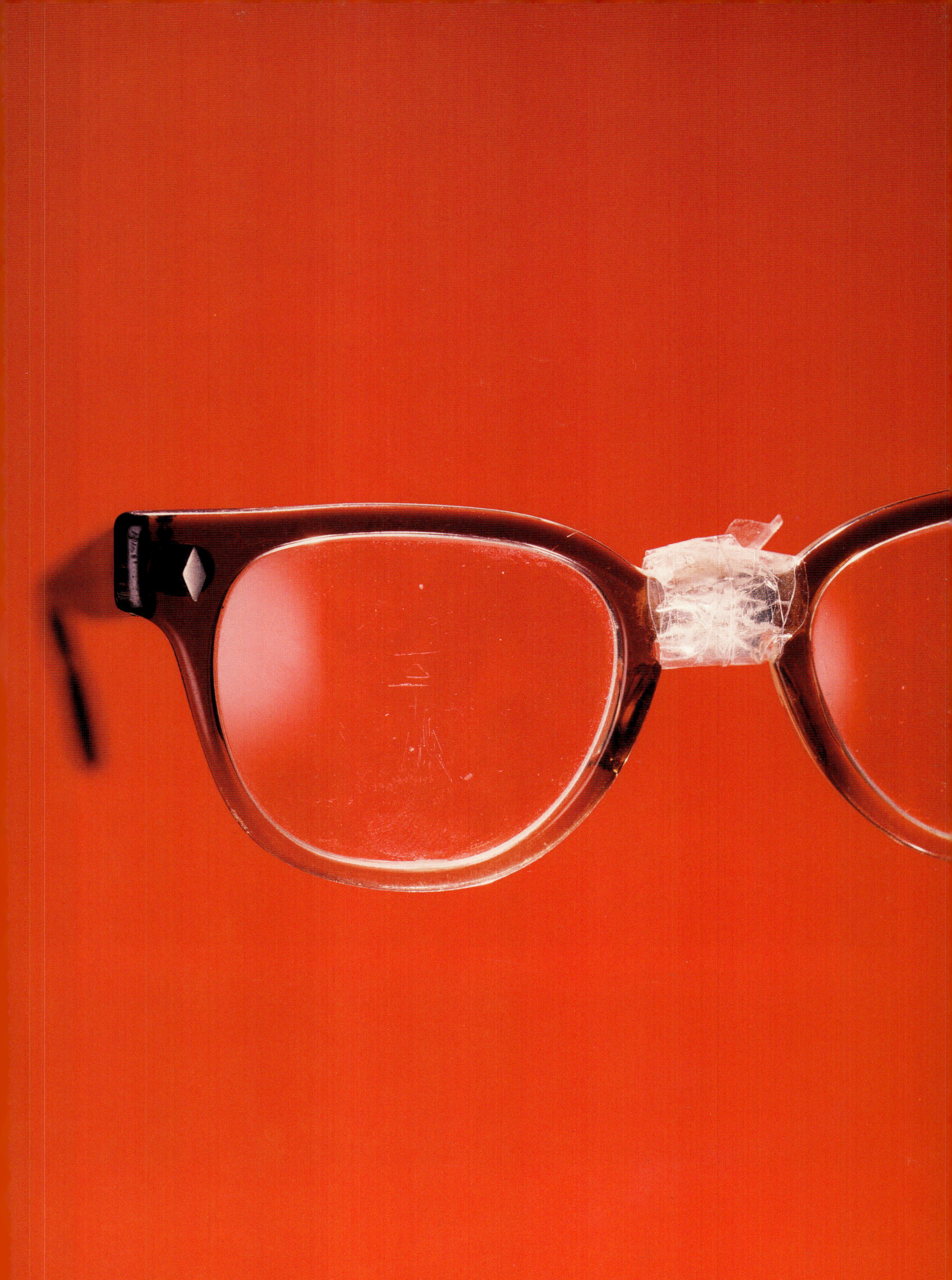

Geoff Spear

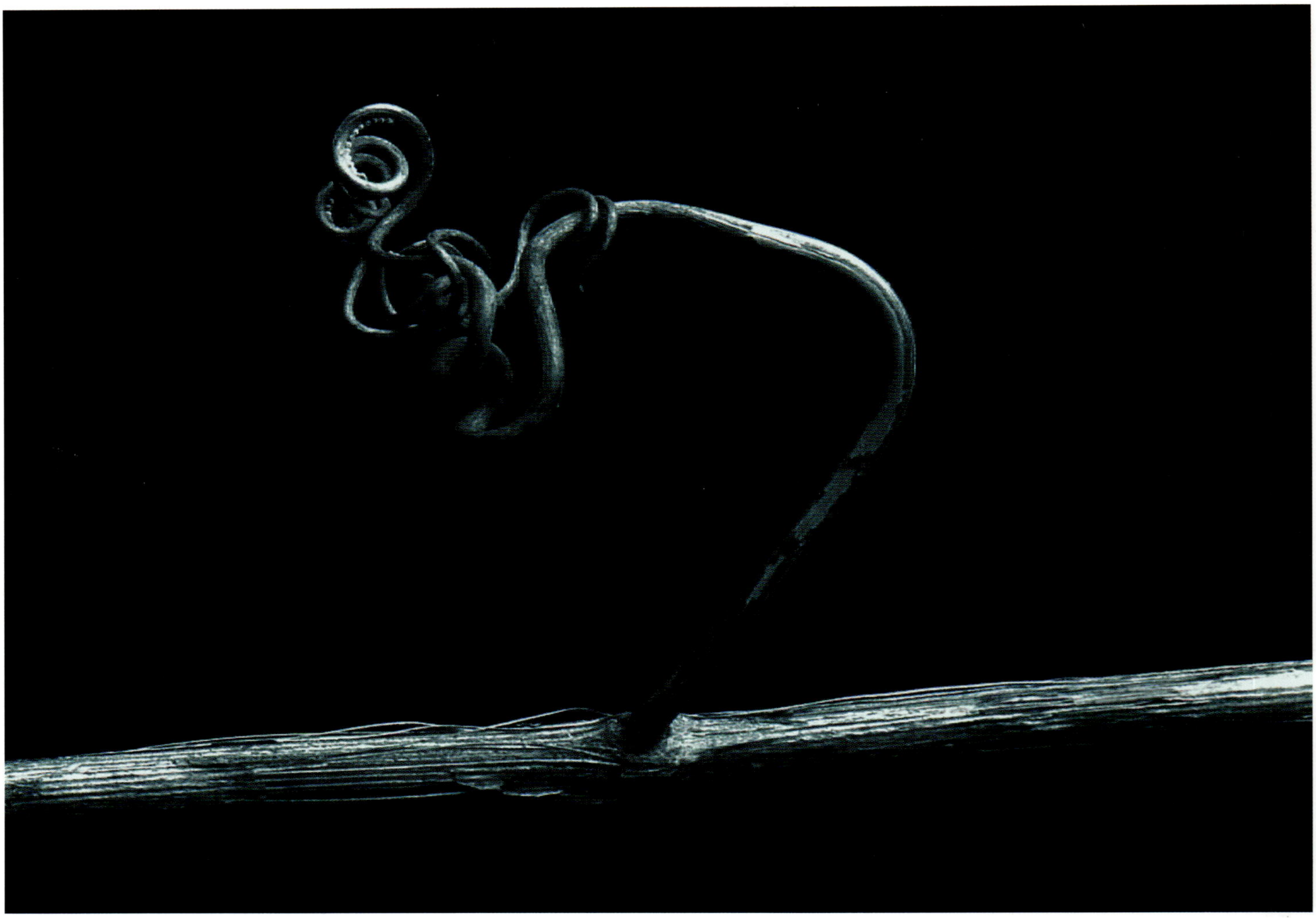

Mark Battrell

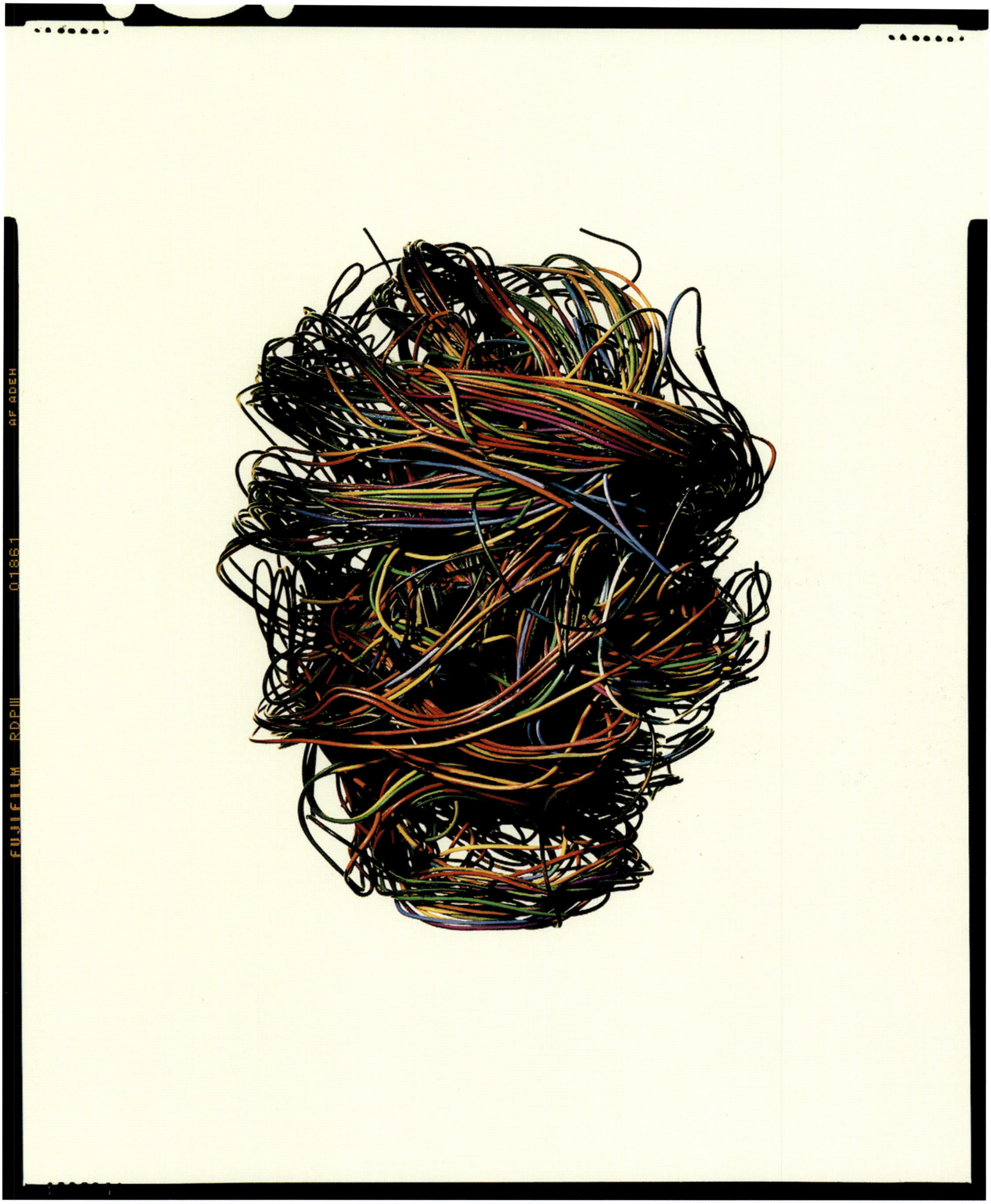

Mark Battrell

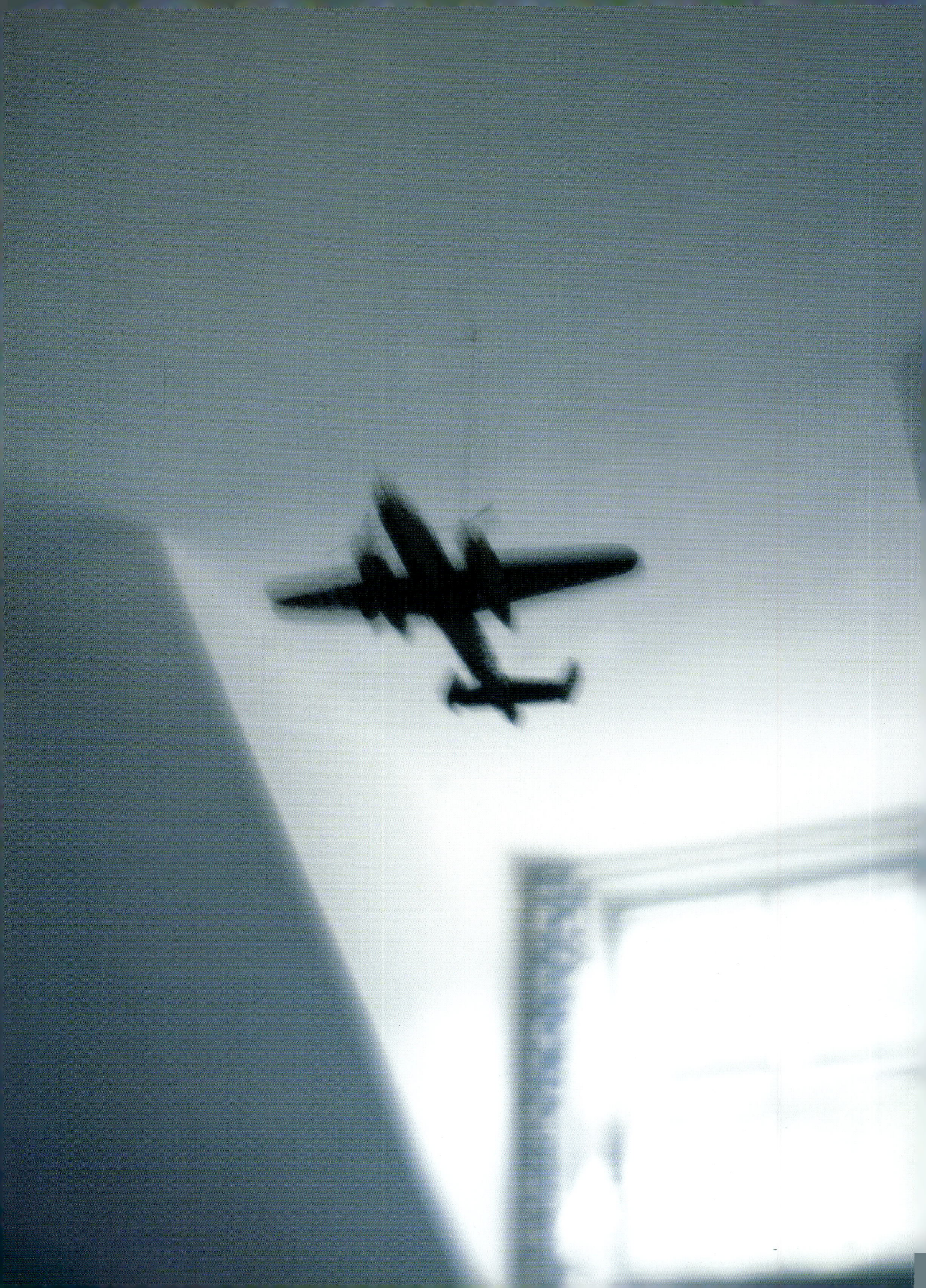

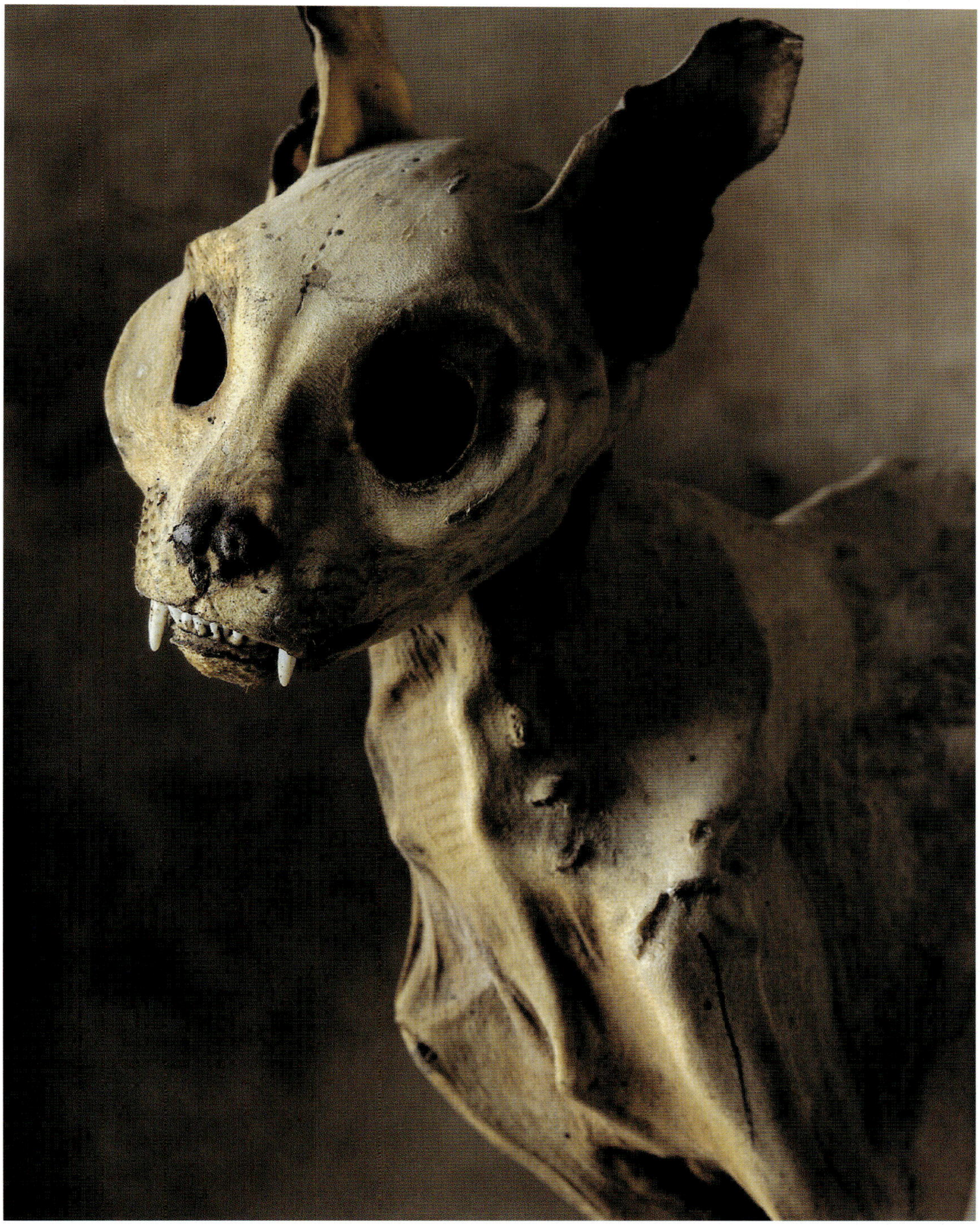

Jim Krantz (opposite) Sean Kernan

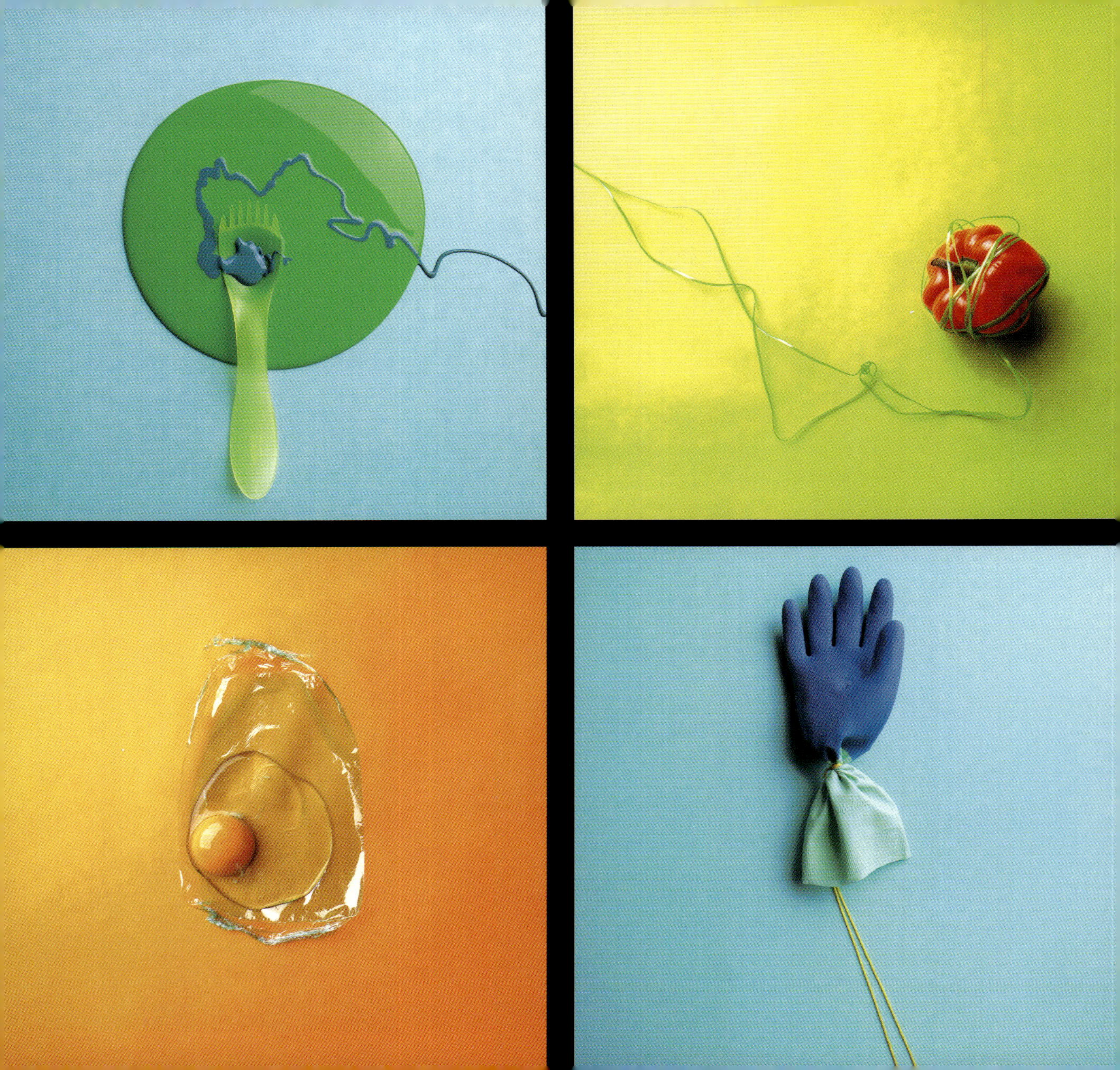

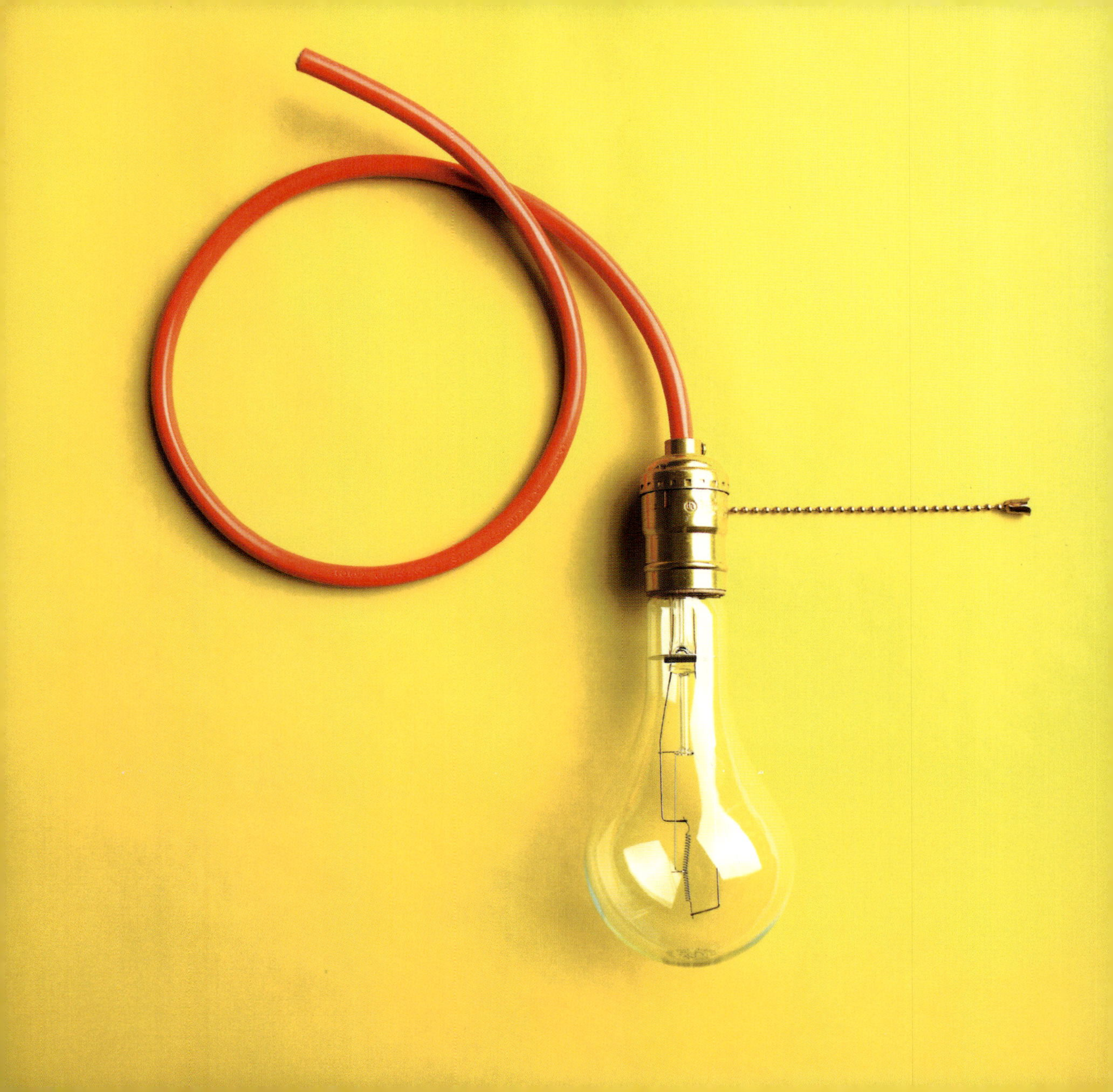

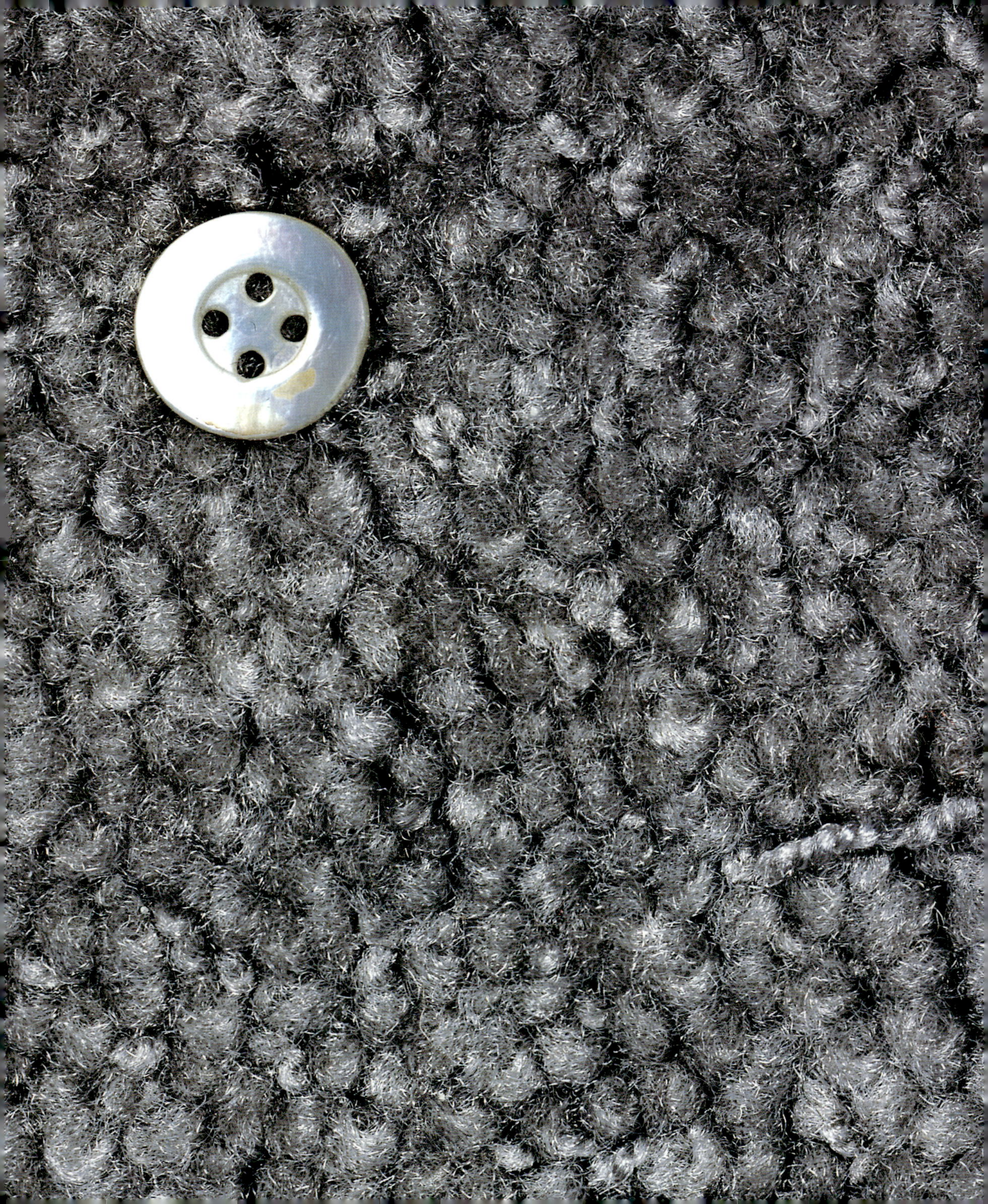

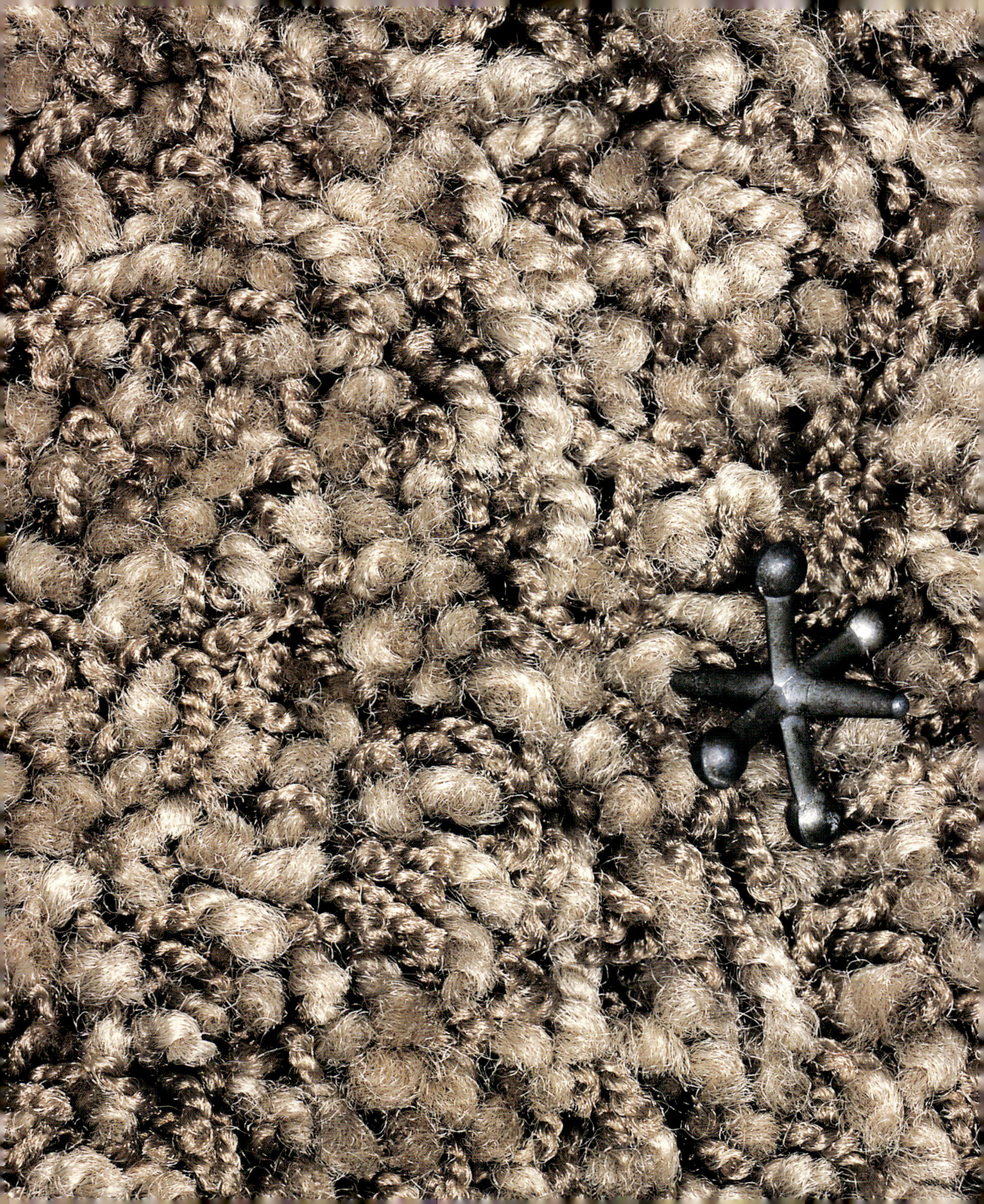

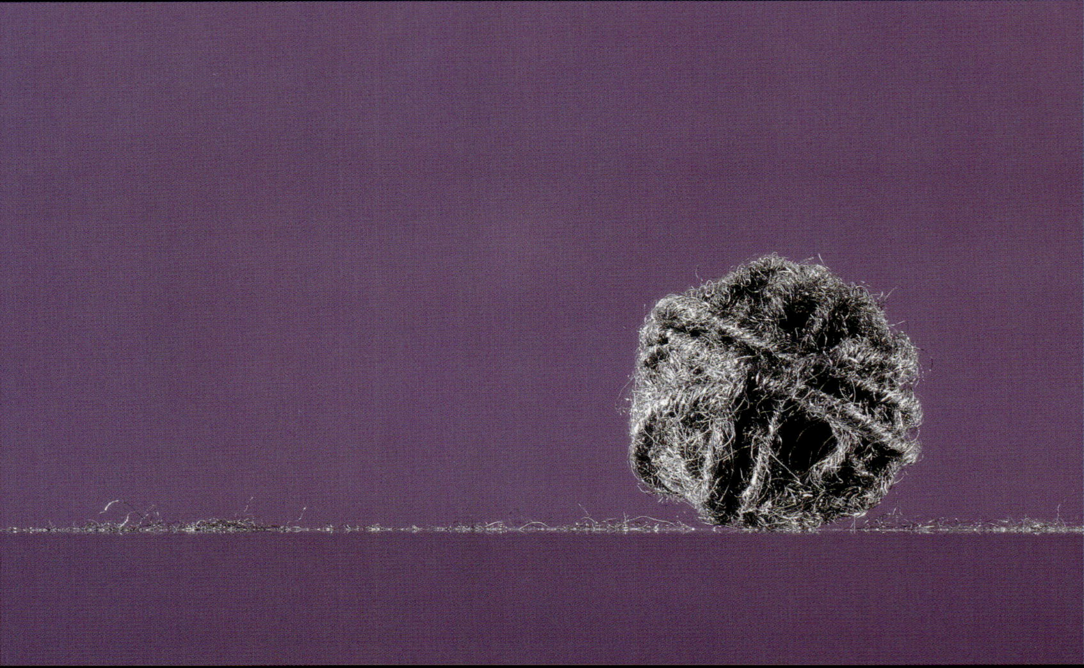

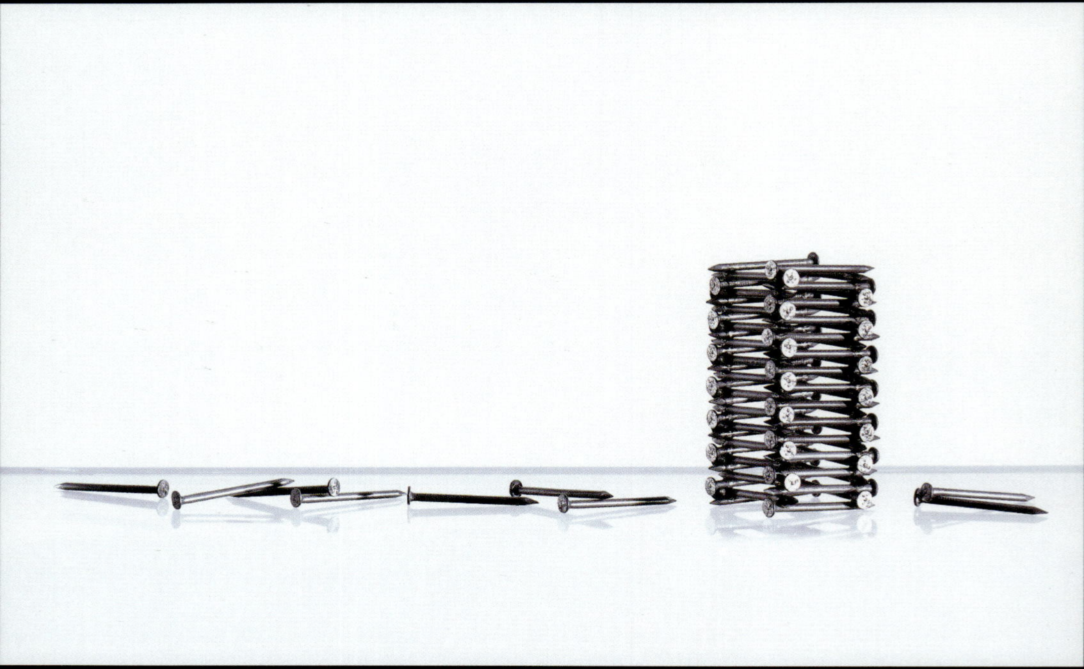

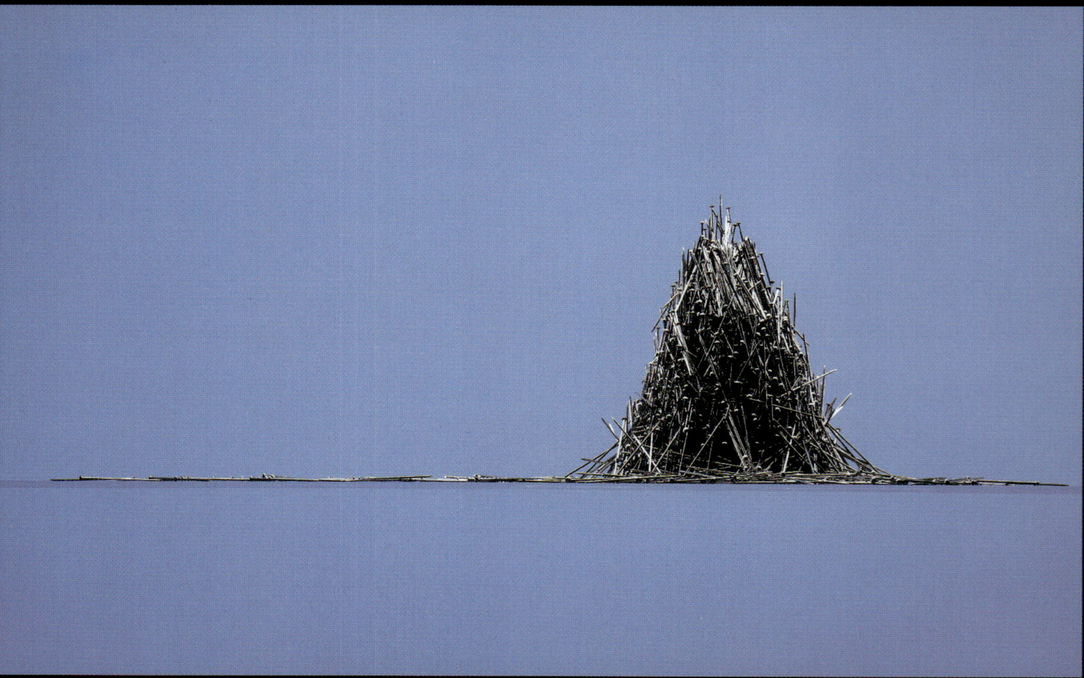

Plamen Petkov

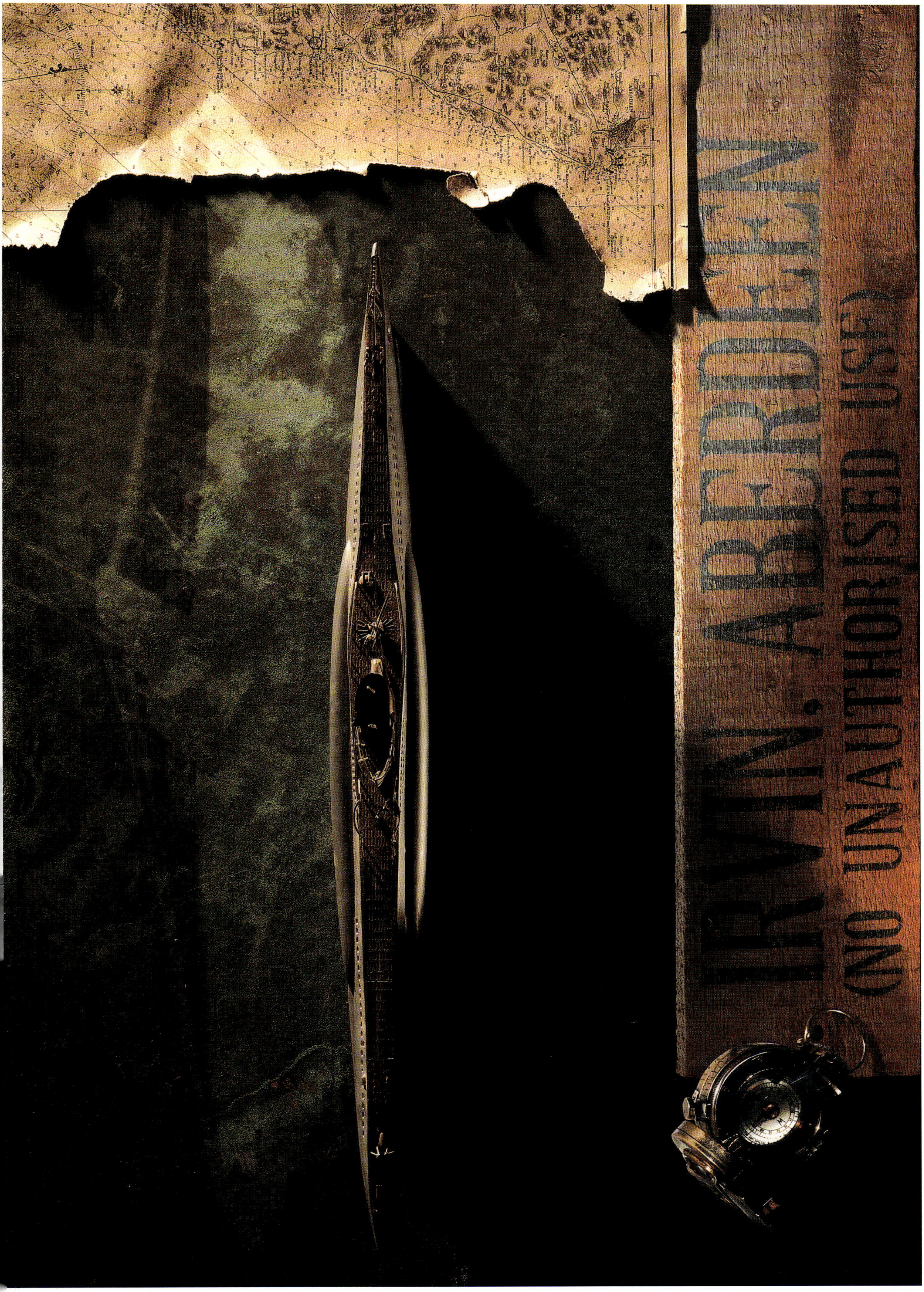

Lutz Pape

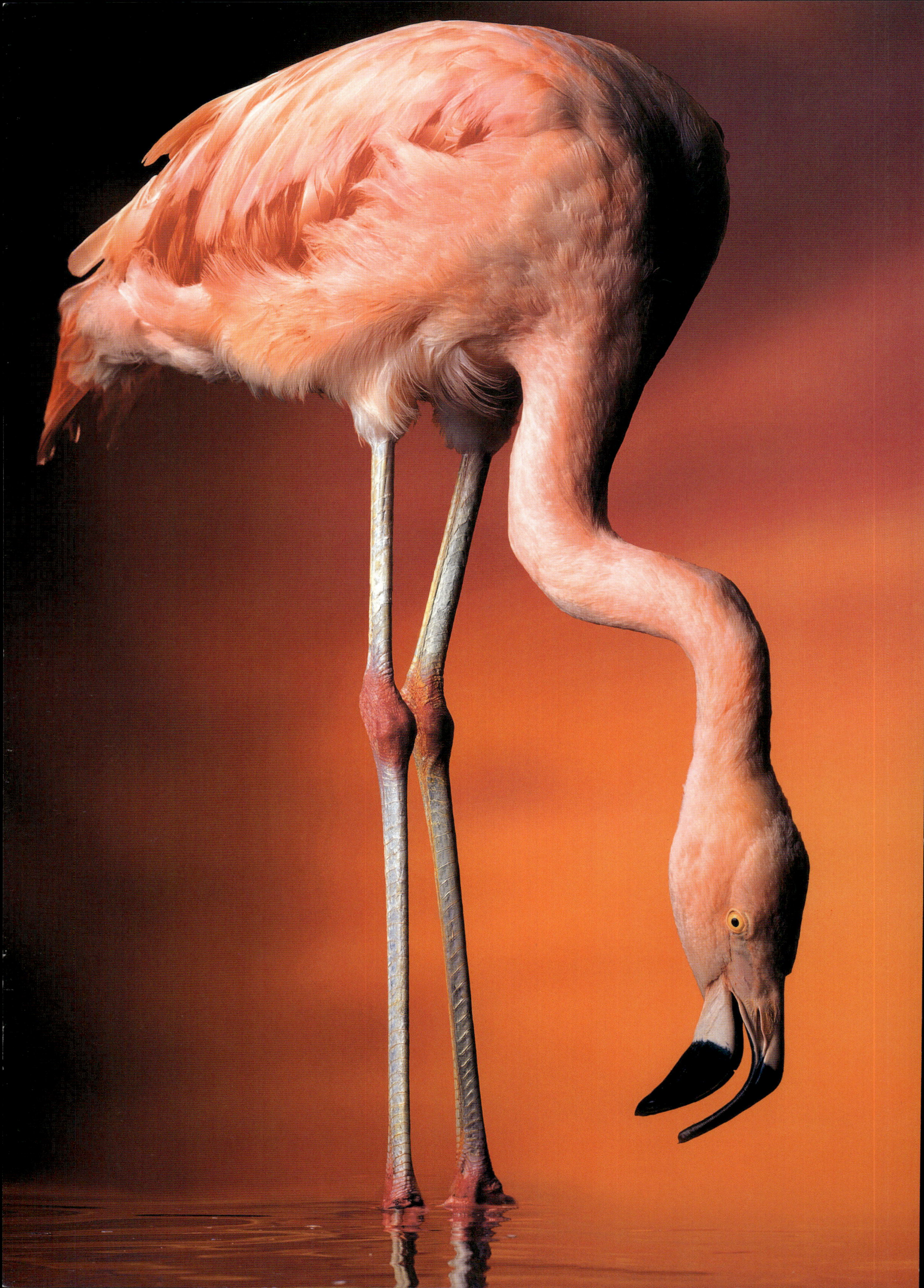

Wildlife

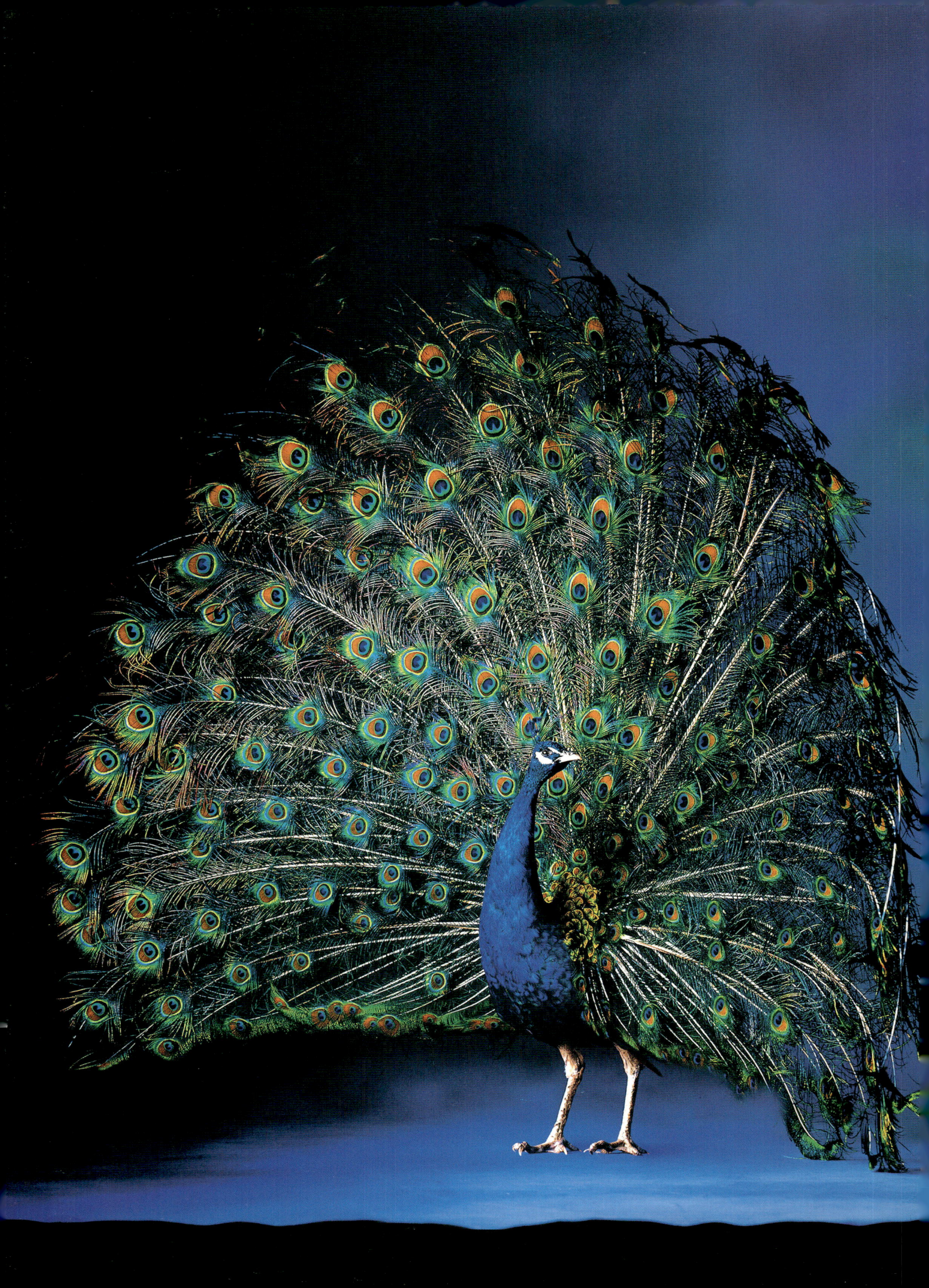

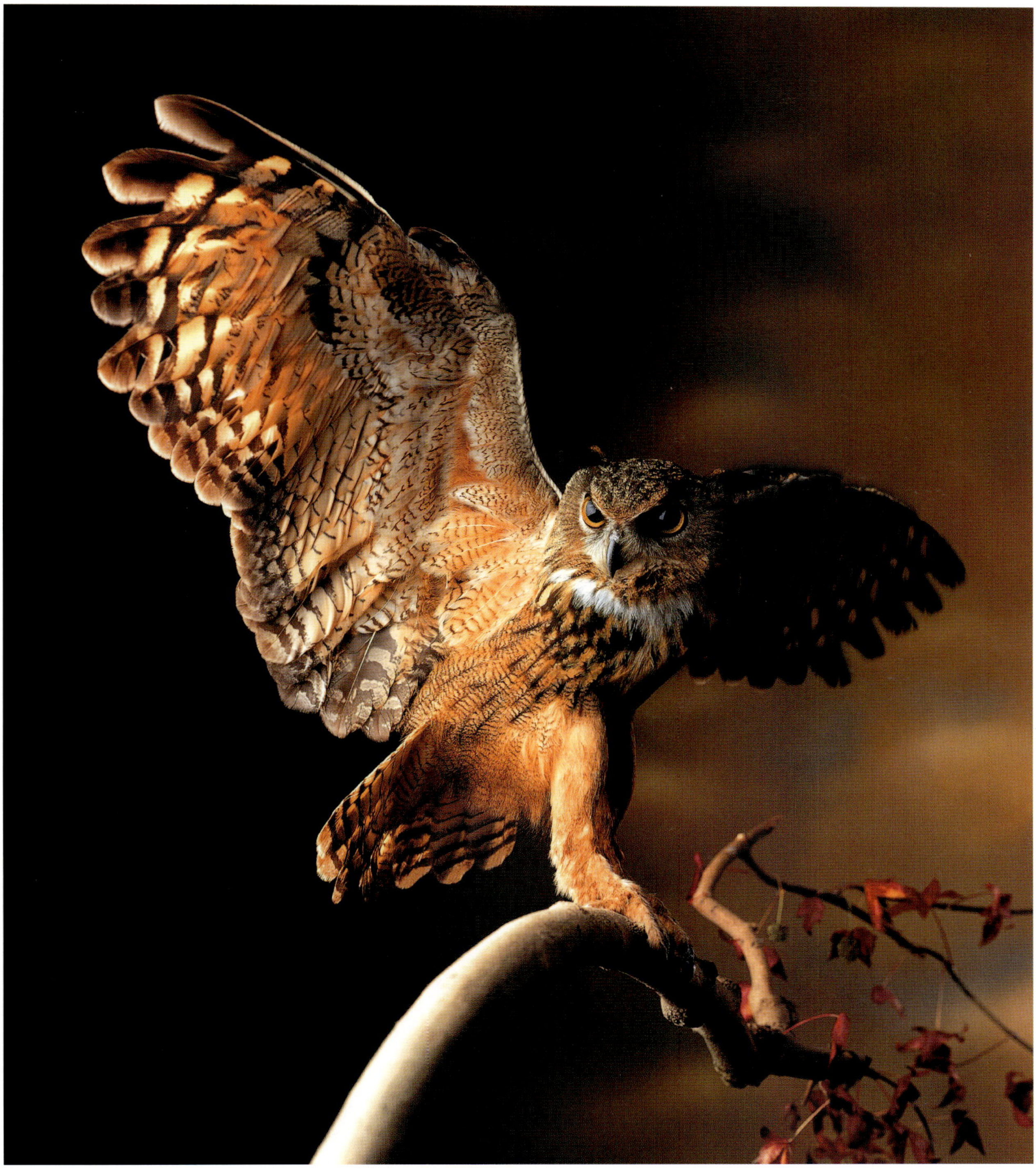

(this spread and opening page) Mark Laita

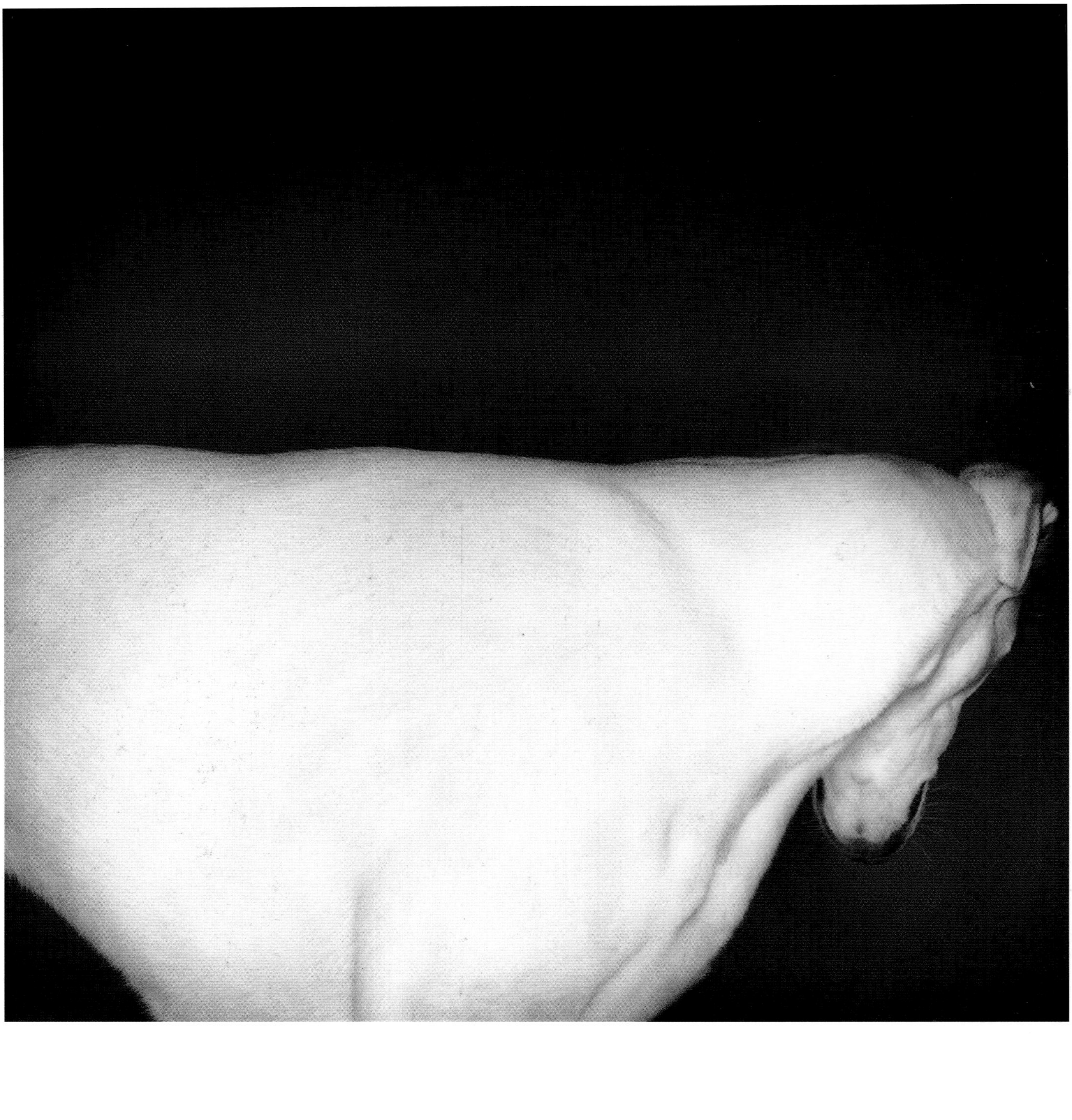

Deborah Samuel

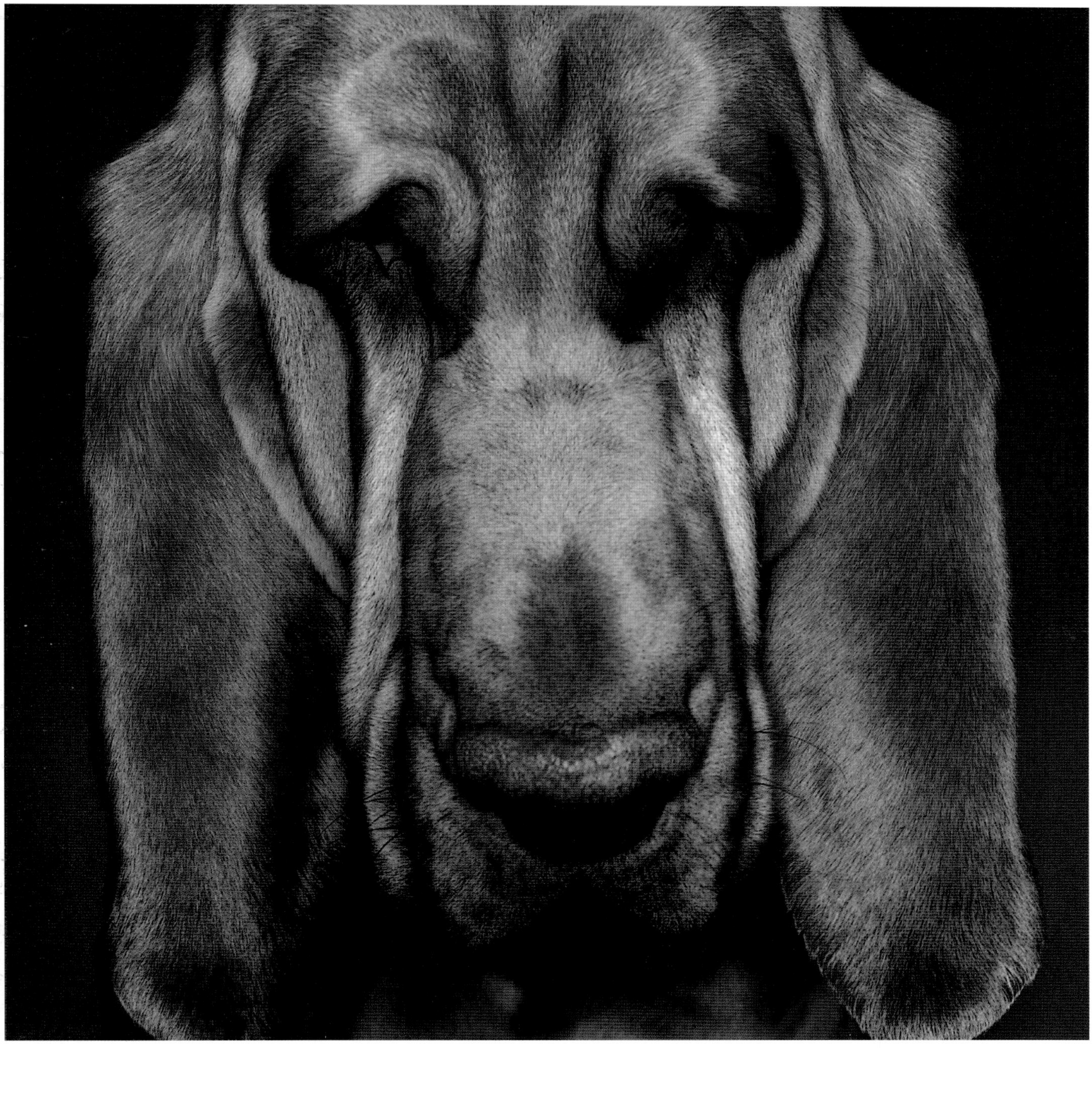

Deborah Samuel

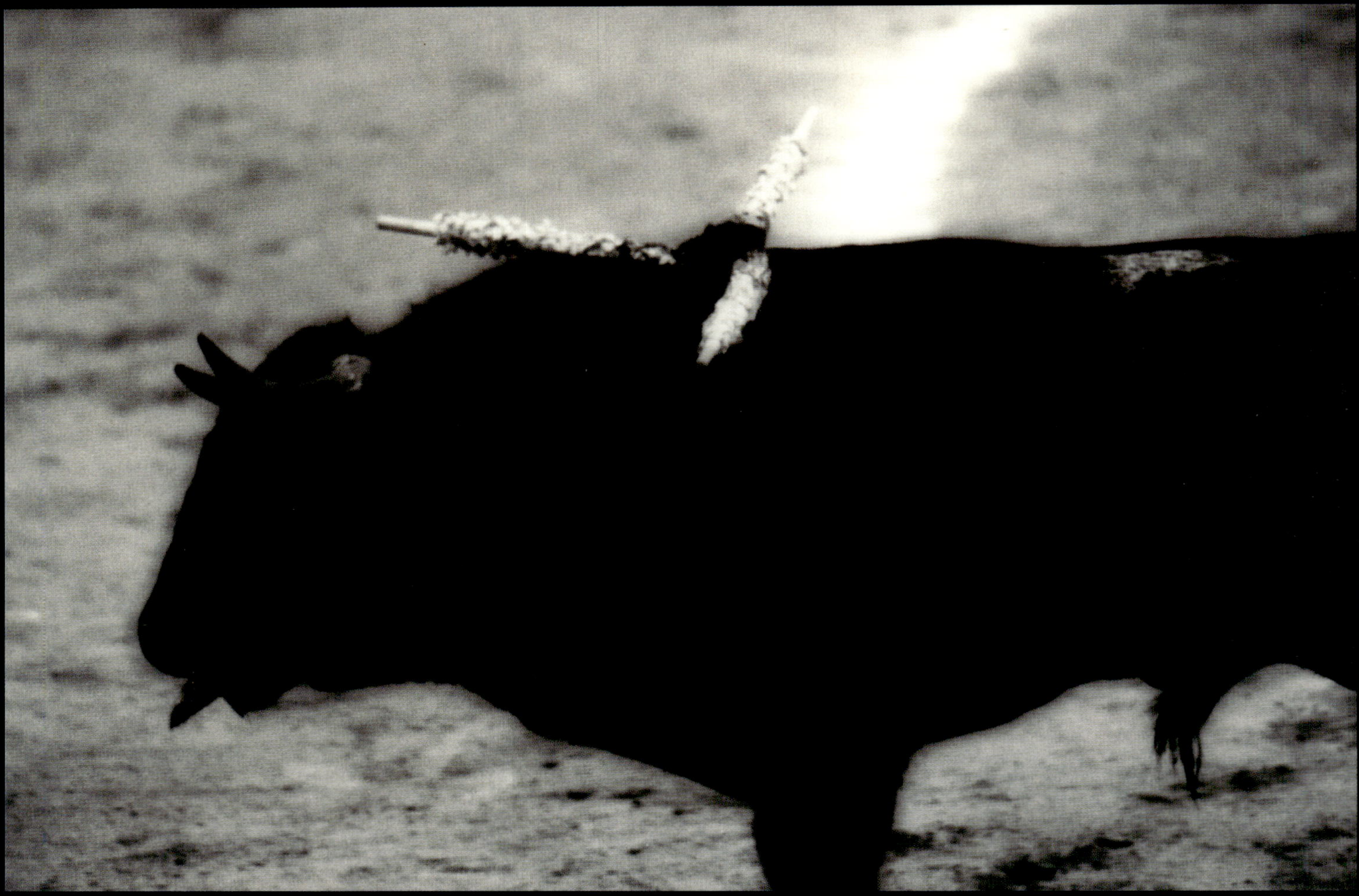

Robert Maxham

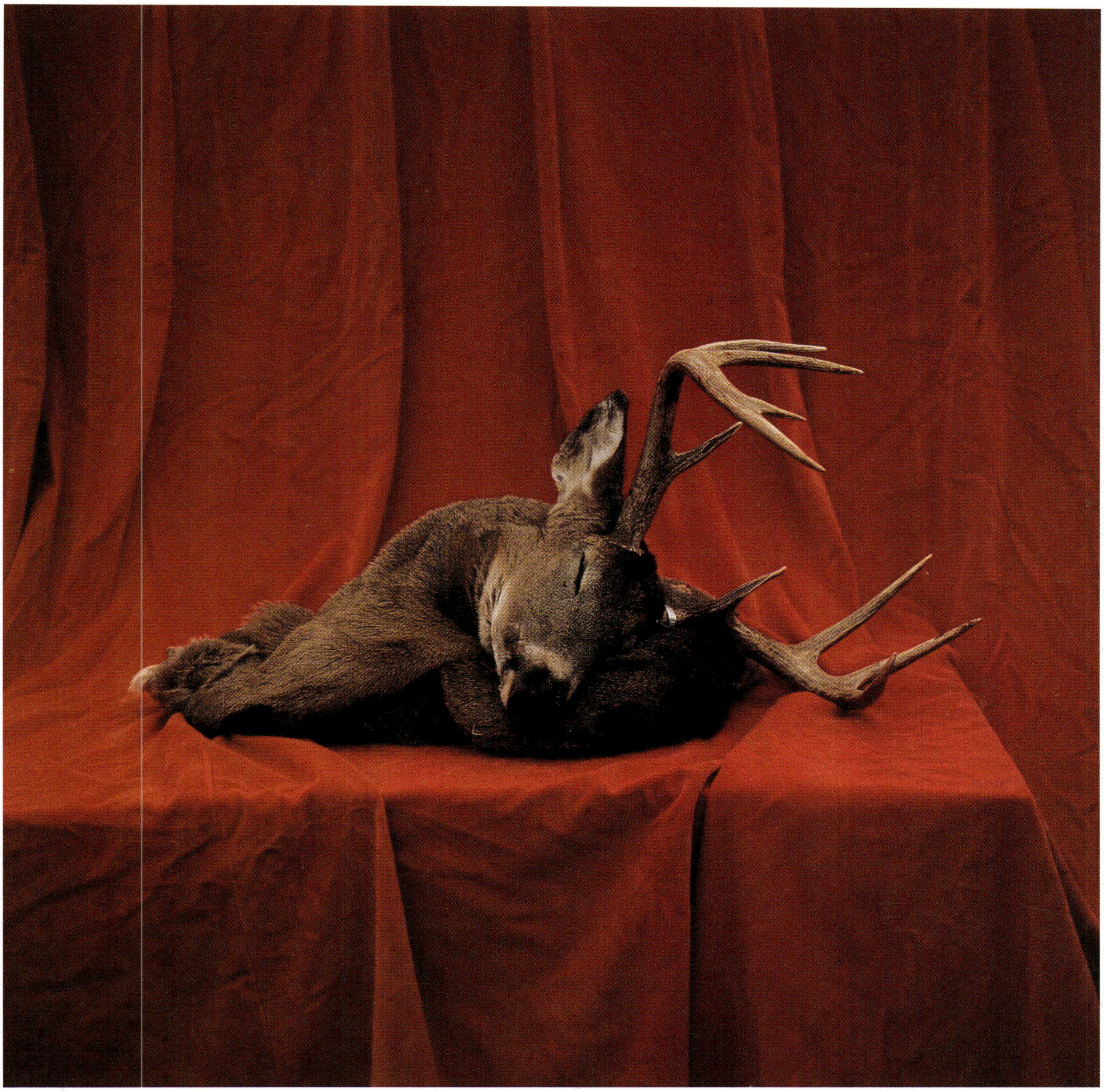

James Schnepf

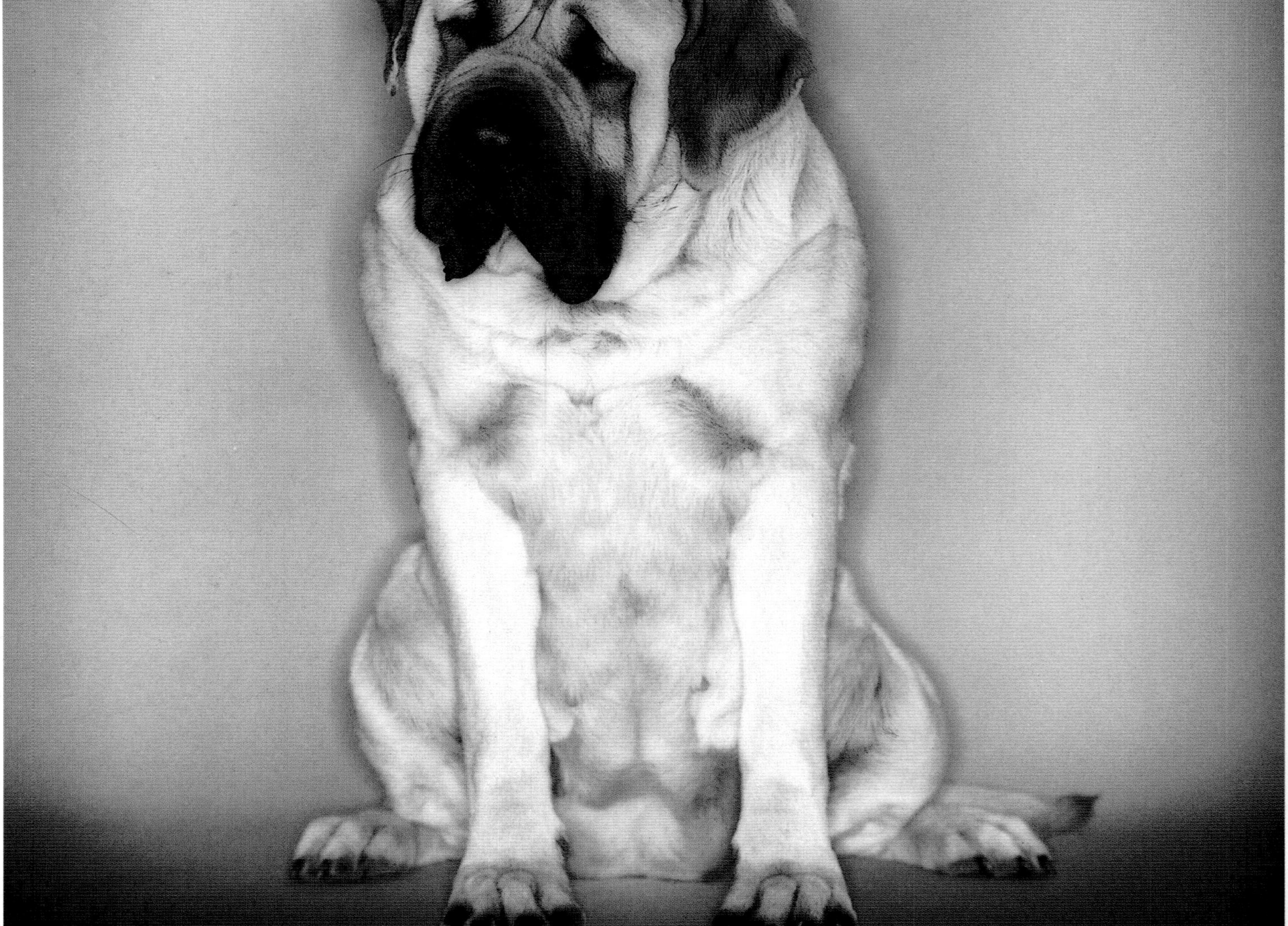

Deborah Samuel

Credits

Page 2
'Fashion Victim'
Photographer: Rafter
Camera: Hasselblad Film: Fuji Provia 100

Page 4
'Savoy Spring 2002'
Photographer: Howard Schatz
Studio: Schatz/Ornstein Studio
Art Director: Howard Schatz
Fashion Director: Kevin Stewart
Designer: Issey Miyake
Client: Savoy Magazine

Page 16
'Street Graphic, Tokyo'
Photographer: Arthur Meyerson
Studio: Arthur Meyerson Photography, Inc.

Page 18, top
'Shutter Wall, Buenos Aires'
Photographer: Arthur Meyerson
Studio: Arthur Meyerson Photography, Inc.

Page 18, middle
'Chairs/Chalkboard'
Photographer: Arthur Meyerson
Studio: Arthur Meyerson Photography, Inc.
Hotel Designer: Dayna Lee
Client: Hotel Derek, Houston Texas

Page 18, bottom
'Colored Wall, Buenos Aires'
Photographer: Arthur Meyerson
Studio: Arthur Meyerson Photography, Inc.

Page 19
'Honolulu Paradise'
Photographer: Andrea Wells
Studio: Andrea Wells Photography
Camera: Leica R7 Film: Fuji Velvia

Page 20
'Striped Architectural Facade'
Photographer: Phil Bekker
Studio: Bekker Photography
Creative Director: Phil Bekker
Art Director: Phil Bekker
Client: Bekker Photography
Camera: Rollei SL66 Film: Ektachrome

Page 21
'MacQuarie Lighthouse'
Photographer: Walter Whitman
Representative: Barbara Bowman Associates

Page 22
'Holiday Houses' (2), 'Irish Convent' and'Light on Wall'
Photographer: Craig Cutler
Representative: Art & Commerce
Camera: Hasselblad Film: Color negative

Page 23
'National Botanica Gardens'
Photographer: Craig Cutler
Studio: Art & Commerce
Camera: Hasselblad Film: 120/Tri-X

Page 24
'National Museum Series'
Photographer: John Gollings
Studio: Gollings Photography
Client: Ashton Raggatt McDougall
Camera: Linhoff Technikarden Film: Kodak 160VC

Page 25
'Move Mountains'
Photographer: Zachary Scott
Representative: Sharpe & Associates
Client: Toshiba Camera: Horseman Film: Provia

Page 26
'Volvo S-80 Interior'
Photographer: Michael Moore
Representative: Kray & Co.
Camera: Contax 645 Film: Kodak EPP

Page 28
'1964 AC Cobra,' '1937 Delahaye' and '935 Auburn Boatlail Speedster'
Photographer: Michael Furman
Studio: Michael Furman Photography
Creative Director: Kevin Thompson
Illustrator: David Phillips
Client: Ticona Camera: Sinar 4x5 Film: E100SW

Page 29
'1937 Dubonnel Hispano'
Photographer: Michael Furman
Studio/Representative: Michael Furman
Creative Director: Kevin Thompson
Illustrator: David Phillips
Client: Ticona Camera: Sinar 4x5 Film: E100SW

Page 30
'Audi AWD Wagon'
Photographer: Michael Moore
Representative: Kray & Co.
Camera: Sinar 4x5 Film: Type 55 Polaroid

Page 31
'Series: Vintage Racecar Details'
Photographer: Greg Myhra
Studio: Greg Myhra Photography
Camera: Holga Film: AGFA APX 400

Page 32
'Rock,' 'Peanuts' and 'Overlook'
Photographer: Chris Wimpey
Studio: Chris Wimpey Studio
Creative Director: Jim Nelson
Art Director: Jason Smith
Copywriters: Jim Nelson and Sheldon Clay
Client: Harley-Davidson
Camera: Toyo 45 Film: Kodak E100

Page 33, top and bottom
Photographer: Stuart Hall
Representative: Bernstein & Andriulli
Art Director: Viv Walsh
Ad Agenciy: Merkley Newman Harty
Client: Mercedes

Page 33, middle
Photographer: Stuart Hall
Representative: Bernstein & Andriulli
Art Director: Matthew Johnstone
Copywriter: Jeff Vinick
Ad Agenciy: Merkley Newman Harty
Client: Fila

Page 34
'Heart'
Photographer: Sanjay Kothari
Art Director: Matt Denning
Photo Editor: Kristen Schafer
Client: Big
Camera: Broniia Film: Kodak SW

Page 36
Photographer: Hugh Kretschmer
Representative: Sharpe & Associates
Art Director: John Korpics
Client: Esquire

Page 37
Photographer: Hugh Kretschmer
Representative: Sharpe & Associates
Art Director: Michael Lawton
Client: Men's Journal

Page 38
Photographer: Hugh Kretschmer
Representative: Sharpe & Associates
Art Director: Laura Zavets
Client: Bloomberg Wealth Manager

Page 39
'Now Online'
Photographer: Graham French
Representative: Chuck Dorr
Art Directors: Wendy Bloemink and Paul Grissom
Designer: David Hayes
Client: Graham French Photography

Page 40
Photographer: Eva Mueller

Page 42, 43
Photographer: Dan Forbes
Client: Harper's Bazaar

Page 44
'Miranda Weese with Bird'
Photographer: Rosanne Olson
Representative: Virtu
Creative Director: John Oberlander
Art Director: Flo Lukey
Client: New York City Ballet

Page 45
'Girl and Aquarium'
Photographer: Bryce Bennett
Studio: Bryce Bennett Communications
Client: Bryce Bennett
Camera: RZ67 Film: E100VS

Page 46
Photographer: Jono Rotman

Page 47
Photographer: Eva Mueller

Page 48, 49
'Beauty Closeups'
Photographer: Safia Fatimi
Camera: Hasselblad Film: Vericolor Kodak

Page 50
'Ingrid'
Photographer: Kenneth Rimm
Representative: CMP/Judi Shin
Client: Wallpaper

Page 51
'Claudia & Jesper'
Photographer: Kenneth Rimm
Studio/Representative: CMP/Judi Shin

Page 52
'Anenais'
Photographer: Sanjay Kothari
Art Director: Yoori Kim
Client: Little Brown Publishing

Page 53
Photographer: Eric Bottero
Representative: Arthouse Management

Page 54
'Bianca'
Photographer: Parish Kohanim
Studio: PKS
Camera: Sinar 4x5 Film: E-100S

Page 55, 56
'Kemp'
Photographer: Parish Kohanim
Studio: PKS
Camera: Contax 645 Film: E-100

Page 57
Photographer: Donna Trope
Client: New York Times Magazine

Page 58, 59
Photographer: Gil Blank
Studio: Gil Blank LLC

Page 60
'Muriel 06'
Photographer: Frank Wartenberg
Representative: Frank Arends
Camera: Mamiya Film: Kodak Epy

Page 61
'Melina Beauty 08'
Photographer: Frank Wartenberg

Representative: Frank Arends
Camera: Mamiya Film: Fuji RDP III

Page 62
'Flower Series'
Photographer: Bret Wills
Studio: Wills Studio, Inc.
Camera: 8x10 Horseman Film: Fuji RTP

Page 64
Photographer: Jon Shireman
Studio: Jon Shireman Photography

Page 65
Photographer: Andre Baranowski

Page 66
'Morning Glories'
Photographer: Parish Kohanim
Studio: PKS
Camera: EOS 3 Film: Ektachrome

Page 67
'From Your Backyard'
Photographer: JoSon
Studio: JoSon Photography

Page 68
'Turkey Leg'
Photographer: David Emmite
Studio: David Emmite Photography
Camera: 4x5 Film: NPL

Page 70
'Steak on Wall'
Photographer: David Emmite
Studio: David Emmite Photography
Camera: 4x5 Film: NPL

Page 71
'Cheeseboard'
Photographer: Geoff Spear
Representative: Greg Sellentin
Camera: Linhof 4x5 Film: Kodak

Page 72
'Baxters Mushroom'
Photographer: Jonathan Knowles
Studio: Jonathan Knowles Photography
Art Director: Guy Vickerstaff
Copywriter: Phil Evans
Client: Baxters of Speyside

Page 73
'Bosc Pear'
Photographer: Phil Marco
Studio: Phil Marco Productions, Inc.
Camera: D1 Nikon

Page 74
'MMMeats #1'
Photographer: Neal Brown
Representative: Sharpe & Associates

Page 75
'MMMeats #2'
Photographer: Neal Brown
Representative: Sharpe & Associates

Page 76
'Time Magazine Special Edition'
Photographer: Lyle Owerko
Representative: Gamma
Art Director: Arthur Hochstein
Photo Editor: Mary Anne Golon
Client: Time Magazine

Page 78
Photographer: Hugh Kretschmer
Representative: Sharpe & Associates

Page 79
'Genoa Protest 2001'
Photographer: Jake Price
Representative: Village Voice
Art Director: Ted Keller
Client: Village Voice
Camera: Nikon F1 Film: Fuji

Page 80, 81, 82, 83
'Farming Series'
Photographer: Reid Lincoln Ashton
Studio: Reid Lincoln Ashton Photography
Camera: RZ Mamiya Film: Kodak 100S

Page 84, 85
'Crouching Tiger, Hidden Thailand'
Photographer: Jeffrey Aaronson
Representative: Network Aspen
Art Director: James Stoffel
Deputy Photo Editor: Nicole Francis
Client: Travel Holiday
Camera: Nikon F5 Film: Fuji Velvia

Page 86
'Sari'
Photographer: Stephanie Flack
Camera: Canon EOS IN Film: Tri-X

Page 87
'Baby Monks'
'Votive Offering'
'Meditation'
'Turbins'
'Bathers en Masse'
'Pilgrim Couple'
'Campfire Women'
and 'Sari Dryer'
Photographer: Stephanie Flack

Page 88, 89
'Touring Cinema'
Photographer: Jonathan Torgovnik
Studio/Representative: Jonathan Torgovnik
Camera: Mamiya 6 Film: Kodak Portra

Page 90, 91
Photographer: Chris Gordaneer
Representative: C-folio.com

Page 92, 94, 95
'Trees'
Photographer: Sean Kernan
Representative: Molly Birenbaum
Creative Director: Sean Kernan
Art Director: Sean Kernan
Designer: Sean Kernan
Client: Sean Kernan

Page 96
'Oregon Coast Series'
Photographer: Lars Topelmann
Representative: Danielle Melanson
Camera: Custom Pinhole Film: Polaroid Type 55

Page 97
Photographer: Shelley Shazis
Representative: Hamilton, Gray & Associates

Page 98
'Home'
Photographer: Barry Gnyp
Representative: Deborah Ayerst
Camera: Pentacon 6 Film: Fuji NHG II 800

Page 99
'Tree'
Photographer: Long Nguyen
Camera: Nikon Film: Ilford

Page 100
'Image 1 Beach 1'
'Image 2 Beach 2'
and 'Image 3 Beach 3'
Photographer: Michael Hall
Studio: Michael Hall Photography
Art Director: Michael Hall
Camera: 4x5 Wista

Page 101
'Lamps'
Photographer: Markku Lahdesmaki
Representative: Stephanie Menuez
Camera: Hasselblad Film: Kodak

Page 102
'Chickens in the Desert'
Photographer: William Huber
Representative: Marilyn Cadenbach
Art Director: Dan Murch
Camera: Pentax Film: 120mm

Page 103
'Trailer'
Photographer: William Huber
Representative: Marilyn Cadenbach
Art Director: Sean Farrell
Client: Hewlett Packard Camera: Nikon F3 Film: 35mm

Page 104
'The Viewer, March 2001'
Photographer: Antonio Bogart
Studio: Bogart & Bogart
Camera: Nikon Film: T-Max

Page 105
'Wooden Boat'
Photographer: Craig Cutler
Representative: Art & Commerce
Camera: Hasselblad Film: Color negative

Page 106
'Tonto Drive-In, Winston AZ'
Photographer: Greg Myhra
Studio: Greg Myhra Photography
Camera: Holga Film: AGFA AFX 100

Page 107
'Blue Pool'
Photographer: Phil Bekker
Studio: Bekker Photography
Art Director: Phil Bekker
Client: Bekker Photography
Camera: 6x12

Page 108
'Pam 82'
Photographer: Paul Murphy
Camera: Sinar 5x4 Film: AGFA RSX 100

Page 110
Photographer: Neal Brown
Representative: Sharpe & Associates

Page 111
'Model Minority'
Photographer: JoSon
Studio: JoSon Photography
Creative Director: JoSon
Art Director: JoSon

Page 112
Photographer: Miro Ito

Page 113
Photographer: Howard Schatz
Studio: Schatz/Ornstein Studio

Page 114
'Untitled'
Photographer: Joseph E. Reid
Camera: Nikon F100 Film: Polaroid OneFilm

Page 115
Photographer: Howard Schatz

Page 116
'Nude Body Nude Series'
Photographer: Howard Schatz
Studio: Schatz/Ornstein Studio

Page 117
'Untitled'
Photographer: Raoul Benavides
Studio: Raoul Benavides Photo
Camera: 8x10 Film: Polaroid

Page 118
Photographer: Eva Mueller

Page 119
'Untitled'
Photographer: Parish Kohanim
Studio: PKS
Film: Delta 100

Page 120
'Salt Flats'
Photographer: Andy Freeberg
Camera: Hasselblad Film: Tri-X

Page 121
'Dancer in Neon #2'
Photographer: Klaus Kampert
Camera: Fuji GX680 Film: AGFA Scala

Page 122
Photographer: Felix Holzer
Studio: Felix Holzer Studio

Page 124, 125
Photographer: Hugh Kretschmer
Representative: Sharpe & Associates
Art Director: Matt Lenning
Photo Editor: Kristen Schaffer
Client: GQ

Page 126
Photographer: Jeff Stephens

Page 127
'René'
Photographer: Michael Castagnetti
Camera: Pentax 6x7 Film: Kodak Plus X

Page 128
'Chef'
Photographer: Zachary Scott
Representative: Sharpe & Associates
Camera: R2 Film: NPS 160

Page 129
'Carl Can't Hide #1'
Photographer: Zachary Scott
Representative: Sharpe & Associates
Camera: R2 Film: Provig

Page 130
'Narrowly Averted'
Photographer: Zachary Scott
Representative: Sharpe & Associates
Designer: Sandstrom Design
Copywriter: Sandstrom Design
Client: Zachary Scott

Page 131
'Bump'
Photographer: Zachary Scott
Representative: Sharpe & Associates

Page 132
'Kenny'
Photographer: William Huber
Representative: Marilyn Cadenbach
Camera: Pentax Film: 120mm

Page 133
'Tricia'
Photographer: William Huber
Representative: Marilyn Cadenbach
Stylist: Suzanne Rubin Camera: Pentax Film: 120mm

Page 134
'OP 04 Mappe'
Photographer: Frank Wartenberg
Representative: Frank Arends
Camera: Mamiya Film: Kodak EPR

Page 135
'Mario 02'
Photographer: Frank Wartenberg
Representative: Frank Arends
Camera: Mamiya Film: Kodak EPR

Page 136, 137, 138, 139
'Blues'
Photographer: Sue Bennett
Studio: Sue Bennett Photography
Camera: Crown Graphic Film: Polaroid

Page 140
'Life Scan'
Photographer: Sue Bennett
Studio: Sue Bennett Photography
Creative Director: Rory Phoenix
Art Director: Jill Regan
Client: Johnson & Johnson Camera: Hasselblad Film: Fuji

Page 141
'T. D. Jakes'
Photographer: Michael O'Brien
Art Director: Arthur Hochstein
Client: Time Magazine
Camera: 4x5 Film: Polaroid 55

Page 142
'Couple'
Photographer: Michael O'Brien
Camera: Hasselblad Film: Tri-X

Page 143
'Kevin Aviance'
Photographer: Stewart Cohen
Representative: Denise Ford

Page 144, 145
'Fight Domestic Violence'
Photographer: Jono Rotman
Studio: Jono Rotman Photographer
Creative Director: Peter Robertson
Copywriter: Susan Hosking
Make Up: Bill Hunt
Client: New Zealand Womens Refuge

Page 146
'Model Minority'
Photographer: JoSon
Studio: JoSon Photography
Creative Director: JoSon
Art Director: JoSon

Page 147
'Bath #291'
Photographer: Barry Gnyp
Representative: Deborah Ayerst
Camera: Polaroid 680 Film: Polaroid 600

Page 148
'Grieg Nori #1'
Photographer: K. C. Armstrong
Studio: Bottle Rocket Pictures
Camera: Mamiya R2 Film: Kodak Tri-X

Page 149
'Grieg Nori #2'
Photographer: K. C. Armstrong
Studio: Bottle Rocket Pictures
Camera: Mamiya R2 Film: Kodak Portra 160VC

Page 150
'David Lynch'
Photographer: Robin Holland
Representative: Village Voice
Art Director: Ted Keller
Client: Village Voice
Camera: Hasselblad Film: Kodak EPP

Page 151
Photographer: Herb Ritts
Art Director: Fred Woodward
Client: Rolling Stone

Page 152
'Jennifer Lopez'
Photographer: Mark Seliger
Representative: Proof Photographic Agents
Art Director: Fred Woodward
Client: Rolling Stone

Page 153
'Britney Spears'
Photographer: Mark Seliger
Representative: Proof Photographic Agents
Art Director: Fred Woodward
Client: Rolling Stone

Page 154, 155
'Belladonna'
Photographer: Jono Rotman
Studio: Jono Rotman Photographer
Designer: Charlie Ward
Client: Dna Designed Communication

Page 156
Photographer: Mark Seliger
Representative: Proof Photographic Agents

Page 157
'Sugar Ray'
Photographer: Mark Seliger
Representative: Proof Photographic Agents

Page 158
'Dave, Groundsperson'
Photographer: Paul Murphy
Art Director: Grant Parker
Client: Fetzer
Camera: Mamiya R2 6x7

Page 159
'Cuban Soldier, Miami'
Photographer: Paul Murphy

Page 160
'Stephen F.'
Photographer: Dale Bernstein
Representative: Jim Hanson Artist Agent Ltd.
Client: Dale Bernstein Photography, Inc.
Camera: Phillips 8x10 Film: Hand-Coated Glass

Page 161
'Wayne G.'
Photographer: Dale Bernstein
Representative: Jim Hanson Artist Agent Ltd.
Client: Dale Bernstein Photography, Inc.
Camera: Phillips 8x10 Film: Hand-Coated Glass

Page 162
'Wayne Reclining'
Photographer: Dale Bernstein
Representative: Jim Hanson Artist Agent Ltd.
Client: Dale Bernstein Photography, Inc.
Camera: Phillips 8x10 Film: Hand-Coated Glass

Page 163
'Joni S.'
Photographer: Dale Bernstein
Representative: Jim Hanson Artist Agent Ltd.
Client: Dale Bernstein Photography, Inc.
Camera: Phillips 8x10 Film: Hand-Coated Glass

Page 164
'Jim W.'
Photographer: Dale Bernstein
Representative: Jim Hanson Artist Agent Ltd.
Client: Dale Bernstein Photography, Inc.
Camera: Phillips 8x10 Film: Hand-Coated Glass

Page 165
'Geno'
Photographer: Dale Bernstein
Representative: Jim Hanson Artist Agent Ltd.
Client: Dale Bernstein Photography, Inc.
Camera: Phillips 8x10 Film: Hand-Coated Glass

Page 166
'Williams Sisters'
Photographer: Howard Schatz
Representative: Temerlin McClain
Creative Director: Chris Cima
Client: Nortel Networks

Page 167
'Butterfly Girl'
Photographer: Reid Lincoln Ashton

Studio: Reid Lincoln Ashton Photography
Camera: R2 Maniya Film: 100S

Page 168
'Motel Lady'
Photographer: Jim Fiscus
Representative: Randy Cole Represents
Digital Imaging: Jester Image Works
Client: Jim Fiscus
Camera: Mamiya RZ Film: Kodak 6100VS

Page 169
'Untitled #2'
Photographer: Cindy James
Studio: Cindy James Photography
Camera: Mamiya RZ Film: E100S

Page 170
'Spencer and Evan'
Photographer: Terry Husebye
Studio: Terry Husebye Photography
Client: Terry Husebye Photography
Camera: Nikon 35mm Film: Kodak Negative

Page 171
Photographer: Ken Villeneuve

Page 172
'Man Screaming'
Photographer: Lars Topelmann
Representative: Danielle Melanson
Art Director: Mike Fazende
Ad Agency: Ogilvy & Mather
Client: Dynergy
Camera: Fuji 680 II Film: Plus X

Page 173
'Ostinato David'
Photographer: Sean W. Hennessy
Studio: Hennessy Photography
Camera: Sinar Film: Fuji

Page 174
'Christan Floating'
Photographer: Parish Kohanim
Studio: PKS
Camera: EOS 3 Film: E100S

Page 175
'Jeanna'
Photographer: Parish Kohanim
Studio: PKS
Camera: Contax 645 Film: E100S

Page 176
'Untitled (#7)'
Photographer: Danelle Dalpra
Studio: Danelle Dalpra Photography
Camera: Hasselblad Film: EPP100

Page 177
'Untitled (#5)'
Photographer: Danelle Dalpra
Studio: Danelle Dalpra Photography
Camera: Hasselblad Film: EPP100

Page 178
'Corey'
Photographer: Rob Stephen
Art Director: Rob Stephen
Client: Vena Cava
Camera: Bronica ETR Film: Fuji RDP

Page 179
'Pat'
Photographer: Rob Stephen
Art Director: Rob Stephen
Client: Vena Cava Camera: Bronica ETR Film: Fuji RDP

Page 180
Photographer: Miro Ito

Page 181
'Soul of a Child'
Photographer: Jimmy Williams
Representative: Natalie Ogura

Page 182
'(T)here Issue #5'
Photographer: Fabrizio Ferri
Representative: There Media
Creative Director: Chris Wieliczko
Client: (T)here Magazine

Page 184
Photographer: Eric Bottero
Representative: Arthouse Management

Page 185
Photographer: Marshall Harrington

Page 186, 187
Photographer: Felix Holzer
Studio: Felix Holzer Studio

Page 188
'Oral B'
Photographer: Steven Moeder
Studio: Moeder Photography
Art Director: Paul Bradley
Designer: Ricardo Salinas
Client: Ideo
Camera: Sinar 4x5 Film: Fuji Provia 100

Page 189
'Giro Helmets'
Photographer: Mark Laita
Art Director: Paul Stechshulte
Ad Agency: Crispin Porter Bogusky
Client: Giro
Camera: Fatif 8x10 Film: Kodak E100VS

Page 190, 191
'VCA Campaign'
Photographer: Mark Laita
Art Director: Jerry Andreozzi
Client: Van Cleef & Arpels
Camera: Fatif 8x10 Film: Kodak E100VS

Page 192
'Technology and Nature'
Photographer: Mark Laita
Art Director: Jean Phillippe Weill
Ad Agency: DDB Paris
Client: Atofina
Camera: Fatif 8x10 Film: Kodak E100VS

Page 193
'Watch'
Photographer: Markku Lahdesmaku
Representative: Stephanie Menuez
Art Director: Steve Glinski
Client: Chrysler Camera: Sinar 4x5 Film: Kodak

Page 194, 195
'Cat Burglar'
Photographer: Craig Cutler
Representative: Art & Commerce
Client: Worth Magazine

Page 196
Photographer: Eric Poggenpohl

Page 198
'Joromir Jagr in DC'
Photographer: Michael O'Brien
Picture Editor: Nik Kleinberg
Client: ESPN Magazine

Page 199
'Pierre Turgeon in Dallas'
Photographer: Michael O'Brien
Picture Editor: Nik Kleinberg
Client: ESPN Magazine

Page 200-201
'Connection'
Photographer: Chris Gordaneer
Representative: C-folio.com
Client: Group Telecom
Camera: Fuji 680 Film: Tri-X

Page 202, 203
'Bare-Knuckle Business'
Photographer: Craig Cutler
Representative: Art & Commerce
Client: E Company Now
Camera: Hasselblad Film: 120

Page 204, 205
'Athlete Series 1'
Photographer: Howard Schatz
Studio: Schatz/Ornstein Studio

Page 206-207
'Swimmer'
Photographer: Chris Gordaneer
Representative: C-folio.com
Art Director: Israel Diaz
Client: Nike
Camera: Fuji 680 Film: Portra VC

Page 208, 209
'Winter Fishing'
Photographer: Scott Spiker
Studio: Spiker Photography
Art Director: Scott Spiker
Client: Spiker Photography
Camera: Canon Film: Fuji

Page 210
'Athlete Series 5'
Photographer: Howard Schatz
Studio: Schatz/Ornstein Studio

Page 211
'Athlete Series 6'
Photographer: Howard Schatz
Studio: Schatz/Ornstein Studio

Page 212
'Scott Johnson at Rodeo'
Photographer: Michael O'Brien
Picture Editor: Nik Kleinberg
Client: ESPN Magazine
Camera: 4x5 Film: Polaroid 55

Page 213
'Catriona Le May Doan'
Photographer: Mark Zibert
Representative: Jooli Kim
Art Director: Donna Braggins
Client: Maclean's Magazine
Camera: RZ 67 Film: E100

Page 214
'Life Scan'
Photographer: Sue Bennett
Studio: Sue Bennett Photography
Creative Director: Rory Phoenix
Art Director: Jill Regan
Client: Johnson & Johnson

Page 215
'Bowling Series'
Photographer: Bret Wills
Studio: Wills Studio, Inc.
Camera: 8x10 Horseman Film: Fuji RTP

Page 216, 218, 219
'Untitled'
Photographer: Jeff Stephens
Studio: Jeff Stephens Photography
Art Directors: Jay Evers and Jeff Stephens
Camera: Hasselblad Film: Colorneg

Page 220, 221
'Circles'
Photographer: Mark Weiss
Studio: Mark Weiss Studio

Page 222, 223
Photographer: Maria Robledo
Studio: Judy Casey, Inc.

Page 224
'Money Bed'
Photographer: Zachary Scott

Representative: Sharpe & Associates
Creative Director: Sue Smith
Client: Business 2.0
Camera: R2 Film: E100S

Page 225
'Broken Glasses'
Photographer: Geoff Spear
Studio/Representative: Greg Sellentin
Art Director: Roberto De Vicq
Client: Harper Collins
Camera: Linhof 8x10 Film: Kodak

Page 226
'Blue Skwig'
Photographer: Mark Battrell
Studio: Mark Battrell Photography
Art Director: Mark Battrell
Camera: 4x5 Sinar Film: Fuji Transparency

Page 227
'I.C. Jesus'
Photographer: Mark Battrell
Studio: Mark Battrell Photography
Art Director: Mark Battrell
Camera: 4x5 Sinar Film: Fuji Transparency

Page 228
'The Dream Room'
Photographer: Sean Kernan
Representative: Molly Birenbaum
Creative Director: Richard Aguan
Art Director: Richard Aguan
Designer: Richard Aguan
Client: William Morrow/Harper Collins
Camera: 8x10 Film: Fuji

Page 229
Photographer: Jim Krantz
Representative: Chris Glenn

Page 230, 231
'Clever Normality Series'
Photographer: Jeff Stephens
Representative: Monaco Reps

Page 232, 233
'Lost Objects'
Photographer: Craig Cutler
Representative: Art & Commerce
Camera: 4x5 Toyo Film: Chrome

Page 236, 238, 239
'Bird Series'
Photographer: Mark Laita
Camera: Fatif 8x10 Film: Kodak E100VS

Page 240, 241
Photographer: Deborah Samuel
Studio: Deborah Samuel Photography
Camera: Hasselblad Film: Tri-X

Page 242
'Toro'
Photographer: Robert Maxham
Camera: Nikon Film: Tri-X

Page 243
'Still Life'
Photographer: James Schnepf
Studio: James Schnepf Photography, Inc.
Camera: Hasselblad Film: Kodak

Page 244
Photographer: Deborah Samuel
Studio: Deborah Samuel Photography
Camera: Hasselblad Film: Tri-X

IndexVerzeichnisseIndices

Photographers

Creative Directors Art Directors Photo Editors Designers

Clients

Anderson Hopkins
40 West 20th Street, #11B
New York, NY 10001
Tel: 1 212 889 2766
Fax: 1 212 889 2786
www.hop2us.com

Andrea Wells Photography
P.O. Box 6637
Bellevue, WA 98008
Tel: 1 425 644 6761
Fax: 1 425 644 6098
www.andreawells.com

Andy Freeberg
678 Northern Avenue
Mill Valley, CA 94941
Tel: 1 415 381 5585
Fax: 1 415 381 6021
www.andyfreeberg.com

Art & Commerce
755 Washington Street
New York, NY 10014
Tel: 1 212 206 0737
Fax: 1 212 463 7267

Arthouse Management
81 Greene Street, 4th Floor
New York, NY 10012
Tel: 1 212 343 2331
Fax: 1 212 343 8841

Arthur Meyerson Photography, Inc.
2710 Bissonnet Street
Houston, TX 77005
Tel: 1 713 529 9697
Fax: 1 713 529 9697
www.arthurmeyerson.com

Barbara Bowman Associates
440 Brannan Street
San Francisco, CA 94107
Tel: 1 415 243 0224
Fax: 1 415 778 6444

Bekker Photography
8205 Landing South
Atlanta, GA 30350
Tel: 1 770 992 5151
Fax: 1 770 992 5151
www.bekker.com

Bernstein & Andriulli
58 West 40th Street, Floor 6
New York, NY 10018
Tel: 1 212 682 1490

Bogart & Bogart
1006 Shepherd Street
Durham, NC 27707
Tel: 1 919 687 4383
Fax: 1 919 688 4880

Bottle Rocket Pictures
#816 1029 King Street West
Toronto, Ontario
Cananda M6K3M9
Tel: 1 416 834 5808

Bryce Bennett Communications
P.O. Box 74
Sofiemyr, Norway 1417
Tel: 47 66 80 04 10
Fax: 37 66 80 04 11
www.bryce.no

C-folio.com
1711 North Honore
Chicago, IL 60622
Tel: 1 312 226 9880
Fax: 1 312 226 9883
www.c-folio.com

Chris Glenn
219 North Justine
Chicago, IL 60607
Tel: 1 312 829 4201
Fax: 1 312 829 4203

Chris Wimpey Studio
1612 West Lewis Street
San Diego, CA 92103
Tel: 1 619 297 3931
Fax: 1 619 297 3954

Chuck Dorr
1123 Broadway, #1005
New York, NY 10010
Tel: 1 212 627 9871
Fax: 1 212 243 4036

Cindy James Photography
500 Expositon, Suite 104
Dallas, TX 75226
Tel: 1 214 823 0595
Fax: 1 214 826 2617
www.cindyjamesphotography.com

CMP/Judi Shin
1180 Avenue of the Americas
New York, NY 10036
Tel: 1 212 655 6500
www.cmpnational.com

Danelle Dalpra Photography
15 Horizon Avenue, Studio 8
Venice, CA 90291
Tel: 1 310 936 7329

Danielle Melanson
2737 Northeast 10th Avenue
Portland, OR 97212
Tel: 1 503 288 6013
Fax: 1 503 281 0075

David Emmite Photography
615 Southeast Alder, #300
Portland, OR 97214
Tel: 1 503 239 5135
Fax: 1 503 239 5170
www.davidemmite.com

Deborah Ayerst
103 East Blithdale, #1
Mill Valley, CA 94941
Tel: 1 415 567 3570
www.debayerst.com

Deborah Samuel Photography
410 Palm Avenue, #A-2
Carpinteria, CA 93013
Tel: 1 805 745 8777
Fax: 1 805 745 8804

Denise Ford
840 Exposition Avenue
Dallas, TX 75226
Tel: 1 214 821 6788
Fax: 1 214 821 0566
www.denisefordagent.com

Eric Poggenpohl
340 South Pleasant Street
Amherst, MA 01002
Tel: 1 413 256 0948

Felix Holzer Studio
Schumannstrasse 5
Munich, Germany D81679
Tel: 49 89 4702 7091
Fax: 49 89 4702 7092
www.felix-holzer.de

Frank Arends
216 West 18th Street
New York, NY 10011
Tel: 1 212 229 1423
Fax: 1 212 604 0216

Gamma
1633 Broadway 40th Floor
New York, NY 10019
Tel: 1 212 767 4567
Fax: 1 212 767 4570

Gil Blank LLC
653 East 14th Street, #95
New York, NY 10009
Tel: 1 917 446 5320

Gollings Photography
147 Chapel Street
St. Kilda, Victoria Australia 3182
Tel: 613 9537 0733
Fax: 613 9537 0187
www.gollingspidgeon.com

Greg Myhra Photography
309 1/2 West Martin Street
Raleigh, NC 27601
Tel: 1 919 828 1699
Fax: 1 919 828 3398
www.myhraphoto.com

Greg Sellentin
325 West 38th Street, #510
New York, NY 10018
Tel: 1 212 736 0488
Fax: 1 212 736 0032
www.gsreps.com

Hamilton, Gray & Associates
3519 West 6th Street
Los Angeles, CA 90020
Tel: 1 213 380 3933

Hennessy Photography
10 Lynn Street
Boston, MA 02113
Tel: 1 617 269 3312
Fax: 1 617 367 7736
www.hennessystudio.com

James Schnepf Photography, Inc.
N34 W5543 Hamilton Road
Cedarburg, WI 53052
Tel: 1 262 375 2600
Fax: 1 262 375 7226
www.schnepfphoto.com

Jeff Stephens Photography
2030 Main Street, Suite 500
Dallas, TX 75201
Tel: 1 214 744 3500
Fax: 1 214 744 3522
www.jeffstephens.com

Jim Hanson Artist Agent Ltd.
777 North Michigan Avenue, Suite 706
Chicago, IL 60611
Tel: 1 312 337 7770
www.jimhanson.com

Jon Shireman Photography
15 East 32nd Street
New York, NY 10016
Tel: 1 212 779 9755
www.jonshireman.com

Jonathan Knowles Photography
48A Chancellors Road
London, United Kingdom W69RS
Tel: 44 20 8741 75577
Fax: 44 20 8748 9927
www.jknowles.co.uk

Jonathan Torgovnik
180 West Houston Street 14C
New York, NY 10014
Tel: 1 212 414 4894
Fax: 1 212 414 4895

Jono Rotman Photographer
PO Box 6857
Wellington, New Zealand
Tel: 64021768626
Fax: 64021698500
jono@rotman.co.nz

Jooli Kim
20 Leslie Street Suite 211
Toronto, Ontario
Canada M4M3L4
Tel: 1 416 469 4900
Fax: 1 416 465 9690
www.methodinc.net

Joseph E. Reid
100 John Street 1409
New York, NY 10038
Tel: 1 917 769 6327

JoSon Photography
350 Turk Street 302
San Francisco, CA 94102
Tel: 1 415 447 6011
www.josonphoto.com

Judy Casey, Inc.
114 East 13th Street
New York, NY 10003
Tel: 1 212 228 7500
Fax: 1 212 228 9339

us Kampert
erkasseler Strasse 108
esseldorf, Germany D40545
: 49 211 5595050
: 49 211 5595051
w.klauskampert.com

y & Co.
53-B Centinela Avenue
ta Monica, CA 90404
: 1 310 453 0053
: 1 310 453 4077

ng Nguyen
2 Tecumseh Drive
on Hill, MD 20745
: 1 703 855 2386
w longnguyen.com

arilyn Cadenbach
5 Upland Road
mbridge, MA 02140
: 1 617 868 2004
: 1 617 868 4077
w.cadenbach.com

ark Battrell Photography
47 West Ohio #302
icago, IL 60622
: 1 312 829 2290
: 1 312 829 2291

ark Laita
15 Main Street
lver City , CA 90232
: 1 310 836 1645
: 1 310 836 1645
w.marklaita.com

ark Weiss Studio
8 Broadway, #502
w York, NY 10012
: 1 212 777 3034
: 1 212 777 3309

chael Castagnetti
0 3rd Avenue, #21-C
w York, NY 10010
: 1 212 251 0269

chael Furman
5 Arch Street
iladelphia, PA 19106
: 1 215 925 4233
: 1 215 925 6108
w.michaelfurman.com

chael Hall Photography
obertson Street
rrabeen, New South Wales
stralia 2101
: 613 2991 31978
w.michaelhall.co.nz

chael O'Brien
8 East 5th Street
stin, TX 78702
: 1 512 472 9205
: 1 512 472 9219
w.obrienphotography.com

Miro Ito
270 Park Ave. South (2-B)
New York, NY 10010
Tel: 1 646 654 6093
Fax: 1 646 654 6570
www.miroito.com

Moeder Photography
71 Marview Way
San Francisco, CA 94131
Tel: 1 415 282 8865
Fax: 1 415 282 8866
www.moederphotography.com

Molly Birenbaum
127 White Birch Drive
Guilford, CT 06437
Tel: 1 203 453 9333
Fax: 1 203 453 1497

Monaco Reps
389 Bleecker Street
New York, NY 10014
Tel: 1 212 647 0336
Fax: 1 212 647 9329
www.monacoreps.com

Natalie Ogura
Tel: 1 919 832 5971
www.jwproductions.com

Network Aspen
319 Aspen Business Center
Studio N
Aspen, CO 81611
Tel: 1 970 925 5574
Fax: 1 970 925 5680
www.networkaspen.com

Paul Murphy
68 Shearman Road
London, United Kingdom SE39HX
Tel: 44 20 7831 6624
www.pmurphy.co.uk

Pencil Fine Art
Postfach 3716
Braunschweig, Germany 38027
Tel: 49 5303 92262
Fax: 49 5303 9709350

Phil Marco Productions, Inc.
100 Fifth Avenue
New York, NY 10011
Tel: 1 212 929 8082
Fax: 1 212 463 0514

PKS
1130 West Peachtree Street
Atlanta, GA 30309
Tel: 1 404 892 0099
Fax: 1 404 892 0156
www.parishkohanim.com

Proof Photographic Agents
247 West 16th Street
New York, NY 10011
Tel: 1 212 727 1445
Fax: 1 212 727 2120
www.proofphoto.com

Rafter
185 West End Avenue, Suite 29R
New York, NY 10023
Tel: 1 212 799 2967

Randy Cole Represents
24 West 30th Street
New York, NY 10001
Tel: 1 212 679 5933
Fax: 1 212 779 3697
www.randycole.com

Raoul Benavides Photo
310 North 2nd Street
Minneapolis, MN 55401
Tel: 1 612 341 6585

Reid Lincoln Ashton Photography
2679 Guoin Street
Detroit, MI 48207
Tel: 1 313 259 6930
Fax: 1 313 259 0939

Rob Stephen
3802 Rosecrans Street, #177
San Diego, CA 92110
Tel: 1 619 574 6998
Fax: 1 619 295 1998

Robert Maxham
223 Howard
San Antonio, TX 28212
Tel: 1 210 223 6000
Fax: 1 210 223 1425
www.maxham.com

Safia Fatimi
22 West 15th Street, #3F
New York, NY 10011
Tel: 1 212 627 3207
Fax: 1 212 691 7942

Sanjay Kothari
450 Broome Street, 3E
New York, NY 10013
Tel: 1 212 226 0015
Fax: 1 212 343 8543
www.sanjaykothari.com

Schatz/Ornstein Studio
435 West Broadway #2
New York, NY 10012
Tel: 1 212 334 6667
Fax: 1 212 334 6669
www.howardschatz.com

Sharpe & Associates
7536 Ogelsby Avenue
Los Angeles, CA 90045
Tel: 1 310 641 8556
Fax: 1 310 641 8534

Spiker Photography
P.O. Box 2509
Col. Falls, MT 59912
Tel: 1 406 892 0501
Fax: 1 406 892 0502
www.spikerphoto.com

Stephanie Flack
8912 Appian Way
Los Angeles, CA 90046
Tel: 1 323 848 8422
Fax: 1 323 848 8422

Stephanie Menuez
Tel: 1 415 382 8817

Temerlin McClain
6555 Sierra Drive
Irving, TX 75039
Tel: 1 972 830 2208
Fax: 1 972 401 9434

Terry Husebye Photography
228 Mount Shasta Drive
San Rafael, CA 94903
Tel: 1 415 444 5844
Fax: 1 415 444 5840
www.husebyephoto.com

There Media
410 West 14th Street
New York, NY 10014
Tel: 1 212 366 4140
Fax: 1 212 202 4791

Village Voice
36 Cooper Square
New York, NY 10003
Tel: 1 212 475 3300
Fax: 1 212 529 4590
www.villagevoice.com

Virtu
400 East Randolph, #3103
Chicago, IL 60601
Tel: 1 312 540 9888
Fax: 1 312 540 0093
www.virtu.ws

Wills Studio, Inc.
347 West 36th Street, 16fl
New York, NY 10018
Tel: 1 212 904 1866
Fax: 1 212 904 1961
www.bretwills.com

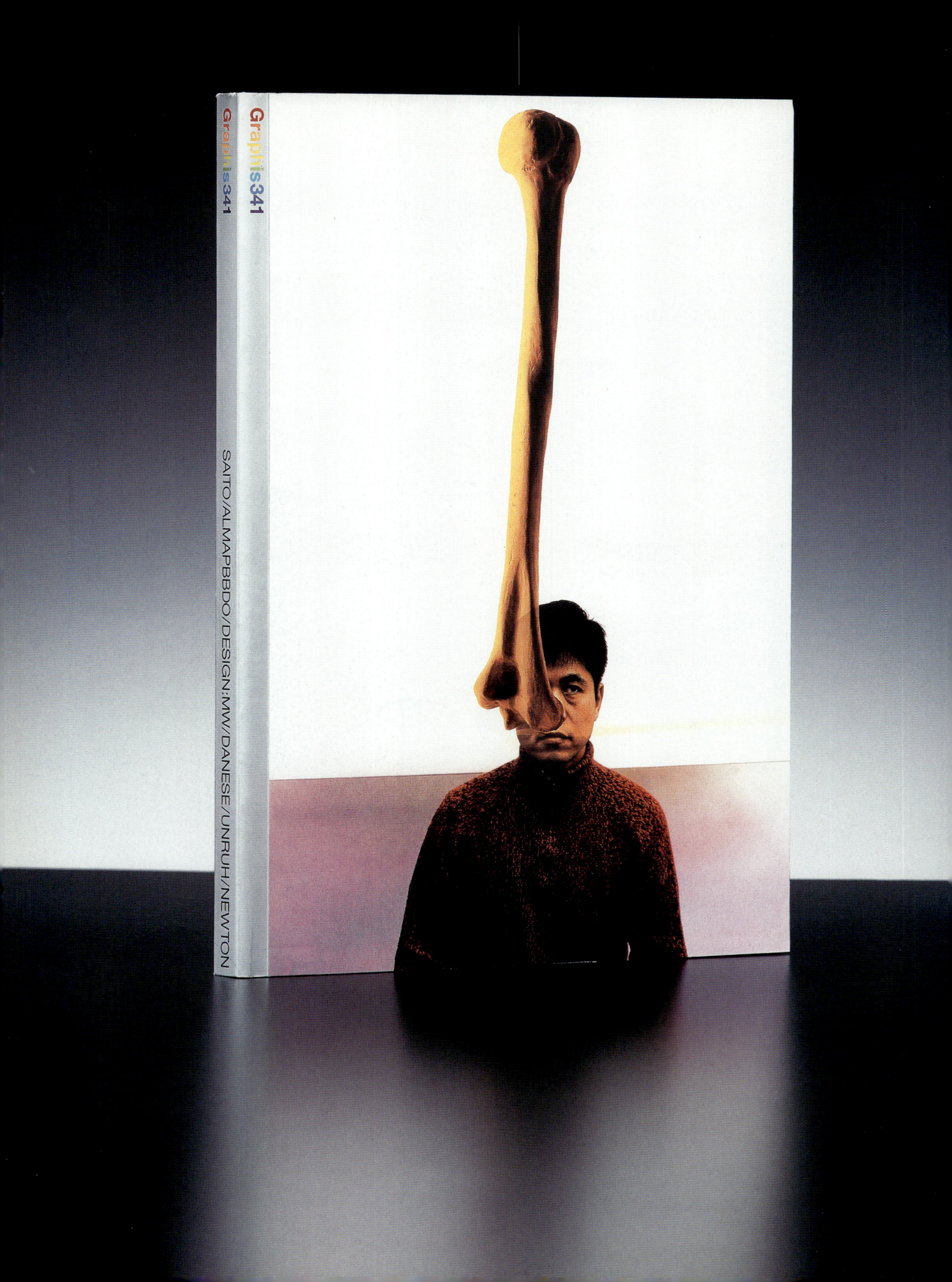
Graphis 341
Graphis 34·1
SAITO/ALMAPBBDO/DESIGN:MW/DANESE/UNRUH/NEWTON